HOMOSEXUALITY:

The Secret a Child Dare Not Tell

HOMOSEXUALITY:

The Secret a Child Dare Not Tell

Mary Ann Cantwell

Rafael Press
San Rafael, California

Published by Rafael Press, PO Box 150462, San Rafael, CA 94915

Grateful acknowledgment is made for permission to quote from *Music for Chameleons*, "Dazzle," by Truman Capote published by Random House, New York, 1975, copyright © 1975 by Truman Capote. The author is also grateful to Oxford University Press for permission to quote various passages from John Stuart Mill *Three Essays* first issued as an Oxford University paperback 1975.

Acknowledgment is also made to the National Gallery of Art, Washington, D.C., for permission to reproduce, for the cover, "Two Children at the Seashore," by Mary Cassatt.

Typography and Cover Design by
Spectrum Associates, Carbondale, Colorado

Printed in the United States of America

Library of Congress Cataloging-in-Publication Data
Cantwell, Mary Ann (Mahern, Elsye C.), 1922–
Homosexuality: the secret a child dare not tell / Mary Ann Cantwell
1. Child Psychology 2. Gay and Lesbian Studies
I. Title.   95-072063 CIP

ISBN 0-9649829-9-4

10 9 8 7 6 5 4 3 2 1   96 97 98 99

First Edition

For David, who is his own man.

Contents

Acknowledgments

So many people have contributed to the writing of *Homosexuality: The Secret a Child Dare Not Tell* that it is difficult to know where to begin to thank them. I must pair John Moffatt, my first writing teacher, for early encouragement, and Cerridwen Fallingstar, for recently freeing my voice. Without them the book wouldn't be.

I thank Neil Postman for the idea of a non-fiction story; Robert Grudin for *The Grace of Great Things*; China Galland for *Longing for Darkness*; and Victoria Ransom and Henrietta Bernstein for *The Crone Oracles*.

Jim Van Buskirk contributed the idea of surveying the parents of homosexuals. His encouragement, and that of T. Berry Brazelton, M.D. and Brian McNaught, were important at a critical time.

The book would not exist without the cooperation of the parents, lesbians, and gays who were willing to revisit painful memories in answering the survey items. In most instances, I do not even know their names, but they know who they are.

The importance of the help generously given by Pflag members, and the very existence of the organization, cannot be overstated. George Neighbors, Jr., Joan Adams, Samuel and Julia Thoron, and Mitzi Henderson are especially to be cited.

The women in the Revolutionary Aging group, and especially Jean Maruejouls, have my profound thanks.

Dr. Judith Rubin, M.D., Jennifer Lehr, and Will Larsen kept me healthy during the writing. Don Ricart, Mary Griffith, Downey Soft, and Byron Fagis were important in the development of ideas. I thank Richard D. Johnson for permission to quote from his unpublished essay, and Kate Mahern for saving the columns.

Rebecca Salome Shaw did a superb job in separating the wheat from the chaff, and in understanding me and the manuscript. Wendy Fawcett did a sensitive job of line editing.

David DuMond, my husband, my back-up, my co-person, was a great help in all matters.

Preface

As a teacher of emotionally disturbed six- and seven-year-olds, I often saw that parents misunderstood or failed to recognize the feelings of their children. When my forty-year-old gay son said that he knew he was different from the age of five or six, I realized that I had been one of those parents.

As I became aware that it was not unusual for children to realize gender variance at an early age, I knew that they suffered alone, with knowledge of their difference. I thought of writing a pamphlet, which a few pediatricians might allow me to leave in their office waiting rooms. I wanted to let the parents of small children know this, as I wished I had known it.

As the months went by and I talked to more and more people, and particularly as I became aware how much time elapses between the child's knowledge and the parent's, I realized that I couldn't afford this comfortable little project. I'd have to write a book.

Often parents would apologize to me, saying, "I had no idea," as though they thought I did. Or they would ask anxiously, "When will the book be out?" They had joined me in wanting to help the children.

It is not just parents who need to know that a significant number of very young children have a problem, one which they can only view as a shameful secret. All of society needs to know.

However as it happened, I did keep my fascination to myself, for I felt a certain guilt: I had a secret, something that was bothering me, something that was really worrying me very much, something I was afraid to tell anybody, <u>any</u>body—I couldn't imagine what their reaction would be, it was such an odd thing that was worrying me, that had been worrying me for almost two years. I had never heard of anyone with a problem like the one that was troubling me. On the one hand it seemed maybe silly; on the other. . .

from Truman Capote's "Dazzle"

Prologue

A Missed Ceremony
May 1957

Dr. Donato stood at the door, bag in hand, ready to go to his next house call. "I can't tell at this point whether he had pneumonia and is now recovering, or if he just came close, and we caught it in time." He gave me a prescription that he assured me would make Mike better in a couple of days. I asked him a question, the answer to which I was dreading. "No," he said, without hesitation, "he will not be making his First Communion with his class on Sunday." Mike's new navy blue pants and starched white shirt hung on the back of the closet door. I saw him looking at them often, and picking up his prayer book and rosary beads. He'd drape the beads around his hands, and hold the prayer book, fingers extended. He was practicing, the way they'd done in the classroom and then in church. He'd put his feet carefully together, and then slowly, leading off with the right, walk across the room: a procession of one.

Sometimes he'd pick up his new black oxfords from the shoe rack and turn them over to look at the smooth, clean soles. It was rare in our large family for one child to get a complete new outfit all at once.

Now he would miss the ceremony. I didn't have the heart to tell him, was thankful that he'd fallen asleep as soon as the doctor finished examining him. I would have to tell him, but I could choose the time. Could I think of some way to soften the blow?

I had to waken him in the night to give him the bright pink liquid. He didn't complain, but I knew that it hurt to swallow. That was why he only took a few spoonfuls of broth. "What day is it?" "Friday," I said, stretching the meaning of Friday night. It was actually early Saturday morning. I knew what he was really asking.

When I held the spoon in front of him in the daylight, he seemed

1

better already. Then he asked his real question. "No," I said, "you can't make your First Communion with your class." I still didn't know what I could offer him in consolation. He began to cry weakly, falling back on the pillow, giving up the dream. Then I was inspired. "You will have to wait, maybe a couple of weeks, but our whole family will go to the altar with you, and after Mass you can put a bouquet of flowers on the Blessed Mother's altar."

His sobs decreased with the mention of a bouquet. He wiped his eyes. "Where will we get the flowers?"

"We'll get them from the florist," I said, taking the plunge, trying to calculate the cost.

I ordered the flowers early that second week, but the Saturday when they were delivered was unusually warm for May. We were at the end of the route. When the flowers arrived it was past five pm, and they suffered from many hours in an overheated panel truck. I didn't know what to do. The flowers were bedraggled. It was too late to get a different bouquet. And I had promised him.

When everyone else was in bed, I went through the bouquet, extracting the most wilted flowers. The finished bouquet was not as full as before, but it was presentable. It'd have to do. I had promised.

After Mass the next day, when the congregation had filed out, Mike walked to the Blessed Mother's altar. I longed for music and candlelight. He reached above his head and laid the flowers on her altar. During Mass I'd noticed that more flowers had drooped. I remembered the dandelion bouquets I'd received from hands which had clutched them so tightly that the yellow heads lay down and formed a circle around the little fist. Mary wouldn't mind.

When I went to early Mass on Monday, I noticed that the bouquet had been removed. Maybe the sacristan always removed such offerings right away, and I had just never noticed. But in my mind the bouquet had been removed because it was not fresh. The gift was unacceptable because it wasn't perfect.

I could see the removal on two levels. When I had time, I went to help the Altar Society clean and adorn the altar. Even the cloths which were used for cleaning were bleached a dazzling white. The starched linen runners with hand-crocheted borders, which covered the marble altar, were rolled on tubes to avoid any crease or wrinkle. On that level I could understand the removal of anything imperfect. But there is quite a gap between our best and perfection. One should offer the purest, the best gift to spiritual powers above one. But in this instance it was our best. I did not mention the removal to Mike, hoping that he would not notice when he went to Mass at eight o'clock with his class. Now, looking back almost forty years, I feel certain he did notice.

What was I to do? Break my promise to a child?

I certainly experienced the removal of the bouquet as a rejection. And now I know that Mike had another reason to feel that he was unworthy: that he had already begun to think that something was wrong with him. When he was seven he only missed the ceremony, not the sacrament. But when he reached adulthood, if he were to remain true to his nature, there was a sacrament which would be denied to him: Matrimony.

Mary must have treasured this dandelion bouquet above fresher ones. But an organization on earth, that claimed to represent Mary and her son, Jesus, had rejected a mother and her child who were offering their best.

PART I

THE DECISION

Chapter One

I've Got To Know
September 1993

I've got to know. I must find out the truth.

Four children, the ages of my grandchildren, pick up stones deposited at their bare feet by the ocean. The Pacific Ocean is well named at this spot, gently rolling in, each gigantic scallop of water and foam depositing a new treasure.

Occasional cars drive by on the road, which can be reached by climbing up steps gouged out of the sand and rock. Beyond the road is the town of Cambria, somewhat of a tourist attraction because it is close by San Simeon and Hearst Castle, the anachronism built by architect Julia Morgan in the 1920s and 1930s.

It's 1993 now, and David, my husband, and I have come here to rest after a strenuous law case that required him to work far into the night for weeks. Cambria is our favorite rock-hound beach, and we are bending to the jadite jewels the same as the children.

Down the sand and stone steps, where we are, you are one with the ocean, remote from the town. The sky is neither gray nor blue. The children complete the picture; a composition worthy of an Impressionist. It is late afternoon and soon it will be time to climb to the level of the road with their treasures: jewel-like stones of great diversity, polished by the constant motion of the water. When dried they will be duller, but a week or two tumbled in slurry water and the shine will return to stay. The children shout to each other, "Look at this one. It's the greenest." The two smaller children have decided to specialize. He's looking only for pure white gems and she's gathering only green ones. I gaze at the children, and the question comes unbidden into my mind. The question has bothered me ever since my gay son said casually awhile back, "I knew in a vague way when I was five or six, but at the same time I knew the need for circumspection."

Mild words that must hide years of quiet suffering. Words meaning that Mike grew up with a problem, a secret he could tell to no one. A heavy burden for a child to shoulder alone. I think of the possibility that one of the stone-gatherers might have that sorrow of secrecy.

A man's voice calls from the road overhead. "Come on, you guys. We got to get dressed. You can't go to the restaurant like that." The children go on bending over their buckets, depositing stones. Another shout or two and they start to straggle up the rough steps. Up the stairs are restrictions. They'll have to put on shoes, comb their hair, conform to expectations.

Was Mike unique in "knowing?" I don't even know that.

I think of the common deception parents perpetrate on small children: Santa Claus. It is a deception born of love, but it is also a denial. The idea of Santa Claus suggests that this world is a better place than it seems. Perhaps there is a double deception going on here.

If children who are homosexual know it at an early age, but also know that the knowledge must be kept secret, aren't they saying to the parents, "There's not only no Santa Claus, there's no Easter Bunny either? Don't try to tell me that this earth is better than it looks, it's worse than you know." If that is true, then the children are taking care of the adults, are protecting the adults from what the child knows.

But who's taking care of the child? That's the question bothering me. Is it possible that a significant number of small children have this secret, and no adults know it? Or is it that the adults know it and attempt to change it? Tommy asks for tap dance shoes, and Santa Claus brings him a football.

Later, I'm in the DeYoung Art Museum and a beautiful young black teacher is explaining the African artifacts to a class of predominantly black students. The kids, twelve- or thirteen-year-olds, are attentive. They know there is a connection here, that this has to do with them. There is none of the usual school-boredom in their eyes.

Many dark faces are reflected in the glass case: twenty-five, thirty — a class. I know pretty certainly that there are two or three here for whom a different kind of connection could be made. If Mike knew when he was five or six, then surely the gay members of this class know.

Puberty is never a time of high security. Zits. Bad hair. Squeaky voice. Then add this: "I am different. In all the world, I am different. What am I to do?"

A memory floats back from thirty years ago, or longer.

Coming out of eleven o'clock Mass, one young man attacks another from the rear. I can't imagine why. They are struggling red-faced in the snow. Fury. "Don't you ever—He tried to—In church—In church." They are of a size and now equally angry. They thrash on the ground, in heavy overcoats like giant furious bears. Some older men come and pull them apart. They walk off in opposite directions, leaving a small battleground surrounded by serene snow. Even in memory the rage is scalding.

My mind is such that I must seek to make sense of what I experience, observe. Was that a case of homosexuality? At the last Mass on Sunday, the vestibule was often packed. Perhaps one young man, in bringing his hand to his face, brushed another unintentionally. But then you would have thought that might have earned a glare, a dirty look. Why were both of these furious bears so invested in what happened, or didn't happen?

Some members of this class may still be alone with the knowledge of their difference, or perhaps they've found some comfort that there are others like them. Have they had a "guilty" secret since they were five or six? I cannot hope to know what happened to the young man attacked from the back.

But I need to know about the children.

How can I possibly find out at what age homosexuals first knew about their difference, when Mike is literally the only gay person I know? Somehow I must get to know other gays. I remember a project I did for a research course in graduate school. Being a third grade teacher, I matched reading scores of six students who produced creative writing with six students whose writing showed little or no creativity. Surveys were sent home to the parents, with questions based on characteristics and conditions that some experts had agreed were conducive to creativity. I no longer have the paper I wrote analyzing the returns, and I cannot remember if there were any marked differences in the responses of one group versus the other.

I do remember that the experts thought that creativity comes from people who have the opportunity to be alone and that creativity requires some naivete on the part of the creator. I wonder now, with television and planned activities, how much opportunity today's child has to be alone.

On the idea of naivete, my question, which I must note was posed more than twenty years ago, was: If a neighbor child told your child that a flying saucer landed in the neighbor's yard, would your child be more likely, less likely, or about as likely as other children to believe the neighbor child?

The reason I remember that question was that *all* the parents answered that their child would be less likely to believe the story. Parents considered naivete an undesirable trait and wanted to think that their child did not possess it. All the parents wanted their children to be reasonable, and logical —not at all fanciful or accepting of possibilities.

Today, I think that survey question would not be a good test of naivete, because so much has been written on the subject of flying saucers that the most you could deduce from the answer would be an *opinion* concerning the existence of visitors from space.

Remembering that experience, I was encouraged to think about a survey. I knew that the most I could do would be to gather information: that my findings could not be extrapolated to apply to all gay people everywhere.

For one thing, the people who would answer a survey would be likely to be healthier, more self-accepting. But any knowledge or insight that could be gained from a survey would be more than was known before. I could at least point out the problem.

When a subject is not talked about, a vocabulary for speaking about it doesn't exist. I wanted to know when homosexuals first knew they were gay. But five- and six-year-olds do not have gay and homosexual in their vocabulary. I would have to question them on an awareness of difference. And maybe the word *aware* was too strong. At what age did you have an inkling? Yes, inkling was a better word.

"At what age did you have an inkling that your emotions and interests did not match familial and societal expectations of one of your sex?"

Yes, that's more like it. The wrong, if wrong there be, is in not meeting or matching an idea that family and society have of who you are, of what you should think and feel. I remember feeling annoyance and anger at the words "appropriate feelings." These words would often be spoken at a meeting to decide where in Special Education a child belonged.

They meant, "is the child's reaction appropriate to the situation now going on," but also "does his/her behavior conform to what I want, expect." But it seemed to me that there are no right or wrong feelings. Feelings *are*. They exist. And if you want to change them, you'd better accept that, and them, and inquire why the feelings are there: where they came from and why they persist. It will not make the feelings "more appropriate" to impose a grid of behavior. You may be able to drive the feelings underground, extinguish the behavior in your presence, but the feelings will not become more "appropriate," only the behavior.

With that in mind I devised the following survey:

LESBIAN and GAY CHILDHOOD

The following is an attempt to gather information about the prepubescent life of gays and lesbians. Please take the time to answer the following questions. Your cooperation could prove helpful to children of the present and future. Answer as fully as possible, no thought or feeling is irrelevant. Use the back of these sheets, and attach more sheets if necessary. Please indicate which item you are responding to. Thank you for your help.

1. Circle the appropriate. I am/have gay lesbian HIV/AIDS.

2. At what age did you have an inkling that your emotions and interests did not match familial and societal expectations of one of your sex? Please expand as fully as possible on the thoughts, feelings or experiences. (The rest of that page is left blank)

3. As a child did you feel that you were more alone than others of your age group? If so, what do you think caused this loneliness? Could you give an example of incidents or feelings regarding this?

(Blank space of several lines)

4. How do you think, or imagine, your childhood would have been different, if you were born into a society where sexual orientation made no more difference than, say, hair color.

(Rest of page left blank)

5. Please tell about anything relevant to your childhood which has not been covered by the above items.

(Blank space of several lines)

Then there were instructions about how to return the survey directly to me. Each survey was accompanied by a self addressed, stamped envelope.

I went to the office supply store to buy paper for the survey project. I wanted a different color for each group represented. The survey asks the respondent to self-identify as to group: Gay, Lesbian HIV/AIDS, but as a fail-safe measure I wanted the surveys distributed to each group to be a distinctive color. Even with the above distinctions, I was later told by a lesbian that they were not clear, because "Lesbians are also considered gay, and therefore the identification of gay should have been gay male." Well, when I learned that, some surveys had already been distributed, and I could only hope that given the choice the lesbians would go for the narrower category. (I was just now being introduced to the various attitudes concerning the word *lesbian*). The color of paper would help me categorize the respondents correctly.

But before that I was stuck on the choice of color. I thought that lavender was connected with lesbianism, but I hesitated using it. Was it one of those things that the *in group* used, and was forbidden to everyone else? Sometimes you couldn't win: couldn't know the right thing to do.

The Gay and Lesbian Parade in San Francisco is usually led by *Dykes on Bikes*. One newscaster identified the group as the *Women's Motorcycle Contingent*. He voted for *safe* but it didn't work. "What is this *Women's Motorcycle Contingent*? We're *Dykes on Bikes!*" was the outraged reply.

I'm trying to break silence between groups who don't speak to each other, except very carefully. I guess it's only natural that vocabulary would be a problem. Once in an interracial seminar we were asked to team up with one person of the opposite color, and tell that person a stereotype which you knew about that group. My black counterpart dug right in: "White people have flat butts." With a laugh of recognition I shot back, "Black people have round butts." She and I had no trouble talking after that.

During the fifties I was active in establishing a Catholic Interracial Council. At that time "nigger" was about the dirtiest word one could imagine. The meetings were very instructive to me because I'd grown up in a small town where the boast was that the sun never set on a "nigger." They came into Beech Grove to work but went away at night. So getting to know black people and what they thought and felt was a necessary part of my education.

At one meeting there was discussion about many words used to put down people of the Negro race. One of the words mentioned was Sambo. I said nothing, but was shocked because one of the favorite books for reading aloud at our house was *Little Black Sambo*.

I awoke the next day in the early morning dark with the conviction that *Little Black Sambo* had to go. I delayed until just before lunch, when I put the book on top of the debris in the wastebasket and went down the walk to the incinerator. Great wracking sobs came from me as I up-ended the waste basket and lit a match. The book was now irretrievable beneath the burning paper. I waited outside until I could stop crying, but still Kevin knew. "What's wrong Mommy?" he asked as I spread peanut butter and jelly on bread.

By the time of the next meeting, I could be calm about telling about my book burning. "*Little Black Sambo* is about an Indian, isn't it?" Harlan asked. I guess my sacrifice was unnecessary since at that time there were no natives of India in Indianapolis to be derogated.

Recently, the miscommunication has taken place between myself and other people of my own group: heterosexuals.

Something goes awry when I mention Mike and his homosexuality. The conversation grinds to a halt, but not immediately. If the conversation were music, one would say that a false note had sounded. The reply—no, it's not a reply—it's just the next thing the person says. They are talking over my shoulder.

And I feel as though I've said something I shouldn't have mentioned. But the discomfort is different from just speaking what is usually not spoken.

It is the nature of the response. The response says that my apology is accepted. The response is accepting my apology, which was not an apology.

I think the proper response to the other person's acceptance of my apology (which wasn't an apology) should be, "Look, I'm talking about my son, and I'm not apologizing. Why would you think that I am apologizing?"

But it takes a while to figure out what's going on. You realize that the person's reply is a *non sequitur,* but you have to figure out what's going on. You have to think about what's happening, and why. With prejudice and bigotry, you don't need to think, they're automatic—it's going against them that takes thought.

There is a variation on this scene.

Once in a committee meeting the affairs of the larger group were being discussed. One of the women, Mildred, had written a letter in the newsletter, a piece which I took to be her out-of-the-closet statement. I said, "I didn't know that Mildred is lesbian."

"Well, she's not!" was the shocked reply. I mentioned the newsletter. "Yes, she's interested in those issues, but that doesn't give you the right to call her lesbian."

Innocent until proven *guilty*. Right?

I was wrong about her sexual orientation. When I talked to Mildred, she identified herself as bisexual.

Next time my reply should be, "It is not an accusation. Why do you consider what I said to be an accusation from which you need to defend Mildred?"

The paper colors I chose were green and blue. I didn't have the nerve for lavender. Better be safe. Then I remember the Women's Motorcycle Contingent. I guess there is no such thing as safe as long as you insist on breaking silence.

With the surveys color-coded, duplicated, and in separate folders, I felt ready to do my research. I'd talked to a lesbian friend, Jill, about the project. She is a professional with many people in her office daily. "I can get you twelve surveys answered in a week." Great. This is going to be easier than I thought. I sent her twelve surveys, and a return envelope with postage for the same weight. With this encouragement, I asked Mike to try to get his friends to do the survey. I sent twelve, and the same type of postage-return envelope. Now I only had to wait for the surveys to roll in.

It didn't quite happen that way.

About a month later I got a call from Mike. He'd managed to get five surveys by appealing to his close friends, telling them that it was for "a project my Mom is doing." Mike is a writer, and he warned me that the going would be rough. "You know that most people hate to write."

So I got five back, not twelve, but there was a bonus even so. Mike and I were talking about the subject of homosexuality.

Chapter Two

How Can I Know?

How can I know what homosexuals think, feel, experience, when I don't know them? I hardly know my son. If I want to ask him anything of significance, whether it has to do with homosexuality or not, I feel that I must frame my words very carefully. But that is partly familial. When the children were growing up, we as a family talked about facts. Things you could see. Prove.

This restriction was not imposed by me, but possibly it was imposed *because* of me. I'm very short of chitchat, always wanting to see beyond the spoken word or gesture. What is behind what you are saying? Never mind about polite manners, tell me how you really feel.

Louie, the father of my children, and my husband for more than thirty years, was quite different in this regard. Did his wish to avoid a tense discussion make me more demanding of the truth, or did my demand make him more avoiding? It would probably be impossible to know, since we've been divorced for more than twenty years, and he has been deceased for more than five. This was the basic difference between us, and the difference grew over time.

He seemed to think the unexamined life the only one worth living. We lived a life of the visible. I felt a thrill of recognition when I heard Joseph Campbell, in his video series with Bill Moyer, describe a certain type of person as "groveling before facts." There was a bitterness and disgust in his voice, and I understood why. Dedicating his life to myth, he must have suffered greatly from fact grovelers.

Within the family I exercised my need for truth in the areas which fell within the province of a mother. For instance, I refused to teach a ritual "thank you" in response to every small favor. I much preferred a heartfelt, "Gee, thanks Mom," no matter how far apart the true thankful feelings came.

By accepting my husband as the head of the family, and as a fact groveler, I accepted his standard concerning the subject of conversations. I was, in effect, saying that he was right: he was the authority. Which left me as wrong: not an authority. This was not analyzed, not conscious. Behind what was permissible to talk about were deep meanings. The meanings could/would stay. We just wouldn't talk about them.

It was not that I *accepted* his rules. Then how did they dominate? Facts are visible, can be looked up in a book, are agreed upon by most everyone. An intuition is private, personal. The weight of the evidence is on the side of fact.

The fact-demander has the power to make the intuitive one doubt the intuition. To think, "The evidence is with the fact, and maybe this is just me." Maybe it is true when he says, "It's just you." He has all the evidence, and this is just what I think, or feel.

It occurs to me now that intuition stands in the same relationship to fact as does homosexuality to heterosexuality. All the evidence is on the side of heterosexuality, and for a similar reason. It is visible: the great bulk of human beings are heterosexual. So that is taken for fact. Homosexuality is taken to be some personal aberration. It is just some quirk in the mind, and is taken to be wrong, because it pertains to a minority, and a hidden one at that.

Blacks, old people, and women are visible. Their reality cannot be denied. Bigots might not like it that these categories exist. But they're visible. The first hurdle is overcome.

But with homosexuality, as with intuition, its invisibility in much of the world allows its very existence to be denied. The homosexual is told, in subtle ways, "it's just you." You have this strange notion: just get over it. And since the ways this is said, at least in childhood, are usually through a person's attitude, the child doubts self. Thinks: maybe it is just me, and if it is just me, then I'm wrong. So if I'm wrong, I'd better try to get over it, to become right, like all those other people. But in the meantime I'd better hide my wrongness.

I need to get this inner truth from a group of people who have one thing in common: the need for secrecy. How could I get them to trust me, when they know they can trust no one?

Do any straight people know homosexuals: know what they feel, and particularly what they experienced as children? Even when a member of the family comes out of the closet, don't we talk about it for a while, "face it," and then put it away in a slightly larger closet?

After all, we've faced it; talked about it. So now let's put it away; not mention it. Let's talk about something pleasant.

No, we don't have to say the above. We all know the rules, and we *all* obey them. It is now a secret shared by a few more people. Now the closet is bigger.

The family dynamics, whatever they were before, close around the subject, and we talk about what we talked of before the closed door was breached.

In our family the dynamic was sports. We talked about sports.

We had ten children: the first six were boys. Mike, our gay son, was the fifth boy. Added to the maleness were my father and brother who lived with us during this time. Being the only female, I had the impression of living in a gymnasium. Later, when I came to teaching I was able to turn this experience to gain, when I could offer a bonus point on the homework to the eighth grader who came back with the answer to my question "What was the birth name of Kareem Abdul Jabbar?" or, "A tall can of corn is slang for what event in a baseball game?" I not only got the answer, but left one dad with the impression that I was a good teacher. The answers to these questions were just junk in my head, left over from years of being subjected to sports talk.

We talked about sports, and things you could see. Cars and refrigerators. Facts.

And didn't other families go on talking about whatever they talked about before the gay member came out and was then retired to a slightly larger closet?

Because of the definite male orientation in our family, and because the rules said that we should talk about visible things, the relationship between Mike and me on the subject of homosexuality has not been an open one. With all of my children, I wanted them to be whatever they were. Probably my greatest pride today is the diversity of my children, one from another. So I never had a problem with one of my children being homosexual. I did have a problem with Mike going away to college, and having a wall between us when he returned home to visit.

I could not see his life: who he was. So I asked him if he were gay. At least that's the way I remember it. He remembers differently. I also remember his denial, and that I didn't believe him.

I said that he had a problem about coming home. He'd arrive for three days, and leave after a day and a half. He said, and I do remember this exactly, because he put it back on me: he said, "It's just that you are like I was before I left." It took me years to figure out that there was truth in that statement.

But at the time, it sounded like what I got from Louie whenever I complained about anything. "It's just you." Any other woman in the world would be happy living in a gymnasium, talking about facts: batting averages, bowl games, scores. For Mike to opt for the female, to admit the female part, was to be estranged from the family. He said, in effect, what had always been said to me. "It's just you."

I did not believe that Mike was *not* homosexual. If he weren't gay, he was nothing: not leading a life. I didn't want that. And I was furious with him for denying it. I could accept him, why couldn't he accept me? In my anger I heard homosexual jokes and slurs coming out of my mouth. I knew why it was happening, but I couldn't stop it. Why couldn't he accept me into his life?

Mike remembers my question a different way. He says that he remembers exactly where it took place. Where he was sitting. Where I sat. He says that I asked, "Do you have a homosexual relationship with Allen?" I do not remember that, but I accede to his memory. And I know why I would have asked such a question.

Mike brought various fellow students home with him. We lived only two hundred miles from campus, a manageable distance for a weekend. But when Allen came to visit, their conversation was not the usual talk that went on in the Mahern household. They were talking about subjects that were real to me: ideas, and how they fit together or conflicted with each other. They were students at the University of Chicago. For me, that would have been a dream come true. I was envious.

Looking back, my question seems to have as much to do with me as with Mike. I was probably noting between the two of them a characteristic which for me is an essential element of intimacy: intellectual play, sparring, cavorting. (This is a happy element in my relationship with David, my husband.) I was saying, "I see that you have intellectual compatibility, are you compatible in other ways as well?" And on that question rode my real concern. If Mike were homosexual, I wanted him to know that it gave me no problem.

I'd waited twenty years after high school graduation to begin taking college courses. Then my classes were scheduled between household chores. So of course I had no after-class contact with other students, whom I imagined were having engrossing discussions as I speeded home to fix lunch.

I imagined that students and professors on campus were engaged in continuous, stimulating, intellectual conversation. I believed in The Ivory Tower, and I wanted to live there. I was not disabused of this notion until years later, when my car broke down close to Purdue University, where Kate was a student. She arranged for me to have a bed for the night next to a very thin wall which brought me a sample of campus conversation. The subject was the darlingness of a certain student. "I mean, he is really, really darling."

Mike and Allen's conversation was an oasis in the desert. I didn't want it to be a mirage.

Mike says that he never denied his homosexuality. It is important to him, that he can say that. But if it is true that homosexuals live in fear of such a question from a parent, why didn't he take that opportunity? He could have said, "No, not with *Allen*." It seems that it would have been so easy at that point. Maybe the question just came at him too quickly.

Or possibly it was because of the family dynamics. If Mike thought that admitting his homosexuality to me was tantamount to admitting it to his father, if he thought that I would force the knowledge of his homosexuality onto his father, he was right. If he thought that his father would have accepted it grudgingly or not at all, he was probably right.

Our family dynamics were not too unusual for the 1950s and most of the sixties. Television showed family dramas in which the adult female played Dumb Mama. It was how the world saw us, how we saw ourselves. We told jokes at our own expense. I knew a young married woman who said that the basic joke between her and her husband was, "Susan is always wrong. Jeff is always right." Once you saw the pattern, it was no longer funny, or tolerable. No matter how bad family dynamics are, change is not welcome, particularly if the problem has been pointedly ignored.

By the time Mike graduated, I had a teaching license, a job as a teacher, and growing independence. There would be another seven years, a divorce, and a move to Chicago with my youngest son, Paul, before Mike would admit his homosexuality to me, late in January, 1974. He was fulfilling a New Year's resolution.

Would Mike have reacted differently to my question concerning Allen if it had come after the divorce, when he knew that my communication with his father was unlikely? I don't know.

Chapter Three

Five Thousand Years

As I write this I am wearing a T shirt that says, "I SURVIVED 5,000 YEARS OF PATRIARCHAL HIERARCHIES."

I am not mad at anyone, finally. I do not want to point a finger. To turn anyone off. But I must tell the truth.

Yesterday I spent several hours going over the newspaper columns I wrote, under the name Elsye Mahern,* for the *Indiana Catholic and Record* during the 1950s. Some weeks ago I faced them for the first time, segregating out into folders the ones I thought I would need, to see more deeply how our family life affected Mike and his homosexuality. The folders labeled Family, Children, Observations (general), Community, and Mike (early, middle, and late) have lain on the corner of my desk since that time.

For days, I have known that I was avoiding the folders. I knew it was time to look more closely at the contents. I moved the folders to the first floor, to the table beside my easy chair. They sat for more days, and yesterday I opened them.

One cannot talk about homosexuality without talking about sexism. I contributed to it. Promoted it. Internalized it. No wonder I have been avoiding those columns.

When I was to be married at the age of eighteen, I insisted on carrying a spray of lilies of the valley on my prayer book, in lieu of a wedding bouquet. The plant encyclopedia describes the flower as "Small, fragrant, drooping, waxy white, bell-shaped, spring-blooming flowers on 6-8 inch stems rising above 2 broad, basal leaves." Lilies of the valley are hardly discernible because of the broad green leaves and because of their droop and tiny size. They are like a very small, shy child, who hangs her head and turns away. You must support the droop with your hand and turn the bell of the flower toward you. It is then possible to see the exquisite shape of the almost microscopic bell with its very edge turned out to greet you.

The difference between this flower and the eighteen-year-old girl who insisted upon it could hardly have been greater.

I had learned about life from the movies. I had learned that people looked at each other. They spoke together of similarities, agreements, conflicts. It was possible to solve problems: it was not necessary to allow life to just take you and shake you. I was movie struck, but Hollywood was far away and impossible. The stage was as close as the church, the school.

My first role was as a maid, when I was a freshman in high school. Only about five or six lines, but the opportunity to express extreme anger. The first and last time my Dad ever saw me act —he rejected the idea that I acted. He said, "Why that's just the way she is at home." All throughout my high school years, I acted in church or school plays, sometimes juggling rehearsals in two plays at once. I also wrote a fashion column for a mimeograph paper which some friends and I published. I wrote for the school paper. I lobbied for a Hawaiian theme for the junior prom, and it was chosen. Lily of the valley? I don't think so.

I knew what was expected of a bride in 1940. We were married in late November, and the flowers were flown in from, as it happens, Germany. Now I see a wry irony in this: my grandmother, Hetty, who imposed upon me the name of Elsye—and from whom I get some of my "starch"—was from Germany. The sweet little bells also came from the Reich.

The flowers were twenty cents a stem. I'd worked for the NYA, the National Youth Administration, a part of Roosevelt's recovery program, at school. Fifteen cents an hour, forty hours a month: $6.00. In that economy, I would have worked eighty minutes for each tiny stem.

The word bride is a corruption of Bridget, which in Gaelic means Fiery Arrow. But I knew I was not supposed to be a fiery anything. The lilies of the valley tell me plainly how totally and sincerely I intended to take up the life expected of me: the life symbolized by the wedding veil.

Eleven months after we were married, Louie Joe was born, and sixteen months later came Timmy, then Eddie, followed by Kevin.

When Timmy was six he developed a tic: blinking his eyes and then opening them wide. At the same time he became insecure, uncoordinated. I took him to our family doctor, who found nothing wrong, but sent us to a pediatrician. He thought I was a nervous mother, but sent us to a further specialist. Before that appointment, Timmy complained of a headache, fell unconscious, and was dead in a matter of two hours. I was somewhat prepared, because I knew something was wrong, and when the doctors couldn't find anything, I knew that it was dire, since beyond their expertise.

Mike was born just a month short of the first anniversary of Timmy's death. Thirteen months later, there was Marty, and two years later Mary, followed thirteen months later by Kate, and after another year Regina, who died at birth. When Kate was nine there was Paul. My childbearing years stretched from 1941 to 1963 and the birth of Paul.

The score was seven boys and three girls, with six boys and two girls surviving. Our first six children were boys. With each son, I received broad smiles, congratulations, approval. I knew I did a good thing: males were better.

Even though I was approved for producing males, I was not myself a male. I was a female, inferior, "dumb" let us say. And let us prove it.

There were a lot of quizzes, fun, and humor. My quizzes, which I played along with willingly, I know, because I wrote about them, had to do with sports and geography. My poor sense of directionality, and disinterest in sports guaranteed that I would do poorly on these subjects. And if you learned by rote, or osmosis, that the Dodgers played for Brooklyn and the Giants for New York, after a time that knowledge turned to ignorance because both teams moved to the West Coast. That out of date information was cause for laughter, and the subject of a column. Written humor is hard to come by, and I wrote about this game. It's difficult now to see how I cooperated.

The directionality was an even easier target. It was only in a teacher training course that I learned that one acquired a sense of right and left at about the age of five or six. I never got that sense. I told my right hand by the strawberry birth mark on my right thumb. Then, in Catholic school, *right* was reinforced by the sign of the cross and genuflection, both of which involved the right hand or knee.

With a sports quiz it was just lack of information, but with directionality there was a weakness within me. At any time on a drive, I could be asked, "Which way is north?" A guaranteed failure.

My spatial difficulty was so severe that, even though I walked four blocks to church every morning, straight down the street, I never knew which side of the street I'd find the church on. I could have set up a problem and logically learned to know about the church. But since it involved only myself, I never bothered.

I simply accepted that Louie knew about such things and I did not. This acceptance was so complete that when he attempted to teach me to drive, and said, "Turn here," I turned to the right, into a ditch.

That was dumb of me. We both accepted that. It never occurred to me that I gave him too much power, that it was not a smart idea for me to try to learn from him, that what I learned from him was not good for me.

Later, when I studied for a mid-term in a class on Modern Europe, he offered to help me by asking me questions on the study sheet. It was a subject he was interested in and I was not. There were dates, treaties, wars, and rulers. But I had studied and missed only two out of a hundred questions. He went to bed early with a bad headache.

Still later, when I taught high school and had not yet learned to use a ruler to enter grades, I entered three grades on what was obviously the wrong line. He was in a good mood all evening.

This was the atmosphere into which our homosexual son was born. Male was good. Female was the subject for derision.

Writing the column gave me a sense of my own individuality. But it was not until Mike was almost twenty years old that I had a real job, and the possibility of being self-supporting.

As long as a woman stays at home, and has no regular contact with the outside world, there is no outer reality check on the relationships within the family. She can be treated unfairly. She can treat others unfairly. It is only when she steps into the world of a paycheck for duties done that the home situation is thrown into relief.

My health had never been good. Among my siblings, I was the most frail, the most prone to disease. When I was raising my own family, low energy was a great problem. In the sixties I attended college with the aid of Vocational Rehabilitation.

During my first year of teaching I functioned fine for the five teaching days, but could hardly get out of bed on the week-end. I did not realize that I was sick because of the dawning insight that at school I was treated with more respect, *and* paid real *money*.

The weekend strain of the difference between life at home and life out in the world made me sick. But I did not realize that I was suffering a foretaste of what Mike would go through to proclaim his nature and take his place in the world. In the end it is good news that it's easier out there than it is at home, but it is painful to realize that you can be more yourself, more accepted by strangers, than by your own family. At the end of *Streetcar Named Desire*, Tennessee Williams has Blanche Dubois say, "I have always depended on the kindness of strangers."

My own mother never left home for the discipline of a job, and her outer life and her view of men and women could hardly have been more divergent. Born in 1900, she worked for a millinery company painting flowers on hats. Her extremely small salary was carried home and handed over to her mother. She was married at the age of 18. She had no experience of freedom or of handling money.

As a married woman her life consisted of using every small resource (she once made me a beautiful dress from two dresser scarfs) in an effort to feed and clothe a family of seven with the money left from her husband's post-payday binges.

Once he got confused in the hall, and urinated against the bedroom closet door. My memory of her on her hands and knees, wiping up the urine, is searing.

Within her mind she had a picture of men protecting women, boys protecting girls. She tried to project this idea onto her children. She told one story of a boy leading his younger siblings up the stairs to bed. The boy saw a man lurking in the hall, and without mentioning it to his slightly younger sister, he led them back downstairs again to get help. What that story taught me was to be afraid in upstairs halls.

Boys were to take care of their poor weak sisters, in such ways as carrying their books home from school. My brother carried my books once, partway home. Mother forgot to indoctrinate me in the graciousness that this gesture should have called forth on my part.

No doubt I had animosity built up from being told that my brother could ride his bike around the neighborhood and I could not. The reason given was, "He's a boy." I got even with him when mother sent me to the field where the boys played to fetch him home. "Mother wants you."

"What does she want?"

I hadn't bothered to find out. So this routine grew into me sing-songing, "Mother wants you, and I don't know what she wants you for." This produced the desired effect.

He was probably in the sixth grade and I in the third, when he undertook to carry my books home from school. This was power too heady for me to resist. I must have taunted him. I can still see the place on the sidewalk, just beyond where Huckleberry's lived, where he set my books down. I walked on without them, sure that he was wrong. Wasn't he supposed to protect me?

He burst in the door and told his story. Mother sent me back to pick up the books. But before she did, she slapped me in the face, and said, "That's just like a girl!"

I think of her evaluation of me, and of the urine on the floor and of the whole summer long when she and I wrung the family wash by hand because the broken wringer needed a part that cost more than a dollar. She laid the wrung bed sheets along her upper arm as she twisted the water from the tail ends. Her large hands had double-jointed fingers, red and gnarled with effort.

I can time the book episode pretty well, because it had to be before my brother had a paper route, and the paper route was then passed down to me. It had to be before the Five Hundred Mile race in 1931, when Billy Arnold won. It was thrilling to cry "Extra! Extra!" along my route and have my customers emerge from their houses and give me pennies in exchange for the paper. My cry was the first they knew. I told them that Billy Arnold won. In my excitement I forgot my paper bag when I went to pick up the papers, and the *Indianapolis Times* was so fresh from the press that my dresser scarf dress was smeared black from where the paper rubbed my leg as I walked along. I was nine then.

It is harder to date the broken-wringer summer. Probably it was the next summer. I would have needed to be ten to be big enough to wring anything larger than socks or washcloths.

When we'd finished the several hours of hard work, I'd be given two nickels. I'd go across the street to the filling station and buy two Cokes. The bottles were like icy jewels, heavy and substantial, as most things in my life were not. We'd drink them on the porch, our dresses clinging to us, soaked with rinse water.

Whenever I think of being with my mother, I think of us with our clothes pasted to us and of those Cokes. Today a few swallows of Coke is the most refreshing thing I can think of on a hot day, but I need to be careful and drink it slowly, or I get a deep aching pain between my shoulder and neck.

We were tired on that porch but satisfied. The family would have clean clothes for another week. We'd done what was necessary.

But it should not have been necessary. I don't understand alcoholism. It seems that denial, avoidance of the truth, is the disease, and drinking is the symptom.

And the same could be said for homophobia. The phobic person does not examine the inner workings of self, but projects all that is dark and unacceptable onto a person or subject in the outer environment.

*In the matter of names. I was born Elsie Cantwell. Hettie, my starchy grandmother, wanted to tell everyone what to do. She wanted my older brother named Jack. When her wishes were not honored, she simply called him Jack for the rest of her life. Grandma wanted me named Elsie. I guess Mother thought it would do no good to resist. It never felt like my name. I especially disliked the name because she sought to social-climb by naming me for a rich woman in the town. When I started high school I changed the "i" in Elsie to a "y." Then I married Louie Mahern. That's how I came to write the column as Elsye Mahern.

When David and I married and moved to California in 1980, I saw my chance. I changed my given name to Mary Ann. I feel a great benefit from the change, and recommend it to anyone who feels that they do not have the right name.

Chapter Four

Mike Through The Columns

Mike was born in 1950, which is the year I started writing "Family Growing Pains" for *The Indiana Catholic and Record,* now renamed *The Criterion.* I continued writing that column until Mike was ten years old. I wrote about the family, the children. They were my children but also my subjects. When I look over the columns today I am surprised how their individuality stands out. I would still know which child was being written about if the name were deleted.

I realized that I did have information about the early life of a gay child, because I had Mike's first ten years delineated.

At first Mike had an advantage with his father. Big hands and feet. Louie was always looking for a son to follow him in his career as an amateur champion swimmer. The first examination was of hands and feet. Large ones are important. All Mike's older brothers had more or less taken after me when it came to water: they feared it. When they first showed signs of not liking the bath, I switched to bathing them on the bath table. I didn't want them to be afraid, and have it attributed to me.

Mike has the hands and feet and he loves the water. Water rolls out from under the bathroom door. Drops cling to the curtains, the walls, and even the ceiling. Mikie's father throws water in his face. He catches his breath, shakes his head, and squeals for more. The only time he objects, cries, screams is when he is taken from the water.

It was at bath time that I found out about the red eyebrows. If he got mad enough, if he stiffened and screamed long enough, his eyebrows turned bright red. This condition was to be avoided at all cost. There was no turning back, it just had to be endured and usually ended with a spent boy, hiccupping loudly.

Only now, in looking back and thinking about the red eyebrows, do I realize how much Mike's determination and will served him as a homosexual, to prevent his life from being worse than it has been. As an infant he didn't want his bath to end. Screaming and crying were his only method of getting his way, but he didn't stop until he'd used up all the cries and screams.

By the time he was in high school he must have realized that he needed to get out, go to another location where he would feel more free to pursue his sexuality. He started to write to colleges for information and catalogues when he was a sophomore in high school. By the time he graduated, he had several full scholarships to choose from. His actions here were not unconnected with the red eyebrows.

Shortly after his birth, Mikie's Grandpa bought him a wheeled device, a circle of metal, which held up a yellow canvas seat. The metal curved down to the floor in four legs ending in wheels. Mike looked like a long legged spider when inserted into this contraption, and he careened, dangerously, banging into legs both human and wooden, grabbing everything within his reach, from the time he was six months old.

When Mike was not quite three his Dad and I decided that something should be done about his looks. He had creamy skin, rosy cheeks, curly blond hair, and large blue eyes. When he went to the store with me, women exclaimed about his eyes, pulled the curl of hair sticking out the front of his cap, and cooed over him.

His cousin Jimmy came over picked him up and said, "You're a pretty boy."

"I know it," he said calmly.

He'd always had a boy's haircut but we decided that a shorter cut would be advisable at least until he quit attracting so much attention. And we'd call him Mike instead of Mikie. The little plaid pants he strutted around in would be handed down to Marty, about whom I wrote in a column, "has an overdose of masculinity and is completely unconcerned in the matter of clothes." I agreed to this make-over. I can't tell whose idea it was, mine or his Dad's. But at least I agreed to it.

The agreement came after we'd gone to the store to buy Louie Joe a suit and Mike a jacket. We heard him say, "Hey, I like this picture!" He was standing in front of a mirror, gazing at his own image.

There was a later haircut which was different, and shocking. I was awakened from a nap by four-year-old Mike standing close to my face and calling, "Mommy." I opened my eyes and screamed. I could see nothing except his bald head. Daddy and Mike's big brothers were standing at the foot of the bed enjoying the show. What impresses me now about that scene is the animosity toward me. Louie always cut the boy's hair. So it wasn't a case that I wanted him to have long curls. (Didn't that used to be the popular idea of the cause of homosexuality? "His mother kept his hair in long curls, and dressed him in skirts until he was four.")

If Louie had consulted me about scalping Mike, I'm sure I would have objected. So he could have just done it and then told me about it, or just waited for me to see. But by waking me from a sound sleep, it seemed to me that he was saying, "Take that." It was somehow my fault if Mike weren't "masculine" enough.

The evidence grows that he was not *boy enough*. When Uncle Paul married Aunt Rose, Mike wanted to know all about her dress and the flowers. He announced, "When I get married I'm going to give my wife lots of flowers." He left the table two or three times during a meal because, "I have to wipe my hands off." Later he would jump up just as often to make sure that his table appointments were just right. When Louie Joe made a sarcastic remark about his efforts, (Mike was eight or nine by that time) he handed it back with, "You're just mad because no one will fix your toast."

By the time he was six he had decided that he'd be a priest, and he wondered how he'd pay for a car because he knew that priests must have one. He wondered what happened to a saint's halo when he got his head chopped off, and how could Mary be Jesus's mother when no one is older than God?

Another column was about my day to drive the kindergarten car pool. When Charles got in the car, he and Mike rolled around on the middle seat of the station wagon, laughing and hitting each other.

When Mary Lou got in, Charles said, "I think I'll just get back here with her." They both climbed into the far back seat. Mike had a friend until the friend went off with a female: a possible pattern in future life. It is poignant to read this from a distance of forty years. Something went wrong here for the child, and he couldn't have known what it was. I might think that I put too much stock in the incident if it weren't for what happened next.

We pick up several more children, all girls. The conversation died for a while and the next thing I heard was one of the girls saying, "You're cute!" I looked in the mirror to see Susie sitting beside Mike with her face close to his. Here was a female looking for a male. "You're cute," she repeated, "you know it?" Mike wasn't playing this game.

For some time Mike and Susie had been competing about cars and family members. Who had the best car—who had the most brothers and sisters: a famous Catholic competition of the fifties. Now he blurted out, "I had another sister. Her name was Regina Marie and she went to heaven right away."

Apparently this bit of information had the desired effect of getting Susie off the subject.

Mike has said that it was in kindergarten when he realized his difference from other boys. It seems almost impossible that a child could realize it much sooner than that. Even if the child had the maturity and insight for comparison before the age of five, most children are not put together in a large enough group of peers who are the same age, or almost the same age, until kindergarten. Most day care centers have a broader range of ages.

At least that was true in 1955 when Mike was in kindergarten. Today children may be in a strictly age-level peer group much earlier, and it may be possible that a child could realize the difference at three or four.

I am fascinated by the picture of Mike in the kindergarten pool, knowing that he knew of the difference in kindergarten. The carpooling day which I wrote about was datelined March 1956, which meant he'd been in kindergarten for six months. Chances are he knew, but he wouldn't have needed to know to show a difference. The difference was there. I think he didn't know at the time of Uncle Paul's marriage, but he showed the difference by his interest in Rose's dress and in the flowers.

In the carpool column he was most exuberant with Charles: they were laughing and punching each other. Then I observed, "the male fun was short lived," because when Mary Lou got in the car Charles scrambled into the far back seat with her.

The scene between Susie and Mike could have been projected twenty years into the future, located in a bar where a woman was trying to strike up a conversation with a man who attracted her: a man who unbeknownst to her was gay. Straight women are often attracted to gay men because they are expansive, expressive, and open, and do not have a hidden, or not so hidden, agenda.

A gay man and a straight woman can be friends. Indeed, a gay man's term for another gay in whom he has no romantic interest is *girlfriend*. "He's just a girlfriend." Mike's refusal to answer Susie, and his changing the subject, would fit that future scenario just as well.

He had heard that "you're cute," line often before, and possibly he'd been taught that he shouldn't say, "I know it," or that he should say, "thank you," when someone says nice things to you. But I'm sure that he hadn't been taught to withhold an answer. That non-answer must have come from within himself. Was his non-response his awareness of attraction to males instead of females? Or was he learning already that his response might be unacceptable?

I'm thinking of those maligned mothers who were thought to have "caused" their sons to be homosexual by dressing them in a way not regarded as masculine. Possibly they had an exquisite insight into their sons' true natures, and were perfectly willing for that nature to grow its own way.

I can't claim to have had that insight, or at least I can't claim to have allowed it to grow its own way. I had internalized sexism: for a male to show traits attributed to females was to be less than male: that is, to be female.

I have said that Mike was unusually attractive, smooth, beautiful. He laughs now, and bemoans that, "I peaked at the age of five." His sister Mary had those same attributes, but they were treated differently because she was a girl.

Mary was the first girl after six boys. When she was born, people said, "Oh, you must be so thrilled." I wasn't thrilled, I was in shock. I knew how it went with boys. I had resigned myself to having boys.

I could not immediately change to ruffles. She was a year old before I managed scallops, and I could, and can to this day, treat ruffles only with great restraint. Mary, Kate, and I all wear classic rather than fancy clothes. Perhaps our styles have been influenced by the extreme maleness of the family.

Even though Mary was not dressed fancily, her beauty was not thwarted. We did not feel that she needed to be plainer, less attractive. When she was three, L.S. Ayres had a photography promotion which amounted to a beautiful child contest. I dressed Mary in a blackwatch plaid dress with a white pique collar, a white flat-brimmed hat with a few flowers across the front, and wrist-length white gloves. A restrained, elegant look. The first photos were not good at all, and I asked that they be retaken. This was done. She won a fifty dollar government bond, and now and then for a few years after that relatives reported seeing Mary's picture in department store ads in various cities. We all were happy to think that Mary was prize-winning attractive.

I am trying to imagine what would have happened if I'd entered Mike in such a contest. He would certainly have had an equal chance at a prize. What would his Dad's reaction have been if I'd advertised his beauty, which was ethereal rather than male, and if I'd insisted on his beauty by asking that the picture be retaken?

There is also an interesting comparison to be made between Mike and his sister Kate. She was born telling people what to do. She was approved and Mike was disapproved: both for sexist reasons. We would be getting into the car, everyone present except Kate. I'd go into the house and call her. She'd appear on the landing between the first and second floors, step down one step and pause. She knew exactly when my mouth was ready to fly open to yell at her, and she'd step and pause again.

I worried about her, because here was a strong female who did not see anything wrong with being a Fiery Arrow. I'd had enough trouble keeping my head down, but she had no intention of trying. I'd never been defiant, at least not that blatantly.

These actions of Kate's were not feminine behavior of the late fifties and early sixties. And she probably was curbed somewhat, but her Dad and I laughed about her actions in secret. Mike's actions and mannerisms were seen as female: second class. Kate was female, but her actions made her almost as good as a male: first class.

I went along with this. Who knows why? Because of internalized sexism. To gain approval from the males in the family. It was a male household, and I was fitting in.

PART II

THE SURVEYS

Chapter Five

Under Way

I heard the mail hit the box. When I looked, the lid was up—a flat package. The surveys I had been waiting for? Yes. I opened the package and began to read. I was most interested in the answers to Item #2, because that was the question which started the whole thing. At what age did you have an inkling that your emotions and interests did not match familial and societal expectations of one of your sex? Please expand as fully as possible on the thoughts, feelings or experiences.

This was the question which started my research. Did other gay children know as early as my son Mike did?

Two respondents gave the age "6 or 7," one gave the age of "5," one the age of "4 or 5," and one gave "first grade."

Since first graders are six or seven years old, that answer makes three answers of six or seven. So the range fell between four and seven years old. Mike was not the only one who knew!

These five respondents represented diverse groups: Catholic, Protestant, Mormon, Black, White; from the United States, Ireland, Trinidad; between the ages of thirty and forty-five.

One would expect a great diversity, and there is, except on the subject of homosexuality. They all knew early: knew of the need for secrecy. They all suffered. Alone.

Since the five surveys were returned to me by Mike, I'd used up my contact with the gay community. He suggested that I call the Gay and Lesbian Center at the San Francisco Public Library.

Jim Van Buskirk, the Director at the center, was very helpful. As I talked about the project, he suggested that I might also survey parents to see when they had an inkling that their child might be gay. He told me about Pflag.

The name Pflag is an acronym for *Parents and Friends of Lesbians and Gays*. That was the original intent, but recently the F has taken on the double meaning of Friends and Family.

I had known about the organization before and had seen their newspaper, *The Pflagpole*. Jim thought that if I wanted to get surveys answered by parents, Pflag would be the most valuable, possibly the only, source.

My own prejudice stopped me from going to a Pflag meeting. I thought that Pflag represented people from Orange County, California, who were saying, "Our children are all right the way they are, they're Republicans, aren't they?" Maybe my idea of Orange County as Republican, with a *just us* attitude, stems from my extremely Democratic background. My mother worked to elect Franklin Roosevelt in 1932. And my ten-year- old mind boggled when I was told that Monsignor Killian was a Republican. How could you be Republican and Catholic, a *Monsignor*?

I voiced my feelings to Jim. He said mildly, "That's what it's all about isn't it?" It's all about prejudice against people, groups.

In my mind, at that time, Pflag was made up of people who had a problem with gays and lesbians. Gays and lesbians were disowned: I'd stand with the disowned. Pflag represented the parents who were struggling to accept their family members, but I couldn't grant them any leeway for that. I was prejudiced against them for having a problem with the subject at all. But beyond the word Republican, I had a problem with what I took as the inference that these gays and lesbians were all right *because* "they are our children." What about the homosexuals whose parents did not speak out? Were they not all right? I thought they were all right because homosexuality is their nature. Because they exist.

I had to begin to admit that I had something in common with these Pflag people. Gay children. What's more, they had done something for their children. I was only now trying to correct a wrong which I perceived. And the final, ignoble motive: I needed them. They had built a system of information which I needed.

I was to learn later that Pflag grew out of the actions of a mother who did instantly accept her son's sexual orientation. In June 1972 Jeanne Manford marched beside her son, Morty, in a Liberation Day parade. She carried a sign saying, "Parents of Gays: Unite in Support for Our Children." There was almost instant applause which she thought was for Dr. Benjamin Spock, who marched just behind them. Then gays and lesbians ran out from the sidelines, crowding around her, asking her to speak to their parents. The Pflag movement grew out of that hand-lettered sign which this grade school teacher had made out of her love for her son and her innate openness and honesty.

Then I read these words in a Letter to the Editor: "I am a gay son who has a father—I am standing on firm footing when I tell you how rare it is to have a father who is the least bit tolerant, let alone accepting."

I later talked to this man, Don, about my project. He and everyone else I spoke with, thought that I would get no replies from fathers. It was all the more reason to try. Don and his mate attend Pflag. That was encouragement to me: if gays can accept Pflag, then I should too. I devised a survey for parents, which follows:

Parent's Survey

CHILDHOOD: GAY WOMEN, GAY MEN

The following is an attempt to gather information about the pre-pubescent life of gays. Please take the time to answer the following questions. Your co-operation could prove helpful to children of the present and future. Answer as fully as possible, no thought or feeling is irrelevant. Use the back of these sheets, and attach more sheets if necessary. Please indicate which item you are responding to. Thank you for your help.

1. Circle the appropriate:

I am the father mother of a gay man gay woman.

2. At what stage, or age, in the life of your child did you begin to think/feel that he/she might be other than heterosexually oriented? Please expand as fully as possible on the thoughts, feelings or experiences.

(With Items # 2, 4, and 5, space was left blank for the parent's replies.)

3. Was the knowledge or insight difficult/impossible for you to think or talk about. If the answer is yes, could you estimate, in percentages, how much the difficulty was due to your own thoughts and feelings about homosexuality, and how much due to society's view of the subject?

My view_____% Society's view_____%

4. How would your life and relationship with your homosexual child have been different, if within weeks of the child's birth you had been told and accepted that there was a one in ten chance that your child is a homosexual?

5. Do you have any ideas/thoughts/feelings about what could have made the childhood of your offspring happier, and your acceptance/tolerance of your child's sexuality easier?

The above was printed on three sheets of paper, with room for replies. At the bottom of the third sheet were instructions on how to return the surveys to me. All surveys, to the best of my knowledge, were accompanied by a stamped envelope, addressed to me.

Note: The early parent surveys were addressed to the parent of gay men or lesbians. As I learned the prejudice against and avoidance of the word *lesbian* I changed the wording of the parent survey to read gay women and gay men.

Revolutionary Aging and Pflag

I wasn't ready for Pflag, but I knew I needed to talk to people. I thought of the Revolutionary Aging group that meets in Santa Rosa. This is a group of older women who meet to discuss age, society, and how they want their lives to be different from the stereotype of women in their sixties and upward. Revolutionary Aging is just one of the interesting groups offered by The Women's Center.

Earlier I'd gone to a one day workshop on Women's Sexuality sponsored by the Women's Center, and was impressed by the open dynamism of the women I met there. There were women there from all walks of life, and all economic strata. Women on welfare, or those who otherwise could not afford even the lower end of the sliding scale cost, were given the opportunity to help with the work in lieu of a fee.

They were all talking about "Faludi's book." This was in 1991, shortly after Susan Faludi's book *Backlash* had been published. I wondered where I'd been: I'd never heard of it. Neither had the booksellers in my neighborhood.

The Revolutionary Aging group was not a disappointment. There was one youngster of forty-nine, but most of the women were in their late sixties up to the mid-eighties.

A doughy, juicy bunch of dames. I can recall no word of self pity uttered during the afternoon. They were not rich, not all healthy: a couple of leg braces glimpsed between shoe and slacks told what went unspoken. These women were different, "revolutionary," I guess you could say. And maybe it was partly the environment in which they lived. Californians take care of themselves, but do not think of age. One woman remarked, "There are six students enrolled at Santa Rosa Junior College who are over one hundred years old."

The women in the room had some physical ailments, but the chief overall characteristic was aliveness.

When one woman declared, "The business of old women is to do justice," I thought of an idea I'd heard more than once. The idea was: when a woman is old she is entitled to tell the truth. An old woman could do justice by telling the truth.

I'd brought my project to the right place.

Another woman expressed her surprise at the pleasure of living alone. "Why did no one mention this before?"

These women were not going to drop their jaws in shock at the mention of homosexuality, nor were they likely to deny it if they had a gay son or daughter. We went around the room, each of us introducing herself and saying why she came to the group, or what she hoped to profit from the afternoon. I talked about the survey, and asked for their help. Two or three hands went up in immediate response.

When the meeting was over and women began to drift toward the refreshment table, I produced the Parent's Surveys. By that time there were seventeen women left in the room and four of us had a gay or lesbian child.

No one knows the actual percentage of lesbians and gays in the population. Ten percent is a figure generally agreed upon. But with four women out of seventeen having produced a homosexual child, I was led to think that the percentage may be considerably higher.

The three other mothers took surveys with them. Margot was in a hurry, but she tossed over her shoulder, on the way out, "Yes, our son came out to his Dad when he was in kindergarten." I wanted to run after her, beat her to her car, hold the door closed until she explained. But I thought that such actions would not lead to her cooperation and my hearing her story.

With this good experience, I was ready to tackle Pflag. The local chapter of Parents and Friends of Lesbians and Gays meets in the evening in the assembly room of a bank. There was nothing attractive about the room. We sat around the outer side of four tables, angled to form a square. The lighting was depressing: nothing here to bring you out after dinner.

Except the people. We went around the room, each of us making a brief introduction and saying something about our family situation. I talked about the project, and mentioned "Family Growing Pains," the family life column that I'd written during the first ten years of Mike's life. I said, "Looking over the columns it is obvious that Mike was homosexual." I implied that one could always tell.

No one disagreed with me, but as we progressed around the square, as others spoke, it became obvious to me that one could not always tell.

One woman visualized sex as on a continuum, with male characteristics at one end and female at the other, with humans all along the line, with various mixtures of female and male. That was a useful idea to me. I have difficulty understanding bisexuals, and cannot spend much time thinking about it while I'm engrossed with this project. Trying to understand gays and lesbians is enough for me just now, but this opened a door for me to begin thinking of bisexuals as people near the center of the continuum.

A frail-seeming woman, announced her name, adding, "I am a life-long Republican." She went on to reveal herself as somewhat of a Ché Guevera of homosexual rights. She talked about calling people when they make homosexual slurs. "Two years ago I couldn't have said anything, and now, I can't keep my mouth shut." This is a different kind of Republican. Later I told a woman from another Pflag chapter about the Republican announcement and she mused, "Republicans usually stay in the closet in Pflag."

Mostly I find meetings as boring as a manual to someone else's computer. Not this meeting. These people are not just going through the motions: they are struggling to change their attitudes. Then I realize, I, too, need to change. It's backwards but I am changing, I'm at least learning tolerance for people who have problems accepting homosexuality in their family. And I remember that I did not respect Mike's unreadiness to come out when I tried to force his closet door.

Janet, a lesbian, is there with her partner. She talks about the importance of being "on the wall:" of having her picture with her partner included with the family portraits displayed in the parent's home.

She is lean, athletic-looking. She talks about the sports activities she and her partner share. When the meeting is over, I ask if we could meet and talk.

I have the idea that lesbians, as children, were praised by men for their sports activity. If that is true, then lesbians' self-concept should have been strengthened, as gay males' self-concept must have been weakened by the disapproval they received from not being able to fulfill the male, (read *preferred*) role. Janet can tell me if that is true.

Chapter Six

The Parade

June 12, 1994. Los Angeles. My husband David and I had gone to Los Angeles to march in the Gay Parade with Mike, his lover, Ronald, and their friends. We were told that the parade might not be as large and festive as usual, because it was the twenty-fifth anniversary of Stonewall, and many gays and lesbians would have gone to New York to celebrate.

Stonewall, which took place on June 28, 1969 in Greenwich Village, marks the decisive time the gay community fought back when harassed, beaten, or sometimes killed. Before the confrontation with the police at Stonewall Inn that early Saturday morning, gays were a free target on which police could vent their frustration and fears. After Stonewall, the homosexual community began to fight back against the prejudice and persecution meted out to them from a certain segment of the modern straight community. How large that segment is would be a matter of conjecture. I choose to think that they are a small minority, with a larger number being led by them, the latter group having had no occasion to think about the issues, and specifically what that persecution entails.

Before Stonewall, there was no opportunity to understand because of the silence on the subject of homosexuality. Straights could do nothing to defend gay men and lesbians because they could not know them. The subject was distant: foreign. Gays were over there, in some strange community, which had nothing to do with us, our family.

After Stonewall, some courageous gays lifted their heads and said, "Yes, I'm gay, and there's nothing wrong with that." They organized. As more and more closets were opened, straight society found that gays and lesbians were not over there: they are our sons and daughters, mothers and fathers. Pflag was formed and parents, friends, and family began to stand by their loved ones.

So now we'd gone to Los Angeles for our first parade. And the reason David and I wanted to march was Don. He's a gay man of fifty, an activist. I saw a letter he'd written to the editor of our local weekly. I telephoned him to see if he'd answer a survey for me. He was suspicious of what kind of book I was writing. He asked to know more about me and the project. I made up a fact sheet and sent it to him. A mother of ten, who'd written for a Catholic newspaper for ten years? I'd be suspicious, too.

We invited him to tea. Of course, he was a little reserved, and when I offered him a cookie, he said, "I'll get one a little later." We continued to talk, a little wary of each other. Finally we got around to Pflag, and he urged me to attend the local meeting. He started talking about marching with the Pflag contingent in a Gay Pride parade. At the same time, he reached for a cookie. Without hearing his words, the change in his expression would have told you that he was talking about something profound. He finished speaking by describing the event as "One of the emotional highs of my life." After that we could hardly wait to experience what had affected him so deeply.

On the day of the parade, we had trouble finding the correct place in the line of march. The people who seemed to know what was going on, who were in charge, kept shouting numbers. But we did not know the number assigned to Pflag. I also didn't know that Pflag chapters would be expressing solidarity with distinctive color T shirts. The shirt I happened to wear was blue-green. So I was marked as an outsider.

The parade started without our finding a place. Finally we spied a Pflag banner coming in the distance. They came abreast of us and the shirts were bright red, orange, Kelly green. With a big smile I noted blue-green shirts marching toward us. Obviously, that's where we belonged, even if only by chance. We fell in four or five lines after the banner. What did the words on the back of the T shirts say? Orange County. I had not wanted to join Pflag, because I thought the members were all Orange County Republicans. So here I was marching with the members from Orange County.

As soon as we were in line and marching, I noticed the applause from the people lining both sides of the street. No one minds being applauded. It was great. Then after a little while a thought crept in, which was not so happy. Why should anyone have to applaud others, just because the applauder is accepted? It should be the birthright of everyone to be accepted onto the planet where they are born.

One should be able to take acceptance for granted. Obviously for the applauders, that was impossible. I thought of a gay young woman in an earlier parade, who left the line of march when she was overcome by weeping because her own parents were not among the parents marching.

There were viewing stands on either side of the street, people hanging out upper windows, sitting on curbs, clapping and cheering us on. Some people held up square signs bearing the numerals 10. I didn't know they were intended to be a number, and tried to figure out the meaning. Was this some kind of a symbol for safe sex? What then? I saw the sign in several different places, so obviously the meaning was commonly known. Then among the cheers, I heard, "A ten! A ten!" It was a rating system. On a scale of one to ten, the parents, family and friends marching were rated Ten.

Directly in front of us in the line of march were three men in blue-green, Orange County Pflag T shirts. They further broke down my stereotype of people from what I thought of as John Wayne country.

I guess I was influenced by Wayne's statue, three stories high, in the lobby of the airport named for him, and by the experience of leaving the terminal and seeing MacArthur Highway.

"MacArthur?"

"Douglas," David replied, no happier than I was.

These trips to Orange County happened about four years ago, when David had a client who urged us to move to the area. We went looking for a house, and wherever we went David asked, "Are there any Democrats around here?"

Mostly people just looked at him as though he'd asked about rattlesnakes or alligators. Once he asked a woman who was selling her own house that question. She considered a moment and pointed to a house across the street and two houses down.

"He teaches at the university," she said, "and she's some kind of an artist. I wouldn't be a bit surprised to hear that they are Democrats." The still-pointing finger and the slowly nodding head agreed with her new insight into her neighborhood.

Now the three men marching in front of us in the parade were Latinos. That was a surprise. In a way, they did fit my stereotype, but I never expected to see them marching in a Gay Pride parade. The man on the left held a sign aloft in his left hand, while he waved to the crowd with his right. He was probably in his fifties, and I have to think of him as Gordo. He looked rock solid, and not much taller than he was wide. On the right side was a man, probably in his early to mid-twenties, deeply tanned. When he turned his head to the left, I could see his mouth. There was something about the set of it which made me think: If I were in a tavern, and a fight seemed to be brewing, I would get as far away from him as possible.

From what I could see of these two men, given a crowd and asked to rate people for bigotry, they would be my number One and Two.

Then, between these two, was this young man with softly curling dark hair. He could have been between sixteen and twenty: remember, I am behind these people, this family. He is smiling, confident, accepted. Who are these men, and how did they get to be so untypical? I've heard that the Latino community is macho, not accepting of gays and lesbians. And maybe the story my mind has made up about these people is fictitious, but there they are marching in the Gay Pride parade.

Society's harm to that young man will be minimal. He has a guardian on either side of him. Those two men, father and brother, can protect him in a way his mother and sister couldn't. The acceptance of mother and sister is somewhat taken for granted: the acceptance of father and brother cannot be.

On an esplanade of grass to the left were a few men huddled together, holding signs with Biblical predictions for the future of people who happen to be born gay or lesbian. They looked so miserable, so outnumbered, so out of place. I thought: Now do you understand how it is to be a very small minority: to be different from the great crowd around you? Maybe one of them did.

A man with intricate camera equipment jumped in front of us, marching backward. The camera seemed to be aimed at our middles. A belly-button freak? Ours were all covered. What then? Was he photographing our clasped hands: mine and Ronald's, one pinky white, the other rich brown? It seemed so long ago that color was an issue: sweet and distant. But of course it still is.

Then I saw the young man, standing a little apart from others nearby. A tightness around the mouth, a look of bright torture in blue eyes, and I am sure about him, as I could not be sure of the Orange County men. He knows he's gay, but he cannot accept himself.

The shades of color in the clothing, the skin, the banners, the sparkle of the sun, the rainbow of colors signifying diversity, the bands playing, the baton in the air, the cheering, the happiness, the smiles, cannot be conveyed except as a pale shadow of the reality of the day.

We came to the end of the line and went to sit on a low stone wall, watching the marchers fan out into the adjoining streets. I found myself sitting beside Tim, who was shortly to visit his mother in Ireland, his first time in several years. She knows he's gay but doesn't accept it: thinks it's all nonsense. He talked to me about it, probably because we marched together. David and I were also planning a trip to Ireland. I offered to visit her, see if I can get her to accept him more. As it turns out my visit with her was impossible. So was his, in a different way. She is still waiting for him to find a nice girl and settle down. He told her, "You know that is not going to happen."

But for now, everyone appeared to be talking to everyone. We were all friends. We'd been through a moving experience together. The earth seemed a good place.

Chapter Seven

The Surveys

I spent about seven months going to meetings, talking to people, handing out surveys. At the beginning I spent so much time gaining people's trust that I finally wrote a fact sheet of what I was trying to do. I needed to show them how much the success, even the completion, of the project depended on their cooperation.

Very little writing was being accomplished, because of all the running around and yakking. Sometimes, realizing my helplessness in getting the surveys returned, I meditated for hours trying to motivate possible returnees. Finally I set a deadline three weeks in the future. I would need to progress with what I had when the deadline arrived, even if my goal of 12 gays, 12 lesbians, 6 mothers, and 6 fathers had not been reached. When that time arrived this was what I had: 9 gay men, 11 lesbians, 7 mothers, and 5 fathers.

With the decision made that the information-gathering was complete, I closed the door and went to work analyzing the results. When did the gay or lesbian person know, and when did the parents know?

The surveys did not always yield an age. The lesbians and gays sometimes gave a grade in school which could be translated into an approximate age. When a spread of ages was used, (5 or 6) I used the later age.

GAY MALES: One gay male says he knew "early." I've discarded that survey on the subject of *when known*, as it is impossible to know what "early" means in this context. The average of when the gay boys knew is 6 years, 4 months and 15 days.

LESBIANS: Two lesbians that didn't give a numerical answer were not counted, nor were the two who declared they were born feminists, not lesbians. I found that the lesbians knew of their difference later: at the age of 6 years, 8 months, and 20 days.

FATHERS OF GAYS AND LESBIANS: All of the fathers reported on some exterior event triggering their knowing: usually "when he/she told me." A number could be derived from 4 of the 5 surveys. The ages given were 20, 28, 19, 21. On average the fathers knew the child was gay or lesbian when the offspring was 22 years old.

MOTHERS OF GAYS AND LESBIANS: The mothers' knowledge came in a different manner than the fathers. Mothers intuited, or observed an event, or in one instance refused her own intuition. Mothers knew on the average at 17 years, 9 months and 22 days.

Then I counted the words used by each respondent. Gay men used an average of 452 words; lesbians used 412 words; fathers used 143 words and mothers used 609 words.

With these results tabulated I was ready to deal with the emotions and personal experience of the individuals.

I wanted to be able to assign a name to each respondent, yet feared that I might accidentally assign the person's real name. I solved this problem by starting with the letter identifying the category and proceeding down the alphabet, skipping the letter Q. Thus mothers 1, 2, and 3 became Mattie, Nell and Olive.

Childhood of Gay Males

Item #2 on the survey for gays and lesbians asks: *At what age did you have an inkling that your emotions and interests did not match familial and societal expectations of one of your sex? Please expand as fully as possible on the thoughts, feelings or experiences.*

It must have been difficult to answer this item because it required looking back and analyzing thoughts and experiences which happened at an age when the child lacked a vocabulary for the experience. No kindergartner or first grader knows the words homosexual, lesbian, or gay. If they have heard words such as *queer, fruit,* or *fairy,* it was probably heard as an accusation, and no one wants to be guilty, least of all a little child.

The answers to Item #2 break into two general categories: recognition of a way of being, or recognition of actions, either actions of the child or actions of peers.

The earliest recognition of being different was from Ned. "At the age of three. My very first experience I remember is laying in a crib at the age of three, surrounded by my mother and father. My brother was going across the street to buy cigarettes. I was in awe of the world, the curtains, looking out the window, people; everything was new to a baby of three. I knew intuitively that I was somehow different."

Gary states simply, "I knew as early as first grade."

Lloyd names the difficulty of labeling feelings from early childhood. "My recollection of the first feelings for another man places that event in the pre-school period as I was still at home with Mom. The gentleman in question was the milkman who came by now and then to deliver dairy products.

"But I must admit that I am not sure if my feelings for him were those of a homosexual nature or rather those of just seeing a pal-of-sorts. And I have faced this interpretation problem many times with each occurrence of feelings inasmuch as I have no idea how much of these feelings are commonplace with all boys growing up (this is not to be confused with my awareness as a young man and now about my feelings; they are quite homosexual)."

Later he writes, "If you could tell me that the 'regular' heterosexuals do not have such feelings, then I can tell you without a doubt that I was homosexual at an early age." Later still he writes, "I expect that I realized that family and society would not approve when I was say 10, about fourth grade."

All of the attractions he writes about are for older men, and he is now, at age 52, in a stable relationship with a man older than himself.

Hank writes, "I would say around 6-7. I knew what I was feeling was not 'normal' and began to understand that I was different from most. From that moment I began to hide myself and build walls so others couldn't hurt me."

"At approximately 3rd grade I realized that I liked boys instead of girls. Girls were OK for friends," states Matt, "but boys—usually older boys made me feel warm when I thought about them. Fourth grade brought a label—homo-queer. I felt that I would be forced to be like the visible homosexuals—very fem and fluttery. It made me uncomfortable. Eighth grade I identified myself as a gay person. I went through high school dreaming of men and wandering around in worlds of fiction (literature). I knew that as soon as high school was over I could move away and be who I wanted to be. I'd made a pact that after moving—all of my friends would know that I'm gay and so far no problems."

Jim writes, "I was very aware that I was extremely different from my male peers. This difference was in no way sexually oriented. I began to note these differences as early as 6 or 7 years old. When I began to masturbate at the age of 14, I was fully aware that I was not fitting into my expected societal niche."

Kirk gives the age of 5 as his first awareness of difference. "I recall being in kindergarten and feeling embarrassed about my answer to the question, 'What do you want to be when you grow up?' I could only bring myself to whisper in my teacher's ear that I wanted to be a hair stylist (I outgrew that desire).

"Around the age of 7, I sobbingly told my mother that I wished I was a girl. (I outgrew that desire also)."

What strikes me about this answer is that at five years Kirk knew that these admissions needed to be made in confidence, that he somehow didn't fit in, and yet his feelings must have had a command about them, that he tell at all.

"I think I was 4 or 5 years old," writes Ian. "I felt as if I were different from other boys my age. As a matter of fact I remember playing with friends (boys) and thinking that I must be very strange. I wanted to be close to my male friends. I knew it was something not acceptable I had to suppress it. Doing so made me hate myself. I tried my hardest to like girls like everyone wanted me to. To the point that I was probably overly aggressive.

"My childhood was very painful and I had no one to talk to. Looking at it now I can see a very lonely and sad child. It breaks my heart to see that child.

"If only someone could have been there for me. But we all know, of course, that my family would h(ave?) never permitted me to discuss with anyone the other side of the sexual coin. Too bad. It could have really helped me in my psychological development."

Oscar says he knew of his difference "Early, but I'm not sure what age. I had no interest in sports, which seemed to be all the neighborhood boys were interested in. It is difficult to distinguish what were societal pressures and which the pressure of my intensely dysfunctional family. I do remember having 'crushes' on classmates in grammar school. At the time I thought I was emulating them, attracted to their sporting skills, ability to draw, etc. Now I realize I was attracted emotionally (and perhaps physically).

"I was teased because I played with girls a lot. Their sensibilities and games seemed much less competitive and more my style. I dressed up as a girl only once—I enjoyed it but never repeated it.

"Years before I came out to myself or my parents, I recall my mother telling me after I got off the phone with a classmate: 'You sound just like a queer when you talk to Andy.' Of course, I was totally devastated and confused. I was always encouraged to read, and escaped some of the pain through books."

Two of the respondents mention taking refuge in literature. A story has a beginning, a middle, and an end: a problem and a solution. Perhaps the dynamism of a story soothed at least momentarily their daily problem, which had no solution. This may have worked on two levels for Oscar: on the outside with his dysfunctional family, and on the inside with his awareness of difference.

Gay Men's Answers to Item #3

Item #3: As a child did you feel that you were more alone than others of your age group? If so, what do you think caused this loneliness? Could you give an example of incidents or feelings regarding this?

It seems that in regard to loneliness or being alone, junior high school brought changes in both the amount of loneliness and the relief from it.

Oscar writes, "Yes, I felt very alone. Did not have real friends until junior high. Ironically many of these friends later came out as gay or bisexual. My loneliness was exacerbated by somehow knowing that something about me was different (I didn't know what) and that difference needed to be hidden (I didn't know why). From parental attempts to correct a slight lisp, to kids telling me I 'run like a girl' the message was subtly and not-so-subtly indicating what behaviors were okay, and which were not. I certainly did not feel I could talk to my parents or anyone at school. If I ignored it, maybe it would go away. This created a cycle of distancing myself from anyone as a form of protection. Then being miserable because I was so alone. If I let anyone see the real me, they would discover my secret."

Gary recalls, "I felt alone once I reached junior high school level. Although I enjoyed close-knit friendships with several males of my own age, most of the male students I encountered appeared to view me with suspicion. I always felt that this suspicion arose from differences other male students perceived in my sexual character."

Kirk answers, "Yes. I was reluctant to play with other boys for fear that they would not like me for being effeminate. I was repeatedly informed that I 'act like a girl.'"

Ian states, "Yes, I was very lonely. I think I must have pushed some people away by over-compensating my internal dilemma. I knew the way I felt and I knew I must keep it hidden. I was scared. Scared someone would find out my secret."

Sometimes the gay youths stood apart because of very real differences in their interests. Jim says, "Yes, I was more alone than my brother and male friends. Even though I enjoyed sports and games with my male friends, often their conversations were boring and uninteresting to me." Hank thinks he was more alone, "Most likely because I couldn't relate to the other boys my age. They talked about girls or whatever and I was going through something I couldn't talk about or reasonably expect anyone to understand."

Ned had a knowledge of difference early in life. He said, "Yes. What caused the loneliness was knowing that I was different. I didn't relate to the little boys my age. They seemed to have regimented ways of thinking, as though they had been programmed by their parents as to what their roles were as boys and girls. I remember not liking roles in the first grade, and feeling everyone should be able to be free from that.

"Coming out (to myself only) as a teenager was rough. There were no role models, and I had been taught 'queers' were sick, unmasculine, and perverts. It was very difficult coming to terms with my gayness—It took years to learn I was not 'sick,' that I had the right to be me, and that being 'gay,' is something you are, NOT something you do."

Matt does not connect his loneliness with being gay. "Yes I did feel lonely. I always felt different, I was overweight and often picked on. Today we would say Nerd. As an adult I learned to be alone but not lonely."

Lloyd seemed to be a happy and secure kid, with emotions which were quite manageable. "Regarding childhood loneliness, I have no recollection of any loneliness at any time. Quite the contrary, I always had my siblings, an older brother and even older sister." He then goes on to recall a neighborhood of ease and beauty, where the houses were not locked. He says, "I was relatively unaware of my sexual orientation until at least late teens and probably denied it even then. The realization that this could be real did not show up until college, even though I had incidents of attraction before then. The full awareness came to me upon taking action on my feelings when I seduced a gay man at age 40 and every cell in my body acknowledged that this was where I belonged."

Gay Men's Answers to Item #4

Item #4: How do you think, or imagine, your childhood would have been different, if you were born into a society where sexual orientation made no more difference than, say hair color?

Almost all of the gay men speak of the loss to self and family resulting from the need to hide. Kirk replies, "I'm sure I would have been a happier child—a more outgoing child. I've been told that I was a joyful baby, unafraid of people. But from roughly the fifth grade (which is when I remember boys in my age group starting to make fun of me) up until now I have always worried about what other people think of my behavior."

Matt: "I probably would have been happier—I certainly would have been able to share more of myself with family and friends."

Ian: "Obviously I would have had a much easier time growing up. I became the person I am anyway. It just would have made it less painful and traumatic if I didn't think the whole world was/is against me.

"I was happy that people liked me because I had blue eyes and blond hair. I often wondered if they would still like me if they knew what was inside me."

Lloyd expresses what he would have had different about his childhood. "I would have liked to have someone with whom I could have chatted about my feelings. Absolutely confidential and certainly not my parents. Was it normal, abnormal, a mental illness, or just childhood curiosity?

"Right now I feel so sad for those of us who could not express their feelings and had to be closeted or out in a cruel world, full of hate and oppression. Each of us learned survival techniques, many of which I still see today in the older generation who learned to keep a low profile, lest they lose their jobs or their lives.

"This homophobia and homohatred is deeply rooted in some folks. They need to feel they are better than someone else, to be a step up on the ladder, to have someone less than they are. Coupled with the Biblical cant to which they subscribe, we will always have leaders who take advantage of their flocks' weaknesses and use that to persecute some minority."

Hank enumerates the differences acceptance would have made: "First I would not have experienced loneliness and isolation. Second, I would not suffer from low self-esteem and poor self-image, as I did while a child and young man. Third, I would not have denied myself and my parents the opportunity to share among ourselves my experiences in relationships."

Gary says, "Oh God! What a question.

"Other than the fact that I probably would have had somewhat of a positive self image, better grades in school, more *true* and *close* friends than I had and an improved relationship with my family, no, nothing would have been different."

Surely the last phrase was meant ironically, because there is added an arrow, starting from the word 'difference' in the question, streaking down to below his answer. At the point of the arrow are the words, "Not to mention a million other things."

Ned still talks of loneliness and offers a reason. "I was lonely because I wanted love and acceptance, but you only seem to get that if you fit into roles and were 'like everyone else.' I wasn't and didn't want to be. In a society where sexual orientation made no more difference than hair color, I would have been loved and accepted for being who I am; affirmed and nurtured; I was not.

"Straight society seems to have contempt for anything considered feminine or effeminate. It appears as though straight society is run by macho white men, who want to keep women and gays down. It hasn't changed much, and this is the base of the problem.

"I literally had to claw my way up to the understanding that I was as good as anyone else, because of the label and bigotry society puts on gay children. I was always depressed and felt life was not worthwhile, still I didn't want to be dead, so hung on figuring, there must be a way."

This study must remain incomplete because we have no way of surveying or interviewing the ones who could not, or decided that it was not worthwhile, *to hang on*: the ones who committed suicide.

Oscar points to a possible way. As to the question of how his childhood would have been different, he says, "Much less painful. I would have been encouraged to express and become the real me. As I was wrestling with these peculiar feelings, there would be role models on television, and in children's books. There would be adults (counselors, if not parents) to talk to and be reassured that everything was okay, that there were many people who did not conform to narrowly defined norms. I feel I wasted a lot of time and psychic energy trying to understand and come to terms with my homosexuality. And I had it relatively easy! When I think of parents who disown their kids, kids who are physically and/or verbally and/or psychologically abused, and who consider/commit suicide, I realize how lucky I was.

"I imagine support groups in school where kids would get together and discuss their problems, facilitated by a sensitive adult. Adolescence is such a scary time anyway and fears of homosexuality make it terrifying.

"The energy I put into hiding could have been put into more productive pursuits: education, creative outlets, etc. I would have been happier, better adjusted, and better able to contribute significantly to society."

Jim finds a positive side to his experience. "I probably would have avoided the extremely emotional period that I went through 'coming out.' However, I do feel a lot of qualities that I admire in myself evolved from my daily conflict and self examination over being gay."

Gay Men's Responses to Item #5

Item #5: Please tell about anything relevant to your childhood which has not been covered by the above items.

Five of the nine gay men responded to this item. Threaded through the five answers is a strong theme of problems beyond homosexuality. While working with the surveys, I have often thought that poor self-image and the felt need for secrecy applies to other circumstances also, and not just homosexuality. But the responses to Item #5 show that the conflict of a homosexual child is not instead of the other problems; it is in addition to them.

Alcoholism is a condition that the whole family often makes a silent agreement to ignore. Still, there is some grim camaraderie: all members are enduring it together. If one child of that family happens to be homosexual, he/she has the family burden plus an extra, lonely problem, which may cause guilt for adding to the burden, even though she/he carries it alone.

Oscar writes, "Having read *Growing Up Gay in a Dysfunctional Family* by Rik Isensee, I believe that the combination of homosexuality and a dysfunctional family of origin are an especially lethal combination. I don't blame my family for the mores of the 50s, but it saddens me to realize how many parent/child relationships have been cripple(d) and/or destroyed because of the misinformation, fear, hatred, bigotry, that existed then and is perpetuated today."

Ian's response to Item #5 confirms what Oscar wrote. "After I had already felt homosexual thoughts I was sexually molested by my grandfather. This is something I deal with to this day. I felt like I brought this on because I was gay inside. I thought it was my fault. I didn't tell anyone until I was sixteen, which was ten years later. Psychologically scarred, I went on with my life trying to deal with myself, my environment and all of my secrets. I loved my mother intensely but I thought I would be in trouble for my feelings.

"These hidden pieces came out violently in my teen years. I thought that I had lost every bit of my family but I was starting my new life. I was on my journey into myself, a lot like breaking the chains that bind you."

Matt writes, "My parents are alcoholics. They did not encourage any aspect of my life. My early life was devoid of physical affection. Luckily many of these things have changed."

Hank experienced teasing. "I overachieved academically to overcome and ignore the hurt which resulted. But on the other hand, I also experienced periods of (brief) introvertedness."

Jim again sees gain from his suffering. "My spirituality truly evolved from my conflict over my homosexuality. Because of my fear of going to hell because I was gay, often I studied, prayed and meditated. These practices allowed me to be receptive to the message that I was OK and my viewpoint needed to change."

Childhood of Lesbians

The surveys analyzed in this section are those returned with the identification of lesbian. But after that identification has been made, they begin to qualify the statement. If the women who responded in this section were a head of hair, it would refuse to be combed.

Since women are denied admission to society's approval, they do not stand with their noses against the glass in wantfulness. They disburse and find many solutions. All differences in female children are frowned upon. Don't be too smart, too inquisitive, too strong, too athletic. There are lesbians, feminists, and a bisexual here, and one true horror story.

Pam circles the word lesbian, probably because it is closer to her truth than the other choice. Then she says, "Before I answer this question (#2), I'd like to say that I don't label myself a lesbian. I prefer women now, but I've enjoyed sex with men in the past and am open to that in the future. Right now it's women for me. So I feel lesbian now. Actually not true. (Then inserted between the lines of the last two sentences, in tiny writing is; 'And I'm working through my incest wound. I feel threatened by men now. Later?') I refuse to label myself. I am a sexual being! I do know that I'll never be straight again. Maybe bi."

With that qualification she starts to answer Item #2: *At what age did you have an inkling that your emotions and interests did not match familial and societal expectations of one of your sex?*

Pam responds, "I think I started rebelling against female role models, like my mother, at age 13. I didn't want to be a subservient slave to men. Previous to puberty, I acted and felt like regular straight girls. I was into dolls and actually wanted frillier dresses than the plain ones my Mom often got for me. I wanted to be a baker or a stewardess when I grew up.

"The only evidence I have of being homosexual, looking back, is a big crush on my camp counselor at age 5 or 6. I got married at 21 to a man and he and I would check out women on the sidewalk. Most of my awareness of my own interest in women happened much later in life. I came out to myself at age 27." Pam connects her own late knowledge to growing up in the Midwest.

"My hope for future generations is that there is a lot of love and acceptance for all people of all sexual persuasions. To just be allowed to be my natural open self would be the greatest gift. I'm going to give it to myself now, at age 29."

Riki feels that she never failed to meet the expectations of her family because they never expected her to be one of the female herd. But that she failed to meet "Societal expectations: Always, as long as I can remember. Because I was a tomboy, I knew at age 4 up that I wasn't acting like girls should. But it didn't bother me, since I had plenty of friends who felt the same about girlie-girl roles—that is we didn't want to be boys, but we did want to have their options rather than ours. I mean, who wouldn't want freedom and pride and the chance to try anything (even if you failed), instead of servitude and the humiliation of being 'protected'?

"I *do* want to emphasize, though, that this above stuff is not, for me, about feeling I was 'born gay.' I feel I wasn't. 'Born feminist' perhaps— but the gayness was a choice I made, based on pride: nothing but a truly equal sexual/life relationship is acceptable to me, in my gut *and* my brain. . .And that means equal in the eyes of *society* as well as in the eyes of my partner. The latter kind of equality I *could* get from an exceptional man, but the former I could never get with a man—society, in my lifetime will always see me as property, as being 'had' by any man I'm with. So I won't be with one."

There are two more respondents who indicate a good degree of acceptance by family: Ursula and Maria. "Always," says Ursula, about realizing a difference. "I can't remember ever not being different. I can't ever remember being 'feminine' or 'cute,' being interested in dolls, dress-up, or any of the stuff girls are 'supposed to' be interested in. There's a picture of me at age 4, wearing cowboy boots, hat, etc. I remember that being a cowboy was my first career ambition. (I was very clear about that—a cowboy, not a cowgirl). It's funny how old pictures (age 3-4) reflect my lack of patience with 'girl stuff' like cleaning and cooking. I hated dolls and had no patience or interest when my sisters played with them. My parents learned early on not to give them to me."

Maria: "I was about 10 years, when I probably noticed my feelings around my identity were a little different than the norm. I guess I experienced it as a relationship with myself in the sense it was a secret that I shared w/nobody. I was always a tomboy (not that all tomboys will/ are lesbian) and my behavior was never criticized by my friends/ family. In fact, I was outgoing, popular, athletic. I believe what helped me to identify with the so called 'secret' was meeting other lesbians/ gay people. I finally found others who shared my feelings, thoughts. I had my first relationship with a [here she uses the feminine symbol] when I was 12.

"It was a difficult period—being a gay teen. I came out to my parents when I was 15 and I'm glad I did. Considering I've been out to my family for 15 years—it's been a long process. I have a great relationship w/my family today and I would have hated to spend years of being in the closet hiding them from reality. I also wouldn't have wanted to compromise myself for fear of rejection. My family is open and accepting. But when it comes down to it—I'm sure they would have preferred me to choose the more traditional role. But I have a wonderful life.

"My partner and I have been together for $5^1/_2$ years and are planning our commitment ceremony next spring. We're both professionals."

Noteworthy here is Maria's perception that had she remained in the closet she would have been hiding not herself but her family from reality. Many gays and lesbians deny self the comfort of honesty because they want to save family members from pain. The acceptance and emotional health of Maria's family sound loudly in her responses.

Sonia, "Can't imagine not being a weirdo as a child. I was a tomboy. I wrote poetry. I asked too many questions. The tomboy part was the least of it—I played with dolls and was attracted to boys while simultaneously being a tomboy—but I always knew I was 'queer' in the non-gay sense.

"When I was 13 we all had our IQs tested in school, and mine was over 150—'genius.' My parents' main reaction was that *this* explained why I was so different. (It personally didn't kick in for me for more than another decade, when I discovered feminism)."

Viki writes few words in a tiny script. "I was in love with girlfriends who were playmates at age 5. I spent summers in our backyard with one in particular who made me feel romantic."

Lilly says, "I was a very young age (4th grade). I just remember playing house with my neighbor friend and liking it. From that point on I would have dreams about being with the same sex. These dreams made me feel good inside."

Tammy remembers starting school as a lessening of freedom. "When I started school, I no longer had the choice to wear pants with my older brother's T-shirts. That's probably the first time my choices, my feelings, became 'a problem' to other people. I always felt different at home and at school from the age of five. I have a sister 17 months older and another sister $16\frac{1}{2}$ months younger. They tormented me, whether intentionally or not, because I didn't care about dolls and dresses like they did. Having no reference point, I never thought about whether or not I was homosexual. I had no idea what the word meant, and, therefore, don't remember whether I ever heard the word. Around five or six years old I remember seeing a woman at the post office. She had a butch haircut and I asked my mother why the woman looked that way. Mom said the woman was trying to be a man."

Wendy writes: "I felt that I was 'different' from the time that I was 7 years old. I didn't fit in the girls group in school. I was athletic and strong. I have memories my entire childhood of being the outsider—not fitting in any group.

"Because of my `athletic' demeanor, I was mistaken for a boy (along w/my short haircuts) and still am called 'SIR' to this day. Being called a boy confused me, on one hand it was a compliment, on the other hand it was demeaning as my `male' tendencies weren't given any positive reinforcement. So—as an outcast—I chose to stay an outsider. My family has always supported me as a person and promoted my independence."

Olivia wrote in a tiny hand which got somewhat larger as she continued. "I always felt more comfortable with boys, age four. Since early childhood girls made me nervous. I was a tomboy though my mother groomed me otherwise, so doing the traditional 'girl things' wasn't in my agenda. Never played with dolls except my soldier doll in early teens. Around ten or so I began to realize that others thought I acted `out of the norm' for a girl. My best friend's mother wouldn't allow her to play with me anymore because I kissed her—my friend, not her mother. I fought like a boy, played ball and all games boys played. For the 50's this was a little suspicious I guess because I was always being told to do more ladylike things. There was so much shame and guilt from my mother that I think she explained away all my behaviors by taking the blame for them as if it was a burden she had to carry and heavy religion the sword by which she fought my psychological damages. Re: my father molesting me age 4, my being raped age ten. Putting everything and all images together would take years. I'm over it—the damage and self-worth that resulted are my muse through the present into the future."

Lesbian's Answers to Item #3

Item #3: As a child did you feel that you were more alone than others of your age group? If so, what do you think caused this loneliness?

Riki simply states, "No I wasn't lonely", and Maria says, "I felt very much in the closet—which was more frightening than lonely."

Sonia makes the point that aloneness and loneliness do not equate. She speaks of the wonderful day she got her own room, and she says, "The people I encountered in books were more interesting than the people I encountered in real-life, white-bread, Eisenhower-New Jersey.

"I was not excluded but was not interested in the boys cliques. Because of this I kept more to myself and didn't hang out with other females."

Three of the respondents mentioned reasons for loneliness not initially connected with homosexuality.

Pam writes, "Yes, I felt lonely. I think it mostly happened because I got so abused at home. I was really shy & self conscious & extra good. I seemed to attract an extra heavy dose of name calling. I felt really ugly & really alone. I usually had only one friend."

Ursula connects loneliness with her disability. "I was in a body cast & brace for years (age 3-8) & other kids (including sibs) saw me as weird or odd. A self fulfilling idea?—I was very bright but socially inept. This wasn't true for any of my sibs."

Olivia connects her loneliness with religion, which "Didn't allow for bad associations. Always lonely. After I told one of the girls in Kingdom Hall I was a homosexual, even pointed it out in our study guide—it got lonely there as well as at home-school. I hurt to have friends, do school functions, join clubs, groups, go to friend's houses. I was allowed once, it's still one of my better memories."

Wendy feels, "It wasn't loneliness, but one of being alone, not fitting in. It wasn't until junior high where we had Team Sports that I joined a group of girls that had similar interests."

Lilly says, "Yes. Knowing that my friends or just even the group I was hanging out with were not gay made me feel alone."

Tammy has feelings which go beyond aloneness. "I was a lonely child. I felt very isolated. I frequently got in trouble at home for asking questions my parents didn't like. In school I tried to fade into the walls, my desk, wherever I'd be invisible. I felt that 99% of the time, whatever I said was wrong and I got tired of being in trouble all the time. Surely my perception couldn't be true. When I talk with my brothers & sisters now, they help me remember good things. But I remember that they were happier than me because they `fit in' better than I did."

Lesbian Answers to Item #4

Item #4: How do you think, or imagine, your childhood would have been different, if you were born into a society where sexual orientation made no more difference than, say, hair color?

Olivia says, "If my mother had been able to recognize my behavior and treated me not with fear but love and understanding maybe my years of hate would have been prevented and I would have close relations with my brothers & sister. Maybe I'd know my nieces & nephews, brother-in-law, sisters-in-law. I'm an outcast and in a way still lonely.

"I don't know what my childhood would have been like because I haven't seen many happy ones in any circumstances.

"I imagine being free to explore without fear my talents, myself, my young knowledge of awaking. I would have been allowed to pursue any career without limitations. I would have been equal to my brother in every way and surely not lonely."

Pam answers with such verve her words fairly jump off the page. "Wow, I was just wondering this during the last question! Except mine is bigger. How would have I blossomed naturally if I hadn't had to close down & contort my natural expression of myself due to violence, incest & strict religious expectations? Let's see. Wow! Really nice! I would have been a lot more physical & unafraid to express myself. I would have played more, sang more, masturbated more & maybe my love for women would have become apparent as I became a teen. I could have dated girls. Wow! How fun!"

Vicki says, "I would've been able to let myself feel things from the heart one on one with people and be able to express it when I felt something special."

Lilly thinks her life would have gone more smoothly. "I would have never felt that I had to be with a man. All it did was make me unhappy." And one can't help observing that the man wasted his time, too.

For Maria, "It's too unrealistic for me to imagine. Difficult for me to imagine anything different than my experience. I may feel different if I weren't as confident, proud and content with my lifestyle today."

Riki and Sonia say their childhood would not have been different. "Not a bit," says Sonia, "I've been in a monogamous relationship with a woman for 16 years, but like many women who prefer women, there was also a Kinsey-middle attraction to men. I want a world where all difference—not just sexuality—is tolerated and indeed celebrated. Nerdy kids, fat kids, short kids, kids who suck at sports, kids who don't fit in for any number of reasons—they all need our help."

Riki explains the different pressures put on boys and not girls. "I wasn't gay as a child, so didn't feel the torment many gay kids did. But frankly, many lesbians I know feel as I do, as opposed to most gay men—who feel they were born gay, and therefore suffered as kids because of sexual orientation.

"Also, you don't really get taunted for being a tomboy, because it's seen as male-identification and therefore a step up in status. *Sissies*, on the other hand, are seen as acting like girls—a female-identification is definitely worthy of contempt. So these little sissy boys take shit tomboy girls never get."

Tammy has a vision of a utopia. "My image is of a family, a society. A place where being `different' is acceptable. Where the caretakers of the children know that `everyone' is different and that's the way we're supposed to be. So acceptance of differences means the caretakers accept each other as different too. Once everyone accepts that different equals normal, then everyone will be acceptable to everyone."

Ursula speaks of the advances made in treating her disability. Then, "All other things being equal—I can imagine lack of jokes about the `queer' priest who taught C.C.D.—I thought he was great until told to stay away from him. Or being able to admire rather than hate a `funny' gym teacher. I think being less *alone* would've helped immensely; having someone, *anyone*, be different like me. And not being forced into `girl stuff' like dolls, clothes, makeup, etc. would've been good."

Wendy says that at least she would have understood herself better. "I didn't come out to my family until 1991, after I had my own child thru D.I. (donor insemination). I was unsure of my own sexuality because I had no role models, or mirrors that I respected & could identify with. I have had only women lovers since I was 18 (now 37), yet could not admit to others I was a lesbian. I loved being different, yet could not get out of the closet."

Lesbian Answers to Item #5

Item 5: Please tell about anything relevant to your childhood which has not been covered by the above items.

The women who chose to answer this item generally expanded on the earlier answers and gave more details.

Maria: "I think gay/lesbian issues should be addressed more openly in the school systems. Trainings should be (word not legible) on homophobia, films/videos and information on the contributions that gay/lesbians have made."

Viki says that because she was lesbian the mothers of friends warned the other girls away from her. "To feel that you are unlovable because you are gay is a terribly helpless place to be," says Tammy.

"I tried to be straight during the 80's while I was raising my son. I came out in 1979 and spent the next decade trying to prove I wasn't lesbian. I ended up with a chronic illness, in psychotherapy and spending 9 1/2 months at a psychiatric day treatment center last year. So I'm lesbian and getting on with my life & applying to grad school in order to get a Ph.D. in psych."

Chapter Eight

The Horror Story

Most of the gay men who knew of their sexual orientation early also intuited that they needed to be quiet about it. Caitlin, perhaps, did not know what her declaration to her mother meant. She seems to have been totally open and totally herself, but mother got the message, and her relationship with her family was never the same again.

"At age 7, I told my mother that I was going to marry my best friend, Janice, when I grew up. She replied that girls couldn't marry girls, that I'd fall in love with a man and marry him and have children. I said no, that I would never marry a man, and I probably wouldn't have babies either. I told her that I loved Janice and would marry her, and that I couldn't see why girls couldn't marry girls. She just said `Because they can't, that's all.' Within a few days of this discussion, I was no longer allowed to go with my father and younger brother on their Saturday `adventures' woodworking projects, going to the dump, working on the car. I protested to my father, and he told me that now it was time for me to `learn to be a girl.' (i.e., I had to stay with my mother and sister and learn to cook, sew, be a proper wife, etc.). I had always gone with my Dad before that. I resentfully went with my Mom, but it was nothing interesting to me, so I started escaping from the house and going off alone to the river to brood and draw. My dog became my closest family member.

"My Mom eventually gave up trying to force me to stay, because I was so uncooperative and ugly of mood in the kitchen. She told me that I was `weird' and `strange' and that there was `something wrong' with me, but she wouldn't say what. She seemed almost relieved when I was absent. So, I became a ghost—no longer free and happy and doing the things I enjoyed (boy's stuff), and unattached to the world of women's duties. The name-calling continued: 'eccentric', 'bohemian', 'crazy', 'odd.' I have always understood that these things stemmed from that talk with my mother about loving girls. To me, it was natural and positive and happy—love is a good thing, *oui*? But apparently, there were restrictions about who was loveable—this, I never understood or agreed with, even though things degenerated into many beatings and much emotional abuse in the attempts to 'cure' me.

"P.S. My family and the culture I grew up in believes in their sincerest of hearts that to be gay is a) a serious mental illness, *AND* b) a mortal sin. So this context explains why they were so determined to change me before I got old enough to understand what they were so nervous about. So, I can't say they were malicious people—to them they were trying to save my life and my soul. But the tactics were very brutal & misguided. As a young adult (20-22), I spent almost two years locked in psychiatric facilities and drugged nearly to death in their attempt to `cure' my homosexuality and `bohemianism' (I'm also an artist). When I finally said enough was enough, that I was lesbian and proud, my parents quit speaking to me entirely for 9 years. It was only two years ago that they initiated contact with me and *apologized*. But when I asked about how they would behave if I'm in a lesbian relationship, all they could say was `we'll cross that bridge when we come to it.' We have casual contact now—I moved 2500 miles away from them many years ago, because I was afraid they were going to kill me. At that time I understood they would literally rather have me dead than risk their friends learning of my lesbianism. At least, if I was dead, they could edit my life AND get sympathy from the world. Alive, I was dangerous because someone they knew might see who I was. As much as I grieved during those 9 silent years, it was also a big relief to be free of the threats and abuse. I did a lot of healing during that time.

"I was very much alone. I was a classic 'tomboy.' I didn't hang out in girl groups because they thought I was strange, and I thought they were silly and boring. I played sports with the boys, but they would always have to fight with me (literal fist fights) if I, a mere girl, won the foot race or game. So, I didn't fit anywhere, really. Occasionally I would have one or two close girl friends— usually, they were `oddballs' and outcasts, too' for various reasons. So, I felt accepted, and was accepting, of them. Again, my closest friends were my dog, other animals & birds, trees, the river. I never had to be anything but myself with them."

Caitlin's response to item #4, how would her life have been different without prejudice against homosexuals, follows:

"1) I might have grown up to be a cabinet-maker;

"2) I might have had more friends. I'm 42 now—when I was a kid in the midwest, *EVERYTHING* was strictly gender determined, so someone like me could never fit because I refused to allow/accept such limits. Maybe I wouldn't have been so lonely and felt so isolated as a person around other people;

"3) I would be more bonded to humans. My friends now describe me as `feral,' and I'm in agreement. I've had to work very hard on human social skills and relationships. I'm often aware of my differences. It took many, many years to stop believing what I'd always been told about being 'crazy' and 'wrong.' Fortunately, I live in a community where I'm much more accepted as myself (and there are many 'bohemian eccentrics' here, so I look pretty `normal' now!). Even so, there is a certain gulf in my freedom around humans—it's not there when I'm with the forest or other creatures;

"4) I would have not lost all those years of my childhood, when I lost my happiness and self-worth due to restrictions and name calling. It has taken so long to become the happy person I am today, which feels also like the happy kid I had been before the nightmare began. But there are scars that still occasionally remind me how vulnerable I was, and we ALL are, to societal beliefs that would destroy that which they cannot understand or accept. The Nazis killed the queers and misfits *first*, as practice for killing JEWS and anyone else they didn't like. I did hard time in psychiatric prison for my 'crimes' of lesbianism/estheticism. I had a cardiac arrest there and was resuscitated. In other words, I nearly lost my LIFE in the most literal sense for being me."

This is Caitlin's answer to Item #5. "No one should have to go through what I did. I have been rejected, scorned, beaten, accused, isolated, confused, and imprisoned and tortured because I was BORN LESBIAN. If I could have been `cured' or 'converted', I probably would have at some early point, just to escape my circumstances. But I know I am the same person as when I was born—I never decided to become lesbian, I just was lesbian. How it would have been to have grown up loved and supported, I have no idea, but I wish that for every child. Now is the time to really live LOVE—life is too short to be hateful and restrictive."

Chapter Nine

Surveys From Parents

I received five surveys from fathers of gay and lesbian adults. As far as I know, none of the surveys were from people who are personally known to me. I mention this because it was predicted that no father would answer. None were doing a personal favor to me. Three of the men identified self, with complete address, something which I was careful to avoid asking.

I consider these men heroes, and a sign of hope.

The survey to which they responded is given in Chapter Five.

Item #1 asked for self identification. Four of the respondents were fathers of gay men and one a father of a lesbian.

Item 2: At what stage, or age, in the life of your child did you begin to think/feel that he/she might be other than heterosexually oriented? Please expand as fully as possible on the thoughts, feelings or experiences.

Ivan states it simply, "When he told me."

Jeffrey says, "I was unaware of his sexual orientation until at 20 years he brought home an obviously gay acquaintance. This caused his mother & I to wonder and after questioning him he freely admitted he was gay.

"After some soul searching and reading some books our son gave us on the subject, and going to a couple of *Dignity* meetings I accepted his orientation. There was never any rejection of him as a *person* or as our *son*."

Harold writes, "Tom died of AIDS at age forty. He told his parents he was gay about 10-12 years earlier, and we knew he was HIV positive about six years or so before he died. His gayness never upset us or caused any concern until HIV came into the picture. All his life Tom had been the same, outgoing cheery, personable individual who got on well with us, his brothers, and both sexes.

"We never thought much about his orientation as that was his individuality. However, we do regret his gayness, because of the consequences and the unfortunate presence of the virus in our communities."

Frank writes, "Approximate age 21 years. Our daughter left home for post graduate college studies. Previously she had all boyfriends and few girlfriends. She came home for the next Christmas with a girlfriend and they were overly friendly. Shortly afterward our daughter told us she was gay and having a lesbian affair. This relationship continued to grow and prosper. Today she is married to her lesbian partner and about to have our 2nd grandchild.

"There has been a lot of work and personal effort and growth on my part about her sexuality. I continue to support her life and all its ramifications."

George writes, "I had little or no idea until he came out at age nineteen. He was always the jock in the family. He also wanted more boy/girl parties than his straight brother.

"On looking back, he was more interested in hanging out with only girls rather than a mixed crowd. Also, looking back, he was quite homophobic in Jr. High school. Also, unlike his brother, he showed very little interest in *girlie* magazines."

The homophobia of George's son in junior high school is an example of internalized hatred of homosexuality. The young person suspects that he might be gay. He would hate to be gay, so rushes to be the first to condemn *those people.*

Item #3 asks: Was the knowledge or insight Difficult / Impossible for you to think or talk about? If the answer is yes, could you estimate, in percentages, how much the difficulty was due to your thoughts and feelings about homosexuality, and how much due to society's view of the subject?

Because the subject is personal and emotional, and homophobia is often internalized, it is not unreasonable that the percentages would add up to a figure beyond one hundred percent. Frank's were one such. He estimated that the view was 99% that of society and 15% his own view. Three fathers marked *difficult* for thinking and talking about it. Two were unmarked regarding the degree of difficulty. One unmarked was that of Ivan, who marked society's view as one hundred percent, and his view was left blank. Jeffrey and Harold marked difficult, and society's view as 90% and *my view* as 10 percent. George marked *diffi-*

cult, and his view as 25% and society's view as 75 percent.

Item #4 asks how would your life and relationship with your homosexual child have been different, if you had been told within weeks of the child's birth that there is a one in ten chance that the child is a homosexual.

Jeffrey says that would make "no difference." Harold finds that to be, "A rather silly situation or suggestion. I don't think it would have made any difference and possibly would have caused more harm than good."

Ivan says, "Your question is, to me, at the heart of the matter—there are so many possibilities in life that singling out one, in this case homosexuality, begs the question—isn't the point—live with tolerance and humanity and help your children to do the same."

Ivan has a larger vision, and if it were possible there would be no need for me to write this book.

Frank says, "1) I would learn more about homosexuality, 2) I would learn more about sexuality, 3) My understanding of these issues would have been more insightful and I would have been a more tolerant person."

Finally George says, "It would have been less stressful, since there would be less surprise, less feeling different and *society* would be blasé about the whole issue."

Item #5 asks for ideas which could have made the childhood of the off-spring happier and the parents acceptance easier.

Harold writes, "Gayness never was a (word not legible) factor in our acceptance and tolerance of our son's childhood. We always realized that every person has his/her own personality and life to lead. The unfortunate part is the existence of a virus that takes advantage of its hosts.

"His childhood was apparently normal & I doubt that anything would have made it significantly better," writes Jeffrey. But he does think that his acceptance "could have been enhanced by better, more complete & unbiased information publicly given."

His idea about information being *publicly given* seems extremely important. If information were publicly given, homosexuality would cease to be a secret.

George writes, "The last question about parents knowing ahead of time would have been helpful. Also, if schools and religious institutions would teach about the a) possibility and b) the OK-ness of being gay, this would have lessened stress on my son. Schools much more than religion.

"If Gay issues were wide open, kids would grow up knowing about it and it would not be secretive, dark, scary, taboo."

Ivan has some thoughts. He says, "Yes, for us all to examine our anger—emotions—with a view toward understanding others and consequences of our *actions—verbal* as well as physical."

Then he adds, "You might consider your subject in a much broader context: What responsibility is paramount in the 'healthy' life."

Frank writes, "Maybe our daughter would have come to grips with this sooner and she would not have done as much experimentation. Maybe she needed the life's difficult lessons in order to define her own person. Same for the parents."

Whose Fault Is It?

The surveys returned by mothers of gays and lesbians differed in several aspects from those returned by fathers. No father spoke of guilt or blame for the fact of homosexuality in the family. Almost every mother alluded to it in one way or another. Whose fault is it? What did I do wrong?

After asking the first question, the mother quickly assigns the blame to herself. Whether it is because mothers have closer supervision of children during their formative years, or whether it is societally induced guilt, would be hard to decide. Mothers are usually blamed, especially for sissy boys. If homophobia is induced in young homosexuals, then it seems reasonable that guilt would be induced in mothers for making the boy a sissy.

In the past the woman has been charged with "making up for whatever is wanting" in almost any situation. If she was blamed for her husband's lack of masculinity, then it naturally followed that she was at fault if her children of either sex were not gender perfect. Did this ever-lurking guilt hone her intuition to become an advance scout for trouble? The responses of these mothers show what perfect guilt machines women are.

A mother's awareness of homosexuality in the family comes in a different way from a father's. The fathers were told, but the mothers intuited, observed, or made connections. The truth dawned on the mothers gradually, and thus they had time to think and study. There was less of an element of surprise.

Item #1 asked for self-identification. Seven mothers returned the surveys, and they were the parents of 3 lesbians, 3 gay men and 1 bisexual female.

Mattie is a woman in her late sixties. She writes "I had only been exposed to *fairies* in my young years, by jokes, and the fact that a married gay man and his wife rented a flat from my mother. We were suspicious, even though they had a daughter. The way he wore his pants, and expressed himself, made us whisper that he was a *fairy*.

"I was never exposed to the sexual orientation of women. I always enjoyed playing the man in any play or at any party where dancing took place. The feeling of leading a girl and having some kind of power I did not understand at the time really felt good. I mention this as my experience because of the blame I thought I must place on someone when my daughter came to me at age 15 to announce she was gay. I forget if that was the word she used or not. My first reaction was, who is at fault here? I always allowed my daughter to wear pants, and have toy guns, she was the replica of me as a child. I was never allowed to wear pants, even though I constantly yearned to do so. Was I at fault for encouraging this behavior, dressing like a boy, or was it her father's fault, whom I had since divorced because of his perverted sexual ways? Whom should I blame?"

Mattie sought information from the library. She tried to understand why she would never have a grandchild from that daughter, and to assuage her embarrassment with the daughter's preference for women rather than men. Mattie identified her daughter as bisexual, and in her adult life the daughter has had sexual relationships with both sexes. Mattie is a perceptive woman and at the end of the survey she wrote, "P.S. I just noticed as I read this, I have left out the word lesbian. I thought it over, and gay I can accept, but somehow the word lesbian sounds dykish or makes me uncomfortable. Didn't realize how much I do avoid the word in my description of a woman's lifestyle. My daughter is very feminine, loves jewelry and presents herself as a *normal* woman. When she was young she did have a different image as far as dress code. Just an 'AHA!' for me."

Nell reports, "I actually did not become aware of my daughter's lesbianism until she was in her early twenties. Due to her own internal homophobia she had well hid her feelings to those around her, herself included. Even though I had my own suspicions of this while she was in her twenties, she did not come out as a lesbian until she was about thirty. In the meantime, she had been married twice, had two children and had many short term male relationships between her marriages. In her own words, as she told me later, every time she started to look at her sexual orientation she became frightened and just immersed herself in another male relationship. Only after she met a woman and fell in love did she finally come to grips with her reality. It was a difficult decision as she had two children and was married."

Nell says that she did not feel anger at her daughter, but understanding, "For I had been living the very same lie since I was a teenager myself."

Pauline writes of her experience, and of her daughter's sexual orientation. "At 23 when she told us—never had an inkling. She was a feminist but always dated boys/men. I was shocked—horrified."

Rose writes, "My first surprise or shock was seeing her with a friend when they were not aware I was around. I was upset—found more information to read. I knew nothing good or bad about being gay. I wondered for a long time what I did wrong."

Margot knew when her son was in kindergarten that he felt himself to be different from the other boys. He was seen by a psychologist, who told the parents that he might be gay and could have trouble at puberty. She and the boy's father accepted the possibility, but did not discuss gayness as he was growing up. She says, "I think he had a terrible time with accepting his homosexuality during his teens."

Sally says, "I was unaware of his orientation until he was in college and brought home an obviously gay acquaintance for dinner."

This seems to be a safe way for gays to test the home waters, bringing home a *friend*. A little like throwing your hat in to see if you are welcome. But once the subject was opened, this mother was going to know the truth.

"When I mentioned this the following day he acknowledged that the guest was gay, but offered no additional info until I questioned him only half seriously if he was trying to tell me something? He said no, but somewhat hesitantly and when I asked out-right if he was gay, he acknowledged he was. He had intended to wait until he had provided books on the subject for us to read in the future before he told us. Now we can *laugh* about the incident and say *Thank you* Francis (the guest) for making the disclosure somewhat easier for our son.

"We, with some early reservation, accepted his orientation and made no changes in our feelings or our interaction with our son and his later partner and love them both as much as our *straight* son and his partner."

Sally was determined to know the truth. On the other hand Tamara refused to know.

"I kept pushing that away, had a feeling he was not heterosexual. Teenager in high school, he didn't date girls—until Stephanie at age 22. I knew he was mad about her, and one month later they were married. We just never thought about it. My husband and I never discussed anything about him. Marriage ended in divorce a year and a half later."

Tamara's son was born in 1936, and her experience seems to be from a different planet. At times she speaks of herself in the third person. "He never told his mother he was gay. I knew but didn't accept it. He had girl friends too, so I was in the dark about it. Just had deep feelings about the possibility. My experience and knowledge in those years about homosexuality was nothing. He wound up with AIDS, even then he never told me. I just knew. He never talked about it to me. His best *friend* who he hooked up with many years before has remained like a son to me. He is gay also."

Mothers' Answers to Item #3

Item #3: Was the knowledge or insight difficult or impossible for you to think or talk about? If the answer is yes, could you estimate, in percentages, how much the difficulty was due to your thoughts and feelings about homosexuality, and how much due to society's view of the subject?

Mattie: "It was difficult at first to acknowledge that my child was different, and I needed a reason why this happened. I was prepared to take *blame* or designate *blame*. I knew there must be a reason for this, as she was a beautiful redhead, and according to our society she should be feminine and marry a man. My thoughts were 10% my view and 90% society's view. My thoughts and feelings were affected more by society's dictation, which led me to question her behavior, but to always love her and respect her lifestyle choice."

Pauline says that the evaluation is impossible for her to make because her view "was from ignorance." Margot answers the item with a question mark only.

Rose answers that 10% was her view, and 90% was that of society.

Tamara's answer is 100% society's view. Sally gives 25% to her view and 75% to society's view. She then explains that the 25% was "Not so much due to my feelings about homosexuality, but rather about the difficulties he was going to have to face because of his orientation and the things he was never going to have because of it. (wedding, children, etc.)."

Nell gives one hundred percent weight to both sides. She explains, "My views, thoughts & feelings were my own but were formed by society's view as I perceived them in my teen years. These views were a direct result of society's views on the subject back in the 1940s.

"I was well aware as a teenager of my own interest in other girls, but growing up fifty years ago in a small conservative community in eastern N.Y. state, there was absolutely no way I felt I could acknowledge that part of myself. Society viewed lesbians as shameful, dirty, evil and sick. I could not identify with those pictures of myself so I denied my true feelings. Marriage, family and career were the *accepted* path and the one I chose to follow. Even though my marriage was OK, my husband a good person and father, I was always aware of my own lack of true happiness. I did not want this to happen to my daughter. I was happy for her when she finally came out, perhaps even a bit envious of her. Little did I know that within a few years unforeseen circumstances would allow me to make those same decisions for myself. My husband's sudden death from a heart attack came when I was 57 years old. After re-organizing my life, I was suddenly in the position of being able to make my own personal choice. This was not as easy or obvious a decision as it would seem. I was still carrying my own internal homophobia and feelings that this was a *bad* life style. Through a supportive women's group of mixed hetero & homosexual women, and help from a close homosexual male friend, I was able to let go of some of my old judgments and fears. Upon deciding to embrace my true self I then came out to my lesbian daughter and her partner. They were very supportive of me and my decision. We remain in a close and supportive relationship. My only other child, my older daughter, has apparently handled this *double whammy* of her sister and mother both coming out within 3-4 years of each other, quite well. We still remain close also."

Mothers' Answers to Item #4

Item #4 asks how your life and relationship with gay child would have been different if you had been told that one in ten children is homosexual?

Margot says, "Probably not at all," and Sally says, "I don't think it would have made any difference."

Rose writes, "It would have been easier, much so. I would have been more knowledgeable and prepared.

"If Janet had not included us in her life and brought her friends home it would have broken our hearts. The more gay people we meet the more we are impressed with them."

Tamara says, "He would have been lovingly accepted." She then adds, "Have never told family about my son." Tamara's son was born in 1936. Her fear and lack of knowledge, the inability of anyone concerned to face the truth, bespeak the times. There was no mechanism in place to help the mother and son make their lives different—more open.

We could judge her harshly if we judge by today's standards. But for that time she did accept him by her deep perception of the possibility. Yet she was paralyzed by fear of the subject, and lack of an outside agency ready to give help.

She and her son lived a life of silent understanding. With a bridge such as Pflag, their lives could have been enriched. We have moved a long way from the 1930s.

Nell writes, "As for being made aware of the 1 in 10 homosexual possibility for my children at their birth, that would have changed things very little for me. Perhaps it would have removed some of the worry I had of passing on this affliction to my children. Such was my thinking back in that time period. If I could have accepted those facts at their birth, then I would have been in a position to accept myself also. It would be my guess that this kind of information, made available to parents in a very matter-of-fact manner, might well help these parents at a later date should their children's sexual orientation be homosexual."

Mattie analyzes her feelings of the time and later. "In 1957 I know I would have been horrified, but would have searched for reasons, and asked questions. I would have been really fearful that her father would disown her, as he was a very uninformed person. It was very difficult for him to accept it years later, when she finally told him.

"In 1994 I have come a long way in my life. I know I would have been able to accept the fact that I have a gay child much easier now.

"I was caring and especially sympathetic, because I know how it felt to want to be a boy/man as a young girl. It embarrassed me to feel that way, acting on that feeling was unacceptable. As I became more feminine and saw that marriage to a man was the social acceptable thing to do, those feelings left. I have often wondered what I would have done if I could have made an honest choice. Some people are adamant about the reason for being gay, that a person chooses to live that life style. I do not agree. I wasn't gay. Even though I had those feelings as a youngster, I could not act on them. So my theory is that it is not a choice. You either are gay or straight."

Pauline says, "I would have been more quickly accepting: not have judged myself as a cause."

Mothers' Answers to Item #5

Item #5 asks for input on what could have made the childhood happier and the parent's acceptance easier.

Sally says, "I don't think there was a problem during his growing up or his disclosure that would have made any difference."

Tamara says, "No, because we did not deal with it in those days. He is gone now, that was in 1936."

Margot did not respond to this item.

Mattie writes, "I think if all of us are accepted as who we are with no discrimination, that may be the day a person's life, if he/she is different, a lot easier to live. It is easier today to be gay than it was years ago. It is still difficult to live. You have to keep your feelings inside, unless you are on a special outing with a gay group or in a place where you are accepted, as in a gay bar. It is easier, but there is a long way to go before anyone who is different will be fully accepted by the *Superior Normal White Race.*

Pauline says, "No—we have gay lesbian friends—no judgment there. She *was* happy. She says she never knew until she met this woman at twenty two."

Rose writes, "If I had known what feelings she had as being different from an early age I would have loved to share those feelings and help her seek answers. As it happened she had to help me seek answers.

"I would have liked to help the Church open up to these kids so they don't have the feeling of not being accepted."

Nell thinks, "The only means by which we can all help each other to lead happy, productive lives, regardless of sexuality, is through ongoing and open communication, love and acceptance. Things only seem threatening when we do not understand them.

"As parents we owe it to our children and to ourselves to learn all we can about any bias that we hold, whether that is race, religion, cultural or homophobic, etc. Only by working on our own unfounded internal fears, views and intolerances can we possibly offer unconditional acceptance to our children.

"We must all be willing to relinquish that human condition of *judgment* in all aspects of our lives."

PART III

THE PEOPLE
WHO TAUGHT ME

Chapter Ten

Janet

I'd met Janet at the first Pflag meeting I attended. She agreed to talk with me. I thought it necessary to speak with gays and lesbians because the wall between straights and the gay community is seldom breached. And I felt freer asking Janet about her life than I do about asking my own son. Maybe short answers will always be the result of a conversation between a parent and a child when the subject has anything to do with sex, hetero or homo. I was glad that Janet agreed to talk with me.

She's wiry, active, physically fit. As she talks, she moves her arms, her hands, her body in the chair—restless to communicate. She's talking about a child she's working with, who was sexually molested by his mother's boyfriend. The mother was unable to keep her promise to keep the man out of the home, and the child was removed. "So, you see, he was abused *and* abandoned. He has these two issues, and then he has conflict within himself. He is in a male body, but if you hand him a shirt he drapes it around his hips to make a skirt."

I think of the good fortune of this child I'll never know, to have finally met an adult who's on his side, who will accept him and be honest with him. Janet continues, "I asked if he'd like to read a story about a boy like him, and he said yes. I don't know where I'll get it, write it myself, I guess."

Janet is dedicated to building and acknowledging family structures among lesbian and gay households. She meets with a regular support group of young homosexuals and bisexuals, aged fourteen to twenty-three, who are free to express their feelings and to realize that though they are a minority, each is not alone. She is active in promoting Camp Lavender, a summer camp for teenage gays and for children of lesbian and gay households.

It was through Janet that I first realized one of the dynamics of how Pflag functions. If the subject is difficult to deal with in your family, then you can move aside and deal with it in another family context. The idea goes something like this: it was within the family that the secrecy arose, but if I can deal with it semi-publicly, with semi-strangers, then I can begin to get the forbidden words out of my mouth, to loosen my tongue to actually pronounce them.

At my first Pflag meeting, Janet was talking of the importance of being treated like other family members. If there is a place where family photos are displayed, then the homosexual couple want to be included. If all family photos are "banished" because of their "guilty" secret, then that is equally hurtful.

I was impressed by her freedom of expression and asked her about lesbians receiving praise as children for their athletic ability. As a child who hated recess, who stood by the door until the banishment from school was over, I often heard men approve of girls who could throw a ball "almost as good as a boy." That's what I thought the approval was about: first class and second class citizens, boys and girls, men and women. The physically active girl would almost make it to the first category.

"I think that was true, up to a certain age," Janet responded. "At least I liked being that way in the early grades. It was fun winning races, and being chosen to be on the team. Being chosen one of the first.

"Then I remember later, in the sixth or seventh grade, feeling like a tank, like I was too big. And I was the same size then as I am now." She indicates her thin but well shouldered frame. "I may have had some baby fat, but mostly I was the same size as now. I felt wrong, *less than*." She was to use this *less than* phrase many times while we talked.

I said that I thought that sixth or seventh grade—eleven or twelve—was about the age when girls who had done well academically began to perform somewhat poorly. "Yes," she said, "my grades began to fall, as well."

Contrary to Janet's, my shoulders are small and sloping, and my early adult life was lived with a man who exclaimed, "Look at those shoulders," whenever a picture of Esther Williams was visible. I felt that significant shoulders were almost a secondary sex characteristic and the admiration was not about her, but about pointing out my lack. So now I was amazed to find that Janet had felt "wrong" for having such shoulders.

"Lots of women have really strong bodies—big shoulders—and I think that people don't really think that's attractive," she continued.

I'm amazed that Janet could feel wrong for having Esther Williams shoulders. I'm thinking of all the glamour ads featuring well-shouldered women in sun dresses or evening gowns. Those ads still produce a spike of envy, because I have accepted, in some part of me, the put-down in the Esther Williams remark.

"It's hard to separate out lesbian issues from people who don't fit in," Janet continues. She mourns that lesbians, even among themselves, are approved if they look like straight women. She mentions a friend of hers who is attractive, very intelligent, who dresses "very butch". The butch friend boasts about her new girlfriend, with long hair, who's very straight looking. "Isn't she beautiful?" she brags, but Janet says, "I thought she looked a little ditzy." Janet thinks it's beautiful to look butch, too.

Janet's mother tells her that she doesn't mind that Janet is lesbian, "because you don't look like one."

Janet says, "By golly, I am a lesbian, so why can't I have the liberty to look like one. Why should I hide, as though there is something shameful, when I don't feel shameful?" Janet is unusually honest and straightforward, and this deception bothers her.

We talk about Janet's mother and myself, both straight women who are almost incapable of small talk, who attend wedding and baby showers only with great difficulty. Janet also dislikes showers. "I feel like a freak—they're talking about a world I'm not a part of. And they never ask me about my life. My work, yes—but not my life."

When Janet expresses these thoughts to her mother, the reply is, "Don't worry, you don't look any different from the others." But Janet's conflict is not about looks; it is about truth.

These two women who are so alike, and so different, struggle to understand and accept each other. Janet cut her hair, which had been long in back and short on the sides what she describes as a typically lesbian hairstyle, which her mother did not recognize. Her mother's idea of a lesbian apparently includes short hair because she has struggled with Janet's new look.

"But she has short hair," Janet says of her mother. It is as though the mother can have short hair, wear flat shoes, and be "who she is" because she knows that she is straight. Because Janet is lesbian, she is not supposed to appear to be what she is.

I speak of my desire to have my children accept me as a human being, and not as some oracle whose word carries thunder. "When my children were growing up I learned to edit my words to them, because if I said, 'Be careful, you'll fall,' it became a prophecy: the child did fall." I don't know if it was a form of prophecy, or the child was practicing some form of obedience.

"I would like," I continue, "to say something to my daughter, Mary, and have it carry no more weight than if her friend Sharon had said it."

"It takes a while," Janet says "I'm thirty-four, and I'm trying to see my parents' humanity. But it takes a while."

She talks about the many ways that people put each other down: "And some of them we have no control over." She always gets back to the need for honesty.

Many extremely good women athletes are lesbian, but there is great pressure on them not to look like who they are. The day before a big athletic event there is Game Day, in which athletes are to dress up and appear at their finest. This is a custom with both male and female athletes. But some women's athletic coaches insist that the athletes wear dresses on Game Day, that they look like ladies.

"If you're a big burly gal, and you look silly in a dress—" the thought is too ridiculous for Janet to complete the sentence.

"Some coaches go so far as to state that they don't want their girls to look like dykes.

"But looking like a dyke is looking like a man, too," Janet continues. "It's hard to separate out lesbian issues from people who don't fit in, and society's attitude toward people who don't fit in the right box."

I am reminded of an unpublished essay by Richard D. Johnson, which came to me along with the first five surveys from my son, Mike. In the essay Mr. Johnson says, "Homosexuals find themselves in two difficult positions: working toward gender rights and fighting homophobia." And he continues, "Our society can be very cruel. It places minorities in categories, then discriminates against them for being in those categories. Homosexuals are viewed as feminine for gays and masculine for lesbians by our society: this point of view sets up a two-edged sword against homosexuals which even federal legislation can't cure."

This same essay quotes Dorothy Sayers: "What is repugnant to every human is to be reckoned always as a member of a class and not as an individual person."

Janet's insistence on honesty seems to deal with this issue of being an individual within a category. She is herself, and a member of a category, known as lesbian. She does not hide her lesbianism, is not ashamed of it, does not need to flaunt it, but demands to be the individual she is.

She struggles to put aside the category of parents and to see the two people who are responsible for her physical being on this earth as the people they are.

Janet's acceptance of a variety of people and lifestyles must be among the most inclusive on earth. Her acceptance is contagious.

At a recent session of her therapy group a young man arrived wearing a skirt. The only question from the other members was, "Do you have a slip on under there?"

Chapter Eleven

A Straight-looking Gay

His name is Mike Salinas. On the phone he said he'd known from day one that he is homosexual. What I was looking for was a gay man who had the appearance of a straight: in other words, a macho-appearing man. I wanted to know how it felt to know that you were different, but for society not to perceive that difference. Would it produce a different kind of, and possibly greater, anxiety to know that people were deceived about you but that the truth would come out in time? Did it make you feel like a fraud?

I had asked several people if they knew a gay deputy sheriff, or a gay biker. We usually got nowhere: they couldn't think of anyone. The conversations ended with me thinking that I would have to visit a leather bar.

The drawbacks about that were many. I'd be viewed with suspicion; I'd fall asleep after one drink, and I didn't know how to read the stereotype. Would a gay man who appeared to be super-straight communicate in monosyllables and refuse to discuss emotions? What if I had to talk to two or three before I found someone?

Earlier I'd written a letter to the editor of *The Slant,* asking for people to fill out the survey. I'd gotten several surveys back from having that letter published. So when Don suggested that I write a letter to the editor of the *Bay Area Reporter,* I knew that to be a good idea. I wrote asking for a masculine appearing gay man who was willing to talk about his childhood and feelings. I also included a fact sheet about the project.

The news editor called, and we played telephone tag for a few days. I thought he wanted to tell me why he couldn't publish the letter. When we finally made contact he said that most people take him for straight, but that he'd known since day one that he was not. He thought that maybe I wanted someone who was more of a jock, a football player perhaps. I knew he was what I wanted. He had the qualifications I sought.

He appeared masculine, was willing to speak about his childhood, was articulate and emotionally open.

Mike sat with a heaping breakfast before him; I offered to wait until he finished eating before questioning him. He declared that he grew up in a farm community and that he could eat and talk at the same time. It was past noon on a Saturday, after he'd indulged in his weekly luxury of sleeping late.

So I asked him about day one.

"I guess that the first time I had occasion to think it through was when my little sister was born. I was seven at the time, and read everything I could get my hands on. There was a pamphlet which explained something like 'When a man loves a woman.'

"It was about intercourse and birth. I knew that what they were talking about was deep and profound, but I also knew that it was not for me. I knew that I didn't have the circuitry for it."

"So you knew that you were different, but you didn't appear to others to be different, were not put down for being different," I said.

"Not for *that* difference, but there were other differences, which I did suffer from. We did not have a television, or a car. My mother was raising three children in a household with no father. We lived in a community of 104 Catholics, and us. My mother had the first divorce in the town, and the second. In those days, and that place, it was like being a whore. We were the whore's children.

"And Mother was not docile. She is absolutely brilliant, and did not fear to take on government agencies, or corporations. She was and is a formidable foe. This skinny welfare mother found that blacks were being charged more than whites in the Public Housing Project. She took on the Board and succeeded in having the rents equalized. When she took on a project, she always won.

"I began experimenting with sex very early. Then in sixth grade I realized that there was a name for the way I am. There were several names, most of them bad. I had to decide if I would hide it, or not care."

When he was about ten, Mike got the idea one night that maybe he could change, be different when he grew up. "I remember going to bed feeling very optimistic. It was all going to be all right. I was going to grow up and be like everybody else. But the next morning I realized that it was not true. That I was different, and that I was going to have to deal with that.

"I was the first feminist at our house, but my mother was a Socialist, and it didn't take her long to catch up. I learned to view life from many perspectives. I started to say many boys are not exposed to that. But the truth is that they are exposed to it, but are not always open to learning because in grade school it is so important to fit in.

"What I wanted to be most in life was a politician—a statesman who would bring progressive change to the world, who brought people together.

"In seventh or eighth grade, I remember lying in bed and realizing that I had no chance of being a politician. Even if I never had sex again, people would be able to say, `he had it once'—and that would be terrible enough. I gave up the idea of politics that night. This was in the sixties when it seemed as though progressive politics were going to win— that we were all going to get along together.

"It makes me wonder how many people decide to settle for less. I don't think my life in journalism and the theater is meaningless, but some people who settle for less have to work in a meat packing house."

Mike Salinas decided that he couldn't hide. He'd had a ringside seat to observe what happens when a homosexual tries to deny his nature and *fit in*. His parents met in the army. "She knew he was homosexual when they married. She wanted a life with children. He was handsome, and I think that she may have thought that she could change him. They both drank heavily when they were married and now they are both recovering alcoholics.

"He may have been bisexual at the time; at least he was married, had a life, children. Then when she was seven months pregnant with me, she left, or threw him out, or he left." Later Mike's mother married and divorced another man. That man fathered Wendy, the sister born when Mike was seven.

Mike decided that he wouldn't/couldn't hide his homosexuality. He made his own Gay Pride T-shirts when he was in junior high. I asked Mike, "How did your mother take your coming out?"

"Not very well," he replied, "She said it was a phase, that I'd grow up and get married. My answer to that was, `and ruin four more lives.' For once she was speechless."

Mike and his mother do not speak, which he says is due to an incident that happened just after his sister Star gave birth to her first child.

But I cannot help but think that the animosity between them has something to do with Joel.

Mike says, "I was stigmatized early for being different, because we didn't have a TV and because I read all the time. I was not built for speed. I was a bean bag, who could just lean back in any corner and read.

"And I didn't please most of my teachers. One teacher sent a note home to my mother asking her to tell me not to ask any more questions. This happened a long time before any stigmatization about sexuality."

Then came the Gay Pride T-shirts. "It was like someone riding by in a car shouting, 'Right hander! Right hander!' If you just answer, `So?' then the persecution, the teasing, is over. I was saying, `I'm gay. So what!'

"I was not one of the obvious sissies, but I didn't avoid them. They seemed more interesting than the other kids. I had nothing against baseball, except it would have taken away from reading time.

"About 6th grade the names start. That's when you know this is serious. If you did something really, really bad— broke something in a store, your parents might take you home and punish you severely, but no one else would touch you.

"But being Queer was something which anyone in the community felt they had a right to punish."

Not far from where Mike lived there was a facility for delinquent boys. It was out in the country, and whenever Mike rode by there in a car his imagination went to work. He'd think, "They're all there together, and here I am alone. It wasn't about sex, it was about bonding, laughing, horseplay, roughhousing." He was more alone than most adolescents. At the time when most teenagers grow a telephone out their ear, he had no one to talk to on the other end of the line.

He had no peers. He was a homosexual, and all he knew about that group was shame and the kind of lurid details in magazines, which were hidden under the counter in drugstores.

At the age of fourteen he realized that if he went certain places, wore tight pants, and acted in a certain way, he could meet and engage with men. What he was advertising was sex, and that's what he got.

Then he met Joel, an older man of twenty-seven. He thought that Joel was doing the same thing as himself, picking up men. When he realized that Joel was trying to pick him up, he was flattered.

They met in a bar, which was twenty-two miles from where Mike was living with foster parents. Mike and Joel went to Joel's apartment.

Joel asked Mike what he drank. Mike says, "I didn't even know. Whenever a man had picked me up before he simply brought two drinks, so I drank whatever he was drinking."

Mike and Joel sat side by side on a sofa and talked and listened to one another. "He was willing to allow a mood to build, before he even kissed me." Joel's thoughtfulness about the drink, and the mood, his humanity, carried through in their relationship.

All this time Mike was carrying out his idea of how a gay person should act. He says, "I became the most flaming queen in the county." Once as they were driving along, Mike was entertaining Joel with funny stories about what had happened with other men. In the telling he was translating the male pronoun *he* into the feminine gender. "And then I said `this' and *she* said `that.'" This went on until Joel pulled the car off the road and stopped.

He faced Mike and said, "I haven't understood anything you've said in the last five minutes. You don't need to act this way. I see you, and I want you the way you are. In yourself. You are not some fake girl. If I wanted a girl, I'd get a girl."

Mike credits Joel with teaching him about homosexuality and life. "I could stop acting the stereotype, because Joel accepted me and cared for me. He was very important to me. A mentor. He gave me self esteem. Taught me many things. I wish I could tell him that."

Mike is aware of the dangers of trying to contact another homosexual whom you have not heard from for some time. The attempt could cause the person to lose a job, or to be outed in a community where it is not safe. There is also the danger of learning of the death of the friend.

Mike moved back to Iowa and lived with his mother. He and Joel wrote, until Joel's letters stopped. Mike thinks that someone threatened to have Joel arrested because Mike was a minor. The informant may have been a member of Mike's family.

Then there was the traumatic time around the birth of the first grandchild. Star's pelvis was small, and her child was born with a broken collarbone. The child had to remain in the hospital, and Star had to go there several times a day to breastfeed the baby. "Mother was ugly to Star because she wasn't getting enough attention."

"I said, `Look, the only joy you can take out of this day is your own.'

I guess she considered that a challenge and escalated her behavior to where she was threatening to take the baby away from the parents because they were cocaine runners. (A totally untrue accusation.) I knew she could be scathing, but that's the first time I'd seen her turn on a family member just because we weren't paying enough attention to her."

I don't know this mother, and yet I do. It seems that she did not know how to lose, to back down, to say "I'm sorry." That may have been her tragedy. But this scene Mike described at the birth of the first grandchild elides into an experience of mine that I've never written or even talked about, because there was no framework within which to fit it.

The occasion for me was the same: the birth of the first grandchild. The birth of my son's son; a daughter-in-law was giving birth. Did that make it easier for me, so that the outcome was not so devastating?

Barbara brought Jimmy home from the hospital when he was three or four days old. They came to our house, because her family lived a few states away. When they were safely ensconced in an upstairs room, I was overwhelmed by feelings that I did not and still do not understand.

I was confused. I was not happy. I think I did not act out my feelings, but I tried to rationalize them, to explain them to myself. Was I jealous? Maybe. Someone else was playing my role. I'd borne ten children. It certainly was *my* role. And now someone else was playing it. If I was jealous, then I must want to be in her position. Right? Wrong! I still had a toddler; I *didn't* want another baby. We can scratch that.

I'd always been the star of the show before, and now someone else was starring. But why was I on stage when I didn't know my lines? I suppose that if you have to give a quick answer to the phenomenon, you could say that I felt that way because I was not getting enough attention. But if that's true, why doesn't it feel like jealousy? And why am I so confused?

The process of becoming a grandmother is very different from that of becoming a mother. Pregnancy forces the truth of the situation upon the future mother through morning sickness, listlessness, and other symptoms. If one is lucky enough to bypass these, the added weight eventually comes. Discomfort grows until the birth is longed for.

Even if the mother is not too interested in the child, which is unlikely, she is desperate to get back the personal possession of her body.

She must prepare a place for the child and the clothes and accouterments necessary to the daily routine. Becoming a mother is unavoidably physical. Motherhood intrudes itself on you, around you, and in you. It is happening to you. You are it whether you want to be or not.

The process of becoming a grandmother is not physical. All the changes take place in another body. And what has been hers for a generation or more is about to pass to another. She is becoming a has-been. Redundant. And what's more: old.

Becoming a grandmother is a process that happens to someone else. It could be happening at a distance, without your awareness even. Because it happens to someone else, you have no control, you are helpless. Motherhood, if you functioned in the role, was pure control at least at first. Diapering. Feeding. Burping. The role became second nature.

My own mother said, before the birth of my first child, "I wish I could do it for you. I know how to do it." She must have had some insight into the passing of the role when my turn came. I had none.

Mike's mother was strong and aggressive. She went after what she wanted. Made things happen. When Star's baby was born, she saw something happening without her involvement, and it was not going right. The baby had a broken collarbone and Star had to travel to the hospital several times a day. Besides being confused, her mother must have been terribly worried about Star and the baby.

Worry couldn't have been foreign to this woman; she had raised three children alone. But helplessness and confusion probably were. She didn't know how to back down, so she attacked Star and the situation.

I imagine myself meeting Mike's mother. We might not agree on much. We might fight like tigers. But we would understand each other.

Chapter Twelve

A Lipstick Lesbian

At the end of my conversation with Janet, she said, "I think you should also talk to a lesbian with long curly hair," implying someone with a different lifestyle. I often meet, in the gay community, the idea that gays may have nothing in common with other gays except their gayness. There is the stereotype, and some people fit it, and then there are people who are very different from the stereotype.

I told my son about Janet's suggestion. He laughed and said, "What you want is a Lipstick Lesbian."

When I found my lipstick lesbian she did not have long curly hair, but I knew her anyway.

Deborah is a professional storyteller. The first time I met her, she was talking about a video she'd made about the three generations it had taken for her family to come out of the closet.

Since she was giving a presentation to a group, I was free to observe her in a closer way than if we'd been engaged in conversation. I was fascinated by the way she looked. In her mid-thirties, she moved with a grace and confidence that does not come easily to a woman as tall as she. Perfectly proportioned, she is absolutely herself. Her brown eyes sparkle with interest as she talks. Large earrings are part of the fascination, but it was her hair that almost made me giggle.

Her short light brown hair stands up from her head in loose scimitars, producing an image in my mind which I didn't understand. And it was weeks later, only when I finished making notes from the tape of our talk, that it came into focus. The image was this: a still-diapered toddler getting up from a sitting position. The feet and hands are on the floor, butt in the air. Then the child achieves balance, not without a huff or two, raises the upper part of the body, and finally, with a world-beating grin raises the arms over the head. Her hair seemed that same triumphant gesture.

Deborah was a bright first child of a family climbing the corporate ladder. She talked in complete sentences from the age of three, and was popular with both boys and girls. She had a good pal-like relationship with boys and enjoyed playing ball and trading baseball cards. She was accepted as an equal.

When she was in junior high, her father was promoted and the family moved from Cleveland to much smaller Mattoon. She did not fit too well in the smaller town atmosphere, and to add to this discomfort her relationship with boys changed; or rather they changed. The boys didn't want to play ball with her anymore. "They were interested in Marianne, who was developing her chest." Deborah had acne and braces, which added to her feeling of not belonging. She'd had romantic dreams about women for years, but didn't realize what this might mean.

She had her first date when she was fourteen, and when she told her mother she had kissed him, Mother said, "You're a whore." There seemed to be a grid imposed on how one acted, what was fitting in each circumstance. Kissing on a first date was not following the plan. Later when she was in college, there was much talk about men as *catches*. He was a *good catch or not a good catch*.

Deborah's parents had married the week after they graduated from college. That was why one went to college: to find your other half. You found him, got married, had a couple of kids, moved up the ladder.

Deborah could bring herself to contemplate marriage, but she couldn't see herself having children. She envisioned some happiness, some adventure. Over there. At a distance. She was always trying to get her parents to agree to foreign study for her, or to allow her to work on a tramp steamer for the summer. Her desire for adventure and diversity has now been realized. Besides being a storyteller and video writer and producer, she is a marketing consultant and a playwright.

She was obviously not on track. One week after *her* college graduation, she hadn't even had sex with anyone.

Later, in her twenties, she did have sex with men, but her words for these experiences are, "It wasn't enough." And she acknowledges that when it came time to take the relationship to another level, to go further, there was no one with whom she wished to go further.

Toward her late twenties she began wondering about her life. Where was it going? She realized that her relationship with other women had always been deeper, more fulfilling than that with men, even though she still enjoyed, and does to this day, an easy bantering relationship with men.

She began keeping a journal, trying to figure out her life, and when she came to the conclusion that she might be a lesbian she hardly dared write her thoughts. It would mean a disruption of everything she'd been taught, everything for which her family stood. She joined the National Organization of Women and moved to Laguna Beach, which she notes has a gay community.

And how did one go about finding out? "You could hardly say, 'I think I might be a lesbian. Would you come and sleep with me, so I can find out?'"

Her arrival at the knowledge that she is a lesbian evolved slowly, as did the rest of her sexuality. She became friendly with a co-worker, and they talked freely. The other woman revealed herself to be a lesbian. She was in a relationship, but she developed a crush on Deborah as time went on. Deborah was not sexually attracted to her, but she recognized that she was on the road to the "more" she had been seeking.

For a homosexual, to find a partner is much more complicated than for a heterosexual. One must recognize one's own kind, or suffer repeated rebuffs. You must find a needle in the haystack, and then it probably is not the needle for which you've been looking. If it is, then there is the question: has this needle been looking for you?

The haystack, in due course yielded up the needle. She had a relationship with another woman for a year before she realized that more than half of her life was hidden from her family. She made a big trip east to "tell everybody."

The reaction of her women friends was, "Yes, we've been wondering when you'd tell us." They seemed to accept her lesbianism totally, but one woman did say that the idea was repulsive to her. Deborah could not understand how her friend could be accepting and repulsed at the same time. She is still puzzled by that.

Does Deborah consider herself bisexual, since she did for a time relate sexually to men? To this question she gives a vigorous shake of her head. She does not.

Deborah's mother seemed to say, yes, I'm your mother and I know these things. She then went down the list of all her daughter's friends, and must have been somewhat surprised to learn that all were straight.

The next morning, when she was to fly out, she noticed that her dad was jovial and calm. She knew that the news had not been communicated.

Mother's Day was soon after, and Deborah sent her mother a bottle of perfume, and called her. She began to say how glad and relieved she was that her mother accepted her lesbianism, when her mother launched into this huge thing against Deborah. "It's not socially accept-able—not legally recognizable—I'll never have grandchildren from you." In spite of this, Deborah managed to say that she'd like to bring Paula home for Christmas.

"Not in my house."

"Then I'm not coming."

With no insight that she was the one forcing a choice, Deborah's mother said, "You're choosing this woman over your own mother." Deborah began to cry and then her mother softened and said that they could work it out. The couple did go home for Christmas.

But in the meantime, Deborah had occasion to call her dad on a different matter. She took the opportunity to ask, "Well, where do you stand on all this?"

"It's a stupid choice."

Deborah told him, "It's not a *choice*."

"It's damaging to your career and she's not from the same socio-economic background."

"Like marrying the janitor's daughter, eh Dad?"

Deborah's sister, her only sibling, stepped in. She said, "I will not let this happen, again. We're not going to push her away."

Deborah and her sister had a gay uncle who lived and died in secrecy. He was just a bachelor who lived with another bachelor in Texas, surrounded by cats and art objects from Gumps, a posh store in San Francisco. No one ever talked about it. No one ever faced his homosexuality. When he died, seemingly from AIDS, the family said he died of cat fever.

Deborah and her sister are determined that history will not be repeated. They will not live in secrecy, nor accept shame from the community.

Like the toddler, Deborah has her own balance, hard won from the center of her being.

Chapter Thirteen

The Kindergarten Outing

I had gone to the Revolutionary Aging group in Santa Rosa, hoping to find women who would be willing to answer a Parents Survey, and particularly women who would take the survey to a father or two, since I was continually warned that fathers would be a problem. I was told that fathers would not fill out a survey. Margot took one, and declared that Stanley would fill one out: that Samuel came out to his father when he was in kindergarten, and that she had to run because of another engagement.

How did this square with fathers being a problem, which I knew they were? Surely most gay men come out to a female member of the family first, looking for reinforcements before facing Dad. I had Margot's address and phone number. I wanted to call immediately and say, "I gotta talk to you. I'm coming right over." Here was this rare bird sitting in a tree, and I could barely focus the binoculars of my imagination on him, but one false or quick move from me, and he could fly away. Maybe he was the only such bird in the world. I would simply have to wait for the bird to fly into my tree.

One day I mentioned to a lesbian friend who has completely broken with her father over her sexual orientation, that I found a gay man who came out to his father in kindergarten. She mirrored my feelings about it by saying, "Well, it would take more than just saying I like to play with boys best."

Yes, how did this happen? He wouldn't know the words to use. I just had to wait. It seemed to be months, but actually it was about three weeks before I got a survey from Margot. That encouraged me to write and ask to speak to Margot, Stanley and Samuel. Here is the story as revealed by the survey and a personal interview with Stanley and Margot.

Margot is elegant in a rather austere way which makes the word pretty seem rather silly. Stanley is small boned, with an air of good humor and barely suppressed laughter. She seems tall, he sprightly. She may be taller than he, but I guarantee that it is no issue with either of them.

It is easy enough to imagine the scene, thirty-five years ago, when Samuel, then in kindergarten, came out to his father. Easy enough to imagine now that Margot has set the scene and relieved me of weeks of curiosity.

"Samuel was about five years old—perhaps six: he was in kindergarten, was home with the flu as was his dad, and one morning I gave both of them breakfast in bed—our bed, and the two spent the morning together, talking, sleeping and reading, and he told his dad that he was 'different' from the other boys in his class—he didn't understand it, but he just felt 'different.' I was not a party to this conversation, but my husband shared this with me, and we agreed that he should talk with a well-respected child psychologist friend—who worked at the National Institute of Health. This man suggested it might be helpful to have Samuel seen by a psychiatrist for some time just to assess his attitudes, etc."

Several months of sessions ensued, with the parents alternating taking Sam to what they referred to as the Imagination Doctor, since Sam had a marvelous imaginary life. Margot says, "It was not at all surprising or shocking to us that this son might be a gay person." At the termination of the visits the parents were told that the next "crisis" time would be puberty.

In the ensuing years the subject was not talked about. Stanley and Margot had friends who were lesbian and gay, and once they visited for a week in the home of a gay couple. Later this couple said that they thought Samuel might be gay. They said nothing to his parents, in spite of their knowledge of Margot and Stanley's acceptance of homosexuals. The gay couple knew of the possibility. Stanley and Margot knew. But no one talked about it with Sam.

Margot says that she told herself that Samuel was not necessarily gay just because he was artistic. He was not necessarily gay just because he had such a vivid imagination. She says, "We had every intention of allowing him to be whomever he needed to be for whatever reason."

Between the ages of six and twelve, the subject of homosexuality was not mentioned. I asked if the subject was avoided because they felt that it would strike the boy as an accusation. Margot thought that there was more to her silence than that. She says, "I probably thought that there was something else. Mu-ther! Wasn't it always the Mu-ther? Or Father was not manly enough." Margot was silently mulling over blame. Whose fault was it?

Their hands-off policy during these years was in the interest of Samuel's freedom, rather than from secrecy. However, in looking back, Stanley feels guilty because, "We didn't discuss it. Let a little of the steam off."

Samuel taught himself to read when his brother, two and a half years older, started to school. He made a dictionary for himself of words he knew, going through the neighborhood borrowing children's books that had this sort of thing, and spending hours drawing and printing for his dictionary.

He and a friend built complicated structures with Lego blocks, and his projects, whatever they were, went on for "weeks, nay months," in the words of Margot.

He was outward going, and his interests were strong and lasting. His older brother was embarrassed by Samuel's "difference." Stanley says that this was serious since it was not just a social gaffe on the part of Samuel, but that according to his brother his whole being was wrong.

The difference between the natures of the two brothers was great. The older boy, when in the fifth or sixth grade, took great glee in bringing friends home for his little sister to beat up. Maybe he thought that the sister's aggression made up for Samuel's lack of it.

When Samuel was in about the second grade he complained to Margot that the boys in the schoolyard were rough with him. "Well, you'll just have to fight back," Margot said.

Samuel said, "But Mom, you always told me that I should be a *gentle* man." Margot says, "I thought, 'That's right. My first statement was correct.'"

Samuel wanted to take ballet, and since he was very self-directed and his parents willing, he did. He had a natural talent and was very quickly the star of recitals. The older brother was not made to attend the recitals, but he must have suffered just from the knowledge that they were taking place.

Margot says that she tried to talk with the older boy, who enjoyed sports and more usual pursuits. She emphasized the enjoyments of each boy, and that their difference didn't make one better than the other.

When Samuel was in sixth grade he decided not to continue ballet, and Margot remembers "being sad that he chose to stop, and speaking with him to try to ascertain if he was making this decision on his own, or was reacting to big brother's pressure, or that he thought we couldn't afford it." Margot is herself an accomplished musician, and part of her sorrow must have been that Samuel would not have the joy of music. She thought, "he's afraid to go all the way," that he was withdrawing from his own nature.

He had an example of what the community thought of people like him in the person of his brother. The whole spectrum, from acceptance to rejection was right within the household.

The week before his thirteenth birthday Samuel and a friend forged their fathers' names on some checks and ran away to the Virgin Islands. From there he telephoned his parents to say, "I'm gay." They said, "Yes, we know." There was a later phone call from the police in the Virgin Islands. The boys were living in a campground and were almost out of money. Stanley went to bring them home.

But homosexuality was only one problem they were dealing with, which will be no surprise to any parent of teen-agers. They moved to a small town where the public schools were bad and the boys, along with a sister, who is ten months older than Samuel, went to a private school.

Samuel and his brother found some common ground to share: drugs, and in the latter part of high school, alcohol. "Our family's problems were very severe," says Margot. "We had family counseling, the two older boys were kicked out of the private school because of the drugs." The sister between the two boys was allowed to stay on, but only because, Margot says, "We really went to bat here. The youngest boy, a third son, was in a country day school, and he was, of course, tarred by the community because of the drugs."

You will know something of the "tarring" a small community would do in such circumstances, and the pressures each member of this family was under, when I tell you that Stanley was the pastor of a local church.

Samuel's older brother continued to have problems with drink and drugs. He was and is often out of contact with the family for months at a time. Stanley tells of visiting patients in a hospital in his role as clergyman. One day as he walked away from the hospital, he saw a street person coming toward him, and with a shock recognized the street person as his oldest son. He said, "I was devastated by the experience."

Samuel is now forty and lives with his mate in southern California. Stanley retired a few years ago and he and Margot returned to their roots in California.

When I visited with them in the spring of 1994, I was impressed by the tranquillity of their home. There was no sense of decorating for effect: the furniture, the pictures on the wall bespoke Margot and Stanley. And from this man and woman I sensed no bitterness against that "tarring" community, and no self-pity over Samuel's HIV positivity.

What I remember most about their home is a collection of crosses, which I did not see when I arrived: the open door hid them. They are of various sizes, colors, and composition. They must have been carefully arranged, but the effect is that each cross came to rest where it wished to be.

Chapter Fourteen

A Victorian Legacy

John Stuart Mill published "The Subjection of Women"* over a hundred years ago. He said that he knew society was not ready to accept his thoughts, but that publishing would preserve them for a future time.

Surely that future time is now.

He talks about civilization, and man's necessity in business dealings abroad to be, or appear to be, reasonable. Other men keep a man in check because the power between men has an equal footing: men are judged to be equal. But there is not equality between the sexes. He says, "The clodhopper exercises, or is to exercise, his share of the power equally with the highest nobleman. And the case is that in which the desire of power is the strongest: for every one who desires power, desires it most over those who are nearest to him, with whom his life is passed, with whom he had most concerns in common, and in whom any independence of his authority is often likely to interfere with his individual preferences."

Then he says, "We are perpetually told that women are better than men, by those who are totally opposed to treating them as if they were as good." He states that we can hardly see what women are in their nature, since they have been so constricted and taught self-abnegation. He thinks that equality of rights would balance the scale, and that men and women would be equally self-sacrificing, because men would "no longer be taught to worship their own will as such a grand thing that it is actually the law for another rational being. There is nothing which men so easily learn as this self-worship: all privileged persons, and all classes, have had it."

He notes that the less respect a man has from the world, the more he is likely to insist on raising himself well above those within his household. Philosophy and religion should keep this ignoble tendency in check, but: "are generally suborned to defend it; and nothing controls it

* John Stuart Mill, Three Essays (Oxford University Press, 1975)

but that practical feeling of the equality of human being, which is the theory of Christianity, but which Christianity will never practically teach, while it sanctions institutions grounded on an *arbitrary preference of one human being over another*." (emphasis added)

A little further along Mill says, "the only school of genuine moral sentiment is society between equals."

He is speaking of equality within the marriage state, between husband and wife, but there is another inequality that grows out of the present inequality of that relationship: that between the father and the adult children of that union. Any condition a wife accepts from her husband is visited upon her children. They do not have more freedom than she, more right to disagree, to be different, to exhibit to the world a characteristic or a nature which would reflect unfavorably on the father's self-image. Her servitude will not buy their freedom. If she is treated as not equal, just as much inequality will be visited upon them.

I think the above is true and applicable to society's non-accepting view of gays and lesbians. But there's more.

Civilization has misused males, heaping upon them responsibility because of their larger size. Surely this has influenced males to think they must control everything. If they are responsible for everything, they must control everything.

One of the early controls must have been that of their own feelings. Emotions fluctuate; therefore they were not to be counted on, trusted. This need for control may be connected with the male's love of games. The rules are a kind of control. Men can dance around on the baseball field or under the hoop, because the feelings are within a framework that can be counted on. There is the scoreboard, the referee, the umpire, the team. Man is not alone here. The team supports him, says he's right: especially if he wins.

Did what was at first control of emotions turn into suppression and denial of feelings? The reason I think that society has dis-served man is because he is cut off from himself: from his most individual personal part, from knowing himself. There is something in many modern males that says, "I must not be touched."

"I must not be touched physically, and I must not be touched emotionally." People who have closed off their feelings are made uncomfortable by enjoyment, enthusiasm in others. Maybe they *are* touched by enthusiasm in others. Perhaps the lock on their box threatens to spring open. So they control the situation. The balloon is burst, the feelings hurt: the enthusiastic one a little more cautious, guarded, respecting of the man's closed box. And to the extent that the enthusiastic one has been beaten back, has learned not to be ebullient in his presence, he has carved out a larger territory of safety for himself.

I know this operates in marriage and in society in general. Isn't it reasonable to think that it would be a part of male society's reaction to homosexuality?

Surely nature intended the differences between men and women to complement and not frustrate each other. One of the basic questions to ask is: how can men live life more fully, accept emotions in themselves and in others? When that is accomplished there will be no problem accepting men who *do* live life more fully, and who *do* accept and express emotions freely.

Most of us were born into a family. We later realized that we fit, or failed to fit, for a variety of reasons.

The family is an individual's first mirror. The eyes of the others regard the person with favor or disfavor. This information, the way the family regards the child, comes into the consciousness before discrimination is present. It comes in as truth, and the child accepts the image in the mirror as self. I am beautiful. I am ugly. I am right. I am wrong. I am good. I am bad.

The family is not quite a monolith, though it is usually a hierarchy, with the father at the top. The members of the family stand each in a different relationship to the wishes/powers of the male head. The family member's view, and the mirror which each projects onto the new member, will be clouded, by that member's relationship to (fear of, rebellion against, or unquestioning acceptance of) the family authority: the father.

Say it's the mother. She sees a son who is delicate, beautiful, not rough. In herself, unclouded by the opinion of others, unclouded by the opinion of the father, she accepts, even rejoices in the being of the son. But she cannot be unclouded by the father's opinion. In some part of herself she lives in dread of displeasing him. Her husband's disapproval is an envoy in her head. The son is sensitive, beautiful. What if he's—? The envoy stops even the thought.

If it's true—if he should be, she can hardly think the word. What will his father think, do, say? She knows some of the restrictions in the mind of her husband. "Boys shake hands with other males once they are seven years old." The father is so afraid of homosexuality, so in doubt of his own worth, that he has sexualized all affection. But of course I'm fantasizing what it is that he's afraid of, because males, the ones who exhibit this behavior, don't talk.

Whatever this lack is in the adult male, she walks carefully around it. Obviously it is not to be touched. But she observes how often after a few drinks the conversation between men turns to homosexuality. The women do not talk of lesbians. What is this difference?

What would he say, what would he do, if he found that one of his sons is gay? She is conflicted, can hardly think of the scene.

The child must get mixed messages from both parents. Much suffering and worry could be avoided, if the subject were faced early and when it was only on the periphery of attention. If someone said, "A certain percentage of children are homosexually oriented, yours may be one of them. The child may know early and need your support, approval." Someone, with some authority, someone outside the family, needs to say this early, to both parents.

If this were done, if someone—a pediatrician, the family doctor, or a public health nurse—would give this information by the time the child is three, it would dispel ignorance, release the tension, get people talking. The idea of homosexuality would no longer be unthinkable.

Children are immunized almost from birth to protect them from diphtheria, whooping cough, hepatitis, polio. Protected from foreign things; germs, viruses which can enter the body and cause harm, even death. Yet the child is left to struggle alone, with a nature which may be different from that of most, or all, family members. Homosexuality, exposed to homophobia, can certainly cause immense suffering and death, often by hanging, most often in adolescence, at the time when the child is trying to express self and go to that next stage of life: to become an individual in addition to being a family member.

Since starting this book, I've learned more about the mother of a gay man who calls herself a "lifelong Republican," and whom I called the Ché Guevera of gay activism.

She had no idea that her son was gay. Then he and his wife of six years called and wished to visit for the weekend. She thought that they were going to tell her that she was to be a grandmother. She was greatly shocked, not because she was homophobic, but because her son was not who she thought he was. For weeks, she dissolved in tears whenever she tried to talk about it. She began attending Pflag meetings, and now she and one of her best friends in that organization laugh when they talk about what sodden messes they were at the same time, and for the same reason.

Being a religious person, she signed up for a series of workshops on sexuality which were held at her church. What she heard regarding the pastor's views on homosexuality disturbed her so much that she came home and walked the floor in anguish. She says, "I was so angry at that man that the only thing I could do for any ease was to pray for him."

When she could get neither satisfaction nor support from her pastor, she went to see the bishop, who told her of other churches where she could receive more support. He told her of a couple of options, and of one option which he felt that she didn't have: the option to stop speaking out.

Whenever I heard this woman recount her month's adventure, I wondered at such a Republican firebrand. Then one night she revealed her motivation. She said, "You people don't know this, but my son told me that when he was eleven and twelve years old he thought of suicide every day."

Things which are hidden do not cease to exist. Termites and dry rot are usually hidden.

The words *hermetically sealed* come to mind. I'm trying not even to think the words *homophobe* and *bigot*. I want to understand the people who are sealed against the idea of differentness. It seems that they are largely, but not entirely, male.

The human male has been misused by civilization: used as a beast of burden because in times past his physical size and strength were all important. And the past hangs on. Many a man wants to retain total control of the household.

And women are not blameless. Many want liberation, the right to earn money, but still treat it as play money and feel they have the right to quit a job: a right neither they, nor society, grant to a man.

Both sexes who live by the standards of a former age fail to examine their lives. I think that honor and emotional openness must go together. Honor implies an inner dimension, attention to that dimension, attention to how one acts and reacts to others. If one cannot look inward, doesn't one reject one's own nature? Rejecting or not examining one's nature, isn't one then at war with that in others?

For gay and lesbian adults who have tried to struggle with their families and feel that the door has been closed to them: I want to say to you, YOU DO NOT NEED TO STAND IN FRONT OF THE CLOSED DOOR. There is no comfort for you on the other side of that door. Not now, maybe later. Do not give pain to yourself, or to those on the other side, by standing there. Everyone will be more comfortable if you move away from the door for now.

There is another possibility. One of Funk and Wagnalls' definitions of family is, "Any class or group of like or related things." Homosexuals need to broaden their idea of family, to be a family to each other. And that is being beautifully done in a number of places.

And there is Pflag. A bumper sticker proclaims PFLAG IS FAMILY. That is true in a sense I would not have believed possible two years ago. Pflag is family in the best sense of the word, possibly family in a sense you have never known before.

David and I went to our second Gay Pride parade in the summer of 1995, this time in San Francisco. One sign stood out: carried by a *man*, I'm happy to say. COME TO PFLAG. *UNTIL* YOUR FAMILY ACCEPTS YOU, WE DO.

We waited for about two hours with the northern California group of Pflag chapters, until our position in the parade moved. (We'd programmed our VCR to record KOFY's coverage, so we were able to watch the parade that evening, and see the part we'd missed.) After we entered the line of march, we realized that the parade watchers were multiples of what we'd seen in Los Angeles the previous year. Along the entire parade route the watchers, cheerers, stood four to six deep. While we waited we noticed rainbow flags hanging from balconies of condos. Many marchers and watchers waved small rainbow flags. These flags celebrate diversity among peoples.

When we'd been marching for a while, a compact, elegant, black man called in a vibrant voice, "There's my Mom." I scanned the marchers. There was no likely genetic candidate, but without a doubt the man had seen his mom. At first I felt a wave of shame that the marchers surrounding us were so white. Would a black family wanting, needing to come to Pflag hesitate because of their color? Possibly. Probably. But they would be welcomed if they did come.

Yet the man had breached all that. He did not call, "There's my Mom," in a way which children used to call a parent's best friend "Aunt Betty." There was a deep true connection which the vibration in his voice shouted out.

Close to us was a woman marching with her son, she waving a rainbow flag. A few blocks further on, the parade paused. While we waited, another dark skinned man called to her, "Hey, Mom, can I have the flag?" Without hesitation she walked over and handed the flag to her little boy. No one watching could doubt the kind of transaction it was. He took it and waved it gaily around. And what happened next was not unimportant. One of the marchers behind us passed another flag up to her.

There's more where that comes from, it said to me. Something powerful, organic, is going on here. Both these men reached beyond color and family to find something which is their own.

Tears came to my eyes when another man shouted from the sidelines, "Happy Father's Day." Homosexuals are not the only family members rejected. Nor does the rejection always go down line in the generation. Children do reject parents. And when that happens, rejected fathers and mothers can also reach out and find what is theirs, have their gifts accepted, do not need to stand before the closed door of rejection.

Pflag is for the human family which wants to increase its humanity. I am usually bored in meetings, but I am not bored at Pflag gatherings. Dynamic people attend, people with problems who want to work through them. Gays and lesbians come, and these are the best meetings, because it whacks away at the artificial barrier between straights and homosexuals. Don't let the name fool you. It's not meant to be exclusive.

David, my husband, who is not Mike's father, attended a few times and then said, "I feel as though I don't belong, because I'm not a gay or the parent of one."

He hardly knew what to say in introducing himself. Most people say something like, "Hello, I'm Roseann and I'm the mother of a gay man." He felt as though he didn't belong because he didn't have that identity. But he worked it out and his answer can work for anyone who would like to grow through Pflag. At the next meeting he said, "Hello, my name is David, and I just think that this is a good place to put a shoulder."

Pflag can use all the shoulders it can get. The shoulder will be better for it, too.

Chapter Fifteen

Please God, Cure Bobby

I interviewed Mary Griffith in the fall of 1994. We went out to breakfast, and then sat in her kitchen talking about Bobby. She told me that an Oakland newspaperman, Leroy Aarons, had written a book about her son which would be out in the spring. The book, *Prayers for Bobby*, has since been published by HarperSanFrancisco.

Mary is an interesting combination of fear and daring. She owned a car but never learned to drive. She is an outspoken advocate for gay rights. She conducts a Pflag meeting, but it is held in her home. Her fear shows me how much her activism costs her.

Bobby was the third child of Bob Sr., and Mary Griffith. Joy was the first child, Ed the second. Then after Bobby there was Nancy. The mother and children attended church regularly. Bob senior, an electrician, drove them to church and picked them up again.

He's a practical man, as the father of a considerable family must be; a pragmatist. He knows that if you wire a circuit correctly, then when you flip the switch on the wall or insert a plug, the wires will make contact, electricity will flow, and you can light a room or power an appliance. A practical man, who likes to know the results.

Bob worked hard to provide for his family. Mary prayed hard. All parents become more vulnerable after a child is born. The baby is so soft, beautiful and dependent. And the parent is responsible for the welfare and growth of this precious gift. Mary's children brought out her spirituality, made her feel closer to God. She read the Bible. It was her cookbook, her child care manual.

She thought of stories from the Bible as she moved about her kitchen, carefully avoiding the floor sitter, the lid banger, the skirt hanger, or removing the climber from the counter.

By the time Bobby was four she had a concern for his welfare. He loved makeup, jewelry, dresses, and lingerie. Joy and Ed had fads and outgrew them. It was probably just a fad. But Mary knew the Bible and her religion too well not to be deeply troubled, even when she could push the thought from her conscious mind. "Homosexuality is an abomination unto the Lord."

Bobby was a sweet sensitive child who at the age of three made a valentine giving his heart to Jesus. When he was four a neighbor called Mary on the phone, laughing. The kids were playing at her house, and Bobby was dancing around joyfully with a crinoline half-slip on his head. Mary thought, now the whole neighborhood knows that Bobby is a sissy.

School forces a kind of conformity on children, or it teaches the child to hide, cover up the difference. Bobby still could not throw or hit a ball, but some of his artistic ability came out. He loved to draw, and had a special way with words. Mary told herself that he was just artistic. Artists are usually different from other people.

But when he was sixteen he confided in his older brother that he thought he was gay, swearing the brother to secrecy. Bobby could not stand for his parents to know his shame. But a short time later, when Bobby attempted suicide by swallowing many Bufferin tablets, Ed told their parents.

Bobby felt close to his brother when he confided in him; now he felt betrayed. He was embarrassed to have Bob and Mary know this about him. Bobby was not a stranger to the Bible. He knew that he was an abomination. They stayed up until four a.m. discussing the problem.

Mary was sure that if they prayed hard enough Bobby would be cured. Mary and Bobby stormed heaven. Mary had *no doubt* that Bobby would be cured.

She could not accept that Bobby was evil. She knew him too well. Knew that he was sensitive to the thoughts and trouble of others, always wanted to help in any way possible. Bobby could not be evil. He was just sick.

Whenever they talked about the problem, Mary exhorted him to prayer, and assured him of her own prayers. Bobby was relieved to talk to Mary about his feelings, but he was lonely. He wanted to know someone like himself, who shared the problem, someone he could talk to in the same way he talked to Mary. He wanted someone on his side of the fence.

When he was seventeen he began keeping a diary. It was dedicated to his parents, but the contents were, in reality, a long love letter to Christ.

Emily Dickinson says something like, I love a look of agony because

I know it's real. These entries were real because they expressed agony along with a wide range of emotions: love, guilt, anger, remorse, and promises to try harder.

Bobby could not find a gay friend, a lover. His pictures reveal him as extremely attractive. But guilt does not enhance anyone's looks. And anyone he would have liked for a friend was carrying his own guilt. To befriend Bobby would have multiplied the guilt.

When Bobby was nineteen he moved to Portland to live with his cousin, Jeanette. Maybe being away from his family might help: change his luck. But moving didn't help. There is an angry entry in his diary, blaming Christ. "Why did you do this to me? Well f--- you."

Then: "July 25. Everything just gets worse and worse. I really had no idea my evil deeds would be catching up to me so quickly. I guess it's true that everything comes back to a person. I must deserve everything that happens to me. The funny thing is that I didn't realize until now how bad a person I must be."

A month later Bobby did a back flip from the rail of an overpass and landed under an eighteen-wheeler.

At Bobby's funeral, the minister told the mourners that Bobby was gay. He went on to tell a cautionary tale of how one winds up when one is caught up in "the gay lifestyle."

After the funeral a pastor of the church met with Bob and Mary for grief counselling. Mary said that she had such guilt, and she wanted to know how she could help others like Bobby. The pastor just shrugged his shoulders.

Mary never went back to church. She was now bereft of her son, her church, and her Bible. It was grief beyond grief, and she was alone. Bob senior was grieving too, but he didn't have the guilt. It seemed to Mary that Bobby killed himself because of the belief that she taught to him. He was dead because they had both taken religion seriously. He was a homosexual, and he couldn't change that. But he was also a Christian, and he believed that he would go to hell for following his nature. And he was incapable of being different.

Reading from Bobby's diary, it is possible to see Bobby's spirituality warring with his religion. "What kind of person does the things that I do? What's wrong with me?

"I hate myself because I'm not perfect. I want to be perfect.

"I get the feeling that you love me so much that I can't even see it when it's right in my face.

"I'm completely worthless as far as I'm concerned.

"But maybe I'm not as selfish as I think. I wish God gave out report cards, then I'd know where I stand as far as being a good person is concerned.

"On judgment day I will stand defiantly before God and declare myself a victim of the world. I was never meant to be here. So, I'm innocent.

"God why can't I find some cute, sensible boy? That's all I want. Am I asking too much? I guess so. This is really frustrating. Most of the time I feel like screaming."

God, why can't I find some cute, sensible boy? Would Bobby petition his Friend, Jesus for a boyfriend if he thought in his soul, conscience, heart, that it was an abomination?

Bobby struggled with the church, and the church won. Two months out of his teens he killed himself. Because he'd turned twenty, Bobby would not be considered a teen suicide, but this period of adolescence is when most homosexual suicides occur. Late adolescence is when identity is formed and one gains some distance from family. Sometimes the distance is achieved through suicide. Sometimes it is the *easier* way out. If you're dead, you don't need to tell the family that you're queer. And some families would prefer that choice also.

The Bible is regarded as the word of God, but it is interpreted by men. The interpretation is usually by a group of people: a synod, a convocation, a committee. This means that the interpretation is a compromise. And the committees change their group minds from time to time on Biblical and other matters of religion.

Take the case of Joan of Orleans.

She heard voices instructing her to lead the army in a battle. One of the voices identified herself as Saint Margaret. What kind of control could the Church have, if one were to receive instructions from within oneself?

The Church told Joan that she did not hear voices. But she did, she knew. She would not recant. She was an ignorant country girl, but this had happened to her. She would not deny what she knew. She was burned at the stake for heresy.

Four hundred years later, another committee, in the early part of this century, reversed the decision. Joan of Orleans was declared a saint, to be called Saint Joan of Arc.

In this reversal, the Church admitted that an individual has the right to follow conscience. It admitted that she was right and the committee was wrong. It is saying that not only do you have a right to follow your conscience, it is *better* than bending to dogma. Guidance is from *within*.

In his play, *Saint Joan*, G. B. Shaw says that if Joan were here today, we'd have to burn her again. Yes, GB, you're right. We are doing it again. We're shooting her and hanging her. She's dying under the wheels of big rigs, and in "accidents" and overdoses.

Sometimes she's a lesbian, oftener a gay youth. If control is to be achieved, conformity is necessary. Society needs to be rid of the evidence of its humanity and diversity. But she doesn't always die. Sometimes when the inflicted shame is at its strongest, when a suicide is attempted, the truth blazes forth in the mind of the victim: There is nothing wrong with me. I have a right to live.

And in an essential way, Bobby Griffith didn't die. About three weeks after his "accident," Mary had a dream. She heard happy laughter. "Bobby, is that you?" And the reply came, "And why wouldn't it be?" Then she saw this kitchen floor baby, sitting by the sink, beside where Mom usually is, and where all the good banging things are. It was Bobby, and as she gazed at him she could see that there was something different about his head. And she knew that Bobby hadn't been sick, that he had been born the way he was: born homosexual.

She knew in her heart that there had been nothing wrong with Bobby, but it took another eighteen months to trust her own conscience. After that time, she went to see a clergyman at the Metropolitan Church, which ministers to gays and lesbians. Mary speaks to groups, does whatever she can to help others like her son. Bobby lives on in Mary's work.

Because Mary refused to be shrugged off, I am writing this, you are reading it, and you have a chance to prevent torture to other young people, and to members of your family.

Long live Saint Joan of Arc.

Chapter 16

Mike and Me

When Mike went to the University of Chicago, he intended to study Political Science. But he soon joined an organization called Doc Films, and that action changed his life.

With Doc Film people, he enjoyed early silent films and the movies I grew up on. Like many others, Truman Capote was one, who grew up in pre-television days, the movies were my surrogate family. I learned about life from the movies: the possibilities.

I thought I wanted to be an actress; I never gave a thought to the writing. The story simply existed. But it was the <u>story</u> which I told after I'd been to the movies. I'd tell the story to my mother in the kitchen. I told it in such detail that I'd say, "Now, you have to look at me for this part." Then I'd make a face of mental torture or physical suffering, or twist my body to portray a dramatic high point of the story.

I recounted so many stories that one day when I begged for money to go to the show, she said, "OK you can go to the show, but you can't tell me about it." Maybe she was fed up with two generations telling her about it. Mother's mother was a movie buff who replayed the story in great detail the next day.

Even today, when I can't always recall the name Denzell Washington or Julia Roberts, I can look at a scene from an early film and usually name all the characters in it. Franklin Pangborn, Carole Lombard, Jack Oakie, Guy Kibee, Margaret Sullivan, Dick Powell, Loretta Young, Eric Blore. The starlets stump me, probably because they were standardized to look alike.

I mention all this because in time Mike realized that he wanted to work in Hollywood. It was not a case of having one of my children fulfill my dream. My early thoughts of Hollywood were considered so unrealistic that I probably hid the idea in shame. I doubt that Mike knew of them.

Mike realized that Hollywood was a crazy place and that he needed to be armed. He wanted to be crazy in the most sensible way. He got a Masters degree in Business Administration, and then went to live in Los Angeles.

He was involved in various business ventures before he settled down to be a screen writer. He wrote the script for "Mobsters," the story of four gangland figures who knew each other in their young years in Brooklyn.

I thought his heterosexual love scenes could have been better and suggested that I could help. After his screen credit as writer could be added the words: heterosexual love scenes by his mother. I guess his sexual interest came through, because a reviewer, in a take-off on Young Guns, referred to it as Young Buns.

He scripted several other stories which never made it into production. Then he got around to following the writerly advice: write about what you know. Among Mike's circle of friends, many are Black. He wrote a script which sparkled and sang. The characters were Black. His agent and those to whom the agent showed it were negative. It was different. It didn't follow the formula. But while he waited for them to decide, he wrote another with Black characters. It was hilarious. It also was rejected. Two of his friends exchanged a look and said, "White people."

He studied the television market, picked a show, and wrote a script which got him hired as one of the writers. His first script aired in the fall of 1995 to good ratings. He's found his work.

Since Mike and I are both writers, you'd think that we would have much to say to each other. And in a sense, we do. We read each others work, and probably both of us value the opinion of the other more than most opinions, because we know that it is informed.

But it seems to me that a conversation is like a dance, or more specifically like dancing together. One person takes a step, makes a gesture, and then the other does. If the two people are open and free with each other, the talk can range over everything that either of them is, or thinks, or feels.

But I think that I can never have that with Mike, nor can anyone in our family. It pertains to his homosexuality, but is not because of it. It is because he needed to hide from us, needed to build a filter, a censor. That censor was in place during most of his formative years. It curtailed his response to me, to us, and also our response to him. We can never get rid of that censor: can never have the relationship we would have had between his being and ours. If you dance with one who limps, to keep the rhythm you need to limp.

It is a sorrow. It is humanity lost, and all because humanity was not accepted. Humanity lost for an inhumane reason.

Epilogue

Tommy's Problem

"Dad, what does cavalier mean?"

"I think it—" a roar rises from the TV and Dad swings his recliner upright. A touchdown has tied the game and Dad's favorite team has a chance of winning with only minutes to go.

"What does it mean, Dad?"

Dad's eyes veer from the TV to Tommy. "Go ask your Mom." Tommy rises from where he has been sitting with his back against the footstool, he and Dad sharing the same circle of light. Tommy goes into the next room and asks Mom the question.

"Read me the sentence," she says, her index finger holding her place in the book she's reading.

"John thought that Walter had a rather cavalier attitude on the subject."

"Oh," she says, holding her book to her chest, "that means that John thinks that Walter is not paying attention to his side of it—that Walter has made up his mind, and that he knows better than John—that he thinks he's above John.

"Hey, Tommy," Mom goes on after a moment's reflection, "I never thought of it before, but I guess there might be a connection between cavalier and cavalry. You know, cavalry ride horses and are above the foot soldier. That could make them think they're better than the soldiers on the ground. Let's find out."

Tommy scrambles to his feet and plops the C volume of the Oxford English Dictionary into Mom's lap. She looks around for a bookmark, sees only a box of facial tissue, pulls one from the box and inserts it into the book she's been reading. It flutters as she lays the book aside. He perches on the arm of the chair and curls into Mom's shoulder.

Both parents are usually ready to help Tommy with words, the football game being an exception for Dad. And why not? Tommy seems to have been born with a different language in his head.

Their three-year-old son is talking, saying something to them, and they can't understand him. "Wa oh ga." They know he is saying something, because the syllables repeat, are the same. But it is something they can't understand, nor can he make himself understood, no matter how loud he gets, or how angry.

By the time this is going on, Bill, the second son, has been born, sits at the table for family meals, and follows, with his eyes and attention, the fork in his father's hand or the knife as Mom butters bread for Tommy. "Bada go Jub." The meaning of Tommy's words has been lost. Mom and Dad never understood them.

Bill begins to talk. "Daaa—Mummum." Tommy is not just a slow talker. Something is wrong. The frustration is almost unbearable for everyone except Bill, who is happy as long as he can watch anything move.

They take Tommy to a specialist, who finds that he has fluid in his inner ear and thus hears everything distorted as though hearing through liquid—which he is.

The operation is relatively simple. The speech therapy that follows may partly account for Tommy's love of words, their meaning and use.

Poring over the O E D, going in depth on a word or idea, discovering the broadening out, the surprising connection of words to each other, this was Tommy's best time with Dad. And those times usually grew out of their sharing the same circle of light from the lamp at Dad's shoulder.

But sometimes in bed, before he went to sleep, or worse, when he woke in the night, Tommy worried, and the worry centered around Dad.

Tommy was on the football team, but he wasn't good at it, nor did he like it. No one knew how disinterested he was in it, and they did not know how avidly he watched the cheerleaders or how he listened to their talk even when his eyes were on the ball game.

Meanwhile, Bill was on a team for little kids, practically toddlers. When suited up, they looked like huge round balls with legs, and everyone laughed at the sight of them. So cute—little men.

The first time Bill faced an opponent in scrimmage, he stumbled against and on top of him. The boy on the bottom howled and continued to scream and cry, his nose and eyes streaming, as he was extricated from under Bill. The three men present shouted and ran around, thumping Dad on the back, pumping his hand up and down as they comforted the crying boy, wiping his nose, saying, "You have to learn to take it."

When they got home, Dad asked Bill didn't he want a glass of milk, and then got it for him, while he excitedly lunged forward demonstrating Bill's tackle to Mom.

Then one day Tommy was called into the game, but he was watching the cheerleaders, and Dad shouted at him. He tried not to run wide to avoid contact, but Dad could tell. That was the first time Tommy saw the pucker between Dad's eyes when he looked at him.

It is that look, that slight frown, which worries Tommy most. It is there often when Dad looks at him. Tommy thinks of how Dad treats Bill at the ball game. "Go get'em son! We need a touchdown." He pats him on the back, or on the fanny. Bill waddles onto the field and as Dad often says, "Does me proud."

Tommy has made up a cheer in his head and choreographed it. He's proud of the cheer and feels good in his chest when he thinks of it.

Tommy knows that Dad will never say about him, "Does me proud." Tommy and Dad share words and their meaning, but it is a quiet sharing. Dad does not laugh and clap his hands over what they do together.

It is as though Dad and Bill share some center that Tommy cannot share. What Dad and Tommy share is a thing on the edge that does not matter much to Dad.

But it is Tommy's center that causes his night worrying. It is there. It is a fact. And Tommy knows that the more Dad knows about his center the deeper he'll frown.

What's going to happen about Dad?

Tommy is not yet nine years old and he has a problem he can tell to no one.

Tommy's self is stronger than the worry tonight. He lets it float from his mind and goes to sleep, chanting the cheer to himself, like a prayer.

But tomorrow when he wakes up, or if he wakes in the night, the problem will be there.

What If. . .

What if tomorrow morning the world awoke with amnesia? Everyone on the earth woke up and yawned, and there was a hole in the brain, in the mind, where certain things had been. We'd not forgotten everything, just certain things.

We'd forgotten what these things were used for. We fingered them with wonder. What are these things for? How strange! A man emerges from the bedroom saying to his wife, "Look what I found in my pocket." He holds out his hand. "Huh," she says, finger prodding the circles. "In the Greek and Roman times," she remembers, "they called things like that coins." The objects look like some cuff links which he has. Later he finds leathery, green papers in his pocket which add to the mystery.

At the office he finds more men staring at those round things. Flat like wheels. They stand around and discuss the coins: a few people have agreed that's what they were called. They talk about this sitting on each others' desks. They can't remember exactly what they did at the office: why they came there every day. The confusion was like a mini-vacation. They drank coffee, and one man began to swing his legs back and forth as he listened to another. He stopped, feeling vaguely as though he shouldn't be doing that, although the why of it puzzled him.

The grocer, the checkout woman, the bag boy, all held extended palms and wondered why they were in the store. The bus driver stopped. "I need to get to school," the slim teacher said. He looked confused "I can take you." "Thank you," she said, "Thank you very much."

Across town a mother walks into the living room and sees on the coffee table a shiny metal pipe, with a curve at one end. What is this, and what's it doing in her house? It's heavy and cold in her hand. Her son doesn't know what it is either. Sleepily rubbing the back of his head, he takes the object and holds it by the curving end. He notices a little tongue of metal just by his index finger. His finger closes around it. Their heads wobble. Is the noise inside or outside of their heads? Dust falling in the room. The morning sun comes through a new hole, big as a salad plate, between the top of the window and the ceiling. They are no longer in sleepy wonder. Mother and son stare at each other, terrified.

All over the neighborhood, the projects, similar scenes are occurring. At a meeting that afternoon a wise one comes forward and declares that these dangerous objects must be gathered and kept in a safe place until they can determine the full nature of the objects, and their use. They also notice and talk about the Roundies. What are they doing in their pockets, and how did they get there? That very evening the Wise One and a member of the committee drive around gathering the Hole Makers. The word spreads before them, and often the Hole Maker is on the table, the members of the household in full cooperation with the gathering project. Companionable words are shared, relatives and family inquired of. People draw closer to each other: they sense a common goal. Confusion makes the people open, inquisitive of any insight the other might contribute. At first it is a need to know, and then they become interested in each other.

By ten p.m., the gathering project must stop, because the back of the car is filled with Hole Makers, and they begin to slide into the front seat. Taking the Hole Makers to safe storage, they plan to find a truck for the next load.

News stories on TV prove the confusion to be worldwide. No one knows the purpose of the Hole Makers or the Roundies. There are dirty men, women, and children in wasteland streets, and here the Hole Makers are endemic. These people quarrel excessively with each other, then they join to forage for food or a place to sleep. One man returned to find the man he'd spat at cradling the returned man's own small son in his arms, whispering a lullaby. He said, "Harumph." Stripping off his filthy jacket, he laid it on the ground so the other man could put his son down. They seemed two fathers of the same child.

At the grocery store, women come asking for a few potatoes, a bottle of milk, and go away with the items gratefully in their arms. The clerks at the store sometimes encouraged the customers to add other items. There seemed to be plenty.

But the supplies were not endless, and planners were looking ahead to see how society would function. More and more people came to meetings. It became obvious that humanity was the greatest resource. The Ecology of Humans was formed.

Experts who had studied the ecology of the earth were called upon to teach what they'd learned to the new Ecologists of Humans. Here is what they taught: While there are extinct species among the plants and animals, and we don't yet know the cost of our loss, it is hoped that it is not too late to still have a full complement of kinds and types of humans to meet the needs of humanity.

Everyone was required to attend training with the ecologists. Each individual was made aware of his or her own need and duty to develop all sides of the personality.

"The earth must develop her resources: humans are the gold of the earth. We cannot afford to stunt anyone's growth. To undercut an individual's self esteem is the worst offense a human could commit. It is an offense to the stunted one, but also to one's own self esteem. Respect for oneself and for others is equal."

This was the tenor of the early lectures. Later the students were broken into groups of not more than ten, with a teacher deemed rich in the element that needed development within the group.

One of the major corrections to be accomplished was the balancing of male and female energy. Men usually were power oriented and women as a result were manipulative. Neither was good, or permissible, in the light of developing humanity.

Two groups of talented teachers rose to the attention of the overseers immediately. Gay men and lesbian women. Both groups had escaped the stereotype, but their suffering at the hands of humanity had sometimes resulted in low self esteem. They were given an extended course at a special academy where they were known as The Gold of the Gold.

While they were at the academy, the groups, which would be their teaching assignment, were being formed. The start of a new round of teaching, and the return of the GGs, as they inevitably came to be known, was high festival, because it meant that humanity had increased by the bringing to a high state the new GGs, and was about to increase more as the GGs taught their pupils to become more fully human. The festival was both planting and harvest. Many people felt a connection with the earth, realized that everything is part of everything else.

When the festival was over and all were happily sated, there were a few days of rest. Then the new learning began.

The teaching of the men and women was very different because most often they had been allowed to flower in opposite directions: men toward mental capacity and reason, women toward emotionality and intuition. But there were extreme cases in which men had become dictatorial, and women capricious. The best of teachers were assigned to these most difficult groups. They were addressed first during the new cycle of teaching, because it was acknowledged that each person in these groups affected adversely a wide range of family and friends.

Each group of nine or ten men were taught by two men. These teachers were mostly gay men, but a few were straight men who by nature or occupation had escaped the lopsided development of the "normal" male.

It was particularly necessary to have two teachers for the men, especially in the beginning, when the members of the class were reluctant to participate. The teachers could keep up a conversation, whereas one teacher alone would find himself chattering and would therefore be a totally unacceptable model for the nor-male. The GGs did indulge in this little joke between themselves: calling their students "nor-males." It would have been inhuman to expect them not to have any joking animosity toward their students when they had suffered at the hands of such types. But they were more than willing to help their students.

The aim during the first few days was for the men to speak in full sentences, rather than in words, or grunts, or feet shuffles. The students were invited to give topics for discussion. When these began to come after two or three days the topics were about sports. This often required the teachers to become students as the fine points of the game were explained. It was during such an explanation that a teacher noticed that the men were no longer knuckle punching each other, but slapping on the back or arm with an open hand. This seemed like progress.

Then one day, when they were talking about their high school years, a tall rangy man with coke bottle glasses said, "A bad thing happened to me." Something in his voice arrested the other men.

"Do you want to tell us about it?" one of the teachers gently urged. He was hunched forward with his elbows almost on his knees. He stayed that way for a long time without speaking, but the men waited.

"I never could play, because of these," he said, fanning one hand up toward his glasses. "I always liked sports, hung around the gym. When I was in high school, one year I was the equipment manager. Got the basketballs in a big net bag and dragged them to the gym. Kept score." His hands hung down between his knees, limply, like so many bones.

"Then I had to get my glasses changed—thicker. The game was tied up. End of second half." The bones in his hands rose level with his wrists and fell again. "The away coach came over. Said I made a mistake. I couldn't see very well. He could have been—." His voice came muffled from his bent head, but it had no competition in the room. "I changed the score. Was just stuffing the last ball into the bag. Our coach came over and said—said—'I knew you were dumb, but I didn't know'—." His hands rose and fell between his knees.

One teacher nodded to the other and to the men, for the end of the session. The men crowded around, talking, touching him. Later one teacher said to the other, "They didn't carry him off the floor on their shoulders. It was more like they carried him in their arms." When they returned to the session, two of the men were smiling. As they sat down, a third man laughed. The sound rolled from him coming past the place from which the short bitter barks had issued at the start of the classes.

The Gold of the Gold teachers of the women had a different problem. In these classes there were two teachers also, but they were not necessary to maintain conversation. The women talked. They talked. It was observed that most of the women in these first, most desperate, classes were women who were familiar only with the society of the household. They had developed methods of operation which worked in the family, or possibly failed to work there. But their whole reference was the family.

At first the teachers were confused. They'd meet after class and ask each other, "What's going on? I can't get a grip on this. And why do I think that what they really mean does not match the words coming out of their mouths?"

At the third class the problem emerged. A woman speaking of a man in her family said, "He's despicable, but of course I don't despise him." The teachers looked at each other with an "Aha" look.

"Well," a teacher asked, "Who despises him?"

"He is worthy of being despised," she said, "but I don't despise him."

"But," the teacher said, "you just said, 'He's despicable.'"

"Why are you trying to twist my words around?" she asks querulously, looking at her watch.

At the next meeting a teacher asked, "What's wrong with this statement?" She'd written it on a chalkboard. HE'S DESPICABLE, BUT OF COURSE I DON'T DESPISE HIM.

"It's the pot trying to call the kettle black," a woman offers.

"Not necessarily," the teacher replied dryly. No other thoughts from the class. They went on to other subjects. The words remained on the chalkboard. And the words remained in the vocabulary of the teachers during their time away from class. "You're despicable," one would say, and the other would answer, "but of course you don't despise me."

On the fourth day a woman opened class by declaring, "It's dishonest," flicking her wrist toward the words on the board. Here was an advocate from the ranks.

The teachers encouraged her to explain.

"Well the person just made a judgment that the man is despicable, then she denies that she made the judgment by saying that she doesn't despise him. She wants him to be despicable, but to have none of the dirt stick to her. He is despicable, but she would never despise him, because she loves everybody, or she doesn't say bad words. It's something like that. It's dishonest." She sat back satisfied with her statement, but not for long.

The room buzzed with outrage. The woman who had originally spoken the "despicable" sentence said sweetly, "You're obviously brilliant, and I'm just a dumb woman with no education."

"I'm not brilliant," the other answered, "but I've been thinking about it for three days. I figured out what was wrong right away, but I couldn't figure out why she says things like that. And in the process I realized that I do it too."

"Do what?" the teacher asked.

"Manipulate." The teacher encouraged her to explain.

"The dishwasher is an example. I wanted a dishwasher. Needed a dishwasher. And I got one, and I'm glad that I got it. But I'm not proud of the way I did it.

"My girls were too little to do dishes, and the boys messed around, squirted each other with water through the holes of baby bottle nipples. It was almost easier to do it myself, except that I didn't have time.

"My husband hated to spend money. He was always promising, whatever I wanted or needed for sometime in the future. Next year. But I needed a dishwasher now."

There was a general murmur among the women. "Of course, you needed a dishwasher. Boys don't know how to clean a kitchen."

"But the way I got it. I appealed to his prejudice. I said that boys should not be doing dishes. Even then, I did not think that. But I said it to manipulate him, to get what I wanted. That dishwasher appeared in my kitchen by magic. Poof! It was there."

"But you got what you wanted," one woman said. "That's the big thing."

"No, that's not the big thing," said the dishwasher woman. "Especially now. If we're going to be fully human we need to be honest with each other. I manipulated my husband, I failed to teach my sons to do a good job in the kitchen, and I lied. I spoke an opinion to agree with my husband. That opinion was not what I really thought. It was not the truth."

This was the beginning. Some of the women began talking about similar problems and realizations. Some fought vehemently against the ideas. And the faces of some women became fists. The latter few were rescheduled for another workshop. The watchword of the teachers became, "Don't you see that this sort of behavior is insulting to men?"

The children were the true Human Gold. They did not need to be changed so that they could flower fully, equal in all parts. They only needed to be allowed their nature. They revealed themselves in imaginative play. From the age of three they were telling stories, singing songs, dressing up in costumes, drawing and painting.

The materials provided them were purposely rudimentary. The child or children provided the shape. A long chiffon scarf could be a turban, a sash, a rope, a tablecloth, and in at least one instance a curtain between the actors and the audience.

By five or six they were writing, directing, producing, and acting in stage performances. Parents were encouraged to notice any particular talent or interest the child might have.

The child could only become herself or himself. If the child did not, could not achieve self, then the child was stunted.

If at around the age of five or six the child showed interest and affection for other children of the same gender, it was taken as a possible sign of homosexuality. This caused happy excitement, because the Gold of the Gold teachers realized that in the past, many, possibly most, great artists, writers, musicians, and athletes have been homosexual, and their contributions to the evolution of humanity have been greater than anyone could estimate.

So here was another person who might be the great contributor of the future. All the children were encouraged to read biographies of great men and women, especially those in their field of talent. The names of the great of past ages flew around the dining hall, like those of sports figures or movie stars. Marta, our best athlete, was the first to notice the lack of women's names among the great of past ages. This was the subject of many discussions. The young people needed to know the ways of the past.

No one could explain it thoroughly, for our memories were still defective about the times before the Roundies and before the Hole Makers appeared and were locked up. All agreed that this imbalance of greatness need not continue into the future.

In the spring and fall of each year, our talented young ones travel to other communities, performing, demonstrating, talking, exchanging ideas. Then we are visited by other traveling bands. This is why we have many marriages and unions between our youth and those of other communities and nations.

Our Marta is not only our best, she is *the* best. Even the young men go back home bragging, "I competed against Marta." Ever since the spring traveling, Marta has laughed easily. The name Joya is on her lips often.

Next week we are being visited by a traveling band. We are excited at the prospect of meeting Joya and hearing her music, especially the songs which she's written for our Marta.

We are further joyous over the possible enrichment to our community, and to the earth itself, which a Holy Union between our Marta and Joya would bring.

All affects all. May we never lose that knowledge.

To find a Pflag chapter in your vicinity write or call:
P-FLAG
(Parents, Families, and Friends of Lesbians and Gays)
1101 14th Street NW, Suite 1030, Washington, DC 20005
phone: 202-638-4200   fax: 202-638-0243
E-mail address: PFLAGNTL@aol.com

For information on how to start a Pflag chapter ask for Gabriella De Anda.

You can find *Homosexuality: The Secret A Child Dare Not Tell* in fine bookstores everywhere, or order directly from the publisher:

Rafael Press
PO Box 150462
San Rafael, CA 94915-0462

- -

❏ **Yes! Here is my order:** (please enclose check or money order)

Send me _____ copies at $12.00 each. Total:_____

In California, add $0.87 each for sales tax:_____

Shipping: $3.00 first copy, $1.00 each add. copy:_____

TOTAL ENCLOSED:_____

Ship to:

Name:_____

Address:_____

City, State, Zip_____

FIREBIRD

FIREBIRD

Iris Gower

G.K. Hall & Co. • Chivers Press
Thorndike, Maine USA   Bath, England

This Large Print edition is published by G.K. Hall & Co., USA
and by Chivers Press, England.

Published in 1998 in the U.S. by arrangement with
Caroline Sheldon Literary Agency.

Published in 1998 in the U.K. by arrangement with
Transworld Publishers Ltd.

U.S. Hardcover 0-7838-0165-3 (Romance Series Edition)
U.K. Hardcover 0-7540-1159-3 (Windsor Large Print)
U.K. Softcover 0-7540-2115-7 (Paragon Large Print)

The text of this Large Print edition is unabridged.
Other aspects of the book may vary from the original edition.

Set in 16 pt. Plantin by Rick Gundberg.

Printed in the United States on permanent paper.

British Library Cataloguing in Publication Data available

Library of Congress Cataloging in Publication Data

Gower, Iris.
   Firebird / Iris Gower.   MAR   3 2000
     p.   cm.
   ISBN 0-7838-0165-3 (lg. print : hc : alk. paper)
   1. Large type books. I. Title.
   [PR6057.O845F57 1998]
   823′.914—dc21   98-14059

To my parents, William and Wilhelmina,
with love

CHAPTER ONE

Her legs ached. Her feet had been turning the wheel for hours, fashioning the large jugs and bowls for which the Savage Pottery had become known.

Llinos Savage rubbed her eyes and listened to the cheerful voices of the young boys outside the bottle kilns. The apprentices were stacking pots ready to be biscuit fired. She envied them, they were so carefree.

The row of pots on the table before her wavered in the waning light. The smell of oxide, mingled with the metallic aroma of black lead, lay heavy on the air.

Llinos climbed down from her seat, running her hands over the pitted wood of the wheel. It had been specially designed for her by her father when he had last been home on leave. A few months later came the devastating news that he was missing believed killed. Llinos had never quite believed it to be true. He was such a big man in every way and the memory of him was still sharp.

She sighed. The fortunes of the Savage Pottery had gone downhill since then. Jeremiah, the man her father had left in charge, had quarrelled with her mother over wages. He had quit his job and

Gwen had decided to save money by not looking for a replacement.

Llinos watched as Binnie Dundee lifted a jug and dipped it into a bowl of brownish liquid, the warm red of the earthenware vessel gradually changing to black. Binnie caught her eye and frowned.

'You look tired, better call it a day.'

One of the candles on a shelf above Llinos's head flickered and died and the aroma of tallow momentarily overrode the other smells.

'I suppose so.' Llinos swallowed the fear that the thought of returning home aroused in her. *He* would be there, the man who thought he could take her father's place.

Llinos shivered as she placed some pots in the sagger ready for the final firing.

'Take these over to the ovens, Binnie,' she said. He rubbed at his hands with a rag and sighed heavily; his eyes were shadowed and Llinos felt a warm rush of gratitude for his loyalty.

Binnie was older than she by several years. He had been taken on at the pottery when he was little more than a child. And he had stayed when most of the more experienced workers began to drift away to find more secure employment.

He opened the door and stepped outside and a cold draught wrapped itself around Llinos's ankles. She snuffed out the rest of the candles and darkness folded in on her. She did not like the dark. Even though she was growing into womanhood, she was still afraid of shadows

She left the shed and as she crossed the yard, she felt the crispness of frost in the grass beneath her feet. She rubbed at her arms, suddenly aware that she was aching.

'*Darro*, Llinos, come as yourself! I thought you was a little ghost there.' Ben Carpenter was just leaving the yard. He stood in the gateway and looked back at her. She smiled at him, he was an old man now but like Binnie he had remained loyal to her.

'Sorry, Ben, did I startle you?'

'Too royal you did. Look, Miss Llinos, you shouldn't be working like this, it's too much for you.'

'Anything's better than being in the house with *him*,' Llinos said softly.

'I know what you mean.' Ben retraced his steps and rested his hand on her shoulder. 'Young you may be but you're a good judge of character. Pity Mrs Savage didn't have some of your good sense.'

Llinos watched as Ben left the yard. 'Yes, a great pity,' she said. Behind her, she could hear the voices of the apprentices. They were laughing and she felt suddenly lonely. Now the boys lodged in a small outbuilding at the far end of the yard. In the past, they had shared a room in the Pottery House but the arrival of Mr Cimla had put a stop to that.

Llinos turned as she heard a light footfall behind her.

'Wonder if your mam will make us supper tonight?' Watt Bevan was the youngest of the apprentices. His job was to clear away the rubbish, the bits of clay left from the potting. Watt rubbed at his thin stomach. 'I'm starving.'

'I'll see what I can do,' Llinos said. 'It will be all right if Mr Cimla's in a good mood.'

Watt sighed. 'Why did your mam have to take up with 'im, we was all right on our own.'

'What we can't change we have to put up with.' Llinos rubbed Watt's hair, which was thick with clay dust.

Binnie came out of the shadows and stood beside her.

'Speaking for myself, I'd like to kill the bastard,' he said quietly. 'And if he lays a hand on any of us again, I might just well let him have it.'

Llinos tried to assess Binnie's chances against Mr Cimla and shook her head. Bert Cimla was big of shoulder, a handsome man but going to seed now that he was enjoying an idle life. He indulged himself in food and ale that he never thought to pay for.

'I'm going indoors. If I can, I'll bring you some bread and cheese.'

'Look out for the rats.' Binnie's smile did not reach his eyes. 'Especially one that goes by the name of Mr Cimla.'

Pottery Row stood on the flat lands beside the river Tawe. As its name suggested, it comprised a short row of houses that ended in a high wall.

Behind the wall huddled a group of pott
buildings. A mill house with the wheel turning
rose above a trio of pot-bellied kilns. And on a
clear night, the glow of the fires lit up the sky.

A little lower on the river bank stood the more
flourishing Tawe Pottery belonging to Philip
Morton-Edwards. The family were rich, influential, solid citizens of Swansea. At the Tawe Pottery, experiments were being made into the
production of a fine porcelain body. If the experiments were successful, the Tawe porcelain
would grace the finest homes throughout England and Wales.

Llinos began to walk resolutely towards the
house. It was pointless trying to delay the moment when she would come face to face with
Bert Cimla. Gwen Savage had met the man only
a few short weeks before. She was besotted by
him and had allowed him to come calling on
her almost at once. Tongues had not stopped
wagging ever since.

The doorway of the house was ajar and Llinos
stood for a moment silhouetted in the light of
the moon. The hallway was in darkness. One
candle gleamed high up on the curve of the
stairs, shedding a dim light. Llinos made her
way towards the sitting-room; with luck there
would be a good fire burning in the grate. She
rubbed her chilled hands together anticipating
the warmth. She paused as she heard a sound
from the dining-room.

Reluctantly, Llinos made her way along the

passage. The smell of ale grew stronger as she approached the dining-room door and her heart sank. Mr Cimla had been drinking. As she opened the door, Llinos saw her mother's face, smiling as she leant towards Mr Cimla, hanging on his every word. She glanced at her daughter and frowned.

'Llinos, have you finished work already?'

'It's very late, Mother.' She sat down at the table, avoiding looking at Mr Cimla, who was sprawled in her father's chair, a tankard of ale marking the polished oak of the table.

'Well, Miss Savage, what have you been up to then?' His tone was honeyed. Llinos did not look at him and she delayed replying to his question for as long as she dared.

'I have been working, as usual.'

'I thought I saw you dawdling with the young apprentices.' He leant forward and she hesitated, looking directly at him for the first time. 'That's right, I promised the boys some supper.'

'Supper?'

'Yes, supper. They've been working hard, they must be as hungry as I am.'

'But, my dear, you are the daughter of the house, those boys are just poor folk.' Mr Cimla spoke in kindly tones but Llinos had seen the sudden gleam of dislike in his eyes.

'That doesn't make them less hungry than I am.'

'Tut, backchatting your elders, that's not nice, is it?'

'Look, Llinos,' her mother intervened. 'Ta.. a jug of soup and some bread to the boys in the outhouse. Have your food with them, if you like.'

Llinos nodded, grateful for the excuse to get away from the claustrophobic atmosphere of the dining-room.

As she carried the tray of food along the passage towards the yard, Llinos heard Mr Cimla remonstrating with her mother.

'You spoil that girl, Gwenie, darling. A little discipline would not come amiss.'

Llinos resisted the temptation to kick the door shut with her foot. Mr Cimla should have been out of the house by nightfall; he seemed to be unaware that he would be compromising her mother by his rash behaviour. Especially now that the last of the servants had left, tired of empty promises of payment of their wages.

'Oh, boy!' Watt looked up at Llinos as she entered the big, roomy outhouse where the apprentices slept. 'Supper!'

'Give that to me.' Binnie relieved her of the heavy tray and placed it on a stool. He rubbed at the red marks on her arms. 'You should have called me, the tray's too heavy for you.'

'I'm all right, don't worry so much.'

'Who's worrying? Where are the bowls?'

'Mam was too busy getting rid of me to think of bowls.' Llinos smiled. 'Go and get some from the china we've packed ready for market day.'

'Are you sure?' Binnie hesitated.

'I'm sure, we can wash them and put them

back when we've finished.'

'I'll go.' Watt moved over to the corner where the finished china was stacked in baskets. He lifted a pile of plates, balancing them on one arm while he tried to locate the bowls.

Llinos saw what was about to happen and she held out her hands as though to ward off the disaster. But it was too late. Slowly, the plates slid away from the pile, crashing one by one onto the stone floor. Almost immediately the door opened and Mr Cimla looked in, his face dark in the candle light.

'I just knew something was going on in here.'

Llinos stood looking at him, her hands on her thin hips. Suddenly, she was so angry that she could not think straight.

'It's because of you we are reduced to eating like beggars. How dare you interfere? What business is it of yours if I choose to break all the dishes in the pottery? It's my inheritance or have you forgotten?'

He smiled scornfully. 'You're only a bit of a kid! Your inheritance indeed, you don't know what you are talking about.' He turned to leave but the tone of command in her voice stopped him.

'While you *are* here, I have something to say to you.' She paused. 'It's not a year since we received news of my father's death. Mother is in mourning and it's not proper for you to come at such an hour. Have you no sense of propriety?'

'For your information, madam, I was just

14

about to leave for home.' He moved into the building and closed the door behind him. Llinos stepped back, frightened by the look on the man's face.

'Just as well I was,' he continued. 'It seems you have been playing high jinks with the apprentices and you have the gall to talk to me about propriety. Look at the mess in here.'

'It was an accident,' Llinos said, staring at him, wondering what her mother saw in him. 'Please leave.'

Mr Cimla paced across the floor with deliberate steps, his eyes never leaving her face. He looked down at the broken plates, at the shards of pottery strewn around the baskets, and shook his head.

'This is a wicked deed. Someone has to be punished for it.' He jerked his head towards the apprentices. 'You, out!'

Watt slid along the wall and edged past Mr Cimla, his eyes wide with fear. The other two youngsters followed him. Only Binnie stood his ground.

'I said out!' Mr Cimla repeated. Binnie lowered his eyes and slowly walked towards the door.

'Now, Miss High-and-Mighty Savage, I think it's about time you and I understood each other.'

He caught her arm and Llinos flinched as he lifted his hand. She thought for a moment that he was going to hit her, then his hand was hot on her neck. 'It doesn't have to be like this between us, girl,' he said. 'We could so easily be friends.'

She jerked away abruptly. 'How dare you touch me.' Her voice was heavy with disgust. Mr Cimla did not seem to hear it.

'You'll grow to like me, lass,' he said. 'All I want to do is to be kind to you.'

Mr Cimla grasped her arm. She pulled away from him tearing her dress from shoulder to waist. She pushed him away.

He made a lunge and caught her, holding her fast; she felt the heat of his hands pressing against her spine and she slapped out at his face with all her strength.

Suddenly he was jerked backwards. Llinos saw Binnie grasping Bert Cimla's hair, pulling back the man's head, a thick shard of pottery held to his throat.

'Go into the house, Llinos,' Binnie said. 'I'll deal with this bastard!'

It took Llinos a few moments to gather her wits. 'Get out of here, Mr Cimla,' she said. 'Or I'll rouse all the occupants of the row with my screams. See what my mother thinks of you then.'

Bert Cimla shook free of Binnie and moved towards the door. He was smiling as he opened it and looked out into the darkness.

'Gwenie!' he called. 'Gwenie Savage, come here at once!' His commanding voice echoed along the row and Llinos met Binnie's eyes ques-

16

tioningly. He shook his head, as bewildered as she was.

Her mother came to the door of the shed, a cloak hastily pulled over her shoulders, her hair hanging loose.

'Good God in heaven, what's happened here?' She stared from one to the other of them, her eyes coming to rest on her daughter.

Llinos opened her mouth but Mr Cimla spoke first. 'I found them together, on the floor, like a pair of animals, they were. Didn't I always say she was too friendly with the boy?'

'Mother, don't believe him, it's not true!' Llinos said. 'He attacked me, he was hurting me.'

'Rubbish! I never laid a finger on you except to try to salvage something of your chastity. Look, Gwen, see how the girl's dress is torn? She's a common hussy, exposing herself to all who care to look.'

'I don't know what to think.' Gwen Savage rubbed her eyes.

'Mother!' Llinos wound her arms around her mother's waist. 'I have never lied to you before, have I?'

'Furthermore' — Mr Cimla was merciless — 'I was the one who was attacked. The boy came at me with a piece of broken china. Get rid of him, Gwen, he's a danger to all of us. It's a wonder you haven't been murdered in your bed.'

Gwen held her daughter at arm's length. 'Come along, Llinos, tell me the truth, what

17

really happened here? How did the plates get broken?'

'Does that matter now?'

'Tell your mother, madam, tell her how you sent the younger boys to get the china. You wanted to distract them while you and he' — he gestured towards Binnie — 'had your bit of fun.'

'How do you know what we were doing?' Llinos challenged, suddenly calm. 'Are you saying you were deliberately spying on me? If so, that is not the act of a gentleman, is it?'

'I just heard the noise of smashing china, so I came to look. I saw you through the window. I saw him hold your arms, rubbing them real friendly he was. You were all set for a nice bit of canoodling before you got down to the real thing.'

'Don't be ridiculous,' Llinos said.

'Binnie' — Gwen moved towards the boy — 'did you touch my daughter?'

'Not in the way *he* says, never. He was forcing himself on Llinos, trying to kiss her, that's why I jumped on him.'

'Come on now, Gwen, who do you want to believe, this young tom cat or me? Do you think I'd want anything to do with your daughter when you are the light of my life?'

Gwen took a deep breath. 'Llinos, go in the house. I'll speak to you in the morning. And you, Binnie, pack up your belongings and get out.'

'No, Mother!' Llinos protested.

Her mother glared at her. 'Go inside the house at once. Any more nonsense from you and you can pack up your things and get out as well.'

Llinos swallowed hard, she was tempted to defy her mother and throw in her lot with Binnie. Her mother read her mind.

'If you go with him it will only convince me that what Mr Cimla said is true and then it will be the worse for Binnie, believe me.'

'I'll sort this out, Binnie,' Llinos said. 'I won't let him do this to us. This is my property, not his.' She held her head high and crossed the yard to the house, holding back the hot tears of frustration and anger.

She watched from the bedroom window as Binnie walked along the row, his small bundle of possessions under his arm, his one pair of clogs on string around his neck. 'Damn you, Mr Cimla, damn you.'

She heard footsteps on the stairs and her mother entered the room, holding a candle high so that she could look into her daughter's face.

'Have you lost your virtue to the boy? Come on now. Llinos, tell me the truth.'

Llinos sat on the bed, wrapping her arms around her thin body.

'Answer me, girl.' Her mother shook her shoulder. 'Don't you know you are a woman now and could conceive a child, a bastard?'

'Mam, Binnie has never touched me, not in the way you mean.'

'You swear this is the truth?'

'I swear.'

Her mother looked at her rumpled clothes, at the tear in her dress and her eyes narrowed. 'Then why is your bodice in such a state?'

'Mr Cimla did it.' Llinos lifted her chin. The light shifted and the flame flickered as her mother's hand shook.

'Liar!' Gwen said harshly. 'I don't understand you, Llinos, you want to ruin my one chance of happiness. How could you be so thoughtless? Haven't I suffered enough, losing your father? Do you want me to lose Bert too?'

She turned and left the room and Llinos sat numbly on the bed unable to see anything in the sudden gloom. Her mother had called her liar, she would prefer to believe a man like Mr Cimla than her own daughter.

Llinos crawled into bed and huddled beneath the blankets and lay wide-eyed in the darkness.

A shaft of moonlight lit the wall opposite the window, outlining the shape of the jug on the sill. Llinos turned and looked at it, it was one her father had made when she was just a child. Why did he have to go to the wars? It was nothing to them what wars were fought on foreign lands. It had not touched them, not here in the peace of Swansea.

She screwed her eyes tightly together and against the darkness she saw the figure of Binnie, shoulders slumped as he walked away down the row, and she felt she had lost the only friend she had ever had.

Hundreds of miles from Llinos, across the stretch of water called the Bristol Channel, a soldier lay awake in the darkness of the night, staring up at the stars. He had been dreaming of her again, the black-haired girl with the pale skin.

Wah-he-joe-tass-e-neen, half Indian, half white man rolled himself more securely into his coarse blanket and looked at the star-studded sky. He could feel her close to him now, feel her sadness. Somewhere she was waiting for him to come into her life and they would meet, one day.

Across the camp, Joe heard the sounds of men shifting in their sleep. Someone coughed and Joe turned on his side and instead of the stars he looked into the flames of the fire.

He knew that she was his destiny. She had not been born on the plains of America where he had been given life but in a small town that touched the edges of the sea.

Joe abandoned any attempt to sleep and considered the strange pattern of his life. At nineteen, he had seen a great deal of the world. Born of an American Indian mother, he had grown up with the Mandan Indians near the river Missouri. But he had gone to school in England, his white father had wanted him to be educated in the ways of the white man. But then Joe was half white: that was what his name meant.

21

Now here he was in France, fighting on the side of the English against Napoleon Bonaparte. He looked across the fire to where his captain lay. Lloyd Savage was a big man in every way. He was big of stature and in strength of character.

He had welcomed Joe as his guide and his batman, treating him with every courtesy. This was not the usual response of the British to one they perceived to be a half-breed.

Lloyd turned in his sleep and in the flickering firelight Joe saw the same dark hair, the sculptured features he had seen in his dream. It came to him then that the girl he had never met, the girl he already loved, was the captain's daughter.

He and the captain had faced war and life and death together. Once they had been given up for dead but, by Joe's wits and the captain's courage, they had survived.

Joe wrapped his blanket closer; he must sleep, tomorrow there was an enemy to face. Tonight he would dream again, she would come to him like a bird in the spring. His maiden, his Firebird.

CHAPTER TWO

It was morning and the dawn light was diffuse. It pierced holes through the grayness of the sky with skeletal fingers, shafting light onto the backs of the sleeping men. It was raining and the dying fires eddied smoke that mingled with the lowering clouds.

'By all the spirits of my ancestors, I hate this country of France.' Joe pushed aside his steaming blanket and bent over the fire, breathing life into it.

'How do you do that?' Lloyd Savage opened his eyes reluctantly and peered into the gloom at the flames leaping upwards. 'How do you get a fire to light in weather like this?'

'You forget, Captain, I grew up with the Mandan, I know many things.'

'And yet your skin is as white as mine, Joe.'

The captain was making a statement, not asking a question. He was a man who respected the privacy of others.

'You know as well as I do that I'm half American Indian. Wah-he-joe-tass-e-neen means half white man.' Joe thrust some twigs into the flames, seeing in the glowing fire pictures of his childhood.

He had known from an early age that his father

was a white man come from England. He knew too that his mother was disgraced when the white man lay with her, gave her a son and then left her.

But Mint-leaf had honoured the memory of her lover and had taught his son the language of his father's land. When Joe had been sent for by his English father Mint-leaf had handed him a bundle of letters — love letters. She hoped that by reading of his father's love for her, the son might find it in his heart to be forgiving. She knew little of men.

In England, Joe had been educated, cared for but never accepting or accepted. He had joined the British army at the age of sixteen and had found himself on the battlefields of Europe.

'You have that far-away look in your eyes,' Savage said. 'What are you thinking, Joe?'

Joe looked at the older man and his face softened.

'My thoughts are worth nothing.' He rarely smiled but he did so now. He shared an affinity with the captain that comes to men who have faced death together.

At the battle of Leipzig they had been holed up in a farmhouse for weeks, the captain and his batman given up as lost. Thanks to Joe's resilience and hunting powers, they had survived to fight another day.

All over the camp, soldiers were stirring, eyes bleary, faces grey. The relentless rain shrouded the land with a sheen of mist and as Joe looked up at the leaden sky, he knew the rain would continue for several more days.

The aroma of pipe tobacco drifted towards Joe as he crouched over the fire, shielding the flames with his hands. They grew to a warm blaze and Joe watched the steam rise from his canteen of water.

He made breakfast as efficiently as he did everything. Good hot beans and sizzling slices of pork would set him and his captain up for the long march that was ahead.

'Smells fit for a king.' Savage edged closer to the fire. 'I'm a lucky bastard, do you know that, my friend?'

Joe would never get used to the way the British soldiers used their language. Bastard was an ugly word, it described men like him, born without honour.

He looked quizzically at Savage. 'I know you are lucky and I know you are not a bastard.'

'You take things too literally.' Savage crouched beside Joe and together they began to eat the hot food.

'You either are a bastard or you are not a bastard,' Joe said reasonably.

'All right, all right, I am not a bastard. Am I permitted to say I'm a lucky hog, then? Will that do?'

Joe shrugged. 'Same thing. You are a man, not a pig.' His eyes gleamed. 'We are eating hog, Captain. What do you say to that?'

'I give up.' The captain held up his hands in

defeat. 'You are too clever for me.' Savage brushed grease from his moustache. 'In any case, I'm too happy enjoying your delicious cooking to argue the toss.'

The camp had come alive, men urinated openly and cursed the rain and Napoleon Bonaparte all in one breath. Joe took little notice. The meal finished, he scrubbed his cooking utensils with earth and then with grass. Later, he would find a stream and then he would wash the battered tins and the tarnished knives before storing them away in his back pack.

Joe realized that his position in the scheme of things regarding the British army was insignificant. He was batman to Captain Savage. But sometimes, his extra powers would be uneasily acknowledged and his ability to track the enemy would come in useful.

He thought again about the battle of Leipzig. Some of the captain's regiment had become separated from the main thrust of the attack. A small group of soldiers were trapped in a gulley with the French ahead by only a few miles. The Prussians were attacking the French from one direction, the Russians from another and the Germans were taking the rearguard defensive. One wrong move by Captain Savage and the troop would be wiped out. It had been a matter of pride to Joe that Savage had chosen him to reconnoitre the area.

On a high ridge behind an outcrop of rocks, a small band of French soldiers had been camped. Joe had taken the scent of them, of strange food, of sweat. It was Joe who had seen the raised rifle and had flung himself down onto the soldier's back.

The skirmish had been brief and when it was over, three dead Frenchmen lay staring sightlessly at the sky. The captain had fought at Joe's side, the rest of the troop had fled.

'Wonder if I'll get any news of home today.' The captain's voice jerked Joe out of his reverie. 'I would like to know how my wife and daughter are faring. Still, they can't come to much harm with Jeremiah in charge of the pottery, good man, Jeremiah.'

Joe swung back his long hair and tied it in a knot, tucking the ends into the neck of his tunic. He tried to envisage the business of making pots in the civilized surroundings of a town and failed. Were the captain's family coping? Joe doubted it. He sometimes wished his dreams would tell him more.

'If they have your resilience, they will do very well,' he said aloud.

'Good Lord, a compliment.' Savage smiled as he finished rolling his damp blanket into a neat package. That was another thing about the captain, he did not expect his batman to wait on him hand and foot as some of the other officers did.

Savage rose to his feet. 'You know what? My little girl will be almost a woman by the time I get home — it's her sixteenth birthday next month. She'll be forgetting what I look like and if this war goes on much longer, so will her mother.'

This girl, this Llinos, she was a fortunate daughter. She had a father who cared about her, who even now, caught up in war, worried about her welfare.

'I know Jeremiah will take good care of the place in my absence and Ben, he might be old but he's a good worker. He'll keep the apprentices in order.' Savage began to walk to the edge of the camp where the horses were tethered. It was clear that in spite of his words he was worried.

He took a deep breath and squared his shoulders. 'We'll ride ahead, Joe, have a scout around before the army moves on.' Respectfully, Joe fell in behind him. Now the boundaries between them existed once more, they were on army business.

'That's a fine glaze, how do you make that colour?'

The voice startled Llinos and she looked around to see Mr Cimla standing behind her. He spoke ingratiatingly, rubbing his hands along the sides of his breeches. It seemed he wished to make amends for his vile behaviour of a few nights ago.

'Yellow oxide.' Llinos spoke abruptly. 'Blow out the candles, would you?'

She put down the pot, unaware of the glaze

running between her fingers, and made for the door. She had no intention of being left alone with Mr Cimla ever again.

In the house, her mother was sitting near the parlour window mending a tear in one of Llinos's petticoats. She looked up as her daughter entered the room and there was a coldness in her eyes.

'For heaven's sake, Llinos, why don't you wipe your feet? We can't expect old Nora to clean up after you as well as everything else. You seem to forget, cuts have to be made, the pottery is not as successful as it once was.'

'Sorry, Mother.'

'I don't know why you go about the place like a slut, that apron is filthy.'

'I've been working since daybreak, Mother.' Llinos sank into a chair. 'I need more help.' Llinos rubbed at her hands but the glaze was sticky and clung to her fingers. 'Now that Binnie's gone, I can't manage.'

'You have old Ben and the apprentices. You are always complaining, Llinos.'

'I can't help what you think, Mother. I can't go on like this.'

Her mother looked at her closely. 'Very well, we shall look for someone respectable to help you in the pottery.' Gwen looked away, lowering her eyes.

'You might as well listen now you are here. I have something to tell you.'

Llinos swallowed hard; she anticipated with a feeling of dread the words her mother would say. She attempted to rise but her mother held up her hand.

'Listen to me! Mr Cimla and I are going to be married.'

'But, Mother, you are married.' The words were forced from between her dry lips.

'Don't be foolish, Llinos, I'm a widow as well, you know. Your father was killed in action at some place called Leipzig, you saw the letter.'

'But, Mother, it could be a mistake. You forget, the letter only said Father was missing.'

'Yes, missing believed killed and not a word from him since. Of course he's dead. Do you think I want it to be that way? I loved your father.'

'I know, but things happen in war. Remember one time when we didn't hear from Father for almost six months? The letters just didn't get through, that's all.'

'For heaven's sake, Llinos! That time we didn't have an official communication from the army.'

She rose and touched her daughter's shoulder. 'Am I to spend the rest of my life struggling on alone, is that what you want?'

Llinos looked down at her fingers and began to pick at the drying glaze. She could think of nothing to say.

'We will not delay too long,' her mother continued, impatient again. 'It will be a quiet affair, neither of us want a fuss.'

'Where will he stay?' Llinos asked.

'He — Mr Cimla — will stay here of course. Unless we sell up the place, that is.'

'You can't sell the pottery.' Llinos spoke more sharply than she had intended.

Patches of angry colour appeared on Gwen's cheeks. 'Don't be so insolent. You are little more than a child, how can you decide our future?'

'You know what the pottery means to me.' Llinos met her mother's eyes. 'In any case, Father willed it to me, didn't he?' Gwen looked away.

'You were just complaining that you can't manage.' She stood in the window for a long moment before turning. Suddenly her eyes were pleading.

'Don't spoil this for me, Llinos.' Her voice softened. 'I'm getting old, this might be my last chance of happiness.'

Llinos shook her head. 'Mr Cimla will not make you happy.'

'Oh, for heaven's sake! It's no use even talking to you. Go away, get out of my sight.'

Llinos climbed the stairs slowly. She was tired, she could not think straight. In her bedroom, she sat near the window and stared out at the stars bright in the night sky. Over to the left, the heat from the kilns seemed to make the bricks shimmer and dance and Llinos smiled; old Ben was on night shift. He had stoked the fires well before settling down to sleep.

Watt would be with him. He loved old Ben like a father. She took a deep breath, the boy

31

would be missing Binnie. She was missing Binnie. There was no-one to blame but Bert Cimla.

He was a common little man. Oh, he did his best to look the part of a gentleman. His boots were well polished, his shirts crisp and clean and yet Llinos could not help feeling Mr Cimla was putting on an act for the benefit of her mother.

He need not have bothered. Gwen was obsessed with him. Mr Cimla had a kind of good looks, Llinos acknowledged, and though he was a little overweight, he held himself well. His hair was dark and curling and if his chin was weak it was well hidden by his neat beard and the large moustache of which he was so proud.

Mr Cimla bragged constantly about his money but if ever he took Llinos and her mother on an outing it was invariably Gwen Savage who paid for the carriage and pair.

Llinos had heard the neighbours talking, especially Celia-end-house, who was more vociferous than most.

'Nothing like an old fool,' Celia had said. She had been peering from under her bonnet as Gwen and Mr Cimla alighted from the carriage, unaware that Llinos was listening.

'Bleed her dry as an orange, he will, and then leave her flat. I've met his sort before.'

Gwen Savage had sniffed and held her head high and Llinos, following her into the house, had despaired of her mother ever seeing sense. Well, now she had done what Llinos had feared all along, Gwen Savage had agreed to marry the man.

With a sigh, Llinos turned away from the window and began to wash in the cold water in the basin on the table. Her back ached and so did her arms. If she thought about it, every bone in her body ached. She climbed into bed, hugging the blankets around her shoulders, growing warm and comfortable as she relaxed.

She lay awake in the darkness, turning over the problem of Mr Cimla and his pursuit of her mother, looking desperately for a way to expose him for the sham he was. But it was hopeless, Gwen Savage was besotted.

Llinos turned on her side and closed her eyes and willed herself to sleep.

He was there again, in her dreams. He was beautiful, exotic, like no-one she had ever seen before. He had long hair that lifted in the breeze, golden skin and eyes that were as blue as the summer skies. He was smiling at her and behind him was a vast expanse of country with high tors and clear skies and rushing crystal rivers.

She knew they loved one another. Knew that they were happy together. He took her hand and his hair was silky as it blew against her cheek. He stood at least six inches taller than she. He was young, yet she knew he was much wiser than many men twice his years.

When she woke in the morning, it was with reluctance. She tried to hold on to the warmth and the joy of her dreams. But it was no use.

33

The sound of her mother's raised voice and Nora crashing pans in the kitchen shattered the stillness. Llinos rose from bed and stood for a moment in the chill of the morning, dreading going downstairs. Gwen Savage had been used to a houseful of servants waiting on her. She could not understand that those days were gone; the fortunes of the Savage family had dwindled to almost nothing. Llinos dressed quickly. She had another long hard day at the pottery before her.

It was a quiet ceremony, performed at the church of St John by an elderly vicar who clearly wanted nothing more than to sit down and ease the ache in his legs.

Llinos sat in the front pew and watched in silent misery as Mr Cimla placed the ring on her mother's finger. Gwen was radiant, her eyes soft as they looked up at her handsome new husband. And then it was over and in silence the couple walked up the aisle of the church towards the open door. There was no organ music, that would cost extra and Mr Cimla had decided that the money could be better spent.

Llinos followed the couple along the streets towards Pottery Row, her head bowed as she watched her mother's skirts sweep along the dust in the roadway. There should have been a carriage but Mr Cimla's meanness had won the day and Gwen had decided against it.

As the wedding party walked along Pottery Row the place suddenly became a hive of activity. Celia-end-house carried a bucket of steaming water to her door and got busy scrubbing the stone steps outside her house. Mrs Millie Cooper was cleaning her windows and some of the other women stood in a group talking. There was an air of expectancy about them that Llinos was quick to notice.

'Good luck to you, Mr and Mrs Cimla.' Celia-end-house came towards them, her hands out-stretched. 'We had a whip-round and made a collection to wish you luck on your wedding.' She paused and Llinos, glancing at Mr Cimla, saw him bow charmingly to Celia, anticipating a fine gift.

'With the money I collected, I've made you a home brew and some cake, something to cheer you on this special day.'

'Thank you, Celia, it's much appreciated,' Gwen said and looked up at Mr Cimla. 'Isn't it kind of our neighbours to think of us?'

He bowed stiffly but did not speak. He was obviously disappointed in the humble gifts. His hand rested on Gwen's elbow, urging her towards Pottery House.

Llinos followed reluctantly. She did not want to go indoors, did not want to sit and watch Mr Cimla coo over her mother. Perhaps after a reasonable time she could change into her working clothes and go to the pottery sheds.

'Pour some of that grog, Gwenie.' Mr Cimla tugged at his stiff collar, unfastening it from his shirt and throwing it onto the mantelpiece.

35

'Here, girl, take this upstairs and hang it carefully, I don't want it creased.' He handed Llinos his coat and sat down in the rocking chair before the fire.

'Come on, Gwen, for heaven's sake, you are too slow to catch a cold.'

Llinos hurried upstairs and thrust the coat away from her with a feeling of repugnance. It smelled of him, of sweat and ale.

She looked at the bed which her mother would share with Mr Cimla and she felt suddenly ill. It was done, her mother was married, Mr Cimla was in their lives to stay.

She hurried across the landing into her own room and with shaking hands unfastened the buttons of her best dress. It was a pretty dress, high waisted, with long sleeves. Pale blue, sprigged with white flowers. The material was far too thin for a day as chilly as this one was but she had nothing else good enough to wear.

She shook out the creases and stood for a moment savouring the moment of stillness, knowing that from now on there would be little peace or privacy. Everything was changed. He would be there day and night, demanding the best food and plenty of attention.

Llinos pulled on her thick working dress. The warmth of the wool settled around her comfortingly. It had been left behind by one of the maids, unwanted, considered too worn to pack, but Llinos was glad of it.

She would have to go back downstairs but soon she would make her excuses and go to work. She would tell Mr Cimla that an order for a decorative jug and bowl had come in and it was needed urgently. She knew already that he would not go easy on her, that she would have to explain her every move to him.

In the sitting-room, her mother was perched on Mr Cimla's knee and his hand was inside her bodice. Llinos stopped abruptly in the open doorway.

'Come on in, child.' Mr Cimla smiled. 'Don't mind us. Your mother and me are a happily married couple, remember?'

Gwen made an effort to move away from him but he held her fast, his knuckles moving beneath the material of her bodice. 'Let the child see, it's only natural after all. We are not doing anything wrong, are we, Gwen?'

'No, but some things are best kept private, Mr Cimla.' Gwen's protest was weak and in response Mr Cimla drew her face down to his and kissed her long and hard. He looked up then and met her eyes and Llinos looked away in embarrassment.

'Got work to do, child?' he said harshly, his hand pushing Gwen's skirts above her knee.

Llinos nodded.

'Speak up then, what are you working on?'

'A jug and basin, a good one, I can charge a fair price for it.'

'*You* can charge a fair price?' His hand paused

in its exploration of Gwen's thigh. 'Haven't you got that wrong, little girl?' His voice carried an undisguised threat.

'We, I mean,' Llinos said quickly.

He shook his head. 'No, no, the word is "I" — me, Mr Cimla. I will decide on what charges I wish to make. Indeed, I shall be making all the decisions from now on.'

He returned his attention to Gwen, who was flushed, her brow furrowed, an uncertain look on her face.

'Now get out, child,' Mr Cimla said. 'I have business with your mother.'

Llinos hurried from the room, her eyes suddenly moist. She had to face facts, her mother was married to a crass, stupid monster and nothing was ever going to be the same again.

'Hey, Llinos, what's this, then, tears, is it?' Ben was standing beside one of the kilns, his pipe jutting from his mouth. He looked at her shrewdly.

'You're troubled, is that it, Llinos? Worried what sort of stepfather that man will make. I don't blame you, either, he's no gentleman.'

Llinos leaned against the old man and buried her face against the rough cloth of his coat. 'Ben, I can't stand Mr Cimla, I don't know how I'm going to live in the same house as him.'

'Aye, some people make your flesh creep and he's one of them.'

Llinos looked up at him and drew away, suddenly aware that she was a Savage and should keep her dignity at all costs. It was all she had left, her dignity.

'Don't let him hear you say that, Ben. He's got rid of Binnie as it is, I couldn't stand it if you went too.'

'I won't go, don't you worry, I'm part of the furniture around here. I've been working at the pottery since it was opened and no-one, not even that slimy creature, will make me leave.'

He smiled down at her. 'Are you hungry? I've got a nice bit of cold pie and a jug of milk in the outhouse. I was just going to have my tea, would you like to join me, Miss Savage?'

Ben made a mock bow and Llinos smiled. Ben might be an employee but he had been like a father to her since her own father had gone abroad.

It was warm in the shed with a shaft of pale sunlight illuminating the unglazed pots on the shelves.

'Llinos, you are going to need some help, the place is undermanned as it is and now with Binnie sacked it's going to be impossible to get enough stock to make a profit.'

Ben handed her a cup of milk. 'Pity your father ever went to fight in the war.' Ben poured some milk into another cup. 'Had to be him that got killed, didn't it? But then the Lord only takes the good ones.'

'I can't believe my father is dead, Ben, can you?' Llinos drank some of the milk; it was cool and creamy and fresh from the cow. So fresh that bits of grass still floated in it.

Ben refilled his pipe. 'That's the way of wars, girlie.' He sighed. 'A handsome man was Mr Savage, you follow him for looks.' He smiled. 'The same dark hair, the brown eyes, oh yes, you are your father's daughter, no doubt about it.'

'When I was a child he used to hold me on his knee and tell me stories before I went to bed. As I grew older, he talked to me about the china. He loved the pottery, Ben, why did he go away?'

'He felt it his duty, I 'spects. But you're right, when your daddy was home we had good times, right enough.'

'And now the good times are all gone,' Llinos said. Once there had been light and laughter in Pottery House. There had been servants to do the cooking, to take care of the chores. Being waited on hand and foot was no less than Llinos expected, she had taken it all for granted, unaware that she had been born to privilege. Well, she had no privileges now.

'Your father' — Ben sucked on the stem of his pipe — 'he was the sort of man who believed in justice. He believed he should help get rid of that Bonaparte once and for all.'

'But we are not going to be attacked by a French army, are we, Ben?'

'The war needs to be fought, girlie, there's not much sea between France and England and it's easily crossed. Seems the French had plans to

40

do just that. Gathered at Boulogne, they did, and it took Nelson to put them off the idea. Just can't trust them foreigners. You wouldn't like to wake up one morning and find a French man at your door, would you?'

'So my father was killed protecting us from something that the French might or might not do?'

'Sounds daft put like that but then war *is* daft.' Ben began to puff on his pipe, sending up spirals of smoke that mingled with the motes of dust drifting across the window.

'Hit her hard, your dad's death did, mind.' He jerked his head towards the house. 'Mrs Savage cried for days when she heard the news. No consoling her. Like a poor ghost she was for a long time. I expect she's always been looking for love since, just like the rest of us but I doubt she'll find it with this Cimla.'

He sighed. 'I'd better see to the fires, can't let them die down or the pots will be spoiled. Better give the boys some food, too.' He paused, a sad smile on his lined face. 'Look, Llinos, don't let life get you down. You'll win through, you got the right spirit.'

When he had gone, Llinos looked round at the crowded shelves, wondering what she could do to pass the hours until bedtime. She did not feel like working, she did not want to mix up fresh glaze or paint a pattern into the fresh clay. She was tired and dispirited. She wanted to curl up and fall asleep and never wake again until

Mr Cimla had gone from her life. But he would never be gone, he was there for ever.

She walked across the yard to one of the sheds and lit a candle. She sat on her seat before the wheel and stared down at the dried bits of clay and began to pick at them with her fingernail.

On an impulse, she pulled a chunk of clay from under a damp sack and began to pound it on the table. She kneaded with her fists, expelling the air from it with such venom that it might well have been Mr Cimla's head she was pounding.

She threw it onto the wheel and her feet worked swiftly, spinning the wheel around. She turned the ball of clay, dampening it from the basin of water at her side, revelling in the feel of the wet clay beneath her fingers. She worked surely, shaping the clay, developing a curved pot on the wheel before her. She dug in her nail and a groove formed at the neck of the pot.

The candlelight flickered above her head and Llinos tried not to think of the future. How could the pottery survive? Gradually, the workers had left, sales had dropped, profit was a thing of the past.

She cut the pot from the base and began another. She had to work, to keep her hands occupied, or she would go mad. It was only when she became aware of the ache in her back and arms that she realized she had been at the wheel for several hours.

The candle was only a stump, the flame

wavering in one last glow before it died. The clay beneath her hands wobbled into a flat nothing on the wheel. Llinos rested her head on her forearms; her fingers were numb, she could not feel her feet.

At last, she climbed down from the stool. She could not delay any longer, she must go back into the house. She looked up at the brightness of the sky; the stars appeared low, almost touching the horizon. It was a crisp, clear night and it was cold.

Slowly, she let herself into the house. It was silent and dark, her mother had not waited up for her. But then she probably had no choice in the matter, not now that she had Mr Cimla to consider.

Llinos washed and undressed as quickly as she could and climbed gratefully into the bed. She pulled the blankets over her shoulders and tucked them under her neck.

From the next bedroom, she heard the creak of springs. She heard her mother's voice low, pleading. She heard what sounded like a slap and then there was nothing but the rhythm of the springs and the sighing of the wind in the tree outside her window.

CHAPTER THREE

Market day was a busy one for the inhabitants of the row. It was the day when most of the housewives did their shopping for fish and vegetables and meat. It was a day when Mr Cimla in his wisdom had suggested Llinos, accompanied by Watt, should drive into town with a cart full of china and sell it in the market place.

'But,' Gwen had protested, 'my daughter can't go to market! Good heavens, the Savage family are above that sort of thing.'

When Mr Cimla insisted, Gwen had meekly submitted to his wishes. Her eyes had been filled with tears and she mouthed the word 'sorry' behind her husband's back. But far from being offended, Llinos was happy to go to market, relieved that she would have a few hours of freedom from the brooding presence of her stepfather.

She stood in the early spring sunshine oblivious of the cold, and though self-conscious at first soon became engaged in a brisk trade. After only a few hours, the supply of jugs and bowls was almost gone. Llinos arranged a few of the flat plates to better advantage at the front of the stall and smiled down at Watt, liking the feeling of being in charge.

'We doin' all right, aren't we, Llinos?' Watt had grown taller in the last few weeks but his face was small and pinched. He looked, Llinos thought, as if he could do with a good meal. Which was not far from the truth.

'We are indeed! I didn't realize what a good saleslady I'd make.'

Even so, the morning's work would bring in scarcely enough money to replenish the diminishing stocks of clay. Sales had been good but bore no comparison to the huge sales of a year ago.

By early afternoon, most of the stock had gone and the weight of the money in Llinos's bag gave her a warm sense of achievement. The Savage family might be living in reduced circumstances but she, at least, was doing something about it.

She felt Watt pull at her sleeve. 'Look out, *he's* coming.'

'So, girl, how are you doing then?' Mr Cimla stood in front of her, his hands thrust into his pockets, his stomach bulging over his breeches.

'Very well, thank you.' She spoke coldly but Bert Cimla was not deterred.

'Come on, then, let the dog see the rabbit, what have we got here?'

Reluctantly, Llinos handed over the bag. Mr Cimla weighed it in his hand and with a smile of satisfaction slipped it inside his coat.

'Right then, when you've finished here, get off home and keep your mother company. I won't be in till late. I might not be in at all come to that.'

He loped away into the crowd and Llinos fought the anger that seethed inside her.

'Come on, Watt, let's get back.' Llinos packed away the few remaining items of pottery. 'I don't see why we should work ourselves to death to give that man drinking money.'

With Watt in the driving seat beside her, Llinos urged the horse in the direction of home. Her legs were aching from standing so long and her feet felt as though they were on fire.

As she rounded a curve in the roadway, she saw a large gleaming carriage coming towards her. In the driving seat was a footman in livery. An elegantly scrolled monogram bearing the initials 'M.E.' graced the carriage doors.

The driver made no attempt to slacken the pace of the horses but drove on as though nothing barred his way. Llinos was forced to turn the cart towards the hedge. The wheels slid slowly to a halt, entrenched in the ditch at the side of the road. Llinos heard the crashing sound of china behind her and bit her lip in anger.

'Blutty hell!' Watt said. 'Our stuff's all smashed, we'll be for it when we gets 'ome.'

The richly appointed carriage drew to a halt a short distance away and Llinos saw a slim young man climb out onto the road.

'It's the folks from the Tawe Pottery,' Watt said in awe. 'That must be Mr Eynon Morton-Edwards home from his posh school.'

Llinos knew the younger Mr Eynon by sight. He seemed nice enough but rather reserved. He would sometimes touch his hat to her in passing but he never spoke. Now, as he approached, she noted that his clothes were immaculate, his boots highly polished and that made her even more angry.

'Your driver is a maniac! I suppose you think that people like us don't matter.' She spoke more aggressively than she had intended. The young man stopped in his tracks, the colour leaving his already pale cheeks.

'I do apologize.' The words, delivered with a fine, precise sense of diction, were so inadequate that Llinos shook her head.

'I suppose that's all you would offer if you'd killed me and Watt here — your apologies.'

'Please. I'm sorry.' He came nearer and Llinos saw he had the sort of boyish charm that had never appealed to her. His fair hair curled over his brow and the brightly coloured scarf at his neck seemed to emphasize the softness of his features. His eyes were dark, almost black.

'Oh, forget it, I'll sort things out here, you go on your way.' Llinos looked down into the ditch. 'Come on, Watt, let's see if we can get back on the road again.'

'Here, let me help.' Eynon Morton-Edwards spoke anxiously. 'It's the least I can do.'

'It's all right,' Llinos said. 'We don't need your help, we can manage on our own.'

The driver of the coach had climbed down

from his seat and was walking reluctantly towards them, a sheepish expression on his face.
'We'll need to pull you out of there, miss, won't
do it by yourself.'

'All right then, if you have to.' Llinos stood
back and rubbed her eyes wearily. She was bone
tired, she could have done without this mishap.
All she wanted to do was to get home, curl up
in her bed and sleep.

When the cart was righted, Eynon Morton-
Edwards looked at the broken pottery. 'Perhaps
I could pay you for the damages?' he asked
tentatively.

Llinos shook her head. 'No, thank you.'

'I'll say good day to you, then.' He returned
to the carriage and with a last look back, climbed
inside. Dust rose from the road as the carriage
moved away.

'Pompous ass!' Llinos said sulkily.

'He was trying to be kind,' Watt said. 'He's
a good artist, mind. They say he paints all the
designs for the Tawe china.'

'Oh, well, it's none of our business.' Llinos
climbed back into the driving seat. 'He's such a
dandy, he looks every inch a spoiled brat, he's
not my type of person at all.' She flicked the
reins. 'Walk on!' she called and the old horse
ambled along the road, head down.

'Poor Brandy,' Watt said, 'poor horse, he's as
tired as we are.'

'Never mind, not far now, we'll soon be
home,' Llinos said, as much to encourage herself

48

as the young boy. The candles gleamed from the windows of Pottery House and her mother was waiting for her with an anxious look in her eyes.

'Where's Bert?' She was peering over Llinos's shoulder, her eyes narrowed. She had changed over the weeks from a woman radiant with love to one who was subdued by a bullying husband.

Llinos shook her head. 'Take the horse and cart round the back, Watt, will you?' she said. 'There will be supper tonight, tell the other boys.' She smiled ruefully. 'I'll get rid of the broken pots.'

Later, Llinos joined her mother in the sitting-room. Gwen was sunk into a chair, her hands clasped in her lap.

'I thought he would come home with you. But he's not coming home, is he?' She covered her face with her hands. 'I love him. Am I a fool, Llinos?'

'It seems that way, Mother.' Llinos flopped into a chair and looked at Gwen with pity. If her mother had changed so had Mr Cimla. At first he had at least affected an air of charm. He had kept himself reasonably clean and groomed. Now he had sunk into a perpetual mood of sullen anger and his appearance left a great deal to be desired. His moustache and beard remained un-trimmed for days and usually carried a residue of anything he had consumed. Worst of all, he stank. How her mother could share the intimacies of the bedroom with him, Llinos could not imagine.

'Are you sorry you married him, Mother?'

'The answer to that is not a simple one.' Gwen's voice was heavy with sorrow. 'He means well and he loves me, I know he does, but he's weak like most men.'

Llinos resisted the urge to say that her father was not weak, he had never raised his voice to his wife or his child and he had made sure they were well provided for. She put her arm around her mother's shoulder. 'Perhaps it will work out, if only he would take some responsibility for our future, it would help.'

'I'll try talking to him,' Gwen said. 'I'll be strong and tell him to mend his ways.'

'Leave it for tonight, Mam,' she said softly. She knew he had the day's takings with him and if she had judged him correctly, he would be spending it all on ale. 'It will all keep till morning.'

Her mother straightened. It was as if she had not heard a word Llinos had said. 'I'll have to say something, he must respect me, a marriage is not a marriage without respect.'

'See what mood he's in tomorrow,' Llinos insisted. 'You never know, he might have taken the money to the bank.'

'What money? Do you mean he has today's takings?' Gwen covered her eyes for a moment with her hand. Llinos could see her mother's veins blue against the thin skin.

50

'He'll be drinking, then. Perhaps you're right, we'd better wait until morning.'

Llinos fell asleep as soon as her head touched the pillow but she was woken a short while later by the sound of singing from downstairs. She opened her eyes; it was still dark. She climbed out of bed, wrapped a robe around her shoulders and stumbled towards the door. She met her mother on the landing.

'What is he up to now?' Gwen sounded frightened. 'He's drunk, he must be.'

Llinos followed her mother downstairs and crossed the hall to the sitting-room. The door stood open and the room was filled with smoke and the smell of ale and with people.

Mr Cimla was sprawled across the lumpy sofa and on his knee was a gaudily painted woman. Her trade was quite obvious even to Llinos and Llinos put her hand to her mouth to stop the angry words from spilling out.

'Ah, here comes my dear wifey and that miserable kid of hers. Come here, Gwenie, dear, meet my friends.'

Gwen lifted her chin. 'What are these people doing in my house, Mr Cimla?'

'I think you mean *my* house, Mrs Cimla,' he sniggered and Llinos clenched her hands together at her sides. How dare he humiliate her mother in this way?

'Nice little girl you got there, Bert.' A man with a bright waistcoat barely covering his barrel chest peered through the smoke at Llinos. He put his head sideways consideringly. 'She's a bit on the skinny side but I suppose she'll fill out given time.'

'Fancy her as a wife, do you, Brendan?' Bert Cimla asked, his eyes gleaming with malicious humour. The man rubbed his chin.

'Don' know 'bout that but I wouldn't mind a bit of fun, like.'

'No, can't have that, Brendan. I wants her off of my hands, see. It's marriage or nothing.'

'Don't be absurd, Bert!' Gwen's voice was unusually sharp. 'Tell these people to leave at once.'

'Shut your cackle, Gwenie, before I give you a back hander. Anyway, Llinos is not a baby, time the girl was wed.'

Gwen was deathly pale. 'You go too far, Mr Cimla.' She stared at her husband. 'Get these people out *now*.'

'Oh shut up, woman!' He pushed the strumpet from his knee and approached Llinos, ignoring his wife. He jerked open her robe and Llinos flinched.

'See, nice little body, she'll fill out good, given time.'

Gwen gave a little cry and ran from the room. Llinos stared after her in consternation. She felt abandoned, as though her mother was leaving her to the not-so-tender mercies of Bert Cimla.

'Moody cow,' he said. 'But, back to business, Brendan, the kid is a thorn in my flesh, cold as ice but you might get a bit of fun warming her up. We'll need a proper dowry, like, she's a fine piece of merchandise is this one, a lady, the like of which you'll never see again.'

'Take your hands off me!' Llinos kicked Bert's shin and he hollered and moved sharply away from her.

Brendan smiled, revealing stained teeth. 'I like a pretty wench who 'as a bit of spirit about her.'

Gwen reappeared as suddenly as she had vanished. She stood in the doorway and Llinos, alerted by the sudden dropping of Mr Cimla's jaw, looked round at her. Llinos recognized the musket Gwen was holding; it was her father's.

'Get out of my house, all of you.' Her voice was hard. 'Get out or I'll shoot you. Move!'

Mr Cimla was staring at her, his mouth open. He gulped and looked down the barrel of the gun.

'Come on, you lot,' he said. 'I'll deal with her when she's calmed down.'

In moments the room was empty. Mr Cimla reappeared in the doorway. 'You made a fool of me!' he said harshly. 'You'll pay for that, I swear you will!'

'Get out and stay out until you can show us some respect.'

Mr Cimla suddenly seemed to become aware of the consequences of his actions. 'Now, look, Gwenie' — his whining voice grated on Llinos — 'I'm sorry if I did wrong but it's so damn quiet up here. I get lonely see.' His voice hardened. 'In any case, you can't turn me out, I'm your husband and I know my rights. You can't put me out into the street like a dog, now can you?'

Llinos watched in dismay as her mother lowered the gun. 'All right, get yourself cleaned up and mend your ways or you are out of here for good, do you understand?'

'But Gwenie, aren't you forgetting something?' His voice held an undercurrent of triumph. 'Your property became mine when I married you. I own everything.'

'That's where you are wrong,' Gwen said wearily. She looked at her daughter. 'Tell him.'

'My father willed the house to me,' Llinos said, a feeling of triumph rising within her. 'Last time my father came home on leave, he made a will. If mother remarries all the property goes to me. It's legal, witnessed before a notary. My mother has nothing except the clothes she stands up in.'

He sank back against the cushions, his face ashen. 'Gwenie, what have you done to me?' He looked as if he might burst into tears. 'Gwen, I thought you loved me, is this any way to treat your husband?'

'Look, Bert, we can still make this work.' Gwen sat beside her husband and took his hands in hers. 'Come on, Bert, we love each other, we will be happy, you'll see.'

Llinos moved to the door and as she left the room she caught sight of Mr Cimla's eyes and the hate in them made her shiver. She would have to be careful; if Mr Cimla found a way to be rid of her he would not hesitate to use it.

'I need Binnie back here, Mother.' Llinos was placing the unglazed pottery in the biscuit kiln, careful to put the lighter pots above the heavier jugs and basins. 'I need the temperature to be nine hundred degrees centigrade. Ben is fetching the coal for the oven. We can only afford to have one kiln working now but it needs stoking to keep the temperature constant. I can't make pots and look after the fires as well.'

She looked down at Watt, who was pulling at a tuft of his hair. 'You are doing your best aren't you, but we must have Binnie back to help you out.'

'Go and get him then, love.' Gwen smiled and Llinos realized it was the first time she had seen her smiling in some weeks. 'Mr Cimla is behaving himself so go while the going is good.'

Ben came into the yard, a bag of coal on his shoulders. 'I'll just see to the oven now, Llinos.'

He tipped the coal onto the yard and began to circle the kiln, replenishing the fires.

'I'm going to get Binnie back,' Llinos said and Ben nodded slowly.

'That's a good idea, we need a boy like him around, knows the business of potting inside out, Binnie does. The apprentices do their best but no-one can work like Binnie Dundee.'

'Do you know where he lives, Ben?'

'Aye, over in Greenhill with folk his own kind.

55

Ask the vicar, he'll know everyone around the area.'

Llinos frowned. Binnie was a Scot, why would he be living in the Irish community of Greenhill?

Ben met her eyes and smiled. 'High church, see, they like to stick together. Good people, mind, took the boy in when he had nowhere else to go.'

'How about driving over to Greenhill now, Llinos,' Gwen broke in. 'I can keep an eye on the apprentices, I've got some spare time before I need to help Nora with the supper.'

Llinos looked at her mother. Gwen was a woman who had been born to be a lady, to be waited on by servants. She was showing a great deal of courage right now and Llinos was proud of her.

'I'll just fetch my cloak from behind the back door. I'll be as quick as I can, Mother.'

Mr Cimla moved swiftly as Llinos entered the kitchen. He slid a bottle inside his coat pocket but the smell of whisky permeated the air. She hesitated, looking at the man in disgust; he was a strong, able-bodied man but he chose to sit around the house doing nothing but drink the meagre profits. She longed to tell him what she thought of him. His eyes slid away as she looked at him. She pulled her cloak around her shoulders and left the house.

It was good to be out in the late afternoon sunshine. Llinos drove along the ribbon of roadway flanking the river, lulled by the rhythmic beat of hooves against the dusty ground.

She'd had the dream again the night before. The man, tall, with long black hair and the bluest of eyes, had been with her, taking her hand, leading her away from the poverty of her life into a wonderful shining world.

Well, it was only a dream but it always left her with a sensation of warmth and well-being. So different from the greyness her life had become.

Still, she should be grateful, things seemed to be improving a little. Mr Cimla had become much more manageable since Gwen had taken a shotgun to him. He still indulged in drinking whenever it suited him but he was at least trying to be discreet whenever Gwen was around.

Splashes of sunlight on the grass of Greenhill gave Llinos the impression that the place lived up to its name. Small houses had been built at random around the church; gardens sported washing lines billowing with freshly laundered sheets.

Ben had suggested speaking to the vicar and though it was a good idea, Llinos felt diffident about approaching a man of the cloth. She dismounted from the horse and walked around the church, wondering if anyone was inside.

Suddenly the vicar was standing in front of her, his long robes brushing the dust of the pathway.

'Excuse me, vicar.' Llinos hesitated and the man smiled encouragingly.

'Speak up, child, I will not bite you.'

'I'm looking for Binnie Dundee.'

'Ah, the young Scot, I think you will find him in Waterford Place. Aren't you Llinos Savage from Pottery Row?'

'That's right.' She looked at him in surprise. He smiled.

'I'm Father Duncan and I am no mystic, child. Your friend Binnie has talked of you so much I feel I know you.'

He dug within the folds of his cassock and brought out a pipe. 'It broke his young heart leaving the job he loved. An unfortunate disagreement with your stepfather, wasn't it?'

Llinos nodded. 'All that has been resolved. I want Binnie to come back with me.'

The cleric stroked his beard. 'Ah well, I don't know about that, he seems fine where he is.'

Llinos bit her lip. She had imagined that Binnie would jump at the idea of returning to the pottery.

'Go yourself and find the lad,' the vicar said. 'Let him speak for himself. You see that newly whitewashed house at the end of the road there, that's where you will find him. God bless you, child.'

Binnie himself answered her knock on the door. 'Llinos! It's good to see you.' He took her hands. 'There's nothing wrong, is there?'

'No, no, there's nothing wrong.'

Behind Binnie stood a young girl with green

58

eyes set wide apart and hair a glorious red. She looked at Llinos with an air of hostility.

'Llinos, this is Maura. I lodge with her and her mother.'

Llinos felt at a disadvantage as she followed Binnie into a spotless kitchen.

'I want you to come back to the pottery,' she blurted out, cursing herself inwardly for her clumsiness. Binnie raised his eyebrows in surprise.

'Things are different now,' she said quickly. 'My mother has put that awful man in his place for good, I hope. Please Binnie, say you'll come back, I can't manage without you.' The words seemed to hang in silence for a long time and then Binnie rubbed his hand through his hair, making it stand on end.

'I don't know what to say.' He looked at Maura and she stared back in angry silence.

'Give me time, will you?' Binnie was apologetic as he followed Llinos to the door. 'I'll come up and see you at the pottery tomorrow, all right?'

'Right, yes, see you tomorrow.' As Llinos mounted her horse and made her way back along the river bank towards the pottery, she was fighting back the tears. She had thought it would be so easy, just ask and Binnie would come with her. Well, it seemed that Binnie had other ideas. He had a new life, a life that included a beautiful Irish girl.

When she reached home, Llinos found her

mother in the kitchen. There was no sign of Mr Cimla.

'You should have offered him a rise,' Gwen said when Llinos told her of Binnie's reaction. 'Where is Binnie working now and how much is he getting?'

'I don't know, I was so taken aback that I didn't ask him.'

'Ah, well, we can always apply to the union workhouse for a boy, I suppose. That's where Binnie came from and he proved reliable, didn't he?' Her voice was muffled. 'I know it's partly my fault Binnie left us; I'm sorry, Llinos, but perhaps it's for the best.'

Llinos was silent for a moment. 'No, Mother, it won't do, I must get Binnie back. A boy from the workhouse would be inexperienced. I need help now.'

Gwen turned to face her then and Llinos took a deep breath. 'Mother! Oh, Mother! Your poor eye is all swollen and bruised. That man has hit you, he's nothing but a cowardly monster!'

Gwen began to cry. She closed the kitchen door and sat down at the table. 'I don't want Nora to hear but it's over, I've sent him packing,' Gwen said. 'I hope and pray he never comes back.'

'Good for you, Mam! Now we can start to live a normal life again,' Llinos said.

'It's not quite as simple as that.' Gwen bit her lip, struggling for composure. 'I have something to tell you.'

Llinos felt a sense of foreboding as she looked across the table at her mother.

'I'm expecting his child.' Gwen's voice faltered. 'A month ago I would have been beside myself with happiness. Now I don't know what I feel.'

Llinos closed her eyes trying to imagine her mother nursing a baby, Mr Cimla's baby. 'Does he know?'

Gwen shook her head. 'No, not yet.'

'What can we do?' Llinos felt panic begin to weave a knot inside her. How could she hope to deal with the work of the pottery and look after her mother?

'There's not a lot we can do, not about the child. But Mr Cimla is a different kettle of fish. If he returns, you must send him away. This is your house and if you don't want him here, he has no right to stay.'

'All right, I'll tell him, don't worry.' Even as she spoke she heard the sound of the front door slamming. She rose to her feet, suddenly tense. Mr Cimla, it seemed, had decided to come home.

CHAPTER FOUR

Joe watched the older man as he bent over the card table in the tent. The scratch of the quill over the paper as Savage wrote seemed extraordinarily loud in the silence of the early morning. Joe felt a moment of sadness. The captain wrote home almost every day. His letters were taken away from the battle lines by the rider but there was never any reply.

Perhaps Mrs Savage did not know if her husband was alive or dead. It was more than a possibility. If a soldier, even a captain, was missing for more than a few days, someone in command would assume the worst. Letters of condolence would be written, families devastated. But that was war.

Joe left the tent silently and crouched over the fire. He was boiling gruel for breakfast, it was nourishing but thin, and to thicken it Joe stirred in the milk he had stolen during the night.

It had been quiet in the cowshed, the farm animals docile, soothed by Joe's gentle tones. He had closed his eyes, leaning against the warm flank, drawing down the milk, enjoying a moment of peace.

Briefly he had seen a candle flicker in an upstairs window of the French farmhouse. As he watched, ready for flight, he heard the sound of an infant crying. Shortly afterwards, the light was extinguished, there was silence and the inhabitants of the farmhouse slept once more.

The captain came out of the tent and stared down into the pot. 'That looks like a hearty breakfast.'

Joe smiled up at him. 'We're having eggs too, a little feast before we march to battle.'

He heard Savage sigh and knew the reason for the heaviness reflected in the captain's eyes.

'Your letters are not getting through.' Joe spoke with finality. 'I saw the rider dead beneath his horse.'

Savage crouched down beside him. 'Do you mean literally, Joe, or in one of your . . . your dreams?'

Joe looked up briefly. 'Does it matter?'

'No, I suppose not. You are probably right. You always are. But I'll keep writing, you never know, one or two of them might reach my wife.'

Joe ladled the gruel into the tin vessels and handed one to the captain.

'Eat while it is hot. It will put heart into you.'

'How old are you, Joe?'

Joe smiled. 'As old as my tongue and a little older than my teeth. Why do you ask?'

'Clever sod.' Savage scraped the bottom of the tin. 'I ask because you seem wise beyond your years.'

Joe finished the gruel and began cleaning his tin and the cooking pot with the sandy earth.

He wiped the utensils with fresh dewy grass and poured a small amount of the precious supply of water into them, swirling it around before tipping it onto the ground. Joe was always sparing with the water, conscious that the next spring might be miles away.

He cracked four eggs into the pot and added some of the milk. 'You'll enjoy this, Captain.'

'My mouth is watering already.'

Joe was silent, intent on the task in hand. He watched the egg solidify. When the meal was ready, the two men ate silently for a time and then Joe looked up. 'What time are we to leave camp, Captain?' he asked.

He watched quietly as Savage considered the question, knowing the answer already.

'Directly after sundown. You and I will set out ahead of the rest.' He waved the letter he had just written.

'This is the last letter I might ever write home, Joe. I have made my prayers to my God. Have you made supplication to your God for our safety? We are going to need all the help we can get.'

'We will be safe, Captain.' Joe finished his meal in silence. 'I'll pack up the kit and then I shall walk out for a while.' He allowed himself a small smile. 'I shall commune with the spirits of my ancestors. That is unless you need me for anything?'

Savage shook his head. 'I have a briefing to attend. The orders will be duly given that we search out the location of the French armies and as usual, you and I will interpret those orders freely.'

Joe inclined his head. What did these generals know? They sat on their fat backsides and directed operations, sending hapless men to their deaths with a few dashes of ink on parchment. Always, the generals kept well to the rear of any attack. Cowards ran the armies of England and heroes fought in them.

Joe allowed that there was one exception. Field Marshal Arthur Wellesley, Duke of Wellington, was a brave man. He led his troops like the good soldier he was, riding his horse Copenhagen into the most fierce of battles.

There had been occasional rumours that the Field Marshal's high handed attitude drew more English bullets than French but Joe discounted them. He had seen the man to be fair and unafraid.

Now, if Joe's instincts were correct, there would be one hell of a battle taking place before too many moons had passed and Wellington would need all his reserves of courage.

Joe rolled the cooking utensils into his blanket and tied it securely. He repeated the operation with the captain's equipment. The small wooden box containing the captain's personal effects was strapped onto the blankets.

Joe was familiar with the contents of the box. There was the captain's pipe, the ink powder and quill and a tiny miniature painting of a lady with a small child in her arms.

The child was grown now, she was a young woman. Llinos. Joe had never seen her, only her likeness, but he knew her, she was in his heart, in his bones, in his soul. She inhabited his dreams. And in sleep, they reached out to each other across the sea and touched each other with their minds.

He would hold her in his arms one day. Their destiny was joined. Llinos, whom he called Firebird, and Wah-he-joe-tass-e-neen would be mates in body as well as soul.

Joe forced his mind back to the task in hand. There was no need to carry food; anything he needed he would obtain on the journey. There were numerous farmyards scattered around the countryside with thin hens scratching in the dusty soil where he would find any number of eggs. Sometimes, if good fortune hunted with him, Joe would catch a juicy piglet and roast it and then there would be enough cold meat to last for several days. He and the captain had not gone hungry yet.

His task completed, Joe moved across the perimeter of the camp and into the outcrop of rocks beyond. There, he sat on the ground and crossed his legs, resting his hands on his knees. He did not close his eyes, there was no need; in any case, he would never risk being taken unawares.

He allowed his mind to roam at will. Not his educated mind, the white man's mind, but the

Indian part of him that knew the secrets of the universe. In the leaves on the bushes and in the clouds in the sky, he saw his images. Now, quite clearly, he saw the captain's wife, the elegant woman in the miniature.

It was the same woman but she was different. She was older, careworn. There was no smile in her eyes. Beside her was the spectre of the great spirit of death. The image changed. The girl, young but with the look of the captain in the darkness of her hair and eyes, was shedding tears. Tragedy was stalking the captain's house and it came in the guise of a drunken man.

Joe stretched his mind towards the night ahead. He saw the army of Napoleon Bonaparte. It was mighty but it was being fragmented, troops deployed in various directions weakening the main force.

The vision faded and Joe saw the sunlight filtering through the sparse trees. Soon the sun, the enemy from above, would be high in the sky. Joe rose to his feet in one swift movement, it was time to begin his search of the ground surrounding the camp.

There were guards posted, always, but Joe felt more secure once he had scanned the horizons to the north, south, east and west for himself. This was a liberty he was allowed. His instincts, as the Britishers called his inner knowledge, had saved the camp from attack on more than one occasion.

As Joe moved silently across the grass, he saw

again the lovely young girl of his vision, her dark hair blowing free like that of a squaw, her eyes full of tears. There was a tugging in Joe's gut that reached to his loins and lit a fire there. He forced the image away. It was high time he had a woman; when the blood was too hot it fevered the brain. That way lay danger. He walked on for a few more hundred yards and then, satisfied, returned to the camp.

During the afternoon, he rested and when night came the moon hung between the clouds, the light dimmed and Joe thanked the spirits for being with him. The captain was riding ahead of him. The horses' hooves were a steady beat against the rain-softened ground. Joe's senses were alert. If danger came, he would be ready to face it. But whatever happened within the next hours, he knew he would live another day to take Captain Savage back home to Swansea.

The shores of Swansea were shrouded in sea mist, the heavy rolling mist that came in from the channel and blotted out the craggy head of Mumbles, covering the valley, mingling with the smoke from the chimneys of the works ranged along the river banks. It had been a miserable market day.

'I'll climb into the back of the cart, we've got a lot of crocks left over today.' Watt clambered up, standing nimbly on the wheel before heaving himself over the side of the cart. 'I can try and hold the stock steady. We can always have another go at selling it next week.'

His voice, muffled by the heavy air, seemed to waft ghostlike around Llinos's head. She closed her eyes for a moment, wishing she did not have to return home. Mr Cimla would be there. He would be wearing his habitual frown. Gwen had forgiven him for the sake of the child and taken him back. But his return had not made her happy.

The conciliatory tone he had adopted for a time after his fall from grace had vanished. His ill temper was, once again, given full rein. He was drinking more than ever; most of the time he sat in her father's chair drowning himself in ale.

Llinos bit her lip, she must be firm, must tell him to leave the pottery. Her mother still clung to the man only because he was the father of her unborn child, yet his presence meant nothing but trouble.

Llinos shivered at the thought of having a confrontation with the man. There would be an unpleasant scene but he would have to go. And what could he do? A great deal, her mind said. He could give her the beating of her life and who would protect her? Well, just in case he proved violent, she would arm herself with her father's musket, that would deter him.

When she arrived home, it was with a sense of anticlimax that she realized she was to be spared a scene. Mr Cimla was out.

Llinos left Watt to deal with the horse and

cart as she made her way through the house. It was quiet and peaceful. A pale sun was breaking through the clouds, spilling in the windows, and her home felt as warm and secure as it had been when she was a child.

Her mother was asleep in the sitting-room. She looked up in confusion as Llinos entered the room.

'Oh dear, I must have dozed off.' Gwen rubbed her eyes. 'I'll build up the fire.' She knelt on the mat and coaxed the dying flames into life. 'I'm so tired lately and Nora is sick, she's gone to bed, which makes matters worse.'

She kissed Llinos and held on to her for a moment as if to gather her strength. 'We'll have a nice bit of bacon and some eggs, shall we, love?'

'I'll do it, Mother.'

'No, I won't hear of it, you are tired enough as it is, your eyes are heavy with shadows.' She smiled and for a moment she appeared like the happy mother Llinos had always known. 'In any case, you are a terrible cook!'

As Llinos washed, the smell of cooking rose through the house and Llinos remembered the sumptuous meals she used to enjoy when the pottery had been a flourishing concern. When her father was at home, the dining table would be groaning with suckling pig, roast partridge or a whole salmon surrounded by chestnuts. Now they were lucky to have bacon and eggs.

Those wonderful days were gone but perhaps

there would be some improvement in her circumstances now that Binnie had come back to work at the pottery. She had been so grateful when she had seen him standing at the doorway, a crooked smile on his face. She had hugged him warmly. Embarrassed, he had disentangled himself and she knew that Binnie had grown up. He was no longer the little boy from the workhouse, Binnie was his own man.

He was as conscientious as ever but, after work, Binnie would hurry back to his Irish beauty at Greenhill. She supposed nothing stayed the same in this world.

When she had eaten, Llinos went outside to call the boys for supper. She had made changes in the last few weeks and one of them was that the apprentices ate in the kitchen.

There was no sign of Watt; the horse was grazing at the dusty grass on the roadside, the cart still loaded. Llinos climbed into the driving seat and guided the horse through the pottery gates.

'Whoa there,' she clucked softly to the horse and the animal ambled to a good-natured halt.

'Binnie!' Llinos called. 'Give us a hand here.' Watt crept out of the drying shed, his eyes huge in his pinched face.

'Binnie's bad, Llinos.'

'What do you mean, bad?'

'He's lying down, all crumpled like.'

Llinos jumped from the cart and hurried into the shed, her heart thumping — had Binnie fallen, had there been an accident? Where were the apprentices and Ben, where was Ben?

Binnie lay on a pile of rags in the corner of the shed, his knees almost touching his thin chest.

'What is it, Binnie, are you sick?' Llinos knelt beside him, unaware that her freshly washed hair was hanging wetly over her shoulder.

He turned towards her and she suppressed a cry of horror. His face was grotesquely swollen, distorted beyond recognition. His eyes were closed, blackened with bruises.

'When did this happen?' Llinos was suddenly clearheaded. She knew, with a burning sensation of anger growing in her belly, that this was the work of her stepfather. 'It was Mr Cimla, wasn't it? Answer me, Binnie, please.'

He managed to nod and Llinos touched his shoulder. 'All right, don't worry, I'll see to everything.' She turned to Watt, who was standing behind her, his thumb in his mouth.

'Go and fetch Celia-end-house, tell her to bring her medicine bag with her. Hurry, there's a good boy.'

Watt seemed to be gone for an eternity. Llinos knelt beside Binnie, her hand smoothing his hair away from his battered face.

'I'll have him for this, Binnie, I swear it. He'll be out of here so fast he won't know what's hit him.' Anger built up in her so that she felt her head would explode.

'*Duw*, what's been 'appenin' by 'ere then?'

Celia bustled towards Binnie holding a candle in one bony hand and her bag in the other. She bent over, the candle raised high.

'Well, son, you've been beat good and proper. Come on, now, Celia won't hurt you, let me see what's what.' She knelt with difficulty and Binnie groaned as Celia ran her hands lightly over his thin body.

'Don't seem to be nothing broken, thank the good Lord.' She rolled her eyes heavenward. 'But there will be bruises inside as well as out. It's rest in a good bed for you, my boy.'

She looked up at Llinos. 'Where's Ben? I'll need his help to get Binnie into the house.'

'I 'spects Ben's gone to the ale house.' Watt's small voice carried across the shed just as the door opened.

'Someone taking my name in vain? Well I went for a drink but I'm back now. What's the trouble?' He smelled of ale and the bitterness of wormwood. The Neath Inn was not renowned for its good brew.

Llinos pointed to where Binnie lay. 'Mr Cimla's handiwork,' she said.

'There's been trouble here!' Ben rubbed his chin. 'I wondered why the apprentice lads were running hell for leather across the fields. That man's mad, he needs horsewhipping, if you ask me.'

Between them, Llinos and Ben managed to take Binnie inside the house. Binnie drifted in and out of consciousness, unaware that he was being tucked into the comfort of Llinos's bed.

'What's happened?' Gwen came upstairs behind them, her eyes wide in the candlelight, her face pale, and her pregnancy beginning to show beneath the light material of her dress.

'Your man's been at 'is tricks again, Mrs Savage,' Celia said. 'Get rid of him before he kills one of you.'

'What's happened? I didn't know he'd been home. What is it, Llinos?' Gwen rubbed her hands nervously over the small swell of her apron.

'He's beaten Binnie within an inch of his life, that's what's happened, Mother.' Llinos could not keep the anger from her voice.

Celia shook her head as though warning Llinos not to upset Gwen. 'Llinos, perhaps you'll stay by here and help me. Go and have something to calm your nerves, Mrs Savage, you look awful.'

No-one noticed that Celia referred to Gwen by her first husband's name. Gwen bit her lip but left the room and Celia turned her attention to Binnie.

It took almost an hour to bathe and clean the wounds on his face and body. The room smelled of witch-hazel and essence of laudanum but at last Binnie was resting easily.

Llinos rubbed her eyes; her back ached and her feet felt on fire. It had been a dreadful day, a wet, cold, empty day and now to return to find Binnie beaten like this was the last straw.

'I hate that man, Celia,' she said. 'I could kill him myself for what he's done to us.'

Celia lifted her brows. 'My advice is to get your father's musket at the ready in case that monster comes back here tonight, though if I'm any judge of 'uman nature, he'll lie low till the dust settles.'

Llinos nodded, not bothering to say that the thought had occurred to her already. She watched as Celia walked stiffly to the door.

'And I'll have my payment now, if you please, Llinos, for I won't set foot in 'ere when he's at home.' She held out her hand and Llinos nodded.

'I'll get your money, just wait a minute, Celia.'

Llinos went down to the kitchen to look in the tin where the housekeeping money was kept and, as she had expected, it was empty. She smiled bitterly, she was well used to Mr Cimla's thieving ways by now and only a few pennies were kept in the house. She looked in her apron pocket at the few pence she had taken that day at market. At least there was enough to pay Celia.

When she returned to the yard, she put the money in Celia's hand. 'He's had his last chance,' she said. 'Mr Cimla will not spend another night under my roof.'

Celia nodded as though she had heard it all before and ambled away. Ben was crouching beside one of the kilns putting coal on the fires; he looked over his shoulder at her approach.

'How is the boy?'

'Resting quietly,' Llinos said. 'I need some money to replace what I gave Celia-end-house. Will you fetch the pot for me, Ben?'

'Aye,' Ben nodded gravely. 'I've hid it in the clay bin this time, I don't think he'd want to mess his pretty hands by looking in there.'

'Why did my mother get taken in by the man, Ben?' Llinos bit her lip and the old man put his arm around her, hugging her to him.

'There's no accounting for a woman's feelings, is there? Anyone with half an eye can see Mr Cimla's no good to God nor man. If I was a bit younger I'd give him a hiding myself.' He sighed. 'I could speak to some of the men down at the alehouse if you like. Some of them would give him a good going over for the price of a mug of grog.'

'No, leave it to me.' Mr Cimla was only violent when there was no-one to resist him. He played on weakness, he thrived on it. Well, he would soon find that Llinos was not as weak as he imagined.

When Llinos returned to the house it was to find her mother sitting in the kitchen in tears. 'Oh, God,' Gwen said. 'What's going to happen to us? I've tried to love Mr Cimla, tried to be a good wife, but nothing I do pleases him.'

'It's not your fault, Mother, no use blaming yourself.' Llinos drank a little of the hot milk her mother had poured from the jug. 'Anyway, I don't think he'll come home tonight. Let's go to bed, get some rest if we can. I'll sleep in the small bedroom for tonight, Mother.'

'I'll fetch you a blanket,' Gwen said. 'It's cold in there, we haven't had fires upstairs for weeks now.'

'I'll be all right,' Llinos said. 'I'm so tired I think I'd sleep on the bare floor if I had to.'

Later, curled up in the narrow bed in the spare room, she lay awake in spite of her weariness. She listened to her mother's light footsteps and the door of her bedroom closing and then a brooding silence fell over the house.

Llinos thought of Watt and the apprentices, hoping they had found enough courage to return and were curled up in the outhouse on their makeshift bed, and the image comforted her. If Bert Cimla did come home and start trouble then one of the boys could run for help.

She had looked in on Binnie before going to her own room. He was asleep and breathing heavily. She pictured Bert Cimla striking out at Binnie in a drunken fury and shuddered.

'Dear Lord, keep Mr Cimla away from us tonight,' she said fervently.

She slept and dreamt again of the man with blue eyes and long dark hair. He was calling her across mountains and seas, his hands held out towards her. She knew that she loved him, that she wanted to be with him, but she just could not reach him.

Llinos woke to the sound of a noise downstairs. She sat up, aware that someone was knocking on the front door. She was instantly alert but she saw the daylight shining in through the window and relaxed, realizing that it was morning.

By the time she had dressed and hurried downstairs, Celia-end-house was in the hallway and standing beside her was Binnie's Irish girlfriend.

'Top o' the morning to you.' Though the greeting was civil enough, the look on the Irish girl's face was one of anger. Even in the early light she was beautiful, her red hair aflame, her skin white as fresh milk.

'Come in, I expect you are wondering where Binnie is,' Llinos said. 'I'm afraid something has happened.'

'What's happened? Is Binnie all right?'

'He's going to be all right.'

'What do you mean "going to be all right"?' Maura's eyes were narrowed in suspicion. 'I want to see him.'

'That man's not here, is he?' Celia asked and Llinos shook her head.

'In that case, I'd better see my patient. Let the girl come with me.' The old woman led the way upstairs and into the bedroom and gestured to Llinos to open the curtains.

'Mornin', Binnie lad. Come on, sleepyhead, some of us folks get up early in the morning.' She poured him a large measure of greenish liquid and Binnie, coughing, drank it.

Maura moved impatiently towards the bed. 'Oh, my Lord, what's happened to you?' She sank onto the floor beside the bed and held Binnie's hand. Llinos hung back, not wishing to intrude.

'It's all right,' Celia said, 'the boy is not going to die, he'll live to fight another day.'

When she had finished dressing Binnie's wounds, Celia moved to the door, jerking her head for Llinos to follow. The door closed, shutting Maura in with Binnie, and Llinos moved slowly towards the stairs.

Celia put her hand on her shoulder. 'Don't worry, lovie, you'll have a little fellow-me-lad of your own one of these fine days.'

Llinos shook back her hair. 'After seeing my mother's miserable married life, I don't think I want a husband,' she said bitterly.

'Ah, all that will change when you meet the right man. I've seen it all before, you can't tell old Celia nothing.'

Llinos was silent. She thought of the man in her dreams; he was beautiful and kind. He towered over her, the wisdom of the ages in his blue eyes. He gave her the most wonderful sensation of happiness. But then, he was only a dream, that was all he would ever be and suddenly, she felt like weeping.

Joe was breathless when he returned to the high point of the hill where the captain was waiting for him.

'Part of the French army are camped astride the main Brussels highway.' He sank down onto the ground, resting his back against the warmth of a rock. 'Infantry men, a light cavalry corps and the Guard, in all about sixty-nine thousand men and above two hundred guns.'

'Well done, Joe.' Savage winced, he had twisted his ankle in a rabbit hole and his foot, inside his boot, was swollen to twice its normal size.

'It looks as if the big battle will take place soon. So far, the three days of hostilities have not achieved much for either side.'

'We must get back to camp.' Savage attempted to rise and stood for a moment on one foot. His courage was not in question but it was clear that his injury would impede him.

'You can't walk in that state, Captain.'

'You're right.' Savage sank onto the ground, his face white. Joe looked around for a tree in full leaf with stout branches and sliced through them with his knife. He placed the branches around the captain, effectively camouflaging him from any but the sharpest eyes.

'Tell Wellington that Mont-St-Jean is the place to be, that's where he should deploy his men.'

Joe nodded; he had come to the same conclusion himself. 'I will not be long.'

He moved silently away without a backward glance. He could have told the captain that the battle would be won within days, that Wellington would prove his mettle and that the Prussians would change sides at the last moment. But he had held back, knowing that Savage could not quite come to terms with what he saw as Joe's 'prophesies'. But they were more than that, Joe had the certain knowledge of the events that would shortly occur at the place they called Waterloo.

He felt the breeze in his face, smelled the hot smells of a French summer and knew it was good to be alive. He smiled to himself; soon he would leave the soil of France behind him for good, for a new life was about to begin.

CHAPTER FIVE

Llinos knocked on the bedroom door and pushed it open to find Binnie already dressed in his freshly laundered shirt and breeches. Binnie's condition had improved rapidly. He was young and healthy and his injuries were quick to heal, though Llinos could still see some slight bruising around one of his eyes.

Since the night of the beating, Bert Cimla had not returned to the pottery but Llinos kept the musket handy just in case.

'How are you feeling now?' Llinos pushed back the hair from Binnie's face and examined the fading bruises.

'Well enough to go back to Maura's house,' Binnie said. 'Take a word of advice, Llinos, don't let that man come anywhere near you, he's insane.'

'I know, Binnie, I hate him for what he's done to you, and to me and my mother come to that.' Binnie touched her shoulder and sighed. 'I'd better go. You do understand that my place is with Maura now, don't you?'

Llinos forced a smile. 'Of course. I'll drive you over to Greenhill, if you like.'

'Thanks.' Binnie had been moody and non-communicative since the beating but now she felt they might just get back to the old footing.

As she drove away from Pottery Row with Binnie seated beside her, Llinos glanced at his set face and wondered what he was thinking. She could not help wondering if he was going out of her life for ever.

'You will come back to work when you are fully recovered, won't you?'

He was silent for a long moment. 'Aye, I'll come back so long as that man keeps away from the place. I swear I'll be ready for him if he tries anything again.' Binnie's voice was low, strained, his anger almost tangible.

'If once I started hitting him,' Binnie said, 'I wouldn't know when to stop.'

When she reached Greenhill, Llinos looked around at the small houses and the narrow courts. She watched as a small boy urinated in the street, and wrinkled her nose.

'It must be difficult to keep up standards in a place like this.'

Binnie looked at her. 'Sometimes you sound such a snob, Llinos, do you know that?'

'I'm sorry,' Llinos was angry, 'but if these people have to use the middle of the roadway as a privy it's no wonder that plagues and pestilences begin here.'

'Go home, Llinos.' Binnie lifted his small bag of possessions from the cart and climbed down into the road. 'If you are too high and mighty to see the clean linen blowing on the washing lines and the gleam of the glass in the windows and the scrubbed steps then it's time you found out what real life is all about.'

'You think I don't know?' Llinos was hurt by his tone. 'I work like a slave at the pottery, I do all the jobs that the apprentices do and more. I go hungry sometimes and when I fall into bed I ache so much I can't sleep.'

Binnie rested his hand on her arm, looking up at her from the roadway, his eyes dark in his pale face. 'I'm sorry, Llinos, I suppose I'm still out of sorts. I'll see you soon, right?' He walked rapidly away and without turning round, vanished into one of the houses.

After their exchange of angry words, Llinos thought Binnie might give in his notice but to her relief he resumed work the following Monday. His presence made the load lighter for Llinos but somehow the old spirit of camaraderie that had existed between them was gone. Binnie was respectful but that was all.

Llinos knew, with a sense of loss, that Binnie's life had changed, he had grown away from her. The easy friendship they had shared had vanished when Binnie had fallen in love with Maura. It was obvious that the Irish girl was far more important to him than Llinos or the Savage Pottery could ever be.

They worked hard that week. Llinos, Watt, Binnie and the apprentices, as well as some of the women from the row, turned out a sizeable stock of pottery. Old Ben needed to work extra time to keep the fires alight in the kilns.

Much of the stock was needed to fulfil existing orders. At last, trade seemed to be picking up.

An enterprise the size of the Savage Pottery should be turning out a great deal more pottery than it was but at least now they were producing enough wares to make it a viable proposition.

On Saturday night, the workers had time off to relax and spend their wages in town. When everyone had left it was silent in the pottery yard, though the kilns still throbbed with heat.

Indoors, Gwen was finishing off a small vest she was knitting for the coming baby and Llinos kissed her mother's cheek.

'I'm going to bed, Mother, don't stay up too long, you'll strain your eyes working in this poor light.'

As soon as she climbed into bed, Llinos fell into a heavy sleep. It had been dreamless until she felt the touch of a hand on her arm.

In her dream she looked up into the face with the bronzed, clean-cut features; she saw the softness of long silky hair. Blue eyes above high cheek-bones looked into hers. He was shaking his head. She sat up abruptly and looked into the darkness, knowing she was being warned of danger.

She sat up in bed, brushing back her tangled hair. She had been too tired to plait it before going to bed. She relaxed a little, she had been dreaming, that was all. It was a strange dream; it had left her feeling warm and yet frightened at the same time.

Even awake, she could still see him, feel him close. She breathed in the fresh grass scent of him. His presence lingered with her.

She climbed from the bed and opened her door and heard the sound of raised voices. Her mother was talking so loudly that she sounded hysterical. Then there was a lower voice, a masculine voice. Llinos felt a sudden sense of dread. Bert Cimla was here in Pottery House.

Llinos stood for a moment, shivering in the darkness. She pulled on a robe, opened the cupboard door and her hand encountered the cold handle of the musket. As she moved quietly down the stairs, the sound of shouting intensified.

The hall was in darkness. Breathing unevenly, Llinos felt her way towards the kitchen, her bare feet curling against the cold stone of the passageway.

She heard a scream and a slap and a sudden anger replaced her fear. Her searching fingers came in contact with the barrel of the musket and she took strength from the coldness of the steel.

As she approached the kitchen, she saw shadows flickering against the walls, grotesque, enlarged figures from a nightmare.

There was the sound of china smashing and another slap and then Llinos heard her mother's voice, low, pleading.

'Please, Bert, don't hit me again, I'm carrying your child, how can you treat me like this, have you no feelings at all?'

'You cheating bitch! You took away my rights as a husband, threw me out onto the street to starve and you talk about feelings!'

There was a thud. Llinos heard her mother whimper and then there was silence. She pushed open the door and stepped inside. Her mother was lying spread-eagled on the floor, her head against the marble hearth.

Bert Cimla looked towards Llinos as she entered the room, his mouth drew back into a snarl. He took a step towards her and then she raised the musket.

Suddenly he was on his knees, looking down at Gwen and trying to lift her. 'Oh, God! I didn't mean it. Gwen, come on, don't be daft. Open your eyes, for God's sake.'

Llinos felt as though events were unfolding before her like a series of pictures. Mr Cimla's shirt hung open, his face was blotched with red, he was staring at the crumpled figure on the floor as though he did not know what had happened.

'Get out of here.' Llinos prodded his back with the musket. 'Get out now before I kill you.'

'You wouldn't dare.'

'Don't you believe it!'

He lifted his hands in the air. 'All right, I'm going. I've finished with you, with all of you. It's about time I moved on and found a proper woman to look after me, not a namby-pamby weakling like her.'

He moved to the door and looked back at Llinos and he was grinning.

'She's not my wife.' He pointed to Gwen's still figure. 'I've already got a wife. That kid she's carrying is going to be a bastard, isn't that funny?'

She heard his echoing laugh as he slammed the door and marched through the hall, and hated him. Llinos knelt quickly beside her mother. 'Are you all right, Mam, can you get up?'

Her mother's eyes flickered; they opened but they gazed upwards, dark pools with no light of recognition in them.

'I'm going to fetch Celia-end-house, Mother,' Llinos said in panic. 'I won't be long.'

Celia came to the door at once. 'Oh Gawd, he's been back, 'as he? Thought I heard a rumpus.' She looked at the musket still grasped in Llinos's hand. 'Got rid of him now, have you? Good for you, girl, good for you.'

Llinos needed to rouse Ben to help carry Gwen back to her room. Once she was settled in her bed, Celia began to examine Gwen carefully.

She looked at Llinos and shook her head. 'It's not good, she's started to bleed. Looks like she'll lose the little one.'

Llinos bit her lip. She could not help thinking that it was just as well if what Bert Cimla said was true about the child being a bastard.

'Go on, you, get some rest, you look all in. I'll sit with your mam, nothing I can do. Nothing anyone can do, it's all in the hands of the Gods now.'

Llinos woke from an uneasy sleep at dawn. She had made up a bed on the sofa in the sitting-room, the musket at her side, but there had been no sign of Mr Cimla. Llinos doubted they would ever see him again. He had realized at last that there were no more pickings to be had from such a poor family.

The kitchen was empty, the fire unlit, and Llinos felt a sense of gloom. Celia was still keeping an eye on Gwen; that in itself was a bad sign.

Llinos ran up the stairs to her bedroom and dressed hurriedly, then she went to see how her mother was feeling. She crossed her fingers as she had done as a child, willing everything to be all right.

Once in her mother's bedroom, Llinos could see that all was not well. Her mother's eyes were closed, her breathing was laboured. Celia was nodding in the chair beside the bed.

'Mother.' Llinos approached the bed and spoke softly. 'It's me, are you all right?' Her mother did not respond.

Llinos touched the thin shoulder. 'Please, wake up.'

She touched her mother's brow; it was cold and yet beaded with sweat. Llinos was frightened. She could hear Ben and the boys outside in the yard and the normality of sounds seemed strangely unreal.

Celia opened her eyes and, like a cat, she was immediately awake. She lifted Gwen's hand; it was limp, the fingers icy. She looked up at Llinos. 'Better get the doctor, love.'

Llinos bit her lip. Things had to be serious before the doctor was called in. She wrapped herself in her cloak and left the house. It was going to be a fine day, the colours of morning were brighter now, the hedge roses splashes of brightness against the greenery. In spite of the sunny skies, she felt a sense of impending doom. Her mother was so sick she might die.

It was as if he was with her then, Joe. That was his name. She had no idea how she knew it but she clasped the name to her heart. His arm seemed to be around her, his dark hair brushing her face. He was tall, so tall. He had become reality to her. She felt the lightness of his kiss against her hair and then he was gone.

Was she going mad? Had the misfortunes of her family turned her mind? She began to run towards the doctor's house as if the demons of hell were behind her.

'What's wrong, Llinos?'

She gasped as Binnie caught her arm. She looked at him, trying to adjust her thoughts.

'Llinos, I was just on my way to work when I saw you rushing down the road like a mad thing. What's happened?'

Her mind was full of confused images, she could not think straight.

'Llinos!' The sharpness of Binnie's voice

brought her to her senses. 'What's happened?'

'My mother is sick, she needs the doctor.'

'I'll go and fetch him,' Binnie said. 'You go back home.'

Nodding dumbly, Llinos obeyed. Once back in the kitchen she occupied herself building the fire, placing coals so that the flames shot up the chimney. She could hear Celia's light tread above her and knew she should go upstairs but she was afraid. A long time seemed to pass before Binnie returned with the doctor. Llinos waited as the heavy footsteps climbed the stairs. She wanted to pray but the words would not come. She put the kettle on the fire and put out cups and saucers, unaware of what she was doing. The clock ticked loudly, filling the room, and Llinos felt she could not stand the uncertainty any more.

When Celia eventually came for her, it was with reluctance that Llinos followed the old woman into the bedroom. A short, rotund man was standing near the bed, his bag open, a bottle of potion in his hand. As she watched, he dropped the bottle back into the bag and turned to face her.

'I'm sorry,' he said. 'There was nothing I could do.' Llinos nodded.

'Thank you for coming, sir,' Celia said. 'I thought it only proper-like, in the circumstances.' Celia saw the doctor out and Llinos stood looking down at the face of her mother. It was unfamiliar now, set as though carved from ivory. The stench of blood permeated the room and suddenly Llinos felt sick.

She left the room, closing the door silently behind her. She needed to get out, to get away from the spectre of death. She needed to walk.

The sea was edged with silver, sparkling with light where sea met sand. Her feet sank into the softness of the dunes as Llinos crouched onto her haunches. If she pressed low enough, perhaps she would disappear altogether. She closed her eyes, they felt frozen with dread and behind closed lids she saw her mother's face, pale, smeared with blood.

'Mam!' Her voice was like the keening of a wounded animal. It carried on the wind, mingling with the cry of the seagulls. Her mother was dead and Llinos knew that the pain and anger she felt against Bert Cimla would be with her for ever.

She curled up in one of the dunes, closing her eyes, feeling the sun shining down on her. She wanted to sleep, to forget the awful thing that had happened.

He came to her and she was not sure if she was asleep or awake. Joe sat with her, brushing back her hair; she felt his presence, felt his largeness blot out the sun. It was late when Llinos left the beach. The silver had gone from the sea and the sand was no longer warm and comforting but full of shadows. She made her way back to Pottery Row, glancing towards the window of the house. She hesitated and then after a moment made her way into the pottery buildings.

The kiln was no longer alight but the residue of warmth from the brickwork was comforting as she leaned against it. The smell of the clay was all around her, the clay that had been her livelihood for as long as Llinos could remember.

She put her head in her hands and felt tears spill onto her fingers. Bert Cimla had come into her life and had changed everything. He had wooed Gwen Savage, tricked her into a false marriage and finally, he had destroyed her.

Llinos wiped her eyes on her skirt, knowing she could not stay in the yard for ever. There was no sign of Ben or the rest of the workers. Llinos guessed they were following the custom of respecting the dead by suspending work until the next day.

Slowly, she made her way into the house. She paused in the silence and saw the moonlight shining across the hallway. She heard the soft ticking of the clock and listened until the sound seemed magnified a hundred times. At last, she made her way upstairs.

The door of the bedroom creaked open and Llinos fought the fear that took away her breath. The floorboards protested beneath her feet, the sound strangely loud in the silence.

Her mother's eyes were closed. A strip of linen was tied around her chin; the bow fastened at the top of her head looked strangely festive. There was no colour in her face and when Llinos

93

rested her hand against her mother's cheek, it was the cold of clay.

Llinos backed away from the bed and out of the room, ashamed of the fear of death. But it was not her mother lying there, it was a stranger. No, not a stranger, an empty shell of something that had been living and breathing only a short time ago.

She went into the sitting-room; it was warm, the fire still blazing in the grate. Celia or Ben must have stacked it high with coals. The fire would be company; she would rest next to it, listen to its voice as the flames licked up towards the chimney.

She felt suddenly weary and stretched out on the carpet, tucking her feet into her skirt. She was an orphan, alone in an unfriendly world.

She closed her eyes and felt him near. Joe, her lover, the man she had never met, never touched. But he was real, he was there with her. She would never be alone again.

CHAPTER SIX

'We've come to offer our help, Llinos,' Celia said. She stood at the back door and Llinos saw that she was accompanied by a deputation of women from the row.

'Come in.' She stepped aside for them to enter the kitchen and watched as the women seated themselves around the table.

'I know that old Nora has gone home to her sisters and that you are alone,' Celia said. 'We can't have that, oh no, indeed not.'

'It's kind of you to worry about me.' Llinos felt at a loss, not knowing how to handle the situation. She stood near the fire and waited for Celia to speak again.

'I have come with good news,' Celia said, 'the best news I could bring you. Mr Cimla has packed his bags and left town and good riddance to bad rubbish. Seems he's found another foolish woman to prey on, a rich widow from the Uplands by all accounts.'

'That is good news, Celia,' Llinos said. 'Shall we have a drink of port to celebrate?' Llinos asked politely, but she was wishing the women would go away.

Celia nodded vigorously. 'There's a good idea now.'

Llinos left the room and the women stared after her. 'Well, she won't starve, not the daughter of Lloyd Savage.' Mrs Ceri Cooper was an intelligent woman, dark with almost gypsy good looks. 'She still got money, hasn't she?'

'How do you make that out?' Celia leaned forward, her arms resting on her swollen knees.

'Well, she got the pottery and all those buildings, they must be worth a bit.' Mrs Cooper brushed back a strand of hair.

'Why don't she sell up and move somewhere modestlike? Anyway, you mark my words, there's money about that family somewhere, I can smell it and I've a nose for that sort of thing.'

'The captain had money, right enough,' Celia said thoughtfully. 'I heard tell he had holdings, shares and capital invested somewhere. I don't quite know what all those things are but they have something to do with money. Still, can't see any bank handing out cash to a young girl.'

'Well, I still think she could sell up and move,' Ceri Cooper said, folding her arms across her ample bosom.

Llinos stood in the sitting-room, watching the sun playing across the decanter of port. From across the valley came the sound of church bells. It was Sunday. She sighed and returned to the kitchen with the silver tray full of glasses filled with ruby liquid.

'Please, help yourselves.' She sat near the fire warming her hands, which felt cold in spite of the warm sunshine slanting through the windows. She did not know why the women had come. They said they wanted to help but when she'd entered the room, they seemed to be arguing about the possibility of her selling the pottery. She would never do that, this was her home and here she would stay.

Still, she was grateful to Celia, she could not deny that. It had been Celia who had ferreted out the cache of burial money hidden beneath the floorboards in the bedroom. Celia who had employed a carpenter to make the pine coffin devoid of ornamentation and Celia who had handed the left-over money to Llinos.

It seemed to Llinos as though her life had been taken over by Celia. The old woman had attended to the funeral arrangements with efficiency born of long practice. Gwen Savage, as she would always be known, had been buried in Dan-y-Graig cemetery, the grave marked only by a wooden cross.

The swiftness of it all left Llinos no time to grieve. She felt numb, as though her senses had become blunted. She had not combed her hair in days and the food Celia forced on her from time to time tasted like sawdust in her mouth.

'What I want to know is what we're going to do about buying our pots now.' Mrs Millie Fishguard was frowning. 'Broke my big basin only last night, I did, got nothing to mix up my bread in, poor show, mind.'

'Don't be so selfish, Millie.' Celia's voice was reproving. 'There's more important things to sort

97

out now besides your pots.'

Llinos felt a surge of sudden impatience. How dare these women come into her house and talk as if she was incapable of thinking for herself?

'I will be all right, I assure you.' Llinos heard the strength in her voice and it gave her confidence. 'I can work the clay, I've been doing it since I was seven years old.'

Celia nodded. 'That's true enough, lovie,' she said, 'but what about the cooking and cleaning? You can't do everything.' In spite of her questions, she looked at Llinos with a new respect. 'And what will you do if Mr Cimla should put in an appearance again?'

'I will deal with Mr Cimla with a loaded musket if need be,' Llinos said. 'As for everything else, I'll manage.'

'Well, what if I oversee things in by here, then. Keep an eye on you, watch you don't come to no harm.' Celia smiled. 'A lady like you needs a chaperone, mind, and with old Nora gone to stay with her sister, you're all alone with apprentices and workmen about the place and that's not proper.'

'That's right enough, Miss Savage,' Mrs Cooper said respectfully. 'I'll be glad if you can keep the pottery going, so will my Jim. I know he's only a casual up here but he's a good worker and strong.'

'Jim has been a great help in the past few days. If it's at all possible, I intend to keep him on.'

She rubbed her eyes with her knuckles in an

unconsciously childish gesture. 'All right,' she said. 'I'll be glad of your help, Celia, at least for the time being.'

'That's settled then,' Celia said and sipped her port with a satisfied look in her eye. It seemed the matter was decided and Llinos took a deep breath; it was time she took control of her life, she had wallowed in self-pity for long enough. If she did not assert herself now, her life would not be her own.

'If you will excuse me, ladies,' she said firmly, 'I have work to do. Finish your port before you leave.'

Llinos left the room and made her way across the yard. It was quiet, no-one worked on Sunday, except old Ben who would, sometimes, stay behind to fire the kilns.

She looked around at the sprawled, empty buildings. This was her heritage and she would fight for survival in the business that her father had founded. Binnie had been one of the first apprentices to be taken on at the Savage Pottery and now he was in charge of it he seemed to have become strong and happy. Yet even though Binnie worked long hours at the pottery, he insisted on travelling home to Greenhill after work every night. And when he left, she felt lonely and lost.

She realized that the yard was deserted. There was no sign of Ben, he was probably down at the alehouse near the Strand. The old man was not a heavy drinker but he seemed to enjoy the

99

manly talk that he found only in the public bar of the Potters Wheel.

Llinos pushed open the door of the outhouse where the apprentices slept. It was empty except for Watt, who was lying asleep in the window seat. Llinos smiled and covered his slight form with a blanket. Tomorrow she would move the boy into the house, he would be company for her. She felt a surge of warmth, at least perhaps she could make life better for Watt and the other workers even if her own life seemed to be falling apart.

She retraced her steps towards the house. The rooms were silent, everyone had left, even Celia-end-house had gone. Llinos picked up some discarded knitting, the small garment on which her mother had been working, and hot tears burnt her eyes. The silence spread round her and grew and she felt frightened and alone.

That night as she lay in bed, staring out through the small window at the stars, she wondered if she would ever come to terms with her loneliness. Would she ever be happy again? And then it was as though a rush of air was sweeping over her. A voice seemed to speak inside her head telling her she would not be alone for ever. One day, she would find happiness and peace.

She held up her hand to the darkness. 'Joe?' she said, but all she heard was the sighing of the wind in the trees.

When she woke, she felt rested. She could hear Celia moving about in the kitchen, heard the rattle of china and she was glad of the sounds, they brought a touch of normality to her life. Today, she would wash her hair, cut away the untidy ends. She would smarten herself up, find some good clothes to wear. She was Llinos Savage and it was about time she remembered it.

She turned and faced the wall where early sunlight formed moving patterns and considered her future. She was a good potter. She had mastered the wheel when her legs had been too short to reach the disk that turned it. But run ning a pottery involved more than a potter's skill. How long would the stock of clay last, lying now under damp sacks in the pottery? When it all was used, where would she order more?

She knew her mother kept accounts, she had seen her sitting in the candlelight studying the books in which she sometimes wrote industriously for hours on end. Perhaps in the pages of neat handwriting Llinos would find the information she needed to carry on.

She would require more hands, too. She had taken on Jim Cooper to help with the heavy work and Binnie was a good foreman. The apprentices were becoming more experienced and worked hard stacking pots in the saggers and carrying them to the kiln. Ben kept the kiln fuelled. They were good men, good workers all of them, but what she really needed was more potters, more painters and more labourers.

She sat up and hunched up her knees under

the bedclothes thinking how much the pottery had gone downhill in the last few years. It was a wonder that it had kept going at all. If she was to make a success of things, she needed to get back into full production again. But where was she going to get the money to pay for it all?

First thing after breakfast, she would begin by studying the books. She would learn the business as best she could, she would borrow money if she had to, she would do anything to save the pottery.

What wares made the most money, what goods should she concentrate on? Millie Fishguard promised to pay her handsomely for the mixing bowl and had ordered a jug as well, but large objects took time to bake. Several glazes were needed to cover the surface, making it an expensive process. Perhaps she should concentrate on smaller wares, sugar boxes, milk jugs, that sort of thing.

Tomorrow was market day and Llinos felt she should make the effort to take some of the stock to town. If Binnie and Watt came along, she could leave them to sell the crocks while she saw Mr Francis at the bank and asked him for his help and advice. He had been a good friend of her father's; surely he would not let her down now?

Celia had the fire blazing in the kitchen, the kettle was singing over the flames and the smell of toasted bread permeated the room. She came in from the back yard, a pile of sticks in her arms.

'Oh, aye, awake at last, sleepyhead? Well, get some food inside your belly, too thin by far, you are, my girl.'

Celia took liberties, she was too familiar, but then times had changed. Llinos was no longer the daughter of a rich potter but an orphan who needed to work or starve. She sat at the table opposite Celia, who was rubbing her swollen knees. 'Just been out to give the boys and old Benjamin some gruel and a cup of hot milk. Good man, Ben, got the kiln so hot you'd think it would take the skin off you.'

Llinos rubbed at her eyes. 'Market day, today,' she said, the words feeling thick in her mouth. She was frightened, not knowing if she could support herself let alone support dozens of workers.

'Aye, it's market day right enough. Shall I come down to town with you?' Celia was settled back in her chair, her skirts lifted now, the flames of the fire playing on her knees.

Llinos shook her head. 'I'll be taking Binnie and Watt. Thanks all the same.' Celia would not make it to the end of Pottery Row let alone to town. Fine medicine woman she was, she could not even heal herself, she was plagued by the bone ache.

Llinos ate her breakfast with little appetite. 'I was thinking,' she said, 'perhaps I could get some girls in to help me with the light work, the decorating and glazing.'

Celia's mouth twisted downwards. 'And where would you find the money to pay them?'

'I was thinking of someone from the workhouse.'

Slowly, Celia nodded. 'Aye, that might be an idea, jest for bed and board you'd get yourself some help all right.'

'How do I go about it?'

'Well how do you think? Go on up there. Tell the guardian that you got work for some of the brats. Glad to get rid of 'em, they'll be, less mouths to feed, see?' Celia snorted. 'Course, they'll keep the names on the books, make a bit on the side, like, but that's not your worry.'

Llinos was not sure she had the courage to approach anyone in the workhouse. It was a gaunt, sprawling building surrounded by a high wall.

'I thought you was going to market.' Celia hacked at the loaf and stuck the blackened prongs of the toasting fork into the bread.

Llinos gave up any attempt to eat and pushed her chair away from the table. 'I'd better see if the boys have got the horse and cart ready.'

It was a soft day, the wind had dropped and late tea roses splashed the hedgerow with brave flags of colour.

'Shall I come with you, Miss Savage?' Jim Cooper asked. 'Those pots take some lifting, mind.'

Llinos shook her head. 'I'll take Watt and I

thought Binnie could come, too.'

'He ain't come in, miss, don' know why. But I'm willing and strong, I'll be a right good help,' Jim said and Llinos bit back a sharp retort. The men must stop treating her as a lady, they must begin to think of her as a boss.

'No,' she said firmly, 'I want you to stay here, Jim, look after the place and if Bert Cimla shows his face, take a pickaxe to him.'

Llinos climbed into the driving seat and helped Watt up beside her. The horse shifted uneasily between the shafts. The weight of the pots was unstable and the load moved a little towards the back. She wondered where Binnie was, it was not like him to miss a shift. Well, she had other things to think of at the moment.

'Take your time, miss,' Jim said doubtfully. 'I don't like the thought of you driving to town with only Watt for company. Are you sure you can manage?'

'You are needed here.' Llinos clucked her tongue and the horse moved forward abruptly, jolting the cart so that the pots rocked from side to side.

Llinos looked at Watt. 'Hold on tight now, it looks as if this is going to be a bumpy journey.' After a few miles she realized how prophetic her words had been; the jolting of the cart against the uneven surface of the road jarred her bones and her head began to ache. Already one of the taller jugs had keeled over and the handle had broken off.

The road led along the river bank towards the town and the market place. The animal was restless, knowing there was a bag of oats at the end of the journey. Llinos pulled on the reins. 'Whoa there.' She leaned backwards in an effort to slow the cart, the shafts creaked with the strain and Watt, sitting beside Llinos, was clinging on for dear life. The load shifted again and, startled, the horse reared, hooves pawing the air.

She saw a rider from the corner of her eye. He came alongside and caught the reins of her horse, talking soothingly to the animal.

Llinos was breathing hard, her hair swung loose, her eyes were misted with tears of frustration. She was a failure, she was sure that half the stock was broken, the hard labour of the past week wasted.

She climbed shakily from the cart, pushing her hair away from her hot face. She could hardly breathe, her heart was thumping as though it was going to jump out of her chest.

'Thank you,' she managed to gasp. She looked up and saw the pale face of Eynon Morton-Edwards looking down at her in concern.

'You all right?'

She nodded. 'Yes, I'm perfectly all right.' She somehow felt resentful of him, whenever he was around there was trouble. She knew it was unfair of her to blame him but nonetheless she turned away from him and began to examine her stock.

'Not too much damage done,' he said and there seemed to be a wistfulness about his voice that was touching. She turned to face him. His head was inches from her own. He was very fair, his eyebrows and lashes almost invisible. There was something soft about him, a vulnerability that he seemed unable to hide.

He smiled at her and she felt churlish. 'It was good of you to help, thank you so much, but I can manage now.'

'You call it managing, letting a pile of crocks run away with you? Look, the load of pottery is insecure. Let me ride with you, I'm going to town anyway.'

She hesitated.

'I'm no threat,' he said, 'I only want to be a good neighbour. I heard of your sad loss and I would like to offer my condolences.'

She closed her eyes for a moment. 'That's very kind of you. But please don't trouble yourself, I will be just fine.'

She knew she was being childish but somehow the sight of Eynon Morton-Edwards, son of her father's rival, offering her sympathy was too much to bear. His pottery was not suffering. His father had not gone to the war and left his wife and child at home alone.

'Look,' he said, 'it's none of my business but if you are going to the market' — he gestured towards the pots — 'which unless you are taking these things for a walk I suppose you are, don't you think you should do something about that hair?'

'What?' Llinos put her hand up and encountered a rough tangle of curls. She bit her lip and twisted her hair into a loop with impatient fingers, wishing he would go away.

He was small and thin and pathetic-looking and she felt sorry for him. He seemed to need a friend but she had enough to do to look after herself without taking on his problems as well.

'I don't know why we have to meet in such unfortunate circumstances,' he said apologetically and it was as though he sensed her impatience. 'Last time we met I almost ran you down.'

'I'm surprised you remembered me at all.' Llinos spoke acidly. Eynon Morton-Edwards was being friendly but why, what did he want?

He took out a small brush from inside his coat and handed it to her. 'Just run it through your hair,' he said. 'It's coming loose again.'

She contemplated throwing the brush back at him and then thought better of it. She brushed her hair with quick angry strokes. 'There, are you happy now?'

'You are really quite pretty,' he said. 'You'd be very pretty if you smiled now and then.' The white crisp collar at his neck emphasized his pallor. Eynon Morton-Edwards was not a strong man, she realized with a rush of remorse. Other people had their problems too and it was about time she remembered that.

'I'm sorry,' he said, 'have I upset you? I only wanted to make friends.' Suddenly, it was as if the dam of ice within her melted. Llinos put her hands over her face and began to cry. She was ashamed of herself, ashamed of her ill temper and more ashamed of crying before a stranger.

Tentatively, he put his hand on her arm, clucking to her as if she was a baby. 'There, there, you'll feel better for a good cry.' He patted her shoulder and she leaned against him, grateful for his kindness. After a while, she wiped her eyes and smiled shakily.

'I'm all right now.' She looked at him. The collar of his fine jacket was damp with her tears. 'Thanks for being so . . . so . . .' The words trailed away.

'Think nothing of it. I often feel like crying myself, only men are not supposed to cry, are they? At least that's what my father has always drummed into me.'

'I'd better get on, sell the pots I haven't broken.' Llinos picked up the reins. 'I'll walk the rest of the way, the market's not far.'

'Miss Savage,' Eynon said, 'I know you've had a bad time of things lately. I wish you would accept my offer of help, it's well meant.' He smiled. 'I assure you, I have no ulterior motive.'

'I know.' She believed him.

'Isn't there anyone to look after you, no cousin or uncle or something?' he asked as he fell into step beside her, leading his horse on the rein.

Llinos thought of Celia, who would be cleaning the house, cooking up a pot of *cawl*, taking over her life. She nodded.

'I've got some help.'

'But it's not the right sort of help?'

She glanced sideways, seeing the softness of his features and the clean fall of his hair over his brow. She knew suddenly that she liked him. She felt instinctively that in spite of who he was, she could trust him.

'I have Celia helping in the house, she's very good, but . . . anyway, what I need is financial help,' she said. 'I'm going to the bank while I'm in town to see Mr Francis. Perhaps he can advise me.' Llinos heard her voice shake and swallowed hard. 'I won't lose the pottery, I just won't.'

'I'm sorry. No wonder you were crying,' Eynon said. 'Would you like me to come with you to the bank? I am very friendly with Mr Francis.'

'No,' Llinos said firmly. 'If I'm to run the pottery and make it the fine business it once was I have to learn to stand on my own two feet.'

'I'm sure the bank will help,' he said. 'The Savage name was always good in Swansea. Once my own father even mentioned the place with respect and he doesn't like anyone to be in competition with him.'

'Why should he worry about competition? He has got the biggest pottery in this part of the country.'

'I know, but he's ambitious,' Eynon said. 'He's trying out an experiment on a new porcelain body, he's quite excited about it. If it works he's going to produce it in large quantities, have the finest painters to decorate the pieces and sell the services to London, perhaps even to the king.'

'The king?'

'Oh, yes, as I said, my father is a very ambitious man.' Llinos drew the cart to a halt. The market sprawled across the dirt track of a roadway, stalls set down on whatever spot took the vendor's fancy.

'Well, here we are, then, Miss Savage. I trust you will sell all your pots and take home a nice little profit.'

Llinos turned to him impulsively. 'If you meant your offer to help then I accept. Won't you stay with me, just for a while?'

'Why not? Let's unload the pottery. Young man, you go and find us a good spot, somewhere we'll be noticed.' They set up the baskets of stock between a woman in a hat and shawl selling cockles and an old man with a basket of vegetables.

'Morning, Miss Savage.' The cockle woman lifted her hand. 'Sorry to hear about your mother, good woman was Mrs Savage. Pity she took up with a bad lot the likes of that Mr Cimla, mind.'

Llinos nodded. 'Thank you for your condolences, Mrs Williams.' She was aware she sounded distant but she did not want to talk about her mother, not to this woman whom she scarcely knew.

The woman was not done. 'Got yourself a helper though, I see, Eynon Morton-Edwards no less.' Her eyes were bright with curiosity. She

111

touched the brim of her black hat in a deferential gesture that was belied by the spiteful look in her eyes. Llinos wondered what the woman had against Eynon.

Whatever it was, it didn't bother Eynon. He held up one of the tall jugs, glazed with the brown and cream that was a mark of the pottery, and called out loudly, urging the crowd to buy one of the finest pots in Swansea.

Llinos's mouth curved into a smile; he had a nerve, he was obviously a gentleman and yet he made a sale almost at once as though he was born to barter in the market place.

By midday, most of the stock was sold. 'Want to go home or shall we stick it out?' Eynon asked.

'Might as well sell the lot.' Llinos smiled. 'I'd better make the most of you while I've got you. When I'm on my own I won't do half as well.'

'Very well, then, hang on here, I'll go and get us something to eat. Are you hungry, lad?' The boy's eyes lit up at the prospect of food and the words of protest Llinos was about to say died on her lips.

When he had gone, Llinos felt suddenly weary. Her feet ached and she sank onto a flat stone and wrapped her skirt around her legs.

'That boy is a strange one.' Moriah Williams was packing; the baskets were empty except for a few cockles that clung to the weaving.

'He's been good to me,' Llinos said.

'Well, that posh school didn't make much of

a man of him, did it? All that painting and stuff, no occupation for a bright young fellow.'

'As I said, he's been good to me.' Llinos spoke icily; the woman nodded.

'*Chwarae teg,* fair play, that's all anyone can ask. Perhaps he's not as bad as that father of his.'

Eynon returned and Moriah Williams nodded to him before putting the large baskets over her arm and making her way through the crowd in the direction of the hills.

Eynon had brought a fresh loaf and a piece of cheese and Llinos realized how hungry she was. She smiled, feeling better than she had done in weeks.

'I expect old Mrs Williams has been talking about me.' Eynon began to eat hungrily. His teeth, Llinos noticed, were clean and white. She said nothing.

'I expect she's told you I'm not a son my father can be proud of, I'm not strong and manly enough; that's what everyone says. Well, I am different to him and I'm glad about it.'

'Being a man isn't about physical strength, is it?' Llinos said. 'I, for one, would be proud to call you a friend.'

He rested his hand on her shoulder. 'You are so sweet and innocent and to you everything is simple. I am a few years older than you and far, far more used to the ways of the world and I expect criticism whatever I do. But if you would like us to be friends, I can promise you I will never ask for anything from you except friendship and trust.'

Llinos nodded. 'Sounds as if I'm getting the best of the bargain.'

Eynon laughed. He finished eating and picked up one of the remaining pots. 'I'm going to sell these before we go, if it's the last thing I do.'

The warm air was cooling into evening by the time Llinos made her way back to Pottery Row.

'Tired?' Eynon asked and she nodded.

'I am tired and I never even got round to seeing Mr Francis at the bank, but somehow I feel happier than I've done for days.' She took a deep breath. 'I know I shouldn't say that so soon after . . . after Mother's death but . . .'

'Your mother is probably looking down at you and urging you to be happy right now.'

At the corner of Pottery Row, Eynon paused. 'May I come in?'

'Yes.'

She took him around the back way and left the cart beside the kiln. He appraised the buildings, his head on one side.

'I've never seen your place properly before; it looks like you've got the makings of a very good business here, Miss Savage.'

'I don't know.' Llinos shook her head. 'I'm not sure I can cope with it all, the books and things, figures just puzzle me. I don't know how much clay to buy, or anything.'

'Well, if I may, I would be pleased to help you with all that. Bookwork does not require physical strength, you see.' He smiled.

'Why would you want to help me?'

'A variety of reasons, not least that I hate to see a sweet young lady like you left to the mercy of others who might not have your best interests at heart.'

Celia was sitting before the fire; the smell of ham soup filled the kitchen.

Eynon sniffed the air as though unaware of Celia's openmouthed astonishment. 'Something smells delicious.'

Celia rose hastily. 'Good heavens! You are Mr Morton-Edwards.'

'So I am.' Eynon sat on one of the kitchen chairs. 'And you must be Celia.'

Celia bobbed a curtsy. 'You are welcome to a bit of supper though it's nothing fancy, not like what you're used to.'

Eynon looked from Celia to Llinos. 'I thank you for your kind thought but is the lady of the house willing for me to stay?'

Llinos knew that Eynon was gently putting Celia in her place and she could not suppress the sudden upturn of her mouth.

'I would be very pleased if you would stay, sir,' she said gravely.

The soup was hot and warming, the bread freshly baked. Llinos touched Celia's arm.

'Thank you for everything, Celia, I do appreciate all you've done for me, but I have to manage on my own some time.'

Celia's colour rose, there was an uncomfortable silence and then she laughed and rose to her feet.

'I give in, I have been acting as if I own the place, eating your food, using your fuel and I'm sorry. I meant well. I surely didn't mean to take advantage.'

'And I didn't mean you are not welcome here,' Llinos said quickly. 'I know the arrangement was that you come in now and again to keep an eye on things for me and you've been here every day. If you ask me, it's I who have been taking advantage of you.'

'Bless you, it's been wonderful, I've had someone to care for, to cook and clean for. My life is lonely sometimes in that old corner house.'

'Well, come in and clean and cook for me as much as you like, Celia,' Llinos said. 'If you feel that sharing my food and fire is enough return for your efforts I will be happy to have you here any time.'

Celia subsided into her chair and Llinos felt that an important issue had been resolved, the boundaries were set between herself and Celia.

'Shall we look over the books?' Eynon asked. 'Or are you too tired?'

'I'm too tired.' Llinos smiled. 'And there is still other work to do. You could give me a hand to stack the kiln if you like. Benjamin will have kept the fires going.'

Eynon rested his hand on her shoulder. 'You stay where you are, I'll see to the stacking.' He paused. 'How much help do you have?'

'Not enough.'

'I see.' He made his way to the door and Llinos rose to her feet.

'I should come with you, there's a lot to do.'

'You should get to bed, there are shadows as big as saucers under your eyes.'

There was silence in the kitchen after he'd gone. Llinos leaned wearily against the smooth wood of the rocking chair and closed her eyes.

'He'll want something, you mark my words.' Celia spoke softly. 'His kind, the rich, they don't do nothing unless there's something in it for them.'

Wearily, Llinos opened her eyes. 'What could I possibly give Eynon?'

'He might want to bed you, child, some are like that.' She sniffed. 'Though I must say he seems the wrong sort, a bit on the sickly side if you ask me.'

'Well then?'

Celia sighed. 'I don't know, perhaps I'm getting too long in the tooth to believe in the goodness of folks. But don't you listen to me, you got to live your life the way you think fit.'

'Well, at least for today I've had some help,' Llinos said. 'Mr Morton-Edwards made sure we sold the pots, every one of them.' She jingled the money in her pockets. 'And it will be wonderful if he can help with the books, too.'

'Just be careful, that's all I'm saying.'

Llinos smiled at Celia. 'You don't think he's

after my money, do you?'

Celia's face creased into a smile. 'There's little enough of that in all conscience. Well, take the young man's advice, girl, get off to your bed. Rest easy while you can, no-one knows what tomorrow will bring.'

Llinos shuddered. 'Don't say that, Celia, it sounds as if something bad might happen.'

'No, no, love, don't you fret, we've had enough bad things around here to last us for a long time to come.'

Later, curled up in her bed, Llinos listened to the familiar sounds of pottery being stacked ready for drying. She was grateful to Eynon, grateful for his friendship. Whatever other people said about him, she trusted him and she was glad he had come into her life. Somehow, she felt less alone.

She sighed and turned over in the bed. She was restless, sleep would not come. This was something that happened whenever she was over-tired. 'Past it' as her mother used to say.

Her thoughts pulled up sharply, it was the first time she had admitted to herself that her mother was really gone from her for good. Tears burned behind her closed eyelids and impatiently Llinos slid out of the bed and pulled on a shawl.

Outside, the sky was heavy with the smoke blowing over from the works along the banks of the river. The smell of rotten eggs in the air seemed worse tonight than ever.

She made her way to the shed, passing the

warm rounded belly of the kiln. Old Ben was asleep on a pile of straw, his toothless mouth open, his moustache lifting with every breath.

'I thought you'd gone to bed.' Eynon dusted the clay powder from his hands. 'You'll have enough work to do tomorrow; there are a lot of pots to glaze.' Eynon caught hold of her hand. 'Would you like me to come up in the morning? We can talk more then.'

'I don't like to take up your time, you must have more important things to do than help me.'

'I should be going to the fancy college my father has chosen but that is not what I want.'

'What do you want, Eynon?'

'What I really want might shock you.'

'I don't think anything you say will shock me,' Llinos said.

'Let's say that for now all I want is genuine friendship from someone who will like me whatever my faults.'

Llinos smiled shyly. 'I think I could fit the bill.' She looked down at her hands. 'Why are you so kind?'

'Nonsense! I'm not kind at all. Now, do you want me here tomorrow or not?'

'I'd be very grateful. I will just have to take time off to go to the bank tomorrow.'

'I've been thinking about that. I'd like to invest some money in your pottery, make it a real going concern. What do you say?'

She felt his offer was made more from kindness than from any real business sense. 'I couldn't take your money,' Llinos said quickly.

'Why not? I have plenty of it. You could set up in opposition to my father, wouldn't that be a fine thing?' He was smiling.

Llinos stared at him, trying to read his expression in the dimness. 'Is that why you are doing this, to get back at your father?'

He laughed and ran his hand through his hair. 'No, Llinos, it's not. It would take many years to build up a business to rival that of my father. No, your pottery will never be a danger to him, don't you worry.'

There was silence for a moment and Llinos bit her lip. An influx of capital would certainly take a great deal of the worry about the running of the pottery from her shoulders. 'It's a kind offer. What if I say I'll think about it?'

'Be brave, Miss Savage.' He spoke softly. 'What you wish will come true, you have a star above your head, I can see it.'

'I'd better get back inside.' Llinos sighed heavily. 'I should try to get some sleep.'

He stared at her with a quizzical expression. 'You have a great deal of courage for one so young. Show a little more and take me up on my offer to help. There would be no strings attached, I promise you.'

'I might have to accept your offer but, please, give me time.' She smiled. 'There is no guarantee that even with money I would make a go of things. I might fail and end up in the workhouse.'

'Well, we'll see that doesn't happen. Good

night to you, see you tomorrow.'

Llinos watched as Eynon walked away along the row, a slim figure in a coat that flared around his knees. She thought about his offer, what if she made him a partner? He knew the business of potting; obviously he had been allowed to watch the process, at least before he had been packed off to his posh school and he was pleasant enough.

He was a strange, lonely man and yet Llinos knew instinctively that in the coming months Eynon Morton-Edwards was going to be very important to her.

CHAPTER SEVEN

The smell of death hung over the field at Mont-St-Jean. Bodies lay in huddled confusion; French and British soldiers engaged in battle only short hours before lay united now in death.

Joe staggered a little beneath his burden; the wound in his side was bleeding again, it was not a serious wound but the loss of blood was weakening. Still, he would not leave Captain Savage on the field of death.

From behind him came the sound of sporadic gunfire. It seemed the French did not realize the battle was over.

Joe lowered the captain to the ground, settled him against a rock and, exhausted, sank down beside him. He saw in his mind's eye the flash of cannon, heard the cries of the wounded and the dying. He saw again an army advancing towards Mont-St-Jean, the Prussian army. Blutcher had come with his troops and Napoleon's defeat was a certainty.

The vision faded as Joe heard the captain groan. Swiftly, he knelt beside him in the dirt.

'Blutcher joined us at the last minute. The war with France is over, Napoleon is defeated,' he said in a low voice.

'We must go back to the field and share in

the victory honours.' Captain Savage made an attempt to rise and fell back, his face contorted with pain.

Joe loved his captain, he would give his life for him if necessary, but he could not share his enthusiasm for what seemed a senseless war.

'Your legs are shattered.' Joe spoke gently. 'I have done my best to patch up your wounds but you are not in a fit state to walk.'

'You go then, Joe, you should not have left the field.' His face was white.

Joe rested his hand on the captain's shoulder. 'It's all right, we left under orders from Wellington himself.'

'The Duke said we should leave? Wellington gave permission? Then we should be grateful to the great man for his humanity.'

Joe did not reply. The Duke had issued no such order but then Joe had reasoned that a man with both legs shattered and a half-breed slowly bleeding to death was no loss to the British army. Joe held the water bottle to the captain's lips.

'Where are we making for, Joe?' The captain's voice was weak.

'The surgeon's tent is about a mile away, we must make it before darkness falls.' Joe frowned. Or before the life force drained out of one or both of them.

He tore the bottom from his trousers and ripped the coarse material into strips. The larger strip he tied around the wound in his side to stop the bleeding and the other smaller ones he kept over his shoulder.

He hacked several branches from a half-dead tree, apologizing mentally to mother earth for the desecration. Working quickly, he lashed the branches together to form a crude stretcher. As he manoeuvred the captain onto it, he knew that time was running out, for both of them.

He looked up at the fading sun for a long moment and then, with a supreme effort, he lifted one end of the stretcher and began to drag it along the ground.

There was no point in trying to keep under cover, the earth that would succour brush would be uneven, difficult to negotiate. In any case, Joe believed that the time was not right for him to return to the spirit in the sky, he had his life before him, his destiny was not yet fulfilled.

It was strange how at times of crisis he reverted to what the white man would call the superstitions of the American Indian. Perhaps it was the same with the captain, who was uttering prayers now to his God. The words were hushed, faltering, but Joe's hearing was acute.

'The Lord is my refuge and strength . . .' The captain's voice was fading and Joe closed his eyes for a moment, hoping that it was only unconsciousness that had claimed the captain and not the cold hand of death.

The walk across the harsh land was sapping the last of his strength, he had no compass, it was only the power of his senses and his sheer strength of will that led him forward.

When the moon-mother slid from between the clouds, he looked up, begging her silently for help. A mist formed before his face, he was losing consciousness. He slumped to his knees and feeling the earth power beneath him drew strength from it.

He heard them before he saw them and knew soldiers were coming. If they were the enemy, he was a dead man; the French who had escaped from the battlefield would take no prisoners. He swayed and the light faded, and the last thing Joe knew was the taste of dirt in his mouth.

'Come on, son, take your hands away from the stretcher, we're only trying to help.'

He opened his eyes. The man bending over him wore an eye patch but his complexion was fresh and his uniform that of a British soldier. Joe sighed and sank back into the darkness where there was no pain.

'You shape it this way, see?' Llinos felt the raw red clay obey her fingers, forming itself into a tall pot.

'Looks easy enough.' Watt was frowning.

'Go on, try it.' Llinos allowed the clay to collapse into a shapeless mound as she stopped turning the wheel.

'I used to watch the potters work the clay sometimes,' Watt said. 'One of the potters let me have a go, I was only a nipper then, mind.'

Llinos suppressed a smile. Watt was about nine or ten years old. 'Right then, get onto the stool and get your feet working so that the wheel spins fast and even. Good thing you're tall for your age.'

Watt tried to grasp the clay as the wheel spun but it eluded him, slipping from his fingers.

'Damn and bugger it!'

'Now, Watt, no good losing your temper. Remember the clay won't respond to a pair of hands that can't hold it firmly.'

Watt looked at her wide-eyed. 'You talk as if the clay has a life of its own.'

'It has, you wait and see. Come on, tackle it with guts, grab and hold it, show the clay who is boss.'

Watt tried again and this time the clay rose rapidly between his clutching fingers only to splay out over the top and collapse onto itself.

Llinos resisted the urge to laugh at the bemused expression on the boy's face. 'You keep trying,' she urged. 'I've got to get some glazing done or we'll never have enough stuff ready for market day.'

Llinos wandered around the shed. Some of the more experienced apprentices were becoming quite skilled, shaping pots with deft fingers. She had at last plucked up enough courage to ask at the workhouse for hands, and three young girls and two boys had been placed in her care. They were not skilled but one or two of them showed promise. If the work was crude it scarcely mattered, the pots were functional rather than decorative.

Soon, she would show the girls how to paint, how to work with transfer patterns. The boys could do much of the heavy work. The Savage Pottery was on its way up again.

A dreaming silence fell over the shed and Llinos became engrossed in the process of mixing the glazes. She had learned from age-old methods that wood ash from beech and holly resulted in a smooth green glaze. Ash or yew tended to make the pot turn a greyish colour. She had experimented with onion skins and other vegetables to make a variety of colours but she preferred the plain terracotta of the red clay which came from Penllergaer.

Binnie came into the shed and looked round the room, a frown of concentration on his face. He approached Llinos and spoke in a low voice.

'We can thank God for Eynon Morton-Edwards,' he said, seating himself at the wheel. He took up a lump of clay and Llinos watched with raised eyebrows as he began to work.

'Without his money we would have had to close down by now.' Binnie was trying, without much success, to shape the clay. 'It would have broken your father's heart if he could have seen the state we were in.'

'Thank God you came back to me, Binnie. Those few days you stayed away I was worried to death that you wouldn't return.'

Binnie's face took on a closed look and Llinos knew better than to pursue the subject. If Binnie wanted to confide in her about his home life, he would.

'How did you get on with my father, Binnie?' Llinos looked down at her hands, wondering why she asked such a question now. Perhaps it was the knowledge that she was an orphan that made her want to fix her past into some form of pattern, a way of preserving the essence of what was herself.

'I always found him a good man to work for, hard, mind, but fair.' Binnie was smiling, Llinos could tell from the tone of his voice. She looked up and saw him cut a pot from the wheel.

'Well done!' She went to admire it. Though a little misshapen, it was, unmistakably, a pot. 'I didn't know you could throw a pot.'

Binnie laughed, his hair falling across his eyes. 'I just wanted to try my hand at it. I don't think I'll ever make a potter, though. I'll stick to my job as foreman if it's all the same by you.'

He rubbed the clay from his fingers. 'How are the children from the workhouse shaping up?'

Llinos wiped her hands on a piece of rag. 'All right. Given time some of them might make good potters. The girls are going to lodge with Jim Cooper and his wife.'

The door creaked open and Ben peered into the shed. 'There's a lady here to see Binnie,' he said cautiously.

Through the open door, Llinos caught sight of Maura, her red hair gleaming in the sunlight.

Binnie shrugged. 'Right.' He sauntered towards the door and as he passed the wheel where Watt was working pushed him playfully in the back. Binnie walked out of the shed but left the door open. As he stood in the slant of sunlight, Llinos could see that his shoulders were suddenly tense. His hands were thrust into his pockets, it was clear something was wrong.

Their voices rose and fell and when Binnie moved slightly to one side Llinos saw the faded bag resting at Maura's feet.

'She's having his kid,' Watt said, rubbing at his eyes. 'Heard 'em talkin' the other day. Looks like her folks chucked her out.'

Llinos stared at Watt in amazement. 'For one so young you hear far too much.' She spoke tartly. 'Please fetch the shovel from the corner and put the dirt and wasted clay into the bin.'

Binnie came back into the shed; he was frowning. 'She's left home,' he said.

Llinos was silent and Binnie shrugged. 'Can she stay here, just for the time being?'

'Well, I suppose so.' Maura would have to lodge in Pottery House, she could scarcely be put in the outhouse with the men.

Llinos saw the troubled look on Binnie's face. 'Of course she can stay, for the time being. Come on, we'd better do something about making her at home.'

'Thanks, Llinos, I'll find a place for her as soon as I can, you have my word on it.'

'I know.' Llinos sighed. 'She'd better have the big front bedroom, there's a lovely view of the river from there. But Binnie' — she added a note of caution — 'I can't afford to keep her indefinitely, you know how pushed we are for money in spite of the influx of funds.'

'I understand,' Binnie said. 'Maura is cleaning for the vicar, she'll bring home some money at least for the time being.'

Llinos led the way outside the shed, aware of Watt listening to everything that was being said. Maura stared at her from large green eyes; her mouth trembled. All the spirit seemed to be knocked out of her.

'Llinos says we can live here.' Binnie put a comforting arm around the Irish girl.

'Sure and have you told her the truth about me?' Maura asked, avoiding Llinos's eyes.

'I understand you're expecting a baby?' Llinos said quickly. 'It's none of my business but I suggest you try to find permanent accommodation as soon as you can.'

Llinos wondered how old the girl was, probably fifteen, sixteen at the most. The silence lengthened and Llinos realized that Binnie was waiting for Llinos to take the initiative. It was a good thing Celia was having one of her rare days off. Her presence in the house would have posed some difficulties. Having had an Irish husband who had left her for another woman she was not over fond of anyone from the Irish quarter of town.

'Binnie, see Maura settled and then come back and get those saggers over to the kiln, we've still a great deal of work to do before we finish for the day.' She was aware that her tone was curt but she could not help feeling she could do without any added responsibilities right now. 'I'd better get back to work,' she said.

Binnie returned a short while later and rested his hand on Llinos's shoulder. 'You don't know how much this means to me,' he said solemnly.

Llinos sighed. 'That's all right. Let's get these pots over to the kiln and then Ben can seal the opening, right?'

It was late by the time Llinos threw off her apron. Dark clouds obscured the moon and there was a chill in the air.

'Come on, Watt.' She ruffled the boy's hair. 'Come indoors, let's see what we can find to eat.'

As she entered the house, Llinos was aware of a delicious smell of roasting meat.

'I think Maura's been cooking,' Watt said. 'She's going to make us all fat if she has her way.'

The house was filled with the smell of a succulent roast, reminding Llinos of happier days when her mother was alive, before Bert Cimla swept into their lives, changed everything and vanished again.

The kitchen was filled with steam. Pots simmered on the hobs and the table was laid with the plates from the dresser, plates her father had made when Llinos was a child.

She looked at them for a moment, at the pale

blue glaze and the symmetrical borders and knew what skill had gone into the making of them. Her mother had treasured those plates, never putting them to the practical purpose they were intended for.

'I hope a bit of pork is all right, miss,' Maura said in her soft Irish voice. She sounded submissive but Llinos knew that the Irish girl had a temper that matched that red hair of hers.

'It's more than all right, it's wonderful.' Llinos turned to Watt. 'Go and wash your hands, they're filthy.'

Watt retreated, grumbling beneath his breath. He paused at the door and looked back at the table wistfully.

'Go *on*,' Llinos said. 'If we are to have a feast we must do justice to it.'

The meal was delicious. The gravy running over the meat and vegetables was rich and dark just like Gwen used to make it.

'You're a good cook, Maura.' Llinos shook her head when Maura held the plate of meat towards her. 'No, thank you. I've had too much already.'

'Sure you've got room for a bit o' pudding?' Maura swung open the oven at the side of the fire and with the edge of her apron took a dish from inside.

The bread and butter pudding gleamed crisp and golden in the candlelight and Llinos smiled. 'All right, just a little.'

Watt sat forward eagerly in his chair, hardly

able to contain his impatience. His eyes were wide with anticipation and Llinos smiled indulgently.

'Can we afford to eat like this, Maura?' she asked. The girl looked at her in surprise. 'Oh, I'm not rich, I have to count the pennies,' Llinos added.

'Well, the bit of pork was a gift from the vicar,' Maura said defensively. 'And the pudding, well, that's only eggs and milk and old bread with a bit of sugar.'

'We'll have to sort a menu out some time,' Llinos said. 'But for now, I think we'll have a cup of tea as a treat to finish off a beautiful meal.'

Maura, flushed with her exertions, rose to push the kettle onto the fire.

Binnie came into the kitchen and his face, old before its time, broke into a smile. 'A good home-cooked dinner, wonderful!' The frown eased from his forehead so that he looked like the young man he was. Too young for the responsibilities of fatherhood. Well, that was not her problem, Llinos told herself.

Later, as she helped Maura make up the bed in the guest room with fresh sheets, she sensed a reserve in the Irish girl that bordered on hostility. For all her words of thanks, Maura did not like Llinos and it showed.

'I hope you will be comfortable here,' Llinos said stiffly. 'But do remember that this is a temporary arrangement, you must find a place of your own before the . . . the baby comes.'

Maura straightened. 'Sure and I'll go now if it is any trouble to have me here.'

'I didn't say that.' Linos put her hands on her hips. 'I am happy to help out but as I said before, I am not rich, I can barely afford to support myself, let alone anyone else.'

'Right,' said Maura. 'I understand you, Miss Savage. Don't you be worrying, I'll find a place for me and for Binnie as soon as I can.'

Llinos raised her eyebrows. 'Are you threatening to take Binnie away from the pottery?'

'Well, wherever I live, he will live, it's natural isn't it?' Maura's face was set in hard lines.

'It's natural to have a ring on your finger before you talk about living together and having a family,' Llinos retorted. She knew she sounded like a prig but something about the Irish girl set her teeth on edge.

'Look, I'm sorry, this is really none of my business. What you and Binnie choose to do with your lives is up to you.' She walked across the room and paused at the door.

'Just remember, Maura, that Binnie has a good job here and fair wages. He might not have any of that if he looks for work elsewhere in town.'

She saw Maura's eyes widen and knew her jibe had hit home. Suddenly, she was ashamed of herself.

'Maura, look, we have to get on as well as we can together, otherwise this is going to be an intolerable situation.'

Maura stared at her hands and her mouth trembled, and in that moment Llinos felt she was years older than the Irish girl.

'I know I'm a spiteful cat,' Maura said. 'It's just that I feel so . . . so strange.' She sank onto the newly made bed and covered her face with her hands.

Llinos took a deep breath and sat beside the Irish girl.

'You are bound to feel strange,' she said. 'You are away from home, you are going to be a mother, everything in your life has changed. It will be all right, Binnie is a good worker, I can afford to pay him so long as we keep up the output on the pottery.' She looked down at Maura's bent head and wondered how the girl could endure to be in such a shameful position. No wonder her family had thrown her out.

She rose to her feet. 'Thank you for cooking such a wonderful meal, it was very much appreciated by all of us. Oh, heavens!' She put her hand to her mouth. 'I should take something out to Ben and the apprentices, they haven't had much to eat all day.'

Maura looked up eagerly. 'Can I do it? I can make up some pork sandwiches and the bread and butter pudding will still be warm.'

'That's an excellent idea, Maura.' As she crossed the landing to her own room, Llinos felt she carried a heavy burden on her shoulders. Her list of dependents seemed to be growing. It was true that Maura would bring in her own

135

money for the time being but what would happen when she could no longer work?

Llinos moved to the window and looked out at the summer night. 'Where are you, the man I dream about every night, why haven't you come to claim me? Were my dreams just stardust?' Her own whispered words startled her. Quickly she drew the curtains against the night, she must get some sleep, tomorrow was market day.

It was the next morning when Llinos heard a knock on the door and opened it to find Eynon standing outside, a bag in his hand. They had spent a great deal of time together lately and had become friends. Although she would never think of Eynon in a romantic way, Llinos felt he was a person she could like and trust.

'You know we talked about me becoming a partner?' Eynon said. 'Well, I've discussed it with my friend Mr Francis and he thinks it is a wonderful idea.' He followed her into the sitting-room and put down his bag. 'Mr Francis believes your father has money in a bank in Cardiff. He tells me he can try to find out how you stand if you will write him a letter of permission.'

'That sounds too good to be true.' Llinos sank into a chair. 'I'll give him a letter of course but I don't hold out much hope of finding myself heir to a fortune.'

'Never mind. Just in case you do, I'd better get my claim in quickly,' Eynon said. 'I have brought the papers for you to look at. If you think it all fair and above board, sign them and thereafter you and I will be business partners. If that's what you still want.'

'Of course it's what I want. If only you knew how glad I am to see you. I've been wondering where the next mouthful of food would come from. The money you loaned me is nearly all gone. Money vanishes once I start paying out wages.'

He patted her hand. 'Well, look on the bright side, it could be that your troubles are almost over.'

She smiled. 'I do hope you are right.'

'The wound is healing well.' The surgeon stared down at Joe's side, a frown creasing his forehead. 'I don't know what miracle cure you are using but there is not a trace of infection.' His fingers touched the scarred flesh. 'Soon you will be as right as rain.'

Joe nodded. He knew that his remedies worked better than those of the doctor. Once he was strong enough, he had left the tent at night and gathered dead-nettles from under hedgerows. It was a paste made from these, not the ministrations of the doctor, that had healed him so quickly.

The captain had not been so fortunate. Both Savage's legs were useless from the knee down. He had drifted in and out of consciousness for days. Now he had a fever that the doctors

137

seemed unable to cure.

Later, Joe would slip out to the fields, fetch some roots and leaves of *langue de boeuf*. From these he would distil a potion that would reduce the fever. He would restore the captain to health, though nothing would give him back the use of his legs. Eventually, when they were both strong enough to travel, Joe would take the captain to his home in Wales.

'We'll be shipping out with the wounded in a few days,' the doctor said. 'A boat will take us to British shores, after that you men are on your own and God help some of you.'

'I'll take care of the captain,' Joe said. 'His family will be happy to see him again.'

Sounds of revelry drifted towards the tent. 'The soldiers are celebrating victory over the French.' The doctor smiled thinly. 'Napoleon Bonaparte is finished, there will be no return from exile, not this time.'

Joe nodded, the little Corsican was beaten. There would be no joy in life for Bonaparte now that his battles were over. Before long, he would set his spirit free from his body and then the vultures, of the human kind, would fight over his remains.

Joe put his head down on his blanket and closed his eyes. He would sleep for a few hours, conserve his energy. Over the next days, when the captain was fit to travel, Joe would need to call on every bit of the reserves of strength he possessed.

The country of Wales was full of the shades of autumn. Trees magnificently garbed in reds and golds bordered the small villages. The sea, a mild peaceful sea, edged the land with rich azure, sparkling in the September sunlight.

'We will soon be at your home, Captain.' Joe guided the horse and trap towards the town of Swansea; soon, his guardianship of the captain would be ended, Savage would be with his family. In a way, it saddened Joe to think of parting with the man to whom he had grown so close. They were almost like brothers, or perhaps father and son would be more accurate, Savage being older than Joe by many years.

'Smell the stink of the copper works?' The captain's voice carried from the interior of the trap to where Joe sat in the driving seat. It had been a source of great relief to Joe to realize that the captain had resources of money to draw on. They had stopped for several days at a place called Cardiff and there the captain had done business with well-dressed solicitors and bankers who had looked down their noses at Joe.

There, too, they had learned of the 'marriage' and the death of the captain's wife. He had taken it badly, falling into a long silence, his head sunk onto his chest. But as they had journeyed towards Swansea, he had brightened.

'Aye, there is still an evil smell about the town but I love the place.'

Joe looked towards the winding river marred

by smoking, intrusive chimney stacks. 'Swansea must have been beautiful once.'

'Oh it was.' The captain's voice was regretful. 'When I was courting my wife, the town was tranquil with only the beginnings of a manufactory to indicate what was to come. But we never foresaw the future of the town and perhaps that was a good thing.'

There was silence for a time and then the captain's voice became eager. 'Just turn up the hill here, Joe, the pottery is only about a mile away.'

Joe guided the animal with a gentle tug on the reins and the horse responded obediently. Joe discovered he had a way with animals when he was a child.

The rise of the hill was gentle but Joe leapt down from the driving seat. 'I'll lighten the load,' he said, looking over his shoulder at the captain.

Savage sighed heavily. 'I wish I could do the same, Joe, but there we are, I have come home to my child as half a man. I have no way of knowing how she will react.'

Joe did not reply. It was not for him to guess the ways of the people who belonged to the captain. And yet, in spite of himself, he was excited at the thought of meeting Llinos at last. Would she be the woman of his dreams or had his imaginings led him astray? Well, he would soon know.

His nerve endings were alive as he guided the horse towards the outskirts of the town. Above him and following the line of the river, he saw the tall, oddly shaped chimneys of the pottery. And he knew, deep down within his being, that here, in this smoky town, lay his destiny.

CHAPTER EIGHT

Eynon Morton-Edwards stared at his reflection in the mirror that hung over the ornate mantelpiece. He was not ill favoured, his hair was a fine colour and his eyes were honest and clear. What was it then that made his father dislike him so much? Was it his physical weakness, his artistic streak or the fact that his mother had died giving birth to him?

His father entered the room. He was dressed for riding and he slapped the crop against his boots as he looked at his son in disgust. 'There you go, preening again. You should have been a girl, I've always said as much.'

Eynon felt his shoulders grow tense. 'I know you have, I've heard the same refrain ever since I can remember.'

'I blame your stepmother, she spoiled you rotten, dressed you in frills and furbelows. Silly bitch!'

Eynon flinched at his father's lack of sensitivity. 'Sometimes you can be so crude, Father,' he said.

Philip's eyebrows rose in disbelief. 'You young fool!' He came towards Eynon and raised his whip, bringing it down across his son's shoulders. The leather, cutting through the soft ma-

142

terial of Eynon's shirt, felt like a redhot iron.

'I'll teach you to talk to your father like that!' Philip hit him again. 'I should have done this a long time ago, it might have made a man of you.'

Philip lashed out at him, but Eynon twisted away and caught the end of the whip.

'That's enough, Father,' he said icily. 'That's the first time and the last that you raise a hand to me. I'm going out,' he said. 'I feel I need some fresh air.'

'Clear off, then.' Philip Morton-Edwards spoke sharply. 'I can't stand looking at you. I'll never get strong grandsons out of you. I can only hope that Estelle does better for me than your mother did.'

Eynon left the room by the French windows and walked along the path that bordered the well manicured lawns of Ty Mawr. He felt angry, humiliated, but what was new in that? His father always had that effect on him. As a boy, all Eynon ever wanted was love and respect but there had been precious little of that in the Morton-Edwards household.

One day, he supposed, he would fall in love, meet someone who would like him for himself, but that day was a long time coming. What a pity he could not fall in love with little Llinos Savage. Indeed, he believed he was half in love with her already. Imagine his father's rage if he was presented with grandsons from the Savage family.

Lloyd Savage had always been a great big thorn in Philip Morton-Edwards' side. The two men had hated each other, they had been rivals, the two potteries lying almost side by side, in direct competition with each other. But it was the Tawe Pottery which had risen to supremacy.

Eynon picked up a stone and threw it across the lawn. The stone skimmed through the bushes, sending small creatures scurrying for cover. It was high time he moved out of his father's house. He would begin looking for a property at once.

Later, he would call to see Llinos, she was up against it, she needed all the help and encouragement she could get.

He returned to the house only long enough to get his topcoat and hat. It was a fine day and there was only a short distance to walk to town but he was, as always, conscious of his weak constitution. He stepped out into the road and looked up at the clear sky above him. Today was a new day, he would put his father right out of his mind. Soon, he would be living in a house of his own, he would be free.

Llinos opened the door of Pottery House and smiled as she saw Eynon standing on the step, his hat in his hand, a jaunty bow at his neck.

'Good morning, Miss Savage,' Eynon said. 'I have come calling on you. I hope I have not chosen an inconvenient moment.'

'Come in and stop fooling around.' Llinos

looked along the row and noticed several of the neighbours watching the proceedings with interest. 'You horror! You'll have everyone talking about us.' She led the way into the kitchen.

'Sit down somewhere, I was just making a pot of tea.' She pushed the kettle onto the fire and picked up the brown teapot. Everything was orderly and in its place since Maura had taken to working in the kitchen.

Maura was making herself too much at home in Pottery House, Llinos thought worriedly. Goodness knows what she would be like if she was at home all day instead of working at the vicar's house.

Llinos made the tea and handed a cup to Eynon. He was relaxing in the large rocking chair, his legs stretched out before him, his polished boots almost touching the fender. With his starched linen and fine topcoat, he looked incongruous in such a homely setting.

'I haven't seen you for a few days,' Eynon said. 'I've had a chill. Did you miss me?'

'Yes, I suppose I did.' Llinos brushed back her hair. Her arms ached, she had been working in the sheds since daybreak. Eynon was lucky he had found her in the house instead of having to search the pottery buildings for her.

'Though to be truthful, I've been working so hard I haven't had the energy to think of anything else,' she said.

'I'm flattered, I'm sure.' Eynon spoke dryly. 'Anyway, if you've been working so hard, what are you doing sloping around the house making tea?'

'I'm entitled to a break now and again.' Llinos heard the indignation in her voice and when Eynon smiled she knew he had been teasing her. Like a fool she had risen to the bait.

She sat down on one of the heavy oak kitchen chairs. 'I'm grateful for the money you put into the pottery, but as my new partner I hoped you would find time to help me with the books.'

She looked at him closely; he was paler than usual and there was a faint red mark running along his cheek.

'What's wrong?' she asked.

'It's a long story,' Eynon said. 'But I'll tell you anyway.' He sat forward, his shoulders hunched, and Llinos saw that he was not as relaxed as he pretended to be.

'My father thought he would thrash some sense into me.' Eynon's eyes were dark. 'Needless to say, it didn't work. The point is, I can't stay under the same roof as him any longer.'

Llinos touched his hand. 'You can stay here with me for as long as you like,' she said impulsively.

His face softened. 'I knew you'd say that, but it wouldn't do.'

'What do you mean?' Llinos looked at him in surprise. Eynon shook his head.

'People would talk, don't you realize that?'

'What would they say?'

Eynon smiled. 'You innocent. They would say

I was bedding you, those who believed me man enough, that is.'

She lifted her chin. 'Let them talk, I won't see you out on the street.'

'I have plenty of money, I won't be out on the street, don't you worry.' He squeezed her hand. 'But thank you for caring. I've known from the very first time I set eyes on you that we would be good friends.' He paused, lifting his head in an attitude of listening. 'What's that?'

From outside in the row, the sound of voices rose to a cheer. 'What on earth is going on?'

Eynon got to his feet and moved swiftly towards the door. Llinos followed more slowly, knowing it took very little for the good people of the neighbourhood to become excited. Just the arrival of the baker's cart was enough to cause a stir.

Eynon's tall frame blocked out the sunlight and the view of the street. Llinos tried to peer over his shoulder but she was too small to see anything.

'Captain Savage has come home!' Celia-end-house was shouting hysterically, her voice high above the cheers of the crowd.

Llinos froze — her father? Was Celia demented? Her father was dead, killed in the war. Her mother had shown her the letter. As Eynon stepped aside, Llinos saw a man standing before her. He was tall and long dark hair hung down his back. He looked into her eyes and she recognized him. Carved as if from granite, his face was foreign and yet familiar. The eyes, blue and heavy-lidded, seemed to look at her without surprise.

'I have brought your father home, Miss Savage.' His voice was low, cultured. It was as much a shock as the words he spoke.

'My father?' She heard her voice high-pitched, unrecognizable. 'My father is dead.'

'No, he is safe, he has come home.' Llinos was aware of the sunlight, the warmth of the stone beneath her feet. It was as though time was suspended and she was looking in on the world from outside. People were telling her that Father had come home but how could that be?

'Llinos! Can this big girl be my daughter?' The voice was low, husky, and it stirred memories of her childhood. It was true, her father was alive.

'Father!' She walked towards him and drank in the pallor of his face and the white of his hair. His face was scarred, older than she remembered, but it was the face she loved.

'*Cariad.*' In spite of having aged, he looked fine in his military uniform, his posture was upright, his back stiff, his shoulders square. He held himself with dignity as befitted an officer. 'Are you going to give me a kiss, then, or have you forgotten me?'

She scrambled up the steps of the cart and flung herself into his arms. As he hugged her she breathed in the scent of his tobacco, felt the heat rise from the coarse material of his uniform.

The scents of him were achingly familiar.

'Oh, Father, they told us you were dead.' She clung to him, her arms around his neck, her face buried against his shoulder.

'There, my little girl, it's all right. I'm back, I'll take care of you now, no need to fret.'

'You know about . . . Mother?' Llinos looked into his face anxiously.

He nodded. 'When I called at my bank in Cardiff I found they had been contacted by Robert Francis of Swansea on your behalf because he thought you were an orphan.' He held her away from him and looked into her face.

'Did she die peacefully?'

'Come on, let's go into the house.' Llinos spoke softly. 'We can talk about it later.'

'Joe, will you give me a hand?' Lloyd Savage looked past her shoulder and Llinos turned to see the tall stranger who was so familiar to her standing beside her.

His eyes, blue as the summer skies, rested on Llinos and she felt again an almost physical blow of recognition. She had never seen him before and yet he was as familiar to her as her own face in the mirror.

He nodded in her direction, as if he understood her feelings, and leaned into the carriage. As he lifted the captain and carried him towards the door, Llinos realized that her father had not come home from the war unscathed.

She swallowed her shock. 'Take my father into the sitting-room, please, it's just there to the right,' Llinos said as the group of neighbours, hushed now, moved to make way for them.

'I can give my own directions, I am not a visitor, nor an invalid to be humoured.' There was a note of reproof in her father's tone and Llinos acknowledged it with a droop of her head.

She saw Eynon look at her doubtfully, wondering if he should leave. She beckoned to him to follow.

Lloyd Savage settled into a chair, adjusted the shawl over his knees. He studied Eynon hard for a moment before speaking.

'I know your father and knowing him I can't help but wonder what you are doing in my house.'

'He is a friend, Father,' Llinos said quickly, 'a very good friend.'

'I see. Llinos, call one of the maids to fetch me a beaker of cordial, would you? I've got a raging thirst.'

Llinos looked at Eynon and shook her head warningly. Time enough to explain there were no maids when her father was rested. When she returned to the sittingroom, Eynon was studying the stranger and there was an odd look on his face. When he saw her, he raised an eyebrow enquiringly.

'Eynon, don't go,' Llinos said, catching his hand. 'Father, I must explain, Eynon is more than a friend, he is a partner. He's put money into the business, without him I couldn't have carried on. The business was failing and Eynon helped me try to save it.'

'Why would you work in opposition to that rascal who is your father?' Lloyd asked and Llinos felt herself grow tense.

'I do not agree with much that my father does,' Eynon said. 'But for all that I will not have him insulted.'

After a moment, Lloyd Savage nodded. 'I respect you for that. I apologize for my rudeness. Please sit down, join us in a cup of lemonade. You too, Joe.'

Joe sat awkwardly, his long legs stretched out before him.

'I should introduce Joe.' Savage smiled at his daughter. 'Like you, I am loyal to my friends and Joe is a dear friend. He saved my life, not once but several times. A year ago at Leipzig I was lost for several days. Missing believed killed. It was probably then that some well meaning general wrote to your mother.'

Llinos looked at Joe, looked into the blue of his eyes and felt the sweetness she had experienced in her dreams. Then there had been no barriers, now there were many. He inclined his head and she saw the dark hair swing forward over his shoulder and felt the urge to touch its softness.

'I am honoured to meet you, Miss Savage.' Like the first time she had heard him speak, it was a shock to hear how cultured his voice was. It was strangely at variance with his foreign appearance, and yet the sound of it sank through her veins and into her being and rested in a secret place there.

'Thank you for all you've done for my father.' She swallowed hard, not knowing if she should hold out her hand to him.

'Give him your hand, then, Llinos,' her father encouraged. 'He won't bite!' She obeyed with an eagerness that surprised her.

Joe's hand was warm and strong. He lifted her fingers to his lips and she felt the colour rise to her cheeks.

'Ah, Joe, this is a side of you I've never seen before,' the captain said. 'Your father must have educated you well.'

Joe released Llinos's fingers and sat back in his chair. 'He did.'

Eynon had been watching silently. Now he leaned forward. 'I suppose you attended one of our fine British schools?' There was a hint of sarcasm in his tone. Joe looked at him steadily.

'As a matter of fact, I did,' he said simply.

'Then your father must have been a very influential man.' Eynon rose to his feet and bowed. 'If you will excuse me, Llinos, sir?' He moved to the door and paused.

'I don't know if you are going to need my help with the books after all, Llinos, but if there is anything I can do, just let me know.'

'Not so fast, young man.' Lloyd Savage turned to look over his shoulder with difficulty. 'Come round here where I can see you, for heaven's sake.'

Eynon came forward and stood waiting for the captain to speak.

'You have put money into the pottery?'

'That's right.'

'Then you and I will have much to talk about, I think.'

Eynon looked at Llinos. 'I have been dealing with your daughter, we are . . . used to each other's ways.'

'I see. Well, you will soon get used to my ways. In any event, we can discuss it at our leisure at another time. In the meantime, I must thank you for looking after my daughter.'

Eynon smiled. 'It was my great pleasure and I trust it will continue to be my pleasure in the future.' His eyes rested briefly on Joe and then he left the room.

In the days that followed her father's return, Llinos felt strangely unsettled. Lloyd had taken over the master bedroom and at first he was outraged that Binnie and Maura were sleeping together in one of the guest rooms. Llinos could not decide if he was more upset about the fact that common workers were living in his house or that the two were not married.

Joe chose to sleep in the kitchen, curled in a blanket. He seemed to have made instant friends with Watt, who now slept beside him.

Llinos in her own bedroom was subject to strange dreams. Dreams of eagles, of flying over large seas and continents. But the most disturbing dreams were those in which she was in Joe's arms. Those dreams she rejected as soon as she woke and yet the feeling of warmth they engendered lasted for many hours.

As the days passed, it seemed that the entire household had begun to accept the changes without further comment, but for Llinos, who had to balance the housekeeping accounts, life was made more difficult. She would have to talk to her father, ask him for money.

But what made everything worse was that Joe kept his distance from her. He had not been out of her thoughts since she had first set eyes on him. He was such a strange mixture, half Indian in his beliefs and visions and at the same time civilized, with impeccable table manners and an air of politeness that did much to keep people at a distance.

She knew she had been drawn to him from the first moment she had seen him. She felt gratitude, of course, whenever she thought of his kindness to her father, but more, she wanted to be close to Joe. She knew that his devotion to Lloyd was part of the problem. Some sense of propriety prevented Joe from appearing overfamiliar with his captain's daughter. But she wanted very badly for them to be friends.

Most days, Llinos came downstairs to find that Joe had kept the fire going in the kitchen. But on this sunny morning, she woke to the unexpected sound of hammering. She rose and washed quickly and then paused to glance out at the early morning emptiness of the row. Birds were singing in the brush at the back of the houses, the sun was shining and yet Llinos was filled with a strange melancholy.

She tied up her hair impatiently and hurried downstairs, she had breakfast to make before she went to work.

'Good morning, Joe.' He was kneeling on the floor, hammering wheels onto one of the good dining-room chairs. 'What are you doing?'

He did not look up. 'Putting wheels on one of your dining chairs.'

'I can see that.' She watched as he manoeuvred the chair over the flags, wheeling it to and fro. 'Ah! I see what you have in mind, now, that's wonderful, Joe.'

'It will give your father some independence. He will be able to move around the house at will.' Joe glanced at her briefly. 'He might even be able to work again. A man has his pride.'

Llinos swallowed the constriction in her throat. Joe was far too perceptive, he saw things that most people did not.

'I'm going to the sheds,' she said.

'You should eat.' Joe stared down at her and she was tinglingly aware of him. She longed to touch the silkiness of his hair, instead she moved away.

'I'm not hungry.'

It was good to be in the sanctuary of the potting shed. With her father's injection of funds, she had been able to employ more staff. Four throwers worked the wheels, turning out pots with the swiftness of long practice. Two more young handlers had been employed and even Watt had a boy to help with clearing up the scraps of clay.

Llinos had reopened one of the disused sheds where three ladies sat decorating the wares. The pottery was doing very well and yet she could not help feeling that something had been lost along the way.

'Morning, Miss Savage.' One of the throwers nodded without pausing in his work. He dipped his hands in a bowl of water and lifted a piece of flannel to wipe around the rim of the tall pot he was shaping.

'Good morning, Freddy.'

She wandered out into the sunlight. There seemed to be nothing she could do, at least not in any practical way. She was a good thrower, she could decorate as well as anyone, but she had been forced to resume her role as daughter of the house, a young lady who had no need to soil her hands with clay. It was a situation she did not much like.

She heard the scrape of wheels against the gravel of the path leading towards the pottery. Her father smiled when he saw her.

'Joe's adapted a chair for me, isn't he brilliant?' He wheeled himself closer. 'You are looking rather grim, what on earth is the matter?'

'Nothing, Father.'

'Then come with me, I'm going to try my

hand at making a pot, something I haven't done in years.'

Llinos felt her face relax into a smile. 'Father, you know you have never been a skilful potter.'

Her father frowned. He had become ill-tempered, easily upset and Llinos realized she must exercise great tact. 'You are a businessman, a man of ideas.'

He sighed. 'You are probably right. I'll only interfere with those who can do the job properly.'

'Well, while you are thinking up ideas, I'd better do some work on the accounts.'

'Llinos, wait. You do like Joe, don't you? His presence in the house doesn't disturb you, does it? Because he's foreign, I mean? I know the people of the row must look at us askance. We not only provide a love nest for an illicit liaison but we accept foreigners into our midst.'

'Father, Joe is more of a gentleman than many men I've met.' She thought briefly of Mr Cimla and shivered. As yet her father had not talked a great deal about the events leading up to his wife's death; it was as if he found the subject too painful to broach and in the circumstances, it was just as well. 'I'm going indoors, I feel cold suddenly,' she said.

The sun was high in the sky as Llinos sat near the open window, the accounting books on the table before her. She looked up as her father wheeled himself into the room. For a moment she was impatient with him; he never seemed to

157

leave her time to herself. Immediately she was ashamed of her thoughts.

'How are you managing our household accounts, Llinos?' her father asked, peering over her shoulder.

'I'm not doing those but, as you've asked, I need more money to run the place. Right now, though, I'm working on the pottery accounts and from what I can see from these figures, matters are improving all the time.'

She pushed the books towards him. 'Eynon's input stopped the decline and your funds give us a measure of security, but the outgoings are a drain on our resources.'

'We must cut costs or we will not be in profit, is that what you are saying?'

'I'm afraid so.' She closed the books. She could not concentrate on figures, not this morning.

'Now, about the household expenditure, our outgoings have increased. Maura is the only one contributing anything to her keep and that is a very small sum. When she has the baby, she won't be able to work, the load will fall on us. The fact is, Father, we are supporting a lot more people now and the household accounts are inevitably rising.'

'You're right. I eat like the proverbial horse myself, and I like the fire built up in spite of the fine weather.'

Her father looked at her thoughtfully. 'I must make sure that Joe earns his keep. Apart from any financial consideration, I don't want him to become bored and leave here. I value his friendship too much for that.' He paused and rubbed his chin.

'Perhaps Binnie and his lady love could find somewhere else to live.' His voice held an edge of irony and Llinos looked at him quickly.

'Don't judge them because they are not married, Father. In any case, they can't leave, they have nowhere to go.'

'Really? Now why am I not surprised by your reaction?'

'Oh, Father, we'll manage but we must make plans, big plans, the sales of our pottery at the market are very good but we are limited to supplying local orders only. What if we approach the larger towns in England and offer our wares there?'

'The larger towns in England are already well supplied with pottery, Llinos.'

Llinos nodded. 'I suppose so.'

'No suppose about it, Mr Wedgwood has a large pottery, his Jasper ware is well known. And then we have the Morton-Edwards pottery on our doorstep, we can't hope to compete with his sort.'

Llinos felt a surge of impatience, her father seemed to be blocking her at every turn. 'Very well, we must concentrate on providing wares that are different in some way. More exclusive perhaps?'

'You might have something there.' Lloyd Savage leaned forward eagerly. 'Joe has some design ideas. Look at these, Llinos.'

He took a sheaf of paper from his pocket and handed them to her. She studied them, head on one side.

'But these are American Indian designs, do you think they would go well on our pottery?'

'Why not?'

'Well, for a start we have been selling only glazed earthenware pots with transfer decoration. If we were to branch out shouldn't the designs be of Welsh origin?'

'If you want to be the same as everyone else, yes, I suppose so. But don't you think that the red clay would lend itself very well to Indian motifs?'

'You could be right. Do you mind if I discuss it with Eynon?'

'Not at all, so long as the boy keeps it to himself. That father of his is not above stealing other people's ideas.'

'Father, Eynon is a clever, sensitive person and I trust him implicitly.'

Her father regarded her steadily. 'Are you in love with him?'

'No, Father, I have no interest in him that way.'

'That, my dear daughter, is just as well. I could not countenance a marriage between the Savage family and one of the Morton-Edwards line.' He paused. 'Oh well, in that case go ahead, discuss your plans with Eynon. I agree with you, in spite of his father's influence, I believe he is a man to be trusted.'

Llinos looked once more at the designs her father had shown her. There was no doubt they were eye-catching. Great eagles soared against jagged rocks, wild horses, manes streaming, roaming the plains. Very much the substance of her dreams, in fact. Had Joe communicated his thoughts to her somehow while she slept?

'I'll talk to him.' She rose. 'In the meantime, Father, you look over the books, see what you make of them.'

He smiled up at her. 'You have become a harridan in my absence, Llinos, do you know that?'

She ruffled his grey hair. 'I've had to grow up very quickly, Father.'

'Aye, if only my letters had got through, your mother's sham marriage would never have taken place. If I ever have the chance to lay hands on that bastard Cimla, I'll kill him.' His voice was harsh and Llinos knew he was making no idle threat.

She went outside and stopped as she saw Joe in the yard chopping wood. Llinos watched him, he was bare to the waist, muscles rippling beneath golden skin. He was so beautiful that Llinos felt a strange desire to weep. He turned as if sensing her presence.

'Joe, talk to me.' She seated herself on one of the neatly cut logs.

'All right.' He smiled slowly, his eyes full of

161

humour, and she stiffened.

'Well, if you're too busy of course.' Now he would think her absurd. 'I thought we might discuss business.' Her tone was sharper than she intended.

'Very well, Miss Savage, I'm listening.' His cultured tones were so at variance with his appearance that Llinos felt she would never get used to him. And yet part of her felt they were bound together, a branch from the same root. It was ridiculous.

She fanned out the drawings. 'These are very good.' She sounded almost grudging. 'I think we might be able to use them if we get a skilled artist to paint them onto the pottery.'

'I can paint the designs myself.' Joe leaned on the axe, his dark hair swinging past his jaw. She looked up at him in surprise.

'Can you?'

Joe sat down beside her and she felt a thrill of exhilaration as his bare arm touched hers. 'I was trained by an excellent master when I was just a boy. It's true I received an education in England but my real education began far earlier than that, when I was on the plains of my homeland.' He looked down at her. 'We made pots there too, you see, though not in kilns the way you do.'

'I don't know much about you, do I, Joe?' Llinos heard the humble entreaty in her voice and regretted it at once. 'Not that your past is any of my business of course.'

162

'Isn't it?' he said gravely.

Llinos rushed into speech to hide her confusion. 'So you think you can paint designs in on glaze? It takes a very subtle touch with colours, they do not always turn out true in the kiln.'

Joe rose to his feet. 'It is entirely up to you, Miss Savage, but I think I should be doing more to earn my keep.'

Llinos felt as though he had overheard her conversation with her father.

'You need never feel obligated to us.' She spoke quickly. 'My father owes you his life.'

But he had returned to his task of chopping the wood, his back turned to her as if for him she had ceased to exist.

Llinos rose and stood for a moment, staring at Joe's naked back. A feeling of inexplicable tenderness washed over her.

'Joe, I feel I know you, I have always known you.'

He glanced briefly at her. 'I know.'

'But why do I feel like this? Aren't you supposed to be all-seeing? Have you no answers for me?'

He dropped the axe and when he turned his face was hard. 'I should have answers because I am a foreigner, is that what you mean?'

She was bewildered by her own feelings. 'I didn't mean that at all. Oh, forget it!'

She hurried across the yard and into the house and stood against the door, panting as though the demons of Hades were after her.

'To hell with you, Joe!' she whispered and then, lifting her hand to tidy her hair, she returned to the room where her father sat, pencil in hand, calmly going over the books.

CHAPTER NINE

'We can't stay here for ever.' Maura looked round the large bedroom knowing that she would never own anything half as grand and yet all she longed for was a little house of her own.

She was beginning to feel the uncomfortable swell of her belly and Maura adjusted her position to accommodate her growing girth.

'I don't see why not.' Binnie was drawing on his shirt, buttoning the flannel around his thin body. Maura ached with love for him, he was her darling and yet he could be so blind.

'We'll be a burden on the Savage family if we stay.' She spoke softly, she didn't want to be overheard. 'That was part of the trouble, really, living in someone else's house meant that they had no privacy.

'We will not!' he said. 'I do an honest day's toil in the pottery. Ben is getting older, he's talking about hanging up his boots. When he leaves there will be even more work for me.'

Maura nodded. 'I expect you are right.' She eased her feet into her shoes. Soon she would begin the walk downhill to the vicar's house in Caerpistyll Street. The reverend father was good to her, but he would not want her around the place once the evidence of her sin began to show.

'But I would love a little house of our own.' She saw him shake his head and momentarily anger flared through her, he was so obstinate. Impending motherhood had extinguished much of her fire but at times like this it flickered into life again.

'How could we afford a house of our own?' he asked. He sank onto the bed and pulled on his boots.

'We'd manage.' She would see to it. She frowned, she had learned early that it was the womenfolk of the family who took the initiative when it came to planning a future. 'I shall ask Father Duncan if he knows of somewhere to rent.'

'But why?' Binnie leaned forward, his arms resting on his knees. 'We're all right here, I tell you.'

She rose and put her arms around him. 'We have to leave because our child is growing in here.' She pressed her stomach to his face. 'Can't you hear his heart beat, hear him breathe? He will have fine lungs and he will cry in the night and sure the whole household will be up in arms. Is that what you want for our future, Binnie?'

'I want what's best for us.' He hugged her. 'I love you, Maura, you know that.'

'But not enough to put a ring on my finger?'

'Now don't start that again. I told you in the beginning that I didn't want to be married. I'm sorry, Maura, having the baby was your idea not mine. We were all right as we were and I won't be trapped into anything against my will.'

'Having the baby was your fault as well as mine!' Maura retorted. 'What was I supposed to do to stop it?'

'I don't know!' Binnie said. 'That's a woman's job. Now go to work if you're going and stop nagging me.'

The argument that was about to start between them had been repeated many times and Maura was tired of it. Binnie would never see things her way, she might just as well hold her peace.

'I'm going, don't worry.' She moved towards him suddenly repentant and lifted her face for his kiss. He bent towards her and she touched his cheek with her fingertips.

'Promise you'll love me always,' she whispered, nuzzling her face into his neck, prolonging the moment of intimacy. He did not reply.

The dew was still on the grass as Maura walked away from the row. The singing of the birds was so sweet it brought tears to her eyes. But then, since the onset of her pregnancy, many things brought tears to her eyes. Motherhood was changing her, she was becoming soft. But not so soft that she would not fight for her future.

The sun was higher now and mist rose from the grass verges. Above her the sky was blue, washed by the rain of the night. It was a beautiful, breathtaking morning and Maura felt glad to be alive and in love.

The hill sloped towards where the church stood like a sentinel, tall among the squat houses.

She saw her sister Mary in the distance and called to her.

Mary half turned and then hurried away and Maura bit her lip. 'Mary!' How could her own sister turn her back on her? It was all Dadda's fault, he had forbidden any of the family to speak to her.

Her father was angry because Binnie Dundee had got her with child. She could accept that — any father would be angry — but to throw a daughter out of the house, that was not a sign of the Christian charity preached by the good vicar.

'Good morning to you, Maura.' Father Duncan smiled as he opened the door. 'And how are you feeling this fine day?'

'Well enough, Father.' She moved into the kitchen. 'Sorry I'm a bit late, I'll get the eggs and bacon cooking right away.'

'Sounds like a good idea.' The vicar caught her chin and tipped her face up. 'Are those tears trembling on your golden lashes, child?'

Maura brushed at her eyes impatiently. 'My sister Mary just turned her back on me, that can't be the right thing to do, not between blood relatives, can it?'

'Ah well, child, folks takes a bit of knowing.' He moved to the large pantry and took out a bottle of cordial. 'Have a little drink of this before you start work, it will set you up.'

'I know I've sinned . . .' she began, but he waved his hands at her.

'Hush, now, keep all that nonsense for your prayers. The Lord knows that you are a good girl at heart. Weak of flesh perhaps but then those who are without sin are the only ones allowed to cast any stones. Seen any stones flying about the streets lately, have you?'

Maura laughed. 'Father Duncan, you are so good for me.' Maura cut several thick slices of bacon and laid them in the pan. The sizzling sound and the mouthwatering aroma of frying bacon filled the room, drawing the newly ordained Father Martin into the kitchen.

Martin was pale-skinned with large innocent eyes. He reminded Maura of a picture of cherubs she had seen in a book once. He was nice enough but ineffectual and Maura could not see him ever running his own church.

Maura made sure the plates were well filled with bacon, eggs and fried bread before making a huge pot of tea. The two men ate in silent appreciation, Father Martin holding out his plate for more.

Maura moved silently around the kitchen, fetching the bowl from under the sink ready for the dishes.

'That was delicious, Maura, you'll make some man a good wife one day.' Martin leaned back in his chair patting his stomach.

Maura felt her colour rise and the old vicar shook his head.

'You must forgive Martin, he wouldn't know tact if it got up and bit him with his own teeth.'

Father Martin raised his head and blinked his eyes rapidly. 'What? What did I say wrong now?'

'Go back to sleep,' the vicar said good-naturedly. 'Most of life passes you by when you are awake so where's the difference?'

'Can I ask you something, Father?' Maura said. The vicar frowned.

'So long as it's not going to be a long job, I've work to do in the parish.' His words might have sounded hard to anyone else, but Maura had known Father Duncan since she was four years old and she was used to his ways.

'I want to rent a house,' she said, resting her hands on the table, aware of the ache in her legs.

The vicar shook his head. 'Haven't heard of anywhere going cheap, or anywhere expensive for that matter.'

Maura sighed. 'It was just a thought.'

'I know of somewhere.' Martin sat up in his chair, happy to be the centre of attention for once. 'It's a small cottage up at Cwmbwrla. It needs a bit of work but anyone halfway handy could do it themselves.'

'Oh, Father!' Maura tried to swallow her excitement. 'Will you put in a word for me, please?'

Martin preened. 'I will, colleen, that I will.' He rose to his feet. 'I was talking to the landlord only yesterday, an old gent on a stick. Moved in with his daughter. He told me about it as he locked up the house. Didn't know what to do with the place, so he claimed.'

'What was the name of this old gent?' Father Duncan asked. 'And where does his daughter live?'

'Oh, I don't know where his daughter lives.' Martin looked dismayed. Maura felt her happiness evaporate.

'Well, what's the man's name?' The vicar repeated his question.

'I remember that, it was Christmas Pryce. Well, isn't it a good thing I have a memory for names?'

'Don't worry, Maura, you get on with your work and I'll sort this out for you,' Father Duncan said.

Martin pursed his mouth and it looked to Maura like a bag with a draw string which had been tied too tightly. She resisted the silly urge to laugh.

'Thank you, Father. I'll get on with the beds.' She left the kitchen and climbed the stairs slowly. She was becoming fat, a sow with bloated paps. How could anyone love her like this? Fear coursed through her. What if Binnie should refuse to come with her to a rented house, even if she managed to get one?

She stood in the bedroom, staring out of the neatly curtained window, and watched as the vicars left the house, cassocks moving in the breeze, giving the impression that they were gliding rather than walking. Maura closed her eyes and said a quick prayer before making up the beds.

171

Joe climbed to the top of Poppets Hill and sat staring out at the panorama of the town and beyond to where the sea stretched as far as the eye could see. It was good to be in the fresh autumn air, to feel once more like a free spirit. Within the confines of the pottery buildings, he was beginning to feel caged.

He should be flying across the plains with the eagles, running with the wild buffalo. He longed for the sounds and scents of the place where he was born and yet he knew he would not leave, his destiny was here with a girl called Llinos.

Nightingale or maybe Linnet, that was what her name meant in English. He had asked the old man who fired the ovens to translate it for him and Joe had been enchanted with the reply. She was a bird of flight and beauty, his Firebird. It was an appropriate name for the woman he would spend his life with.

Llinos did not know it yet, at least not with the conscious part of her mind. Perhaps, deep down in the recesses of her soul, there was some hint of what was to come. She had recognized him at once just as he had recognized her. And yet she could not identify the feeling. She had never met him except perhaps in the dreamtime world.

'Afternoon. Taking the air, are you?' The voice was familiar and Joe turned, without surprise, to see Eynon Morton-Edwards coming towards him.

'It's beautiful up here,' Joe said. 'You can see for miles from the vantage point of the hill.'

Eynon sank onto the grass beside Joe. 'You are an odd mixture, old chap.'

'I expect I am, half native, half white man, you could say it was an odd mixture.'

'I didn't mean that, well not quite,' Eynon said. 'You speak in cultured accents and yet you look as if you are . . . poised for flight.'

'Fanciful but not too far from the truth,' Joe said. 'You are very perceptive.'

'I know that the people of the row view you with suspicion,' Eynon said. 'They are startled by the darkness of your hair and the red gold of your skin.' He smiled. 'And I think the fact that you are so obviously well-educated adds to the confusion.'

Eynon sighed. 'And then of course there's me. If you are viewed with suspicion then I am far worse. A misfit, a weakling. I don't think the townspeople have thought of the correct set of adjectives to apply to me.'

'Then we must be friends,' Joe said. He looked directly at Eynon. 'As long as we are not rivals, that is.'

'You mean for the affections of Miss Savage? Well, you know I'm very fond of Llinos, *very* fond and surely you can't seriously see yourself as a suitor . . .' He stopped speaking as Joe held up his hand.

'Don't say any more. We shall not quarrel.'

After a moment, Eynon nodded. 'Agreed. If

you love her I'm sorry but I think I'm in love with her too.'

'Then together we can do what is best for her.'

After a moment's silence, Eynon changed the subject. 'The pottery is getting back on its feet, sales of the Indian designs are booming, I believe.'

Joe rose without answering and moved to the brow of the hill. On his skin the breeze was soft and warm and tasted salt from the sea. Wales was a lovely place but one day, perhaps, he would take Llinos to the plains of Dakota where she could taste real freedom. He had left America as little more than a child but his roots were there and they drew him back.

'You are far away.' Eynon's voice drifted into Joe's consciousness and he ignored it. He wanted to stay within himself, inside his own thoughts, to quieten the restless spirits that plagued him when he did not spend time alone.

'Sorry, old chap, I'm disturbing you,' Eynon said. There was something in the tone of Eynon's voice that touched Joe, a pain, a loneliness that could find no expression in words.

He relaxed. 'Not at all. Come along, let's walk across the hills to the west of the town, away from the stink of the manufactories.'

They fell into step, side by side, and Joe walked as he had done as a child, his feet connecting with the earth but lightly, drawing from beneath him the energy of hidden worlds and from the sky above him the fire of the spirits.

It worried him sometimes that he was this dual personality. On one hand, a perfect English gentleman and on the other, a primitive. He glanced at Eynon, who was content to walk silently at his side.

'So I seem strange to you, do I, old chap?' He consciously mimicked Eynon's own form of address.

Eynon was too honest to prevaricate. 'You do,' he said and then felt compelled to enlarge on his rather bald statement. 'You are strange in a fascinating way.' He paused for a moment. 'You have a quality of strength, of oneness with the whole universe, that lesser souls like me can only envy.'

Joe nodded. 'I look foreign?'

'In a way. Your hair is blue-black and longer and straighter than is worn by most men. You do not look foreign so much as exotic and different and yet walking along the Welsh coastlands with you, I feel you are more part of the place than I am.' Eynon sighed. 'I am a sad case, I fear, Joe. My emotions are too close to the surface.'

'No emotion is ever lost. It can be channelled into good use, one way or another.'

'But my emotions are so mixed. I've quarrelled with my father and that worries me. But it's no use, we just don't get on at all. I've moved out, found a house of my own. I hope I've done the right thing.'

'I'm sure you have. And it's not so unusual

for father and son not to see eye to eye. I don't get on with my father either. Rather, he does not get on with me. He has spawned a heathen, a hybrid, so he tells me, and how can I disagree with what is true?'

'And yet he took care of you?' Eynon said.

'He took care of me in the material sense, yes. In the spiritual and emotional sense, he repudiated me.'

'We have a lot in common then.' Eynon sounded as if the thought brought him comfort.

'I'm sure we have a great deal in common.' Joe half smiled. 'Look, there's a coffee-house over there, on the corner. Shall we have a drink?'

'Are you sure you want to?' Eynon asked. 'Being seen with me, I mean. I'm not popular, I'm thought of as odd, a man who likes to paint instead of indulge in commerce.'

'Well, we are good company for each other, I should think.' Joe led the way inside the gloomy interior of the coffee-house. The aromatic smell of ground beans filled the room and Joe sniffed appreciatively.

'Good,' he said and took a seat near the mullioned windows. 'The coffee here will be hot and strong, just as I like it.'

Eynon sat opposite him, turning his back on the room. 'I hope no-one makes a scene,' he said.

'Why should anyone make a scene?' Joe spoke loudly and a few heads turned to look his way. Eynon glanced nervously over his shoulder.

'They do, sometimes. I no longer frequent public bars for that reason. In drink, some men lose their senses and become abusive.'

'But coffee does not have that effect, surely?'

Eynon laughed mirthlessly. 'It doesn't take much to incense some men.'

The coffee as Joe had predicted was hot and strong. 'Too much of this will send the nerves hopping,' Joe said, looking into his mug.

'What a strange thing to say.' Eynon leaned forward, elbows on the table. 'What makes you think that?'

'It's a fact. This stuff is a stimulant, it sends the pulses racing.' Joe smiled. 'It has the same effect on me as being near Llinos does. Well almost.'

Eynon reached in his pocket for his pipe. 'Anything to say about tobacco, old chap?'

'Breathe in any weed you want to,' Joe said. 'It's none of my business. At home, my people smoke pipes too. It's supposed to be a ceremonial act but I suspect that it's one that brings pleasure.'

The rise and fall of the voices in the room was soothing. Joe leaned back in his chair and though his eyes were open, he saw nothing of his surroundings. His thoughts were of Llinos, her hair, dark like the wing of a raven, her eyes deep and dark. When they rested on him, they were lit from within.

He wanted her badly. Now, even thinking of her set his loins on fire but he had learned

177

patience at an early age. He had learned too that waiting enhanced the prize when it was won.

Joe became aware of a voice talking close to him. 'The new slavey for the Morton-Edwards family, are you?'

Joe focused his gaze on the man who stood behind Eynon's chair, staring down at them, a sneer pulling down the corners of his mouth.

'Talking to me?' Joe said easily.

'Not talking to the wall, am I?'

'You could be for all the sense you are making.'

The colour rose to the man's face. 'Don't be insolent to me, you half-breed.'

'Come on, let's leave.' Eynon attempted to rise but the man held him down, his well-manicured hands pressing on Eynon's shoulders.

'Might I ask your name?' Joe sounded so affable that the man blinked rapidly.

'What do you want my name for?'

'Afraid to give it? Are you one of these people who hide behind anonymity when you insult people?'

'James Clarence at your service.' The man half bowed which seemed a ludicrous gesture in the circumstances.

'That's all right then.' Joe rose to his feet. He knew he was a tall, well-muscled man but he knew too that it was the set of his face that made James Clarence take an involuntary step backwards.

'I just like to know who it is I am about to hit,' Joe said easily.

'No need for violence.' The colour had receded from James Clarence's face. 'Can't you take a bit of good-natured chaffing?'

'Before I hit you, I will give you the opportunity to withdraw your ill-conceived remarks and apologize for inflicting your unwelcome presence on me and my friend here.'

'Withdraw? Apologize?'

'Good, you know the words. Do you understand them or should I explain?'

'I . . . I . . .' The man was blustering.

Joe leaned forward. 'Come along, old man. For someone who claims to be so superior to others, you do not seem to have a very good command of language.'

James Clarence admitted defeat. 'If my words caused offence, I withdraw them and apologize.' He bowed again, a mere inclining of his head, and moved away. Joe resumed his seat.

'There are some ill-bred people in here, Eynon.' Joe's voice rang loudly in the now silent room. 'I suggest we drink our coffee and seek out a more refined set of companions.'

Once they were outside, Eynon sighed hugely. 'Wow!' he said. 'Didn't you make that obnoxious Clarence look foolish? I've never seen the man with his tail between his legs before.'

'You must learn to take care of yourself,' Joe said. 'I will teach you some Indian tricks so that you can fight your battles. But very often, words are the best weapons. You have them, use them.'

'We are not all strong like you, Joe,' Eynon said.

Joe tapped his head. 'Strength begins up here.' His hand moved to his heart. 'Courage is here, in your heart.' His hand rested briefly on his stomach. 'Here is your powerhouse, your fire. Keep it burning, Eynon, or you will be swamped by life.'

'I can see that you are going to change a great many things around here, Joe,' Eynon said. 'I will take you up on your offer to teach me to defend myself but for now, if you don't mind, I'm going back home.' He paused. 'Give my love to Llinos. And, Joe, thank you.'

'For what?'

'Just for being a good friend.'

Joe watched Eynon as he walked away, hands thrust into his pockets, his shoulders slumped. There was a great sadness about him and if Joe's instincts were correct, there would be a great deal more sadness to come Eynon's way.

He turned to follow the course of the river and his spirits lightened. Soon he would be with Llinos, he would drink in her beauty knowing that one day she would be his.

CHAPTER TEN

Llinos crossed the yard, stepping aside as a line of clay carriers moved past her. At the door of the potters' shed she watched one of the women wedging the clay. The girl was a stranger to Llinos, newly taken on, but she seemed to know her business. She lifted a square of clay above her head and dashed it down onto the wooden slab in front of her. She repeated the process until the clay was completely free of air.

'Morning,' Llinos said. The girl turned. She was older than Llinos had first thought, her face was drawn and pale.

'Mornin', Miss Savage,' the girl said. She continued with her work without pause and Llinos, knowing she was disturbing the girl's rhythm, turned away.

All around her was the hustle and bustle of a thriving pottery and Llinos viewed it with mixed feelings. Times had been hard when the pottery was short staffed but she had been busy, in charge with no time to think. Now, somehow, she felt redundant.

She was glad her father had returned from the war, there was no question about that. She loved him dearly and she admired the stoic way he dealt with his disabilities. Sometimes, the wounds on his legs gave him pain, the skin breaking down into open sores. She had seen Joe make a paste from a mixture of boiled roots and herbs and coat the red raw flesh with the soothing balm. Some days, her father would be fit enough to oversee the work in the pottery, at times he would even take charge of the accounts, but much of the time he just sat silently lost in a world of his own.

Joe was so good with him, so patient. When Lloyd needed him, he was there. She swallowed hard. Joe. She was in love with him. He had not encouraged her feelings or even acknowledged them but sometimes she caught him looking at her as if he was trying to see inside her head.

He was a beautiful man, handsome, intelligent and different to anyone she had ever met. It was just a foolish dream, she knew that. Even if by some miracle Joe returned her love, it was an impossible match. One of which her father would never approve.

She moved to the paint shop and breathed in the familiar smells of oil, paint and lead. A line of pots stood on the long table in preparation for decorating. The printer, a man in a long apron over greasy trousers, glanced up at her briefly and nodded. Almost without pause, he continued to lay his colour on a metal slab which he was heating on the stove.

He reached for a pad of cloth and began to transfer the colour from the slab to the copper-plate engraving with the deftness of a practiced printer. Llinos knew the process by heart, she had used it herself many times. She watched as the printer took a wet piece of tissue paper and laid it on the plate. He scraped away the excess paint with a blade and wiped it back onto the slab. He was clearly not a man to waste good paint.

He took the copper plate, covered it with paper and passed it under a heavy roller covered with thick flannel. Llinos could not count the number of times she had watched in wonder as the pattern came out of the roller fixed to the paper.

'Miss Savage, could you help me?' The voice was subdued; one of the girls from the orphanage stared at Llinos, her eyes large in her pale face. She shifted awkwardly on the bench, holding a pattern up for inspection.

'I think I've made a mistake with this scroll by here.' She sounded near to tears. 'Have I ruined it?'

Before Llinos could speak, one of the older women came forward and snatched the pattern from the girl.

'You stupid child! Can't you get anything right? I'm going to have a fine job transferring this mess onto a pot, aren't I?'

'Let me see.' Llinos might be young but in her good gown and hair in ringlets she was every inch the daughter of the owner and as such must be obeyed.

'It will be all right. A scroll missing will not be noticed.' Llinos returned the pattern to the woman. 'What's your name?'

'Mrs Smedley. Good transferer, me, but I can't work with that rubbish. This pattern won't come out proper, like. It will be unbalanced, anyone can see that.'

She stabbed angrily at the paper with a padded stump of cloth and the paper pattern was torn.

'Look.' Llinos was determined to keep her temper, though it was easy to see that Mrs Smedley was deliberately being difficult. She picked up the bowl the young girl had been decorating and placed the pattern onto the surface. 'You must dab, like this, sharply but not fiercely and don't rub, that's what tears the paper.'

Llinos demonstrated with expert hands and then handed the bowl to Mrs Smedley. The woman shot her a glance of sheer venom.

'Thank you, miss, I see what I was doing wrong now.' Her voice rang with sarcasm. 'Here, Lily,' she addressed the girl in sullen tones. 'Take this pot to the barrel of water over there and get the paper washed off. Try to do something right, for a change.'

Mrs Smedley looked directly at Llinos. 'I hear we are having some more of those new heathen patterns to work with,' she said in a deceptively mild tone of voice.

'If you mean the American Indian designs you are quite right, they seem to have become quite popular.' Llinos faced the woman eye to eye.

She was suddenly aware of how tall she had grown in the past months. She was no longer a child, she was a woman with the longings and urges of a woman. Urges that were directed to the most unsuitable of men.

'Don't know what the folks of Swansea make of it all, eagles and strange cattle prancing over their pots. Not used to it, see?'

'The fact is, the pots are selling.' Llinos paused, attempting to moderate the sharpness of her tone. 'At least we are providing something different.' She added a note of caution.

'If we are to compete with the bigger potteries across the country we will all have to pull together or we'll all be out of work.'

Llinos left the paint shop and retraced her steps across the yard. There seemed no place for her now within the pottery sheds. Everything had been organized efficiently without her. It was a strange feeling.

She saw Watt carrying a bowl of scraps on his head, stumbling over the rough ground. 'Watt! Isn't that a heavy load for you?'

'No, miss, it's easy. I'm taking it to the bins ready for the horse and cart.' He grinned cheerfully and for a moment, Llinos felt a flicker of regret for the difficult months after her mother's death when she had tried to keep the pottery alive on a shoestring.

'Well take care you don't work too hard. And, Watt, I'm Llinos, remember? No need to call me miss.' Llinos returned to the house and hung her apron behind the kitchen door. The sun was shining in through the windows, there was a dreaming silence about the house as if everything in it was asleep.

Then she heard sounds of movement, the creak of her father's chair as he manoeuvred it along the passage and into the room he had converted into an office. Somehow, the bond between herself and her father was not as strong as it should be. He quarrelled with her often, finding fault with what she wore, how she spoke. Worst of all, he criticized the way she had been running the pottery in his absence, it just was not fair of him.

Still, she should remember what he had been through and humour him. Perhaps she should find out if he needed anything. As she put her hand on the latch, the door sprung open. She made an involuntary move backwards as she came face to face with Joe. His dark hair was tied back from his face. There was a smudge of paint on his cheek. It was clear he had been working on the Indian designs.

His sleeves were rolled up and the skin of his arms was red gold in the sunlight. She breathed in the scent of him even while she tried to appear unmoved by his nearness.

'Your father would like something to drink.' He moved past her towards the deep pantry. 'There should be some cordial left in the jug.' He looked at her over his shoulder. 'You really should get help with the housework. The place

186

is too big for you to manage alone.'

Suddenly she felt anger so intense she thought it would choke her. She lashed out at Joe as though he was the source of all her frustration. And, perhaps, he was.

'Oh, is it?' She felt her cheeks grow hot. 'Well, how kind of you to say so. I managed quite well before you came here, remember? In any case, I don't appreciate being told what to do in my own house.'

He half smiled. 'Do you wish to waste your talents standing over a stove or scrubbing floors? Is that your ambition in life, Miss Savage?'

'Don't patronize me.' She knew she was being ridiculous but now she had begun, she did not know how to stop. 'You come here, a stranger and take charge of everything.' She gestured towards the cup in his hand. 'You don't even leave the smallest of jobs for me.'

Her anger evaporated suddenly. She sank down into a chair and covered her face with her hands. 'I have no place here any more, I am no use to anyone.'

She stiffened as she felt his hands rest on her shoulders. She was aware of him as he stood behind her. She felt the heat of his fingers through the thinness of her gown. She wanted to turn and fling herself into his arms.

'Your destiny is shaped for you,' he said. 'Just as surely as the patterns are shaped on the clay, so your life will follow its own design.'

She rose from the chair and stood close, looking up at him. He read her easily and shook his head.

'The time is not yet right, Llinos. Be patient.' He touched her cheek lightly with the tips of his fingers and then he turned and left the room, closing the door quietly behind him.

There were tears in her eyes and they fell hot and angry between her fingers. She wanted to scream and cry, she wanted to run in the breeze to be caught and held by Joe and to be pressed into the sweet grass. She wanted . . . she wanted the impossible.

'I shan't be coming here for much longer, Father.' Maura hung the drying-cloths on the line above the mantelpiece and stared outside to where a pale sun was silvering the leaves of the conifers.

'I know.' The vicar put his hand on her shoulder. 'You need to conserve your energy for that new life you have in there.'

'And I need to save you embarrassment,' Maura said drily. Father Duncan smiled.

'I'm past being embarrassed at my time of life, Maura.'

'Still, people will talk.'

'So they will, but have things ever been different? Folks will make it up if they have no real gossip to exchange.' He patted her gently.

'I'm sorry that offer of a rented house came to nought, child.'

'I wasn't surprised,' Maura said. 'The Pryces

are a good church-going family, they wouldn't want to give a home to a fallen woman.'

'Tosh! They did not think you would pay them the high rent they were asking, that is the be-all and end-all of it.'

'But I must get out of Pottery House before the baby is born. The Savage family have been good to me for Binnie's sake, but I can't expect them to support me and my child.'

Father Duncan pushed the kettle onto the flames and perched on the edge of the table.

'Will Binnie not marry you, Maura?'

She shook her head. 'I won't lower my pride to ask him again, Father. Please, I don't want to talk about it.'

'Right then, let's change the subject. Tell me about this man, this so-called heathen the folks of the town are so busy talking about.'

'Joe? He's not a heathen.'

'But he is a foreigner?' the vicar persisted.

'Sure he's a foreigner — in some ways.'

'Well, he is not a Welshman nor yet an Irishman nor even an Englishman so what is he?'

'He's half American Indian.' Maura smiled. 'His father is a rich English gentleman; he had Joe educated in a fine school. And whatever else he is, Joe is wise and gentle and beautiful and if I was not head-over-heels in love with Binnie I would throw myself at his feet, so I would.'

Father Duncan chuckled. 'Not advisable in your condition, my dear child. How does he speak, then?'

'He speaks like an English gentleman,' Maura said. 'He has a voice like a crystal stream falling over rocks made of diamonds.'

'Well, I can see you are smitten.'

Maura looked at the vicar soberly. 'Joe is a good man, he saved the life of Captain Savage and brought him home. He has made a chair with wheels so that the captain can move about the house and when the captain is sick, Joe tends him as if he was a baby.'

'No-one can ask more of any man,' Father Duncan said. 'But I have heard that the Indian goes into trances, conjures up spirits of his ancestors, worships the buffalo, that sort of thing. If the man does that then is he not a heathen?'

'I don't know about that.' Maura was on the defensive. 'He does not go to church, not any church, but he is a very . . . a very . . .'

'Spiritual man?' the vicar supplied.

Maura nodded. 'Sure an' that's just what I would call him — spiritual. And Father, if Joe worships God in his own way, surely that's his right?'

'Ah, I was displaying my idle curiosity, I didn't know we were going to have a deep theological discussion.' Father Duncan pushed himself upright and made a pot of tea. 'Sit down, child, let us talk a little more before you go on your way home. I may be a man of the cloth but I too get lonely for company at times.'

Maura obediently sat at the table, easing her legs apart to accommodate her enlarged stomach. The baby kicked inside her and she touched her belly in wonder.

'You have a lively boy in there, it would seem,' the vicar said easily. 'I know it's a sore subject but what if I talked to your man, asked him to come to church and marry you before the birth of your child?'

'He does not want to be tied down, at least that's what he says. He tells me the baby is my fault and says that at least he's standing by me.' She had been half expecting a lecture and she did not need it, however kindly it was meant.

'Do you want me to have a word with him, then?' Father Duncan said.

Maura shook her head. 'I'll speak to him again myself, I promise.'

'Make it soon, Maura, that little one is not going to wait much longer. Now, let's drink our tea and talk about something else, shall we?'

Later, as Maura made her way uphill towards Pottery Row, she wondered how she could persuade Binnie to marry her. It was not so much the ring on her finger, although that was important too, it was the fact that she did not want her child born out of wedlock. Once a bastard, in the eyes of the world he would always be a bastard.

She shivered, the day had grown sunless and cold and she suddenly felt like crying. She belonged to no-one, she had no home of her own and soon she was bringing an illegitimate child into the world. How did she get herself into this mess? But she knew well enough: her flesh was too weak and her love of life too strong.

As she reached the edge of the town, Maura saw a group of women standing on the corner near Bristow's boot and shoe shop. They fell silent, staring at her in open curiosity. One of them spoke, not even attempting to lower her voice.

'She's one of them Irish peasants from Green-hill. Got herself with child and no ring on her finger, ought to be ashamed.'

As Maura walked on, head in the air, she heard the woman call out.

'Whore! Not fit to be seen by decent folks.'

Tears came then, hot and burning. Silently, they ran down her face and into her mouth. She stumbled round the corner and into Pottery Row, anxious to be indoors, out of the sight of prying eyes.

'Maura, what's wrong?' Llinos caught her by the shoulders. 'Tell me, Maura, what's happened?' Suddenly Maura was sobbing as though her heart would break.

'Come inside,' Llinos urged. 'We'll have a nice hot cup of tea.' She guided Maura into the kitchen. 'Everything will look better when you've had a little cry.'

'No, it won't,' Maura said. 'Some women in the street, they called me a whore and they are right. I'm going to give birth to a bastard and all because I fell in love with a man who will not marry me whatever I say. How can I bear

192

it, how can I walk out with my child and face the world?'

'To hell with them!' Llinos was surprised by her own bitterness. 'They talked about my mother and Mr Cimla and made things ten times worse. Look, Maura, as long as the gossips are not paying for your keep then what you do with your life is none of their business.'

Maura rubbed at her eyes. 'Maybe, but don't you make the same mistake as I've made, miss.' Her voice was thick with tears. 'Loving a man can tear you to pieces and giving in to your passion without thought brings you nothing but trouble.'

She took the handkerchief Llinos offered. 'But you are sensible, miss. You have been well brought up and you would not let yourself down as I have.'

'I am no better than you so don't be silly. We are all capable of making mistakes.'

'I know you are in love with Joe but you wouldn't be so daft as to go to his bed, would you?'

She saw the colour rise in Llinos's face. 'I'm sorry if I'm being forward, but being in love myself I know the signs.'

Llinos walked towards the window, her back to the room, and Maura could tell by the squareness of her shoulders that Llinos wanted her to mind her own business.

'Look,' Llinos said. 'When Binnie finishes his shift on the ovens, I'll talk to him.'

'I don't know if it would do any good. I
don't think Binnie would take kindly to anyone,
well . . .'

'Interfering?' Llinos smiled. 'Me and Binnie
go back a long way, I think he will listen to me.
I promise I'll be tactful.'

Maura swallowed her tears, she knew Llinos
meant to be kind but talking to Binnie might
only make him angry.

She rose to her feet. 'I am looking for a place
for me and Binnie to rent, miss. I'd like you to
know that. We don't want to be a burden to
you for ever.'

'Oh, good heavens, Maura!' Llinos turned to
face her. 'I wouldn't hear of you leaving, not in
your condition.' She paused. 'I know I said you
had to find a place before the baby came, well
now I've changed my mind. You can stay until
you find something suitable. I understand your
wish to have a house of your own and I'll even
help you find one, but first let us get your baby
safely into the world.' She rested her hand on
Maura's arm. 'You can't be alone, not at a time
like this. Anyway' — she spoke more briskly —
'until I employ some servants you are the only
other woman in the house. If you leave I'll be
alone with all the menfolk. That would set
tongues wagging.'

'I never thought of that.' Maura smiled, she
knew that Llinos Savage's future was secure, her
father had come home and he was rich enough
to employ a house full of women servants if he

chose. There was no question of the privileged Miss Savage being compromised. Still, Maura would be grateful to stay. She did not want to be alone at the birth time when it came.

'Thank you for being so kind,' she said but the words almost choked her.

The next morning, as Llinos strolled along the roadway into town, she was remembering Maura's words with a prickling of fear. The Irish girl was right, to love an unsuitable man was to look for trouble. She stopped outside Prosser's coffee-house and peered inside. Eynon was there before her as she had known he would be. He was nothing if not punctual.

He rose and joined her in the street. 'Morning, Llinos.' He smiled down at her as she linked her arm with his. 'You are inviting gossip, you know.'

'I don't give a fig for gossip,' she said. 'Come on, let's sit in the park in full view of anyone who cares to look.'

'I haven't seen you for almost a week,' Llinos said and Eynon nodded.

'I know, but there is no need for me to come up to the pottery these days, is there? My little investment is paying dividends even while I sit here enjoying this fine winter's day.' He paused. 'In any case, Joe is always around and I don't see any fun in torturing myself.'

'I don't know what you mean,' Llinos said huffily.

'I mean I see Joe as a rival for your affections, Llinos. Surely you are not so blind that you can't see we both want you?'

'Since when? You and I are friends, that's all.'

'You must like me a little, Llinos, otherwise you would not be sitting here with me.'

'I wanted to ask a favour of a friend, Eynon, that's why I asked you to meet me.'

'I guessed so. Things getting too much for you at the pottery, are they?'

'Just the opposite. I have not enough to do. I feel useless in my own home.'

'You need some servants up at Pottery House now that the funds are coming in. You would have your work cut out then, seeing they do their work properly.'

'Nonsense!' she said impatiently. 'Supervising servants is not what I want. Joe thinks the same idea of me as you do, he believes I have no ambition.'

'Do you have ambition, Llinos?'

'I don't know. All I know is potting, it's what I was born to, what I love. But now there are skilled workers in every department of the pottery and all I can do is stand by and watch.'

'If you don't like your life then you must change it.' Eynon spoke quietly. 'I did. I moved out of my father's house and since then my life has been much more peaceful.'

Llinos put her hand on his arm. 'I know it took a great deal of courage to buy a house of your own and I admire you for making the break.

196

But admit it, Eynon, you are lonely sometimes, aren't you?'

'I can't deny that.' He stared down at her ruefully. 'The house echoes with emptiness. What I need is a family to fill it.'

Llinos smiled. 'That leads me very nicely to what it is I wanted to talk to you about.'

'So it is not the love of your life, then? You are not here to talk about Joe?'

Llinos pushed at his shoulder. 'No, I am not! No, it is not about love, at least not my own. Are you going to be quiet and listen?'

'I'll be quiet.'

'It's about Maura and Binnie. Once the baby is born, Maura will need a job where she can take the baby with her. No, don't speak, let me finish. The little family will also need a home, somewhere they can spread out a little.'

She smiled up at him. 'Now your house is a very large one and at the moment there is just you in it, except for the servants. Do you begin to see what I am getting at?'

Eynon laughed. 'I get the message loud and clear. You want me to give a home and a job to the little Irish girl, her lover and her illegitimate child. Don't you think I invite enough gossip as it is?'

'Oh, I didn't think of that.'

Eynon put his hand over hers. 'I'm joking. I think it is a great idea. My house will be full, I will have the little family that I long for albeit an adopted one and I will have someone to oversee the mundane household tasks.'

Llinos sank back against the wooden slats of the bench. 'I thought it would be a good idea.'

'Have you spoken to the happy couple about this?' Eynon asked with raised eyebrows.

'No.' Llinos sighed. 'I thought I would talk to you first, see if you would agree.'

'Very kind of you. I wouldn't put it past you to turn up with a cart full of possessions and a list of my orders written large. Know something, Llinos, you are a formidable lady.'

'Am I?' Llinos pulled a face. 'Well, if I am, a fat lot of good it does me.'

'Look, now we've sorted out everyone else's problems, what about yours?'

'I agree with what you said earlier, Eynon. If I don't like my life, I must change it. The pity is I don't know what I want to change it for.'

'What is your greatest strength?' Eynon asked. 'Is it making the pots, decorating the pots or the administration of the entire enterprise? What do you really want to do?'

'I suppose I want to oversee all those things. I think my ambition is to make the Savage Pottery as well run and as successful as your father's pottery.'

'And I thought you said you had no ambition!'

'No, Joe said that. He was trying to tell me the same thing as you but in a different way. I've done a great deal of growing up over the past months,' Llinos said.

Eynon squeezed her hand. 'You have become

a woman, no, a lady, since that first time I saw you.'

He lifted her fingers and kissed them. 'I love you, Llinos, do you know that?'

Llinos rose from the seat. 'Come on, enough flattery. It's getting chilly sitting here. Let's walk.'

They left the park and Llinos thought with a tinge of wistfulness that to anyone watching they might have looked like a happy couple deeply in love. Was she destined to always meet men who were unsuitable in one way or another?

She smiled up at Eynon and he, unaware of her thoughts, smiled back. She slipped her hand through his arm and sighed inwardly. One day, perhaps, she would forget Joe and fall in love with another man but somehow, she did not believe it.

CHAPTER ELEVEN

'You should have talked this over with me, Llinos.'

Binnie was staring at her across the kitchen table, his face flushed. It was clear he was very angry.

'You and me been good workmates, good friends,' he continued, 'but that doesn't give you the right to run my life.'

'I'm sorry, Binnie, I didn't think . . . I was only trying to help.'

'Do you want me and Maura out of here so bad that you'd push us in with that toffee-nosed fop?'

'It's not like that,' Llinos protested. 'Anyway, I thought you liked Eynon.'

'He's all right for a Morton-Edwards but living with him, well that's something different. Anyway, for a start, I don't want to get married.'

'Well you can be unmarried at Eynon's house just as well as you can anywhere else, can't you? For heaven's sake, Binnie, stop thinking of yourself and your pride, think of Maura and the child she is having. Your child.'

He rubbed at his thick, coarse hair. 'I don't know, Llinos, I just don't know what to do or what to think. Perhaps I'm not ready for . . . for all this.'

'Well, that is just your bad fortune, then, isn't it?' Llinos was growing angry. 'You were ready to take Maura to bed, weren't you? Man enough to make her pregnant. Are you not man enough to face up to the consequences?'

Binnie sighed and sank into a chair. 'This has been my home for so long.' He rubbed at his eyes and suddenly he seemed like the youth he was.

'But everything changes, Binnie. Mr Cimla changed things for us, didn't he? He threw you out and Maura's family were good enough to take you in. Are you to repay them by failing their daughter when she most needs you?'

'Oh, for God's sake, Llinos, don't preach!'

'And don't you blaspheme!' Llinos brushed a stray curl of hair away from her face. 'I'm sorry, Binnie. You're right, it's none of my business.'

He looked across the table at her. 'Truth to tell, I don't know what to do.'

'Take your time, Binnie, just take your time and let me know what you decide once you've thought about it.' Llinos sighed heavily. 'How can I expect to sort your problems when I can't deal with my own?'

'What problems have you got, Llinos?' There was not a little sarcasm in Binnie's voice.

'Plenty! For a start I no longer have a place here,' Llinos said. 'I've been used to taking charge; used to working hard, taking all the responsibilities for running the pottery. Now there is nothing for me to do, I feel lost.'

'Aye, I can see that right enough.'

Llinos reached across the table and took Binnie's hand. She saw the warmth in his eyes, knew how much affection and loyalty he still felt towards her.

'I will be even more lost if you and Maura move out but I thought it was best for you.'

'It's good of you to put me and Maura before your own feelings but . . . oh, I don't know.'

'This is a good chance, Binnie,' Llinos said. 'Maura will have a position with fair wages and a roof over her head and, better yet, a place where her baby will be welcome. You won't find such security anywhere else.'

'I like Eynon well enough.' Binnie was uneasy. 'But then I'm not comfortable when I'm around him. He's too posh, not one of us.'

'So you are a snob, are you, Binnie?' The irony in Llinos's voice was not lost on Binnie and he flushed.

'All right, I'm a fool. We'll take him up on his offer.' He squared his shoulders. 'Where's Maura, have you spoken to her?'

Llinos shook her head. 'I wanted to know how you felt first.'

Binnie rose to his feet and on an impulse touched her cheek. 'You are a wonderful person, Llinos. One day some man is going to be very lucky.' Silently, Joe appeared in the room and Binnie drew his hand away. He nodded affably to Joe and went outside into the yard.

After he had gone, a heavy silence hung over the kitchen. Somehow, Llinos was reluctant to meet Joe's eyes. After a moment, he took her hand and drew her to her feet. She stood before him, aware that she was trembling. He tipped her face up and studied her and it was as if he was memorizing every feature. His eyes were so blue, so unreadable, and she knew.

'You are going away?'

He nodded. 'Just for a time.'

She wanted to beg him to stay. 'Why, where are you going?'

'My father is sick. I was reluctant to impose my presence upon him but now I regret it. I may have left it too late.'

She did not even ask how he knew, she had become used to his strangely powerful intuition. 'You will come back?'

'As soon as I can.' He placed his hands along her cheeks, his fingers capturing her. Slowly, he bent and touched her lips with his.

His mouth was hot, passionate and yet gentle, drawing an instant response from her. It was the first time she had experienced a lover's kiss and it was a shimmering light. An awakening. She felt she would never be the same again.

He released her. 'I'll be back as soon as I can, I promise.'

She felt frightened, reluctant to let him go. 'Joe . . .' She put her arms around him, burying her face against the crisp shirt front, breathing in the exotic scents of him. Briefly, he held her close and she felt his heart beating against hers and then, on silent feet, he left the room.

'*Duw*, don't those pots look lovely then?' Lily had grown adept, her small fingers handling the brush with a skill she had not known she possessed.

Llinos smiled at her. 'Are you happier working with the paints than with the paper patterns, Lily?'

'You can bet your last penny I am, Miss Savage.' Lily's eyes shone wickedly. She lowered her voice. 'At least I'm out of reach of Mrs Smedley's sharp tongue.'

'Well, that's an improvement. Here, let me show you an easier way of creating a flat edge. Take your brush, see, this one here.' She chose a brush from the pot and showed it to Lily. 'See, it has a broad, flat edge. Press into the paint like this, sharply. Now, a quick movement of the hand and you have your rock outlined against the sky. Drag the paint downwards, see how it thins, appearing like the crevices in the mountain?'

'You are clever, miss.' Lily's eyes were admiring.

'It's just practice. Right, I'll leave you to it.' Llinos was aware that her presence sometimes had the effect of creating tension among the artists. Some of them were highly skilled, used to handling paint on china but, to a man, they had their own views on how a job should be tackled.

One of the painters was a local artist born less than a mile from the Savage Pottery. David Briars executed the most intricate design with an ease that impressed Llinos. He was more used to the flower designs used on fine porcelain than the bold Indian patterns he painted now on pottery and yet his work was exquisite.

'That's lovely, David.' Llinos admired the Indian brave, head raised to the skies, hair flowing, and saw in the noble features something of Joe. 'May I have that one when it's finished?'

'You certainly may, Miss Savage. It will need to be fired first but then you know that.'

Llinos smiled. 'What's that there, in the distance, a figure, a spirit?'

'It will be the Indian's woman.' David smiled. 'A flight of fancy on my part. Shall I paint her out?'

'No. But leave her as she is, insubstantial. Ephemeral.' She left the smell of paint and clay and walked out into the cool air. She wanted to hide away and cry. She was missing Joe more than she could have believed possible. It was as though he had become part of her. No, as if he always had been part of her. And now that part was missing.

When she crossed the yard she found her father sitting in the doorway of the house. 'Come here, my dear, there's something I want to talk to you about.'

It was dim in the parlour after the winter sun outside. 'What is it, Father?'

'I have been thinking about your future, Llinos.' An icy finger trailed a line down her shoulders.

'Yes?' she asked.

'Well sit down, for heaven's sake!' He was edgy and it showed. 'I think it is about time you attended some sort of ladies' school. I want you to be trained in all the things young ladies should know.'

'I don't want to go away.' Her tone was flat.

'Well, I do want you to go away,' he said. 'Look, Llinos, I'm a cripple but I am not blind. You are becoming too friendly with Joe and it will not do.'

'I am proud to have Joe as a friend,' Llinos said defensively. 'He's a fine man. Well-educated with excellent manners. He is intelligent and more than that he has senses that we do not have.'

'I agree with all that but he is a half-breed, never forget that, Llinos.' Her father's face was set. She could see that he was determined to have his way.

'He saved your life, have you forgotten that?'

'I have forgotten nothing.' He spoke sharply. 'I repeat, Joe is a half-breed, he is not a suitable companion for you.'

'I love him, Father.'

'Love him? What do you know about love? Llinos, you are little more than a child.'

'I am a child who needed to grow up rather quickly, Father. Remember, I kept this pottery working almost single-handed.'

'You are going to school,' he said. 'I will brook no refusal, Llinos.'

She was about to speak when there was the sound of a crash from upstairs. Llinos spun quickly towards the door.

'Maura?' She was taking the stairs two at a time, her skirts lifted above her knees.

Maura was kneeling on the floor, the shards of a broken jug around her. 'I'm sorry,' she gasped, her arms hugging her swollen figure. 'I should have called someone before, I've been having pains for hours, the baby is coming.'

'All right, there's nothing to worry about. Just keep calm and everything will be all right. Here, let me help you onto the bed.'

Maura shook her head. 'No, I can't. Let me just kneel here a minute till the pain passes.'

'I'll fetch Celia, she'll know what to do.'

Maura shook her head. 'No! You can't leave me, there's no time to fetch anyone else, you'll have to help me.'

'But I don't know anything about childbirth and neither do you, this is madness.'

'You've got to help me!' Maura insisted, clutching her swollen belly. 'There's nothing else for it.' She bent her head to her chest, her eyes tightly closed, and cried like an animal in pain.

'All right, I'll do what I can.' Swiftly, Llinos brought water from the kettle, clean cloths from the cupboard and newspaper to protect the mattress. That was if ever Maura consented to lie on the bed, she thought drily.

'A pair of scissors, you'll need those for cutting the cord.' Maura had relaxed as the intensity of the contraction abated.

Llinos swallowed hard. She hesitated and Maura looked up, her eyes desperate.

'Sure 'tis easy enough, seen the old biddy in Greenhill bring two of my sisters into the world, 'tis I do all the hard work.'

Linos pushed up the sleeves of her dress. 'What shall I do?'

Another contraction contorted the face of the Irish girl. She shook her head, unable to speak. Llinos knelt beside her and rubbed the girl's spine in rhythmic movements. Maura looked up gratefully as the pain eased.

'I'd best get on the bed or my babe will be born on the floor.' Awkwardly, she manoeuvred herself into a lying position, half on her side. Sweat beaded her forehead. She screwed up her eyes as another contraction caught her and growled deep in her throat. 'I need to bear down, help me, please.'

Llinos acted on instinct. 'Here, put your foot against my shoulder, it should help.'

'Push my petticoats aside, let the baby have room to come out.' Maura gasped. 'Oh my Lord, help me!' She did not speak again. Her eyes were tightly closed, her face red with effort. Sweat darkened the red of her hair and, watching her, Llinos wondered if the Irish girl was going to die.

The dark crown of the baby's head appeared and Llinos looked at it in wonderment. 'It's coming!' Llinos's voice was urgent. 'Have courage, it won't be long now.'

She felt her own belly grow tense as though her efforts could be added to those of the Irish girl.

'I must rest.' Maura fell back against the pillows, her face beaded with sweat. 'I'll bear down again in a minute but I must have rest.'

The head of the child seemed to recede and Llinos wondered desperately if she should have done more to help bring it into the world.

'It will take a bit o' time,' Maura said, 'don't worry, I'll tell you what to do when the time comes.'

Maura was right. The labour was protracted. Together the two girls fought with nature. Maura was weakening; even to Llinos's inexperienced eyes it was clear that some action needed to be taken.

When the urge to bear down came again, Maura's whimpering turned into the strange, inarticulate sounds of a creature in pain.

As the baby's head came forward, Llinos grasped it firmly. 'Come on, then, push it out! I'm helping you. One last effort, Maura, just one last effort.'

Miraculously, the head of the child emerged, eyes closed, doll-like features turned towards Llinos. 'I think it's a girl,' she said softly.

'Turn the shoulders round,' Maura gasped. Her hands clutched the pillows, her face drained now of colour.

The baby was slippery but Llinos held the shoulders firmly as with a last effort from Maura the infant slipped into the world.

'The afterbirth will come soon,' Maura said. 'You must tie the cord in two places and cut it.' Maura could scarcely speak, her strength was spent. 'Don't worry about the blood, 'tis normal enough to lose a little at the moment of birth. Can you do it?'

'I'll cope.' Llinos hesitated, trying to control the trembling of her hands and then, with a firm stroke, she severed the cord. It pulsated with a life of its own and Llinos marvelled at what she had helped to achieve.

The baby began to gurgle and Maura lifted her head. 'Put your finger in its mouth, hold the child face down, that's right, clear its throat.'

The baby let out a hearty cry. Llinos looked down at the small creature with a sense of awe. She wanted to laugh and to cry all at the same time. She had helped in this miracle of new life and it was a wonderful feeling.

'It's a girl! I knew it would be. Here, Maura, do you want to hold her?'

Maura nodded, a smile widening her lips. Her eyes shone as she cradled the child against her breast.

'The afterbirth, you must wrap it in paper and

burn it, 'tis cleaner that way.'

Llinos worked methodically. She changed the sheets and made Maura comfortable in the clean bed that smelled of lavender.

'Now, I think we both deserve a nice hot cup of tea,' Llinos said.

Maura smiled. 'You more than me by the look of it.' She took a deep breath. 'Will you send Binnie up to see me, please? I want to show him his daughter.'

As Llinos left the room there were tears trembling on her lashes. She felt exhilarated and yet drained of energy. She ran downstairs and out into the yard anxious to find Binnie. He would be so proud of his new daughter. Once he saw her, everything would be all right, he would marry Maura and they would live happily ever after.

'So, the doctor complimented you on your midwifery?' Lloyd Savage tapped a pencil against the arm of his converted chair. 'I must confess I never thought you could be so practical in an emergency, I congratulate you.'

Llinos bent and kissed her father's springy grey hair. 'There is a great deal you don't know about me, Father.' She spoke gently but her words held an undercurrent of reproof.

'So it would seem. I still think that you would benefit from some proper schooling. It is not appropriate for my daughter to be taking on tasks that rightly belong to the peasant stock.'

'That "peasant stock" as you call it comprises my friends. Binnie, Watt, old Ben, how would I have survived without them?'

'You see?' Her father turned his hands palms upwards. 'That is just the point I'm trying to make. You will become a hoyden, unfit to take your place in society.'

'You don't fool me, Father,' Llinos said. 'It's just Joe, isn't it, all the rest is simply an excuse.'

'It is, of course, and can't you see the sense of that, girl? Anyway, I have written to Caswell Ladies' college; they have a place for you there.'

'I will not go.' Llinos spoke flatly. 'If you try to force me I'll leave home.'

'And how will you live without my support?'

'I will live as I did when you were in France.' She looked at her hands. 'I can pot with the best of them, you know that, Father.'

He was frowning angrily. 'You mean you would take up a position with the Morton-Edwards lot?'

Llinos considered the question. 'If I had to.'

'I do not believe this!' Lloyd Savage crashed his big hand down on the table. 'My own daughter turning against me.'

'Father, I am not turning against you,' Llinos said. She was dismayed at the direction the argument was taking but she must have her say.

'I will not be dictated to, not when I kept this pottery going almost single-handedly.'

'You keep saying that but a fine mess you were in when I came home.' Lloyd was angry.

'Your mother dead, the pottery almost ruined. You need me, child, and I won't have you disobeying me.'

'I am not a child, Father, can't you see that?'

'What do you think you are then? A woman? Well, you are too young to think you know what life is all about.' He swung his chair away from her. 'I have seen men die in their own filth. I have heard the cries of the wounded pleading to be put out of their misery. I have lived and I have faced death and here I am with my chit of a daughter defying me.'

'For heaven's sake, Father, don't start feeling sorry for yourself!'

'How dare you!' He was white. 'That's the last straw, get out, then, go.' His voice was low.

Llinos stared at his back for a long moment then turned and hurried up the stairs. The situation had got out of hand. Why had she allowed it? She should have kept her dignity, been adamant but polite. He was her father and he deserved respect. She sat on the bed. 'Oh, Joe, where are you now when I need you?'

Later, Llinos retraced her steps to the sitting-room but it was empty. She looked outside. There was no sign of her father, he could be in any of the pottery buildings. She heard a faint sound, it seemed to come from the room he called his den. Tentatively, she knocked on the door.

'Father, let me in, I'm sorry.'

'It's too late to be sorry. I have nothing to say to you.'

Angrily she turned away. She would show him that he could not treat her like a child.

A few minutes later, she had packed her bag. As she left her room, she came face to face with Binnie; his eyes were shadowed.

'I wanted a boy, Maura was sure it was going to be a boy,' he said.

'Well, your daughter is healthy and beautiful, be grateful for that, Binnie.'

His eyes widened as he saw the bag. 'Where are you going?'

'Anywhere out of here. Look, Binnie, your future is up to you, I can't help you any more.'

She touched his arm and then made her way down the stairs and out of the house, leaving the door open. The row was unusually empty of people. Even the door to Celia's house was closed. Llinos walked along the cobbled road with her head high. She did not want to go to school, she wanted to work at . . . what *did* she want to work at? She no longer knew. The pottery was her life blood, she could not imagine being in any other occupation. It was all she knew.

Her mind was racing. Where would she go? There was only one answer. She struck out towards the streets beyond the town where the scattered houses stood in large grounds facing the sea. It was a long way from Pottery Row but the walk would do her good.

Eynon greeted her with a lifting of his eyebrows. 'To what do I owe this honour, my little friend?' He drew her inside the high-ceilinged hallway of his house. 'I see you have come to stay and on foot, too. What's wrong, Llinos?'

She dropped her bag on the floor and put her arms around him, resting her head wearily against the starched front of his shirt.

'I've left home.'

'I can see that but why, what's happened?'

'My father wanted to send me off to school.'

Taking her hand, he led her into the sitting-room. It was a beautiful room. At one end were French doors leading to the garden. At the other, in the huge bay window, stood a spinet, the wood shining like golden syrup in the sun. Eynon was rich, far richer than the Savage family had ever been. Much wealthier than ever Llinos had imagined.

'Can I stay for a few days?'

'Of course. Need you ask?'

Llinos rubbed her eyes. 'I'm sorry to land myself on you without warning but . . .'

'Look, you are my dear friend, my little *cariad*, I would be hurt if you did not come to me for help. I'll ring for some tea and you can tell me all about it.'

Llinos watched as the young maid set the fine china on the table.

'Thank you, Mena,' Eynon said. 'Tell cook there will be a guest for supper. Oh, and make sure there is a decent fire in the guest room, would you?'

After the maid had gone, Llinos drank some of the hot, fragrant tea gratefully. 'Am I wrong to disobey my father, Eynon?'

'Well, going off to school does not seem such a terrible fate to me, I must say.'

'But I have to stay in Swansea. I could not bear to go away to some strange school where I would learn to stitch and sew and to speak foreign languages. Dead ones too, like Latin and Greek. What do I want with all that?'

Eynon shook his head. 'I don't know, my sweet Llinos, but I think you might have talked things over reasonably with your father before you went rushing off.'

'He became angry with me. He told me if I did not obey him I was no longer his daughter.'

'He is in pain, you must remember that, Llinos. Pain of any kind makes people behave in strange ways.'

Llinos knew he was right. She had seen her father ease the bandages on his legs and knew he was missing Joe's administrations.

'It's because of Joe, that's the real problem, isn't it?' Eynon said, picking up on her thoughts. 'Your father is afraid you will lose your head over Joe. Have you, Llinos? Lost your head over Joe, I mean?'

'Would it be such a bad thing if I had?'

Eynon rubbed his chin where a light stubble of fair hair curled against his skin in an apology for a beard. 'In the eyes of the townspeople, yes, it would. Joe is a native American. He even looks foreign. On the other hand, you would be the one having to live with him and in my book he is a fine, honourable man.' He smiled wryly. 'I'm sure I don't have to list his virtues.'

'I know them all, every one. Oh Eynon, I'm so confused.'

'Sleep on it, you'll feel better then,' Eynon said, and Llinos nodded even as she doubted his words.

Later, lying in bed in the strangely huge and elegant room, Llinos tried to sort out her tangled thoughts. She could not stay here and live off her friend, not indefinitely. So what were the options? She would either have to return home and agree to her father's demands or she would have to find a position where she could earn herself a living. That meant approaching the owner of the Morton-Edwards' Pottery, Eynon's father and her own father's rival.

She sighed and turned over on her side, watching the dappling of moonlight on the wall.

'Joe, please come home and tell me what to do,' she whispered and wondered if, somewhere in England, he would be picking up on her thoughts.

CHAPTER TWELVE

In the tall house on the borders of England and Wales, in a small town with a name taken from the river Wye on which it stood, Joe was sitting beside his father's bed, his head raised, his senses alert as he listened to the hoot of the night owl and the rustle of small creatures in the grass outside.

It was silent in the house, even his father's breathing seemed to be hushed. Peter Mainwaring was asleep, but by his pallor it was clear he was entering the last phase of his earthly life.

Joe had kept vigil at his father's side without respite for three days and three nights. He had seen the sun rise in the morning and watched it set at nightfall. During this time, his father had not spoken, he might not even be aware of his son's presence.

Joe's sisters, two ladies older than he by many years, had allowed him into the house with great reluctance, consistently refusing to acknowledge him as a brother. But he understood them. They were frightened by the thought of being alone with no male protector except a half-breed step-brother.

His father moaned a little and Joe leaned forward to touch the dry, hot brow. Peter Main-waring opened his eyes and after a moment they focused with recognition on his son. He made an attempt to lift his hand and Joe took it, engulfing the fragile fingers in the warmth of his own strong hands.

'You came. How did you know?' The voice was threadlike, insubstantial, but Joe's hearing was acute.

'I knew, Father.'

Peter inclined his head. 'Yes, of course you did. So like your mother.'

'Don't try to talk.' Joe leaned closer. His father's breath was fetid, death was grasping him and drawing him downwards.

'Last chance to say I'm sorry, Joe.'

'No need.'

'I hurt you and your mother. I have always regretted it.' He paused, struggling for breath. 'But I have done my best to make amends. I have left you funds enough to go to see her. And when you go to her, tell her I always loved her.'

His eyes closed and he sank once more into the cloud of unconsciousness. His skin had taken on a greyish tinge, it was parchment thin. Death was ready to take him by the hand and lead him into the world beyond. Joe rose to his feet. It was time to call his sisters.

They came unwillingly. Charlotte and Letitia, joyless beings, both.

'Time to say your farewells.' Joe stepped aside

and watched the women kneel at the bedside, heads bowed in prayer. He did not doubt that the prayers were pious ones but a touch of a hand, a last look into the face of their father, might have served him better.

He left the room. It was over, his father would not open his eyes again. He packed his small roll of clothes, fastening it with a leather thong, and then made his way downstairs. There, he sat and waited.

He was joined shortly by his sisters. Charlotte was weeping but Letitia, the eldest one, stood erect, her face unrelenting as she spoke to Joe without once looking at him.

'You can leave us now, Father is dead.'

'You don't wish me to stay and make arrangements for the funeral?'

Letitia shook her head. 'No! We do not want you at the funeral. You would be an embarrassment.'

'Then I shall be on my way.'

Letitia sniffed. She had made her feelings more than plain but she intended to make them even plainer. 'There will be no need for you to call here again, ever.'

'Oh, I will return, do not doubt it.' He spoke mildly. His eyes rested for a moment on Charlotte, her head was bent and she turned away as if she, too, wished to disassociate herself from him.

'Goodbye to you, my sisters,' he said and let himself out of the house.

He began the long walk towards the nearest town where he could pick up a post-chaise. He wished impatiently that he could fly like the eagle and cover the hillsides and the wooded glades. Swoop over high waterfalls and low, winding rivers.

In the hours of night, Llinos had called to him and he had heard her. Now he was free to go to her but though his legs were long and his stride wide, his progress was slow.

'Don't worry, Llinos, I'm coming home.' The wind took the words. A large bird pecked at them, swallowed them and flew like an arrow towards Wales.

It took him more than two sunrises to reach the post house in Swansea. He left the coach happy to have his feet back on solid ground after the rocking and buffeting of the journey.

He tipped his hat to the other occupants as he took his leave. His fellow passengers had taken him for an English gentleman. One of the elderly ladies had enquired whether he had served His Majesty abroad, remarking on the tan of his skin. He had concurred with a nod of his head but had deflected the questions by enquiring about her heavily bandaged wrist.

Thereafter the conversation had consisted of a list of ailments to which the old lady was a martyr but he had borne it gracefully, allowing his thoughts to wander towards home and Llinos.

It did not take Joe long to reach Pottery Row.

The water wheel was turning swiftly, the rush of water swelled by the thawing of the winter ice. But as Joe looked at the straggle of pottery buildings, he knew that Llinos was not there.

'Joe! Good to see you back!' Captain Savage pumped Joe's hand with a great warmth. 'These old legs of mine been giving me hell and tarnation. Can't wait for you to mix up one of your potions. I'll get the maid to make you something to eat.'

Joe set his roll down on one of the oak chairs. 'Maid?' His eyes regarded the captain steadily.

'Yes, I've taken on some staff at last.' The captain looked away but not before Joe had seen the pain in his eyes. 'Llinos has left home.' His statement was bald, the words clipped.

'I've employed an old woman as housekeeper and a young girl to look after the place. The Irish girl and Binnie went with Llinos.'

'Why?'

'I'll tell you all about that later. Now how was your father?'

Joe sat astride a chair. He felt an ache in his chest and a fire in his loins, he was in love with Llinos. He desired her with all his being but he knew there would be many battles to be fought before he could possess her.

'My father has gone to whatever he sees as his heaven,' he said. 'His passing was peaceful enough. The great spirit was kind to him.'

Captain Savage rang a bell and the strident noise echoed through the house. The maid came at once, her eyes on Joe, appraising him, trying to place him in the scheme of things at Pottery House.

She dipped a curtsy as Captain Savage told her to bring a jug of ale and two tankards.

The girl went swiftly about her business, her eyes pale blue, her lashes fair and long, sweeping her cheeks modestly. She was aware of Joe's scrutiny and made the most of it. At last, her task completed, she bowed her way out of the room.

'I'm sorry your father has died. As to the great spirit being kind, you know I can't abide all that foolishness. It might have been all right abroad, in France and in that hell-hole they called Mont-St-Jean, but this is a good Christian country. Remember, your father was good enough to educate you to our ways, at least you could pay them lip-service.'

'Llinos?' Joe persisted.

Captain Savage wheeled himself to the window. 'She's run out on me,' he said briefly. 'The reasons do not concern you.'

'Yes they do.' Joe spoke mildly and the captain looked at him with narrowed eyes.

'How do you make that out?'

'She and I are destined to be together. You can't change it, Captain, however much you would like to.'

'Over my dead body. You are a . . . a foreigner, Joe, half native, I can't have your blood mingled with mine, you must see that?'

'You have no choice in the matter, Captain.'

Lloyd Savage was suddenly pale. 'You have seen my future? Tell me the worst, Joe.'

'I didn't mean that, Captain. No man knows the time of his death.'

Lloyd Savage wheeled his chair towards the window and looked out. He saw the pale sunshine washing the cobbled roadway, saw the budding leaves on the trees.

'You are right, none of us know how long we shall be spared. I was a pig-headed fool to drive Llinos away.' He turned to face Joe. 'Will you fetch her back for me?'

Joe placed his bundle on the floor. 'I don't think she will listen to me.' He smiled. 'She's a headstrong girl but I will talk to her.'

'Just say that I'm sorry and I want her home.'

Slowly Joe nodded. He rose to his feet. 'First I must bathe, wash away the dust of the journey.'

'She will come home, won't she?' Lloyd Savage's voice shook.

Joe faced him, his eyes steady. 'I don't know. But I'll do my best to convince her that she's needed here.' As he left the room Joe's last glimpse of Lloyd Savage was of a man with his head bowed in despair.

'He's back in Swansea,' Eynon said. Llinos was looking at him but not seeing him. The antipathy in his voice was enough to tell her who he was talking about. Joe was home and the joy she felt was reflected in her face.

He resented Joe, his good looks, his strength, his wisdom. Joe had called at the house several times and Eynon had told the maid to send him away. But the man would not take no for an answer for much longer. Any day now, Joe would barge in and carry Llinos off with him.

Eynon swallowed hard, searching for words to express his love for Llinos before it was too late. He wanted to marry her, to make love to her; the time she had spent under his roof had been enough to convince him of that.

'I know.'

'What do you know?'

'I know Joe is back. Wake up, sleepyhead!'

He ached to touch her cheek, to kiss the sweet lips, but he had no doubt he would be repulsed.

He could well understand her feelings for Joe. He was handsome, confident in his masculinity and yet with a sensitivity that was rare in a man. He was everything Eynon was not.

'Llinos, I have to say it, Joe is not suitable, not as a marriage prospect.'

A tiny smile lit her eyes. 'Then should I take him as a lover?'

'That's disgraceful, Llinos.' There was a touch of acidity in Eynon's voice. 'Don't voice those sort of opinions to Joe, he might take advantage of you.'

Llinos smiled. 'Joe knows exactly how I feel about him and if he was going to "take advantage of me" he has had every opportunity.'

'Ah, well, I didn't know he was a paragon of

virtue as well as everything else.' Eynon felt anger flow through him. He had been attracted to Llinos from the first time he met her, why on earth had he not made the most of his opportunities before Joe came on the scene?

Llinos sighed. 'I love him, Eynon, nothing can change that. I want to own him, body, mind and spirit.'

'Just like a woman, asking for the moon, the sun and the stars.'

Eynon picked up the small brass bell from the table and rang it vigorously. Almost at once, Maura came into the room carrying a silver tray.

'Mena is gone to see her mammy, sir. I said I'd finish off in here, is that all right, Mr Eynon?' She set the tray on the table and the rich aroma of coffee drifted into his face.

'That's fine, Maura. How's the baby?' He had heard the infant in the night crying pitifully. Maura's face was shadowed.

'She's not right, sir. She's got a terrible cough, shakes her little body it does.'

'I shall send for Brayley, he's an excellent doctor,' Eynon said reassuringly.

'Thank you, Mr Eynon, you are so kind, and sure I don't deserve it.'

Eynon smiled. 'No, I'm not being kind, I just want to make sure I get a good night's sleep tonight!'

When Maura left the room, Llinos stood beside Eynon's chair and wound her arms around his neck. He allowed his head to fall against her soft breasts, his thoughts in confusion. Was she teasing him or was she unaware of her own attraction?

'You *are* kind, Eynon, you're a good man and I love you to death.'

'You love me like a brother, though, is that it?' He spoke bitterly.

She kissed the top of his head and moved away from him. 'Eynon, I have imposed on you far too long. Perhaps I should move out.'

Eynon lifted his hand to protest but Llinos rushed on. 'I went to see your father's foreman yesterday. I've got a job at the Tawe Pottery, I start at the beginning of the week.'

'I see. Doing what, exactly?'

'Wheel turner.'

'A wheel turner? Llinos, you are worth better than that.'

'It's a start. Soon, I'll graduate to better things.'

'I expect my father thought it a fine joke to take on Lloyd Savage's daughter.'

'I didn't even see your father. Why should he notice me?'

'Don't fool yourself, nothing gets past my father. He'll know exactly who has been taken on at his precious pottery.'

'Do you really think your father would allow me to work for him knowing who I was?'

Eynon shook his head. 'I have given up trying to work out how my father thinks. Anyway, I don't care about him. Work for him if you must but I want you to continue to live here with me.'

'No, Eynon. It's been agreed that I share one of the houses in Morton-Edwards Street with some of the other girls who work at the pottery.'

'Oh aye, my father's little hand-picked harem. You must be mad.'

'Not mad, just proud. I can't live on your charity for ever, can I?'

'You could work for me instead of for my father.'

'Doing what?'

'I could think of something.' He knew as soon as he had spoken that he had said the wrong thing. 'I do need someone to run the house and that sort of thing. There's the er . . . there's the household expenses, they need monitoring.'

'I won't take a trumped-up job out of charity, Eynon. So you see, there's nothing more to be said. I have a job and a place to live.'

She smiled at him. 'Don't worry too much, Binnie has already got a job at the Tawe Pottery, he'll keep an eye on me. You know how grateful I am that you've put up with me this long.'

'Look, Llinos, why don't you marry me?' He felt elated as he spoke the words. 'I love you very much, you know that, and I want you to stay here with me. It would be the ideal solution, can't you see that?' He rose to his feet and faced her, his heart thumping. 'Think about it, we have a great deal in common. We like each other's company and . . .'

He fell silent as he saw Llinos shake her head.

'No, I don't want you proposing to me out of charity, Eynon. What if you should later meet someone you could fall in love with? In any case, I won't marry anyone but Joe, you know that.'

His feeling of euphoria faded. 'Knowing you, Llinos, you will get what you want in the end,' he said.

'Or die in the attempt,' Llinos said softly.

It was a strange almost uneasy feeling working in the huge buildings that sprawled along the banks of the river Tawe. The potting house was much larger than she had expected. It hummed with the sound of turning wheels and the slap of clay upon wood.

Llinos was crouched beside the fly wheel, looking at the boots of the potter, noting with boredom that one of his laces was untied. Her mind drifted, as it always did, to thoughts of Joe. Why had he not come to see her? Was he angry at her disobeying her father?

'Hold the wheel!' Billy Sullivan's voice drifted down to her and she guessed he was cutting another pot from its base. Impulsively, she leaned forward and tied his laces together and sank back on her haunches.

She heard the creak of his chair as he rose and then before her startled eyes, she saw him crash to the floor.

Other booted feet came into her line of vision and, aghast at what she had done, Llinos peered round the wheel to see if the potter was all right.

'Bashed his head,' a voice said gruffly. 'Get some water, throw it into his face, he'll be right as rain in no time.'

To her relief, Llinos saw the potter open his eyes and sit up. *'Duw,* what happened?'

'You fell, man, take a bit more water with your ale, I would.'

'Wasn't my fault,' the potter struggled to rise. 'Hell and damnation, my boot laces are tied together!'

Llinos was grasped by the collar and dragged forward. 'What do you think you were doing, girl?' the potter said.

'I'm sorry, I only meant it as a joke.'

'A joke that nearly cost me my brains, you half-wit!'

'All right, take it easy, Billy.' Binnie came forward. 'It was only a bit of fun, man. Llinos didn't mean any harm.'

'I don't know about that, I could have broke my bloody neck!'

'I'm sorry, it was a stupid thing to do,' Llinos said. The crowd of men parted and a man in high boots, well-cut coat and tall hat appeared before her.

'What on earth is going on?'

'Fool of a girl tripped Billy up. Tied his laces together, thought it was a joke, she did.'

'Come here. What's your name?'

'Llinos, Mr Morton-Edwards, sir.'

'Savage's daughter, oh?'

'Yes, sir.'

'I thought so. You forgot to curtsy, child.'

Llinos felt humiliated as she curtsied to Mr Morton-Edwards. Did he have to come into the pottery right at this moment?

'Come with me, girl.' Morton-Edwards strode away and Billy gave her a push.

'Don't stand there catching flies, girl, do as the boss man says.'

Llinos hurried to catch up with Mr Morton-Edwards, following him out of the building and into the cold splash of sunshine outside.

He kept walking without glancing back at her until he reached the elegant red-brick building which housed the offices. It was only then that he looked at her.

'Go wash your hands and then come into that room there.' He pointed to a polished oak door and as Llinos bobbed another curtsy, he disappeared inside.

It took her a few minutes to find a place where she could wash. The room was long and tiled in cold black and white and some basins stood on a long shelf that ran the length of the room and beside each basin was a jug of water.

She removed her apron and left it hanging from a hook on the shelf before locating the room Mr Morton-Edwards had indicated.

'Come here, let me look more closely at you.' She stood before him and he regarded her steadily. He reached out to tip up her chin and she moved a pace backwards.

'A haughty little thing, aren't you?'

She felt her colour rise. 'Sorry, sir.'

'That's all to the good,' he said, nodding his head. 'Sluts there are aplenty, good girls are more difficult to find.' He leaned back in his chair and regarded her steadily.

'You are bored turning the fly wheel.' It was a statement. She nodded her head.

'Why do it then?'

'I need to earn a living like everyone else.'

'You are too well-spoken to fit in with the peasant stock. What does your father have to say about you working for me, not pleased, eh?'

'I suppose not.'

'You can read and write and do figures, of course?'

'Of course.'

'You have not answered my question. Your father, what does he think of you coming here?'

She was silent, regarding him with suspicion. She remembered with a chill feeling Eynon's warning about his father's harem.

'Well I won't probe into your business any more. But tell me, what other skills do you have?' He smiled as she looked puzzled. 'It's not a trick question, Llinos. I am not looking to steal your virtue, whatever you might have heard to the contrary.'

She relaxed a little. She could tell by the up-turn of Mr Morton-Edwards' mouth that he possessed a sense of humour.

'Well, I can pot, glaze, paint, indeed I can do almost anything involving the making of pottery.'

He nodded. 'I thought so. Trust Savage to make use of his own flesh and blood in any way he can.' He leaned back in his chair. 'My son has had every advantage, the only time he came into the sheds was when he wanted a little fun. What he learned here was what he wanted to learn, but I would never think of expecting him to do menial tasks. He's a delicate boy but then you know that, you and he are friends, I understand?'

She felt suddenly hot. Embarrassed, she looked down at her hands. Clay still clung under her nails and self-consciously she picked at it. 'Yes, we are very good friends,' she said defensively.

'Good, my son needs friends.' He sat up straighter. 'I understand you have been staying with my son since you left home.'

'You are very well-informed, Mr Morton-Edwards.'

'Where my only child is concerned I make it my business to be well-informed. How did you find him? Is he well?'

Llinos smiled. 'He is very well. He has asked me to marry him.'

Morton-Edwards' eyelashes flickered momentarily as he digested her words. 'And you obviously declined, preferring to work at a menial task rather than be the wife of such an ill-favoured man.' His voice revealed much. He was bitter where his son was concerned.

'I love Eynon,' she said, 'and I would be honoured to be his wife, but I don't love him in that way. He is kind and truthful and caring. Physical strength is not everything.'

After a moment Mr Morton-Edwards nodded. 'I see.' He sat up straighter. 'Perhaps in time you will grow to love him, I can only hope so. A good woman would make a man of him. Well, we shall talk no more about it.'

He took out his pipe and pushed a wedge of tobacco into it. 'Back to business. I hate to see a young lady of obvious breeding and talent wasting both those things turning a fly wheel. What would you like to do, Llinos?'

'I enjoy most of the jobs necessary for making pots but now, here in your pottery, I would love to learn about the new porcelain you are making.'

'I see. Go on.'

'I am fascinated by the excellence of the few pieces I've seen but it still needs some work,' Llinos said. 'I'm sure that in a few more months you will be producing the best porcelain in the world.'

'Ah, praise indeed.' He hesitated for a moment and then looked up at her. 'Very well, you shall work with Mr Wright. He is a very gifted man, though I am probably telling you something you already know?'

'I know of Mr Wright's work, he not only creates porcelain bodies but he paints exquisitely, too. I admire him very much, I would be honoured to work with him.'

'But you will not go running back to your father's pottery and tell him of my designs and use them on the earthenware products, would you?'

Llinos shook her head. She thought of the bold colours and the strong patterns of the Indian designs used at the Savage Pottery and smiled.

'Oh, no, my father is well served with his own patterns.'

'Very well. One more thing, are you happy sharing a house with some of my other workers or would you like a room in my house as befits a lady of your station?'

'I would prefer to keep to the arrangements already made to share with the other girls,' she said carefully. Mr Morton-Edwards smiled.

'I do understand, you need to be independent, but if you change your mind don't hesitate to tell me.'

As she left his room, she was smiling. Her new employer was not half the devil she had been led to believe him to be. He was kind, fatherly and he had a keen sense of humour. Mr Morton-Edwards was a man she could grow to like and admire.

Later, as evening was beginning to fold the hills in shadow, Llinos walked towards the top of Poppets Hill. She was breathless by the time she crested the peak. Once there, she stood admiring the vista of the town spread out before her. Beyond was the curving bay, the sea darkened now under the greyness of the sky.

'Beautiful.' The voice was so close that, for a moment, Llinos thought she had imagined it. Her heart began to beat so rapidly she found it difficult to breathe. She spun round, her eyes glowing.

'Joe. Oh, Joe, you've come to find me.'

She was tinglingly aware of him standing beside her. He towered over her, his hair flowing around his strong features. His eyes were shadowed, his expression hidden from her.

She had to control the urge to throw herself into his arms. 'Your father, how is he?'

'He died shortly after I arrived at his home.'

'I'm sorry.'

'No need to be sorry, it was his time.'

'Oh, Joe.' She made a move towards him, she was so very conscious of the scent of him. 'Joe . . . I . . .' He turned fractionally away from her and her hands clenched together in frustration.

'Joe! Why do you treat me like this? You know how I feel about you. One minute you are kissing me and the next you are barely polite.'

His eyes gleamed for a moment. She had the feeling he was laughing at her. 'You know something, Llinos? You should not be here alone with me, it is not seemly for a young lady of breeding.'

'You forget,' she said without looking at him, 'I am no longer Llinos Savage, daughter of a pottery owner, but a humble working girl.'

'Don't working girls behave properly then?'

'Some of them do, Joe. But you know that. You're teasing me.'

'Yes I am. But I'll be serious. Why did you run away from your father, Llinos?'

'You probably heard from him why I ran away, why ask me?'

'He's sick and in pain. Don't be so hard and unforgiving. He needs you.'

Llinos looked at him sharply, trying to read his expression, but it was too dark now to see his face.

'He's hard and unforgiving to me, trying to force me to go away to school.'

'It's for your own good. Look, Llinos, he loves you but he's had no opportunity to be a father to you until now, all he wants is to do the very best for his child, is that so wrong? At least speak to him, Llinos, you owe him that much.'

'I will speak to my father, but I will not be sent away to school whatever he says.'

'Our lives follow a course just as the river does. We have very little say in the larger scheme of things.'

Llinos was suddenly irritated. 'Spare me the homespun philosophy, Joe. I'm not going away so save your breath.' Frustration gripped her. She wanted Joe, wanted him to lay her down in the sweet grass and make her a woman, his woman.

'You are too damned honourable for your own good, do you know that, Joe?'

'Swearing oaths is not very ladylike.' Joe was

laughing openly at her now and that infuriated her.

'I want you, Joe, and I will have you.'

She heard him sigh into the darkness. 'If we were together now, how long would it last? We both have lives to live, destinies to fulfil.'

'I do not subscribe to your beliefs in the iron hand of fate. We make our own fortunes, we shape our own destiny.'

'I'm not arguing. Come on, I shall see you home to wherever it is you are lodging.'

'To hell with you!'

She was running away from him then, leaping over uneven clumps of grass, taking the risk of falling down the steep sloping hill. If she did not put as much distance between herself and Joe as possible, she would be begging him to hold her in his arms and make love to her.

By the time she reached the lodging house in Morton-Edwards Street, she was breathless. Martha Reeves was there to supervise the girls and she looked reprovingly at Llinos with her wind-blown hair and her bonnet bouncing from its ribbons.

'I suggest you go up and tidy yourself before supper,' Martha said.

Llinos hurried upstairs to a small attic room. It was sparsely furnished with only a table and two beds. A high window let in a pale diffused light. Kicking off her shoes, she curled up on top of the blankets and squeezed her eyes tightly shut. But nothing would take away the image of

Joe, his hair blowing in the breeze, his eyes so blue looking into hers.

He was the man she wanted more than anything in the world and all he did was to laugh at her. She thumped her fist against the pillow.

'I'll show you, Joe, just you wait.' But quite what she was going to show him, she did not know.

CHAPTER THIRTEEN

'This girl, Savage's daughter, she might be of use to me.' Philip Morton-Edwards, glass in hand, stood before the ornate fireplace.

Estelle looked up at him. 'In what way?' She was impatient with her husband; sometimes he did not have the wit he was born with. But she was a second wife, she needed to handle her husband with care. She had not yet produced a son, one who would take the place of the namby-pamby boy produced by the first Mrs Morton-Edwards.

'I don't see how a chit of a girl born of some lowly tradesperson could possibly be of use to us.'

Her husband's sardonic gaze disconcerted her for a moment. Had she spoken too forcefully? Philip did not like women to be too forceful.

He held out his glass and dutifully she put down her embroidery and freshened his drink. He swallowed it in one gulp.

'You are an ignorant woman, do you know that? Savage is *not* a lowly tradesperson, he has a good name hereabouts. Apart from which, the man is some kind of war hero. Mark my words, it does not do to underestimate your opposition.'

Was there a hidden meaning to his words?

Could it be that he was subtly threatening her? Estelle shivered, watching nervously as Philip looked down into his glass.

'My son seems taken with the Savage wench. By all accounts he's been courting her for some time.' He laughed drily. 'She might even be able to persuade him to marry her, I bet that's what she's angling for.'

He stared at his wife with open hostility. 'That way, I might just get myself a child about the place again.'

Estelle looked down at her hands, they were shaking. 'But my darling, I will give you a son — in time.'

'I doubt it! No, Eynon is my heir, he will carry on my name. And anyway, his mother's family tied up her estate so that he should benefit from it.'

She had not thought of that. She knew that traditionally the estate would pass to the eldest son of course but surely her own sons would benefit, too?

'We'll have children, I assure you, I'm a healthy woman. Even if we have daughters, you will be pleased, won't you?'

'You talk nonsense, woman! Don't you understand anything? A man is judged by his male heirs. If you can't give me any then I will have to look to another woman to do it.'

'Eynon is a weakling, he will never father a son.' As soon as the words were spoken, Estelle regretted them. Philip stepped towards her with a slow, deliberate movement and before she could move he had slapped her face.

For a moment she saw nothing but a haze of lights against the darkness of pain. Her vision gradually cleared; she watched her husband refill his glass once more.

'Get up to bed.' He growled the words. 'Get yourself ready for me, at least do something to earn your keep.'

She hurried from the room and, lifting her skirts, took the stairs two at a time. She was afraid of Philip when he was in this mood. He seemed driven, as though by an inner torment. In some ways she could even feel sorry for him.

She undressed quickly, waving away her maid. 'Leave me.' She did not explain, she did not have to. Becky knew these moods, knew when the lord and master of the household intended to claim his conjugal rights. Becky had witnessed the bruises on the body of her mistress more than once. In the morning she would bring witch-hazel, she would apply it as a salve, thanking the good Lord that she was a widow this many a year.

Estelle shivered beneath the bedclothes, dreading the moment when Philip would come into the dressing-room next door. He would be undressed by his manservant, they would share a coarse joke at her expense and then Philip would stride naked into the room.

She closed her eyes and shuddered, no decent woman should have to endure the humiliation she suffered at the hands of her husband. Tears trembled against her lids and she brushed them away. Crying would serve only to excite and inflame Philip, he loved the sense of power that her tears gave him.

She closed her eyes tightly, praying that he would drink too much and fall into a state of oblivion as soon as his head touched the pillow. It was a false hope.

She heard him next door, heard his voice and heard the laughter of his man. Then Philip came into the bedroom and bid the servant to light the multitude of candles in the ornate holders.

The manservant glanced towards her. There was a knowing look in his eye, it was almost as though he could see her naked form beneath the bedclothes.

Before the man had even left the room, Philip had thrown back the sheets. Then, without preliminary, he was kneeling astride her. 'I will get me a child on you if it is the last thing I do!' He ground the words between his teeth, spittle falling onto her face.

'Please, Philip, you are hurting me!'

'Not woman enough for me, eh? Why, the whores down Market Street could do better than you.'

Estelle turned to face the wall, she would just have to pray that Philip's lust was sated quickly. She was out of luck; it was a long, wearisome time before Philip lay gasping beside her.

The blessed darkness folded around her and

she lay still, frozen in fear, until she heard her husband's deep, even breathing. Assuring herself that he was asleep, she climbed wearily out of the bed and in the dressing-room began carefully to wash herself.

In the morning, Philip breakfasted early. He looked well, as though the excesses of the night had never been.

'My dear son is coming to see me this morning,' he said. 'He was reluctant to pay a visit until he read my missive informing him that I wished to discuss Llinos Savage with him.'

'Will he agree? To marry the girl, I mean?'

'I think he will agree once he has heard what I have to say.' When Philip laughed it was an unpleasant sound, and Estelle shuddered. Perhaps she should run away from Philip and his increasingly sadistic demands. What good were fine clothes, rich food and cool sheets to sleep in when it all had to be shared with a sadist?

Eynon arrived as the servants were clearing away the remains of breakfast. She glanced at him and saw him frown in sympathy at the dark shadows around her eyes. She forced a smile and moved quickly out of the room.

When Eynon had received the parchment inscribed with his father's bold hand, his first instinct had been to throw it into the fire. After a moment, he had unfolded it and began to read. He knew then that he had to see his father, to try to protect Llinos from whatever mad scheme his father had thought up.

'Sit down, Eynon,' Philip said. 'We might as well be civilized.'

Eynon sat on the very edge of one of the plush chairs. 'Well, Father, what about Llinos Savage?'

He saw Philip smile. 'I understand you asked the girl to marry you. I just wanted to say that I think it's a splendid idea. I couldn't be more pleased that you want to assure the continuation of the Morton-Edwards line.'

'Marry Llinos? But, Father, surely you would have a daughter of one of the more illustrious Swansea families in mind for me?' His sarcasm was not lost on his father.

'None of them would have you.' Philip spoke bluntly. 'On the other hand, this girl, Llinos, she would consider you a catch. She seems to like you and she might be able to tolerate your . . . your . . . ill health.'

'You think so, Father?' Eynon heard the edge of anger in his voice and wondered why he had even bothered to give his father his time.

Philip smiled expansively. 'She's a pretty little thing, this Llinos.'

'Well, Father.' Eynon rose abruptly. 'Llinos refused me, didn't she tell you?'

'They all say no to start with. Women like to be wooed. Buy her gifts, shower her with diamonds. You inherited enough money from your mother's family, heaven knows.'

'It wouldn't work, Father, I'm telling you.'

'Look,' Philip was growing angry, 'time is run-

245

ning out, Estelle is getting older. I only have you to carry on my name, you must give me grandsons, make it up to me in some way for the disappointment you have caused me. If you don't succeed, then I will ruin the girl, you understand me?'

'I understand you all right! Llinos thinks I exaggerate your wickedness but if she stays in your employ long enough she'll learn that I have spoken only the truth about you.'

'But, Eynon, you are mistaken. Llinos is convinced of my goodness. I have won her over, she trusts me, she shares my ambition. And she knows how easily children fall out with their parents. Indeed, it is the case that all my employees hold me in high regard, don't you know that? They think I'm the finest boss who ever walked on earth.'

'They put on an act because you pay them well. And perhaps it's only your so-called loved ones who see you as you really are.'

His father gave him a long look and Eynon shifted uneasily. 'I'm going, I need some fresh air. I should never have come. I might have known you and I wouldn't ever see eye to eye.'

Eynon left the house, resisting the temptation to slam the door shut behind him. He walked briskly along the banks of the river and past the pottery. It was a vast huddle of buildings, crowded behind a high wall. The mill-house wheel was turning, making a mist of the crystalline water as it fell to rejoin the river.

Llinos could be working in any of the sheds; she was so good at all aspects of pot making. She could design patterns, use glazes to great effect and she knew the firing inside out. Where was she? He must find her and talk to her.

There was no sign of her. He realized that even as he approached one shed, she might be moving into another. At last he gave up the search. Later, he would go to the house where the female workers were lodged and talk to her there.

Despair filled him as he walked up the hill towards home. His father was hateful, he seemed to find just the right way to hurt him. And yet the idea of marrying Llinos made him ache for what might have been if Joe had not come onto the scene.

Yet perhaps his father was right, perhaps if Eynon used persuasion Llinos might come, in time, to consider him a good catch. Give her time to grow up a little and she might realize that a union with a half-breed, even one as handsome and charismatic as Joe, was out of the question.

At least Llinos would be safe with him. She would not need to work in the sheds, at risk from other men, including his own father. There was a great deal they might share. But not love, she could never love him. Llinos loved Joe and would love him until she died. Still, he would accept the role of second best if it meant having Llinos as his wife. And yet, deep inside him, he knew it was only a dream, a dream that would never be fulfilled.

'Why have you come to work here then?' The question irritated Llinos, she was tired, she wanted nothing more than to sleep and perhaps to dream about Joe standing with her on the hillside facing the broad band of the sea.

'Go to sleep, Janet,' she said.

'Aw, come on, jest talk for a bit. I don't get much chance to talk to anybody.'

'I'm tired, I don't feel like talking.' She turned over in the lumpy, narrow bed, her face to the wall. She stared at a grey patch where the white-wash had peeled away. She felt lonely, homesick. She wished for the days when she, Binnie, Watt and old Ben had worked to keep the Savage Pottery alive. Those were happy days. But those, she reminded herself, were days without Joe. Days when she had been sleeping, unaware of the rich hot blood that fired through her veins whenever she set eyes on him.

'You know that old letch got an eye for you, don't you?' Janet's voice was remorseless, keeping Llinos from sleep.

'Shut up, I don't know what you're talking about.'

'Mr Morton-Edwards got his eye on you, or I'm a Dutchman.' Janet sniggered. 'Ruined more than one wedger and pot girl, has our bossman.'

Llinos sat up. 'You are being silly, Janet, of course Mr Morton-Edwards is not interested in me. Even if he was, I am not interested in him.'

'Makes no difference.' Janet sat up and hugged her legs. 'I remembers poor little Clare Brazil, lovely girl she was till he got his hands on her. Took her away to the infirmary they did, never saw her again.'

Llinos shook her head. 'Nonsense!'

' 'Tain't nonsense. You ask anybody in the pottery, calls this 'is harem, they do. Just take care, what he says goes round here, mind.'

Llinos sighed. 'I'm too sleepy to argue.' She snuggled down beneath the blankets and closed her eyes.

'Promise you'll take care and I'll shut up and go to sleep.'

'I promise,' Llinos said but already she was drifting off into a rosy haze of dreams where she was with Joe, running free through the grass of a land she had never seen; bathing in crystal rivers, drying naked and shameless under the sun.

Mr Morton-Edwards sent for her before work in the morning and Janet leaned over the scrubbed table and nodded knowingly. 'Keep your hand on your halfpenny, love,' she whispered so loudly that one of the other girls sniggered.

Llinos tied back her hair and put on a fresh apron before walking the short distance to the big house. The manservant let her in the back door and instructed her to wait until she was sent for.

The cook crossed the flagged floor of the passageway and stared at her curiously. Llinos bit her lip, she already felt humiliated, it was as though she was of no account. But then why should she be? She was simply a working girl now, one among many who slaved for the poor wages handed out by the clerk each week.

At last the servant came for her and took her into the main part of the house. It was opulent beyond her expectations. Rich carpets hung on the walls. More carpets covered the floorboards, which gleamed with much polishing. If she had thought Eynon's house was luxurious, it was nothing compared to his family home.

She was led into a sitting-room where Mr Morton-Edwards sat at a large desk, a pen in his hand. She listened to the scratch of the nib and saw the quiver of the feather quill. She clasped her hands together, standing quite still in the doorway.

'Do you know why I have sent for you?' He smiled and he appeared so far from the monster which Janet had painted as to be absurd.

'No sir,' she answered crisply.

'Well, I have been speaking to my son about you.' He smiled and tapped the desk with his pen. 'You know he is head over heels in love with you?'

'He and I are friends. Eynon was wonderful to me when I was alone and worried about the fate of the Savage Pottery. I owe him a great deal.'

'Good, good.' He smiled and sat forward in his chair. 'Well, you are very young and there is a great deal of time ahead of you to decide who you do, and do not, wish to marry but just in case you choose my son, I feel I must insist on you coming to live with Estelle and me. The house in Morton-Edwards Street is no fit place for the young lady I hope will one day become my daughter-in-law.'

'But, Mr Morton-Edwards . . .' She stopped speaking as he held up his hand.

'Don't say another word.' Philip Morton-Edwards stared at her, a thoughtful look on his face. 'How good is your penmanship?'

'Very good, sir,' she replied. She was wondering where the meeting was leading but her suspicions had faded. There was no sign that Mr Morton-Edwards had any unworthy ideas about seducing her, on the contrary. Janet, it seemed, had been talking nonsense.

'I wondered if you would agree to write my letters for me, as well as working with Mr Wright, of course. There will be some correspondence with the court of King George.' Mr Morton-Edwards smiled. 'My humble pottery has been honoured by an invitation to make a special dinner set for the king's table and my own writing simply will not do.' He held up a sheet of paper and Llinos, seeing the untidy scrawl, smiled.

'You are right, sir.'

'There we are then.' He seemed satisfied. 'For

heaven's sake, get out of those working clothes. Dress in your usual manner, like the lady you are.' He softened the words with a smile. 'You will not be doing any of the menial work, leave that to others, my dear. Now, I'd better get on, off you go.'

'Thank you, sir.' Llinos remembered to bob a curtsy and moved towards the door.

'Oh, Miss Savage' — he had turned away and his head was bent towards his paperwork — 'You have not yet agreed to live under my roof. Just think, I would expect your father to pay any daughter of mine the same courtesy if the roles were reversed, would I not?'

Llinos paused. 'It's very kind of you, sir. May I think about it for a little while?'

He was silent for a long moment and Llinos wondered if she had angered him. 'Very well. In that case, I shall expect to see you here, reasonably dressed, at nine o'clock in the morning. In the meantime, please feel free to take the rest of the day off.'

It was strange to have the day to herself. Llinos walked up towards Poppets Hill, her favourite spot, and sat staring out to sea. She closed her eyes and thought of Joe, hoping to draw him to her with the strength of her thoughts. When she heard footsteps approaching over the softness of the grass, she lifted her head in expectation.

She was ashamed of the way her heart sank when she saw that it was not Joe but Eynon coming towards her. He sank down beside her and put his arm around her shoulder.

'What's happened, why aren't you at work?'

'I have been given the day off.' Llinos rested her head on his shoulder. Why was it she felt so safe with Eynon? She closed her eyes, smelling the sweetness of the soft grasses as the breeze rippled through them.

'Binnie and Maura keeping well, are they?'

'Aye, well enough. The baby seems a little better now and Maura is a fine cook. But I don't want to talk about them.'

Llinos lifted her head. 'What do you want to talk about, Eynon?'

'I want to warn you to be careful of my father.'

'Not again. Why are you all so against him?'

Eynon looked down at her. 'So, someone else has been talking to you about him?'

'Oh, yes.' Llinos laughed. 'Janet who shares her room with me thinks he's the devil in disguise.'

'Perhaps he is.'

'Nonsense! Only this morning he asked me to work with him writing his letters, that sort of thing. He wants to treat me like the lady he believes me to be.'

'Do not trust him, Llinos. What my father wants he gets.'

'Is there anything wrong with that?' Llinos was aware that there was a note of sharpness in her voice. 'He is ambitious, that is why his pottery is flourishing. He loves success and goes all out to achieve it. I can't see anything wrong in feeling that way.'

Eynon frowned. He was staring out to sea, a look of deep unhappiness on his face. She felt a sudden affection for him. Whatever differences existed between his father and himself they were cause for pain. She put her hand on his cheek and Eynon took her hand and pressed it to his lips.

'Be careful, Llinos.'

'You keep saying that! Is there something you are not telling me, Eynon? Does your father change into a monster with horns when the sun goes down or what?'

He kept her hand in his and pulled her to her feet. 'I'm sorry, I just do not like or trust my father. I love you, Llinos, I don't want to see you hurt.'

'Oh, Eynon! I don't get on with my father but I wouldn't want to influence anyone against him.'

'Don't let's quarrel,' Eynon said. 'Come back to live with me. You will be well chaperoned and I can take care of you. I hate to think of you in that scrubby lodging house at the mercy of anyone who wishes to accost you.'

Llinos was becoming impatient. 'I can take care of myself.' She drew her hand away. 'I know we are friends, Eynon, but do not presume to try to run my life. That was the mistake my father made.'

'But the house in Morton-Edwards Street is

damp and shabby, you are used to better things.'

She began to walk away from him, impatient now. 'You needn't worry, I'm moving into Ty Mawr tomorrow,' she said. 'I should be comfortable enough there, don't you think?'

Eynon caught up with her. 'Llinos, you can't mean it. You are walking into the lion's den.'

She shook her head, he was fanciful to the point of absurdity. 'I love you as a friend, Eynon, but you mustn't try to tell me what to do with my life. Can't you see that your own dislike of your father is clouding your judgement? He has shown me nothing but kindness and respect. I have not found him to be half as bad as you make him out to be.'

'He wants you to marry me.' The words spilled from Eynon's lips.

'Really?' The sarcasm in her voice was undisguised. 'So he can't mean me any harm then, can he?'

'You don't understand the way he thinks.'

'I don't understand the way you think, Eynon, that's the truth. Step back from it all, Eynon, look at the situation with clear eyes. I'm sure you'll realize that your own differences with your father are clouding your judgement.'

Llinos ran away from him, her feet hardly touching the softness of the grass. She was tired of people who wanted to manipulate her. She did not know what Eynon was making such a fuss about. All his father had done was to offer her a chance to be independent. What on earth could be wrong with that?

Her mind was made up. She would go and see Mr Morton-Edwards and tell him that she would accept his offer of a room in his own house. There were plenty of servants and what was more he had a wife. How could he be accused of having designs on her? It was absurd. She slowed her steps as she came into the coolness of the valley. For a moment, she leaned against the rock face and closed her eyes.

She would give up her independence in a moment if she could be with Joe. But Joe did not want her or he would have come for her by now. More sedately, she began to walk towards the bustling streets of the town. Men! She must put them all out of her mind and live her life to suit herself.

'You must go to her, convince her.' Eynon's voice was high-pitched, bordering on panic, and Joe stared at him in compassion.

'Do you think I could persuade her when you couldn't?'

'Yes, I do.'

Joe pushed away his coffee cup and watched as a mote of dust caught in a shaft of evening sun drifted downward towards the table. 'She has to live her own life, make her own mistakes.'

'No, my father will take advantage of her somehow, believe me. Go to her, Joe, before it is too late. You love her, don't you?'

Joe turned to look through the dusty window

of the coffee-house and to the open sky beyond. He felt the call of the plains in his blood. He wished himself anywhere other than here in this dreary little township that was being desecrated by the onset of the thing they called progress.

High chimneys were beginning to sprout along the banks of the river. Soon the cool clear waters flowing to the sea would carry the debris of the copper works. It would grow dark and deep and muddied.

'What do you think your father has in mind?'

'He wants me to marry Llinos, to try to prove my manhood. And to perpetuate the Morton-Edwards name, of course. To achieve all this, he will manipulate her mercilessly. He is hard and ruthless and he will stop at nothing to get his own way.'

Joe looked at him steadily. 'So he wants you to marry Llinos. You could hardly call that unnatural. And you, do you want to marry her?'

'I would like nothing better. She doesn't want me, however. When my father realizes his plans will come to nothing, he will turn against her, he might even be violent.'

Joe nodded, he was inclined to believe Eynon. Philip Morton-Edwards seemed to be a man who would get what he wanted no matter who was hurt.

'I'll speak to her.' He rose to his feet. 'Now go home, Eynon, rest, you look worn out.'

It was cool in the evening air, the breeze lifted his hair from his neck and Joe was conscious of the stares that followed his progress along the street. He walked softly, like the Indian he was, his feet scarcely leaving an impression in the dust of the road.

His blood quickened when he thought of being close to Llinos. But there was a barrier between them, a barrier that even he might not be able to remove.

When the rain came down from the heavens, he looked upwards and wondered if the great spirit was shedding tears for the puny strength of Wah-he-joe-tass-e-neen.

CHAPTER FOURTEEN

She was there again. Floating high above the land where the plains spread as far as the eye could see. And where a crystal river cut a swathe of bright ribbon through the rich earth. Llinos did not know this land but she knew that she could be happy here. Even in her dream, she recognized that she was looking down on the country where Joe had been born.

Joe, her love. His face was close to hers, he was bending towards her. The touch of his lips was fleeting, the kiss of a butterfly.

Abruptly, Llinos sat up in bed. She became aware of the lumpy mattress, the coarse sheets and the snores of Janet, who slept on the opposite side of the small room.

She wrapped her arms around her body, she was cold and there was a feeling of emptiness inside her. She washed and dressed in the clothes she had worn when she left her father's house. A good, high-waisted dress and a cut-away jacket. Today she would be leaving the lodging house and moving into the lush room that had been prepared for her in the Morton-Edwards household.

She looked towards the window, sensing something, a prickling feeling in her spine. She felt a presence, a warmth filled her. Had her dream been telling her that Joe was seeking her out?

She hurried downstairs and out into the cool of the early morning air. Dew hung like jewels on the crocus heads in the small garden. He was there. She moved towards him, her eyes searching his face.

'Have you come to fetch me?'

He held out his hand. 'Let's walk together beside the waters of the sea and listen to the talking of the shells on the ebb.'

With her hand in his she felt happiness surge through her. The sun was rising, pouring the warmth of red gold light over the earth. Joe's skin shone like beaten copper. He was so beautiful she felt she was looking into the face of the sun.

They sat together on an outcrop of rocks and stared across the sea to where the dimly outlined shape of the Devon hills formed a link between earth and sea and sky.

'It's so beautiful.' Llinos, her fingers still curled into Joe's warm, strong hand, felt that this breathless time would be with her for ever. Whatever lay before her, she would remember this moment when she had sat with Joe in the light of early morning.

'Eynon has been to see me.' Joe did not look at her and Llinos swallowed her disappointment. His words were like a shower of cold water washing away her happiness.

'I see.'

'Llinos, why do you allow this man Morton-Edwards to run your life? You who are so set against the advice of your friends allow yourself to be persuaded by a man you hardly know.'

'You are all wrong about Philip.' Her words sounded thin and frail and she was not sure if she believed them. 'My father, Eynon, and now you, all of you trying to tell me what I must and must not do. You seem to forget that for a time I was independent of any man. I don't think you understand or care how I feel now.'

'We care.' His words fell like stones hitting a deep pool. The 'we' hung between them like a barrier.

'Come home, Llinos,' he said. 'Your father is a stern man but he loves you.'

'And if I come home my father will insist on sending me away to school. What have I to do with school at my age?'

She looked at Joe and saw the smile tug at the corners of his mouth.

'I might seem young to you but some women of my age are wives and mothers. Just look at Maura.'

'Yes, look at her.'

'What does that mean?'

Joe's eyes were blue against the tan of his skin, they seemed to search deep inside her. 'Do you think Maura is happy, fulfilled?'

'Why shouldn't she be? She has Binnie and her baby.'

'And you think that is all there is to life?'

'No, but . . .' She bit her lip. 'Why, what's wrong with Maura?'

'She is a woman with a child and no wedding ring on her finger. She has become an outcast among her own people.' His voice lowered. 'I know how that feels.'

'Joe . . .' Llinos wanted to touch him, to hold him close to her. He sat beside her, lean and yet broad of shoulder, his dark hair hanging past his collar. He met her eyes reluctantly now, reading the longing there.

'Joe . . .'

He rose to his feet. 'Listen to reason. You would be safer in your father's house.'

Llinos closed her eyes, his unspoken rejection of her hurt so much she could hardly bear it. 'Go away and leave me to live my life as I see fit.' Her voice was surprisingly controlled. She stood up, adjusting her skirts with an angry twitch of her fingers.

'Goodbye, Joe.' She walked away without looking back. If she allowed herself to look at him she would lose all her pride, throw herself into his arms, beg him to kiss her and to promise her his undying love. She was a fool.

That evening, Llinos sat in the large drawing-room of Morton-Edwards House and listened to the lady of the house playing the pianoforte. Mrs Morton-Edwards played with feeling. The pathos in the music was reflected in the droop of her slim neck. Absorbed in the music, Estelle was unaware of the lines of sadness that drew her mouth down at the corners. There was no sign of Mr Morton-Edwards.

After a time, Estelle rose and folded away the sheets of music. 'I'm sure you've had enough of my playing by now.' She smiled but the lines of sadness lingered on her face.

'Would you like to talk a little or are you tired?' Estelle sank into a chair, her head resting against the cushions.

'You play beautifully and no I'm not tired, Mrs . . . Estelle, perhaps you are?'

Estelle shook her head. 'I will have to wait up for my husband.' There was nothing overtly hostile in her manner or her words and yet Llinos had felt from the moment she had entered the house that Estelle did not welcome her presence there.

'Am I intruding?'

'My husband wishes you to live here with us and I obey my husband in all things.' Estelle was very pale. 'Perhaps it might be better for you to retire early, Llinos. You are little more than a child, you need your sleep.' Estelle smiled and a little warmth touched her eyes. 'A very pretty child, if I may say so, you should be wooed by a handsome beau, not sitting here with stuffy old me.'

Estelle rose and pulled the silk cord of the bell. It jangled faintly from some deep reaches of the house. Shortly after, a maid knocked and entered the room, bobbing a curtsy.

'Show Miss Savage to her room and help her

with her toilet,' Estelle said. 'Then bring me a hot drink, I feel quite chilled.'

In her room, Llinos stared around at the rich hangings, at the tapestry-covered walls and the silken covers on the high four-poster bed. It was all strange and unfamiliar and she wished she was home at Pottery House with the hum of the fires around the kilns for company.

She dismissed the maid and undressed herself. She shivered as she climbed up onto the bed, staring at the flickering of the candles placed strategically around the room.

Last night she had lain in the lumpy bed at the lodging house listening to Janet's snoring. Last night she had felt safe. Last night she had dreamed of Joe.

She was woken by a touch on her cheek. She sat up quickly to see the dark outline of a man leaning over her. For a moment her heart felt it would pound its way out of her chest.

'Don't be frightened, it's only me.' The voice of Mr Morton-Edwards was slightly slurred, the reek of wine hung on his breath. Llinos shrank against the pillows.

'It's all right, I mean you no harm, I have just come to talk to you.'

'Surely it would be more proper to talk to me in daylight when I'm not in bed?' Her voice was sharp and she heard the man chuckle.

'Fine spirited girl, I knew you would be.' He moved slightly away from her and Llinos breathed more easily.

'I suppose it was impulsive of me to come to you in the night like this, but I felt I should share my good news with you at once.'

'What news?' In spite of herself, Llinos was intrigued. She sat up straighter and held the blankets to her chin.

'My Mr Wright has produced the most perfect porcelain body. Much better than anything we've turned out before. You can see right through it. This is going to make my pottery the best in the land, rivalling even that of Mr Wedgwood.'

'That's wonderful.' Llinos sat forward eagerly. 'I can't wait to see it.'

'You won't have to.' Morton-Edwards chuckled again. 'This sample plate was waiting for me when I returned home, I've brought it straight up to show you.' He held up a plate; it shimmered whitely in the candlelight. He held it before the flame and the thickness of his fingers showed through the undecorated porcelain.

'It's beautiful!' Llinos said. 'How is it done?'

'Mr Wright has been experimenting with soaprock and bone ash. I'm not quite sure how he did it but tomorrow we will have a demonstration.' He paused. 'We do have one problem, a great deal of the porcelain is cracking in the kilns, the mixture is not quite right. Not yet, but it will come, given time.'

He handed her the plate. She took it and turned it towards the candlelight. 'It might need a little more bone ash,' she said consideringly.

'Ah, I knew you would be interested.' He smiled in satisfaction. 'In addition to writing my letters, you can write down the recipes of the china composition, that way we can keep a check on what works best. Do you like that idea?'

'I do indeed!' The very feel of the china beneath her hands was enough to tell her that this was something very special. The name of the pottery would be spoken of far and wide; the Tawe Pottery would be famous. For a moment she wished it had been her own potters who had made the discovery. She pushed the thought aside.

Mr Morton-Edwards moved towards the door, he was a little unsteady on his feet but he seemed in a good humour. 'You are a lovely, intelligent, not to say gifted young woman, Llinos Savage,' he said. 'I only wish I had met you twenty years ago.' He chuckled. 'As I didn't, I shall have to be content with hoping you will become my daughter-in-law.'

He moved to the door. 'I shall see you bright and early, then. We shall go straight after breakfast to the sheds and there you shall meet my clever Mr Wright.' He paused in the doorway. 'Good night, Llinos.' He closed the door before she could reply. She shook her head, sleep had left her. She would never marry Eynon; Mr Morton-Edwards was hoping in vain for something that would never be.

She slipped from the high bed onto the floor and made her way to the window. Outside, the garden was silvered by moonlight. The trees stood in regimented rows and the gardens, symmetrically laid out, were the place the night creatures could call their own.

From somewhere in the distance, she thought she heard the cry of a fox and then it was silent. The dreaming silence of a still night.

Llinos sighed softly. She would probably remain a spinster all her life. If she could not have Joe then she did not want any man.

She pressed her face against the coldness of the window pane, she would not pine away of unrequited love but pour her energies into what she knew best, the manufacture of china. Perhaps she might even be witness to the creation of the best porcelain ever made.

Philip turned restlessly in the huge bed. He too found sleep impossible. He thought of Llinos. She was a beauty all right, her long dark hair hanging like a cloud around her shoulders and her skin finer than any porcelain he had ever seen. It would be a wonderful pleasure to take away that shining virtue. Still, for the time being he would concentrate on the fact that she would make Eynon a wonderful wife. True she had no fortune to bring him but then the boy had money enough.

Philip lay beside Estelle, listening to her quiet breathing. How could she sleep so peacefully when she had failed him so badly? There was no doubt in his mind that he had chosen the wrong woman; she was sickly, just like his son, and Philip could not abide anyone who showed weakness of any kind.

She had been a lively girl once but now she was like a waif about the place. He wished he was rid of her and then he could live a little, seek out openly the company of other women. He was heartily sick of Estelle.

He turned to look at the plate on the polished table. It was a key to so many things, to fame and even more riches and just perhaps the key that would unlock the heart of the virginal Llinos. He had seen the light in her eye, seen the enthusiasm shine in her face. She loved the china as much as he did, she was excited by his new discovery.

He sighed. He must do all he could to foster a liaison between his son and Llinos Savage, for he just knew she would bear children easily. Sons, sons who would become real men, not weaklings like Eynon. And if she would not agree to the marriage then Philip would enjoy administering her punishment.

He heard Estelle sigh in her sleep and he felt in that moment that he hated her. It was her fault they had no children. Given a real hot-blooded woman he would have a houseful of children by now. If only Estelle would have the decency to die, then he would be free to marry whomsoever he chose.

A small grain of an idea settled into Philip's brain. With Estelle dead he could start afresh.

He could begin his life without encumbrances. He lay awake for a long time and slowly, a plan began to take shape in his mind.

'You see, it looks even better against the sunlight.'

Llinos, her sleeves rolled above her elbows, her hair tied back from her face, took the plate almost reverently. It was light and fine to touch and as she held it up to the sunlight she could see her fingers through the porcelain.

'There's not much soaprock in this, is there?' She looked towards Mr Wright. The old man pushed back his greying hair and shook his head.

'About a sixth and about twenty-six pounds of bone with half again of sand, I suppose.' His voice was gruff but the faint West-Country nuances softened it. 'See how fine it is.'

'Aye, the problem is that it vitrifies suddenly and sometimes fuses to the saggers,' Philip Morton-Edwards broke into the conversation. 'Anyhow, I shall leave you to sort all that out, I have a business meeting in town.'

The workers in the large shed touched their caps as Morton-Edwards walked past them without a glance. Once he had gone, the atmosphere in the room lightened. Men talked quietly together, there was a clatter of saggers being stacked and one man began to sing softly, it was a haunting sound.

'What are you doing here?' Mr Wright asked

269

slowly. 'The sheds are no place for the daughter of Captain Savage.'

'I'm writing down the recipes you're using,' she said. 'I thought you would appreciate some help to keep a check on your experiments.'

'Here to keep an eye on me, are you, his nibs doesn't trust me, thinks I'll hold him to ransom by keeping the exact ingredients secret.'

'Not at all!' Llinos protested.

'In any case, shouldn't you be home under the care and protection of your father?'

Llinos looked at him in surprise. 'I really do not think that is any of your business, Mr Wright.'

'No, maybe not.' He turned away. 'Very well, let me show you how I propose to make the glaze, shall I?'

'Wait, is there something I should know about Mr Morton-Edwards? What are you trying to warn me of?'

'As you said, girlie, it's really none of my business.' He regarded her steadily. 'You have a great deal of common sense, use it.'

The edge of excitement Llinos had felt at the prospect of being involved in making the fine china slipped away from her. Everyone was warning her about Philip Morton-Edwards, could they all be wrong? It seemed unlikely. Ah well, she had a job to do and it was about time she got on with it.

That evening, Estelle did not put in an appearance at dinner. The long, elegant dining-room was ablaze with candles, a gold and silver bowl filled with flowers stood at the centre. Mr Morton-Edwards sat at one end of the long table and Llinos at the other.

'Is Estelle unwell?' Llinos broke the silence which had begun to feel uncomfortable.

'My wife is of a delicate constitution, you will notice many such absences. I apologize for her.'

'No need,' Llinos said quickly. 'May I see her, later?'

'I would not recommend it. She needs complete rest though I believe hers is a monthly indisposition that most women bear with a great deal more stoicism.'

'I see. Some women do have . . . difficult days of the month.'

'Let us talk about my china.' Philip Morton-Edwards changed the subject. 'Do you think we can solve the firing problems?'

Llinos was more comfortable now. On familiar ground, she talked animatedly, warming to this man whom everyone else seemed to regard as a monster. He was a stern man but then no more implacable than her own father.

Philip provided decent housing for his employees and paid them fair wages. He was filled with a burning ambition for the china but then so was she. It was something they shared, a meeting point, a bond almost.

Philip unexpectedly turned the direction of the conversation. 'I'm surprised that a beautiful girl like you is not already spoken for. You know I harbour hopes that you might one day accept Eynon but, tell me, are there no other suitors in the offing?'

'Not at the moment.'

'Many young ladies of your age are mothers already.'

She recognized the argument; it was the same one she had used with Joe and yet now she was uncomfortable with it.

'I don't know that I will ever marry or have children.'

He regarded her steadily. 'Some might say you talk like a woman scorned. Are you?'

'Really, Mr Morton-Edwards, you do ask such personal questions.'

'Then please answer me honestly.' He was watching with nothing but genuine interest in his eyes and she suddenly felt the urge to confide in him.

'I fell in love with the wrong man.' She met his gaze. 'My father thinks he is wrong and so does he.'

'By "he" I gather you mean this Indian chap?'

She looked at him in surprise and he laughed. 'There's not a great deal that escapes me. That is one of the secrets of my success, Llinos dear.'

'Do you think it wrong?'

He shrugged. 'I don't know the man. I understand that even though he is half Indian he is well-educated and from good stock on his father's side.'

'But you see him as my father does, not quite one of us.'

Philip put down his gleaming cutlery. 'And you, Llinos, see him from the point of view of a young, romantic girl. He is handsome as the devil, charming too I've no doubt, but his way of life is of necessity different from ours. If you did marry him and have children they too would be half-breeds.'

Llinos sighed. 'In any case, he does not want me so there's an end to it.'

'Poor Llinos. So you have decided, as I have, that the china is the better passion. China does not disappoint, it does not reject, it responds to any care and attention that is lavished upon it.'

Llinos saw Philip Morton-Edwards then as others failed to: he was lonely, misunderstood, searching for a perfection he might never find. He lowered his head and stared down into his glass and Llinos felt his sadness flow towards her. She hesitated and then crossed the room and touched his shoulder.

'Please, don't be unhappy.'

He put his arms around her waist and pressed his head against her breast.

'I am so lonely, Llinos, so misunderstood.' His voice was heavy and Llinos stifled the urge to pull away from him. He was in pain, how could she hurt him more? She brushed his hair as if he was a child and for a moment he clung to her. Then he released her and sighed.

'My bout of self-pity is over now, Llinos,

please leave me while I ease my mind with a good drink and a smoke.' He smiled up at her. 'And Llinos, thank you for your kindness.'

In the drawing-room, Llinos sat staring out into the moonlit garden. She must see Eynon, tell him that his father needed him. Estelle was delicate and must not be worried and in any case, she had no interest in Philip's work. He needed someone to talk to, to share his achievements with, and that someone should be his son, not the daughter of another man.

When Philip joined her, he was cheerful. His eyes sparkled and he entertained her with stories of his boyhood in Cornwall. He told her of the china clay extracted from the ground and poured aboard ships. Told her of the sea-green pools formed in disused workings.

'Well, my dear, I'm going to retire,' he said at last. He touched her shoulder lightly in passing.

'Perhaps we two lost, misunderstood souls can be of help and comfort to each other, Llinos, what do you say, can we be friends?'

She let her hand rest on his. 'I think we already are.'

CHAPTER FIFTEEN

Eynon Morton-Edwards' house was built of grey stone. It stood on a promontory of land above the curving bay on the outskirts of Swansea. It had once been a vicarage and had housed a large family of children in the five bedrooms that ran the length of the landing. Now it was home to Eynon, Binnie Dundee, Maura and her young baby. The only other servant had quarrelled with Maura and had left the house in a fit of temper, declaring the work of such a big house was too much for her.

Llinos stood before the ornate gate and looked along the curving, tree-lined drive, wondering if she would find Eynon at home. She had decided to walk the stretch of the bay from the pottery to Black Pill and the village beyond. She was young and healthy but even so, her feet, in the inadequate leather slippers, had begun to ache.

As she had left the Tawe Pottery, she had seen her father. He had turned his head away from her and his rejection hurt. Now, pausing to catch her breath, she thought about her father's attitude more calmly. She realized that he was as proud and angry as she was; it was difficult for him to give in and admit he was wrong.

It was inevitable that she should see him

sooner or later because the Savage Pottery stood cheek by jowl with the larger Tawe Pottery. If only he had held out his hand, or if he had smiled, Llinos would have gone to him, tried to talk to him. But he had done neither.

She pushed open the gates and walked slowly along the drive. It was a fine day, though the breeze coming in from the sea was a little chilly. When she reached the arched front door, she knocked briskly. She was looking forward to some sympathetic company and perhaps some refreshment after her long walk.

She heard footsteps and then the door was flung open. In the background was the plaintive sound of a baby crying.

'Llinos Savage, what are you doing here?' Maura looked ill. Her skin, once blooming, was devoid of colour. She had grown thin, the bones showing through the insubstantial material of her gown.

'I'm here to see Mr Morton-Edwards.' Offended by Maura's lack of courtesy, Llinos's tone was icy.

'Well, come in! Sure there's no need for you to stand on the doorstep like a tradesman.'

She led Llinos towards the open door of the drawing-room. It was a room Llinos had liked at first sight, it was long with high windows at one end and French doors on the other leading out to the garden beyond.

'I'll see if Mr Morton-Edwards can see you.'

The crying of the baby from somewhere in the

back region of the house began to intensify and Maura closed her eyes wearily.

'Oh, mother of God! If only the child would be quiet, just for me to get my breath.'

She disappeared and Llinos sat on one of the plush chairs staring out of the window. Joe had been right, Maura was not living in blissful happiness. She looked harried, sickly and unhappy.

Joe. The thought of him brought a warmth to the pit of her stomach. The warmth spread through her and her body tingled with what she dimly recognized as desire. She wanted Joe to hold her, to make love to her, and yet she wanted so much more of him than that. She wanted his unconditional love, she wanted to be his soul mate. She had thought he felt the same. Why then was he keeping his distance from her?

'Llinos, it's good to see you.' Eynon entered the room and pulled her to her feet, studying her at arm's length. She could not help noticing how thin he looked in his linen shirt. He was so pale and there were shadows beneath his eyes.

'Are you well, Eynon?' she asked and he nodded, drawing her towards the sofa.

'I am well enough, how about you?' He looked at her, his eyebrows raised. 'Have you run away? Has my dear father shown his true colours?'

'Oh, Eynon! Don't start all that again. I wanted to see you and spend some time with you. Do I have to have an ulterior motive for visiting you?'

'So you are not here to talk about my father?'

'Well, I wouldn't say that. I would like to talk to you about your father as it happens.'

'I thought so.' He sat but there was a closed look on his face, a set to his mouth so that for once he appeared almost hard.

'He's not as bad as you make out, Eynon,' she said. 'I have been living beneath his roof for two weeks now and he has shown me nothing but kindness.'

'He's not stupid, he will not show his hand, not until he's ready. Anyway, why aren't you slaving for him today?'

'I'm entitled to my day off, aren't I? In any case, your father treats me more like a daughter than an employee.'

'A daughter, eh? That will change. It won't be long until he's trying to inveigle you into some underhand scheme or other. He damages everything he touches.'

Llinos took a deep breath and tried again. 'He has found this new method of making porcelain. You should see it, Eynon, it's so beautiful, it's like snow when it is just beginning to melt. It's so fine you can see your fingers through it.'

'When you say my father has found this wonderful new method, you doubtless mean that one of his overworked employees has come up with a recipe which my father will make his own.'

'I'm assisting Mr Wright,' Llinos said. 'And we are not overworked. We're experimenting with varying degrees of bone and soaprock. Your father *is* funding the venture, don't forget.'

Eynon rose to his feet. 'I'll fetch us some cordial, you look hot and flustered.'

He left the room and, impatiently, Llinos followed him through the hallway and along the passage to the kitchen. The scene that greeted her was one of chaos. Dishes stood piled along the table at the side of the stone sink. Bits of food had been trodden into the flags of the floor. Over all was a smell of rancid food that almost made Llinos gag.

'Good heavens, Eynon, why are you living like this? Where are your servants?'

'Well, Mena was all the help I had beside Maura. She walked out, quarrelled with Maura about the baby. She said she couldn't stand the noise of the child crying any longer. To tell you the truth, I'm sick of it myself. I've had the doctor here several times and he says there's nothing wrong, the child is just teething.'

'Oh, Eynon, what a state on the place!'

'Maura can't cope with the housework and the baby,' he said mildly. 'She's unhappy, Binnie comes home less and less. God knows where he spends his time.'

Maura entered the kitchen and stared at Llinos defensively. 'The baby cries and cries. The only one who can do anything with the child is Mr Morton-Edwards. I'm at my wit's end so I am.'

'For heaven's sake, Eynon! You must get yourself more staff, you can't go on this way, you'll all die of some horrible fever. Come on, Maura, boil up some water. While I'm here, I might as well make myself useful.'

She took the hem of her gown and twisted it into a knot above her knees. 'I'll clean this place up for you, starting with all these dishes, and when I return to town I will try to find you more servants.'

Eynon laughed. 'I wish you would marry me, Llinos, it would solve a great many of my problems.'

'Be careful, I might just take you up on that. Go on, Eynon, you take care of the baby, Maura and I will get on with the cleaning.'

It was not as easy as Llinos had imagined. She had kept house after her mother died but she never had to cope with so much filth and grime as challenged her now. The water for washing the dishes cooled rapidly, gaining a film of grease in the process. Maura kept the fire going, carrying the boiling water to the sink but her heart was not in it. She sank against the door frame and wiped her eyes. 'I'm weary, I can't stand this any more, sure an' aren't I only human?'

Llinos shook the water from the last of the dishes and stared round her. There was still a great deal to do, the cupboards needed cleaning and the floor had to be scrubbed.

'Go on, have a rest, I'll carry on here.'

Maura nodded. 'Do what you can, 'twill be in the same mess tomorrow or the day after, any road.'

Left alone, the task was doubly hard. Llinos needed to keep the fire going as well as carrying the water and doing the cleaning. It would have been better if she had brought in a band of young girls who were used to domestic work. The job would have been done much quicker and far more efficiently. But it was too late to think of that now, she might just as well finish what she had started.

She lost track of time as she scrubbed woodwork and cold flagstones until her fingers were raw. When she rose, her back felt as though it was breaking in two.

'When are you going to stop?' Eynon stood in the door, Maura's baby in his arms. 'You don't want to kill yourself, do you?'

'It's finished now. Doesn't it smell much sweeter in here?' Llinos opened the door to the back garden, allowing the fresh air to fill the kitchen.

'Where's Maura?' Eynon said as the baby began to cry. 'I think the little one needs feeding.'

'She must be resting. She looks terrible, Eynon. Are things that bad between her and Binnie?'

He shrugged. 'Go and find her. One thing I can't do is give this child suck.'

As Llinos climbed the stairs, she became aware that the bottom of her skirts were clinging damply to her legs. Llinos went into the bedrooms one by one but there was no sign of Maura in any of them. Llinos frowned, a suspicion beginning to form in her mind. She opened the cupboards, looking for Maura's belongings, for any sign of the girl's presence. There was nothing. Slowly, Llinos descended the stairs.

'She's gone.'

Eynon looked at her. He had been crooning to the baby but now his eyes were wide with panic.

'She can't be gone, what can I do with a baby?'

'She is gone. Now keep calm, Eynon. Nothing is insoluble. We'll get a wet-nurse from town, just for the time being, until Maura comes to her senses.'

'You are so damn sensible it hurts!' Eynon said and Llinos looked at him in surprise.

'Is that a fault then?'

'No, but it would be nice to see some reaction from you for a change, some indication that you actually feel for people.'

Llinos closed her eyes, if only Eynon knew how deeply she did feel and how hard she worked to keep her feelings hidden.

'I'll go into town, I'll send some women up to you as soon as I can. In the meantime, can you manage the baby alone?'

Eynon smiled then. 'I suppose so, except I'm not exactly the right person to be nursing the child.'

'Oh, I don't know, I think it suits you!' Llinos kissed his cheek. 'I'll have servants with you before nightfall, I promise. Until then, you'll just have to manage.'

She fetched her cloak, sniffing appreciatively at the clean smell of the kitchen, pausing to admire the order which she had created out of chaos before closing the door behind her.

'My son can be all sorts of a fool.' The words though harsh were tempered with a smile and Llinos looked across the table at Philip Morton-Edwards and knew she was warming to him. He was so kind, so humorous.

The early sun slanted across the room, giving the silver on the sideboard a glow as if a light shone through the metal. It was a fine morning and soon Llinos would go to work in the pottery, doing the job she had come to love, experimenting with bone, sand and soaprock.

'Eynon is too gentle for his own good.'

'I agree with you there.' Phillip's expression had changed. 'I think he should have been a second son, then there would have been no pressure on him to follow in my footsteps.

'He is too soft by far,' Philip continued. 'He allows folk to take advantage of him.' He spread his hands. 'I ask you, what other man would allow himself to be saddled with another man's bastard child?'

'But he can't help his nature,' Llinos protested. 'He's loving and kind and honest, he's my dear friend. Don't you love your son for what he is, Mr Morton-Edwards?'

'Of course I do. But he has no time for me and that I find hard to bear.'

'I'm sure any misunderstanding between you could be cleared up if only you spent time talking to each other,' Llinos said.

Philip did not reply. Llinos sighed. 'Anyway, I think Eynon is happy with the arrangements I have made for servants from the village to go and work at his house.'

'Let us change the subject. What of the porcelain, how are the experiments coming along?'

Llinos leaned forward eagerly. 'We are having less breakages, now. The new recipe seems to be working well.'

'And you are not tempted to pass my recipes on to your father?'

'I would not do that, sir.' Llinos heard the indignation in her own voice even as she registered Philip Morton-Edwards' reaction to it. He was smiling.

'I know you well enough by now, Llinos Savage, to realize you would never betray a trust. I am teasing you.'

She looked down at her hands, smiling ruefully at her own foolishness. 'I think I have a great deal of growing up to do yet, sir.'

'I disagree, you are a very mature young lady.'

The door opened and Estelle entered the dining-room still wearing her nightgown and robe. She was paler than ever. She seemed to be fading away with each passing day.

Philip rose to his feet. 'My dear Estelle, should you be out of bed?'

'I am tired of lying in my room day after day.' She sounded petulant and yet her voice lacked energy and life.

'Come sit with us, have something hot, you will feel better if you eat.'

She took a chair beside her husband and stared down at the table. 'I'm not hungry, Philip. I think I should have the doctor.' She glanced up half fearfully.

'Of course, my love. I shall have Perkins run into town at once.' He rose and left the room and Llinos watched in concern as Estelle twisted her thin robe between her fingers.

Estelle looked up. Her eyes were wide; they appeared unfocused. 'He's poisoning me,' she said flatly.

Llinos was not sure she had heard correctly. She searched Estelle's face and saw she was serious.

'You are mistaken, I'm sure Mr Morton-Edwards loves you too much to wish you harm.'

'You don't know him, Llinos, you see only the civilized side of my husband. You can't know what a beast he is in the bedroom. Pray God you never find out.'

'The doctor will come soon, tell him how you feel,' Llinos said uneasily. Suddenly an air of foreboding seemed to inhabit the sunlit room.

'You don't believe me, you think I'm mad. I can see it in your face so don't deny it.'

'No, no, you are sick, you will feel better once you see the doctor, I promise you.'

'Don't make promises you cannot keep, Llinos. And take my advice, get out of this house. There is evil here and it's embodied in the man who is my husband, God help me.'

Philip returned to the room. 'Perkins has gone post haste, darling.' He bent over his wife, helping her to her feet. Carefully, he guided her to the door. She cast a last anguished look towards Llinos as though begging for her help.

Llinos felt disturbed all morning. Not even the excitement of working with Mr Wright on the glaze for the new porcelain could erase her feelings of uneasiness.

'What's wrong, girlie?' He rubbed his hands against his stained apron and looked at her. 'You seem distracted.' She shrugged.

'It's Estelle — Mrs Morton-Edwards, she's very sick.'

'Well, the boss will see to it that she has the best doctor money can buy. No good you fretting about the ills of those older and wiser than you, girlie.'

A sense of release surged through Llinos. She felt unburdened, as though Mr Wright's words had exonerated her. Though from what she did not quite know.

'That's it, little lass, smile, be young and carefree while you have the chance. You should be falling in love, flirting with a beau, not worrying your little head the way you do trying to solve the ills of the world.'

He pushed back his untidy bush of grey hair. 'Right, now let's look at this glaze, is it going to work, do you think?'

'Well, put it like this,' she said cheerfully, 'the

'lead-alkaline silicate, the borax and the china stone in the quantities you specify make one of the finest glazes I've ever seen.'

As she worked with Mr Wright, Llinos became absorbed. She watched his old but deft fingers at work and forgot all about Estelle and her sickness.

That night her worries returned. She had not seen Estelle at dinner and she had thought Mr Morton-Edwards looked more anxious than usual. Her queries concerning the doctor had yielded little response and he had retired early, leaving her alone in the drawing-room.

She rose restlessly and moved to the window. It was a fine night and the long gardens were half in shadow. In front of her, beyond the gardens, the two potteries sat side by side, the Tawe Pottery sprawling over much of the land close to the river while the smaller Savage Pottery crouched self-effacingly on the higher ground.

Suddenly the urge to walk around what she still thought of as her own pottery was too strong to resist. Llinos took up a cloak and let herself out of the house.

The Savage Pottery was silent, all the sheds were in darkness. As she walked through the yard, the warmth from the tall bottle kilns reached out towards her. She heard the gentle roaring of the fires and was filled with a feeling of nostalgia. If only she could turn back time to when she and Binnie and little Watt had worked like slaves to run the pottery, how many times had she wished that? But if she could go back in time, then she would never have met Joe. How she longed to see him, to talk to him about her doubts.

He appeared at her side silently. She was no longer startled by his strange habit of answering her thoughts. She pressed her hands to the outside of the kiln, feeling the heat of the bricks beneath her fingers.

'What's the matter, Llinos?'

'There's a great deal the matter, not least my father's attitude to me.'

'You hurt him when you walked out and when he asked you to come home you refused. What do you expect from him?'

'Nothing!' Llinos faced Joe. The moonlight made a raven's wing of his hair. Light touched his high cheekbones, skimmed the contours of his jaw. He looked like the noble Indian he was. He appeared like a stranger she was meeting for the first time.

She pushed the thought away, Joe was not a stranger, he was the man she loved.

'I expect nothing from my father. He's made no attempt to understand me. He wanted to force me to be his little girl again and that was impossible.' She was suddenly angry.

'But you, Joe, I expected something more from you. You take everyone's side but mine. You insist on reasoning everything through. Why can't you just give in to your feelings, Joe?' Her anger evaporated as suddenly as it had come.

'Joe, can't you just love me?'

He took her in his arms, his cheek was against her hair. She breathed in the scent of him, savouring the moment. He was so near and yet he was far away, somehow untouchable. She no more possessed him than she could possess the wind blowing in from the sea.

'I love you, Joe, I want to live with you.' She looked up at him. 'Take me away to your land. We can live together on the plains, fish in the rivers. You can build us a house, we can forget all this.'

Joe took her face in his hands, his palms were warm and firm against her skin.

'You have your own destiny to fulfil, Llinos. You are young, the world is before you. Don't throw away your chances as if they were nothing.'

She put her arms around his neck, forcing his head down to hers. 'Stop talking, Joe, please.'

He looked into her upturned face and then, almost roughly, his mouth was on hers. She felt incandescent as though flames lapped around her, enveloping her in shades of red and orange and gold.

'Llinos, my nightingale, my Firebird.' Joe was whispering, his lips against her neck. She knew with a piercing joy that he desired her as much as she desired him.

'I love you, Joe,' she said softly. 'I have to be with you or I will die.'

He released her abruptly. 'No, Llinos, you will

not die. You will grow up into a beautiful woman, you will have many admirers. You are destined for great things, a great many joys and a great many sorrows and even I cannot alter the path of your destiny.'

'Excuses, Joe! You are not man enough to flaunt the opinions of men like my father, men who judge you as an inferior being because of your heritage. I love you, Joe, I love you because of what you are not in spite of it. I would give up everything for you.'

'And that I will not allow.' Joe was a stranger again, he half turned from her, his long hair lifting a little in the breeze. 'I'm a man without means, don't you realize that, Llinos? What could I offer you?'

Llinos stared up at him, and was struck again by the almost primitive beauty of him.

'Joe, whatever you say, I will never love another man. If I can't have you then I won't marry anyone.'

She turned and ran from him, her feet scarcely touching the dusty earth. She hated Joe and she loved him all at the same time. Why could he not see that she cared nothing about money, she had been without money before, it was love she wanted, his love.

When she returned home, it was to find the Morton-Edwards house full of lights. A carriage stood in the driveway and maids scurried from the kitchen to the upper regions of the house carrying a variety of bowls and cloths.

Llinos stopped in the hallway, brushing back her hair from her face, wondering what was happening. She caught the arm of one of the maids.

'What is it, what's wrong?'

'Begging your pardon, mam, it's Mrs Morton-Edwards, sickly she is, real poorly. The doctor is with her now.'

She shook her head. 'The vicar's there, too, not that I hold with all that nonsense, mind. Don' know what Mr Morton-Edwards was thinking about fetching him in, what good can he do now?'

'Is she very sick?' Llinos asked anxiously. The maid nodded.

'I don't hold out much hope, bringing up awful black stuff she is.'

Llinos felt a sense of horror, it was almost as though she was facing her dead mother again. She forced herself to climb the stairs, telling herself to be calm. The door to Estelle's room was open. Inside, kneeling beside the bed, she saw Philip, his head bent as though in prayer.

She moved towards him, half-afraid to look at the woman in the bed. The doctor stood silently shaking his head. On the opposite side of the bed, a vicar, Bible open, intoned prayers.

'Llinos.' Philip saw her and lifting his hand urged her closer. 'I am losing her, my dear wife is so sick . . .' His voice broke.

Llinos leaned towards the white mask of Estelle's face, seeing her eyes open briefly. Then

Estelle sighed and her head rolled to one side. The doctor glanced at his pocket watch.

'Your wife is at rest now, sir,' he said.

Philip rose to his feet. His face was set, he appeared to stumble.

'There is no more you can do now, Mr Morton-Edwards.' The doctor caught Philip's arm. 'Allow me to give you one of my potions so you can rest.'

'All right, Doctor, if you think it will help. Llinos, come with me, please.' Philip held out his hand and Llinos took it.

'I'm so sorry,' she whispered, 'so sorry.' She went with him to his bedroom and stood uncertainly in the doorway. Philip threw himself down and his servant pulled off his boots.

'Leave me.' Philip waved his hand. 'No, not you, Llinos, stay with me just for a while, I beg you, I don't want to be alone.'

She looked at the doctor, who had followed them into the room. He held out a cup with some liquid in it. The vicar had remained in the bedroom reading from the Bible.

'Drink this, sir, you will feel better then.' The doctor nodded to Llinos. 'Stay if you will, I shall send one of the maids to sit with you.' He spoke softly but Philip heard him.

'I want no-one but Llinos.'

'I'll be all right,' she said. The doctor looked at her doubtfully and then back at the man on the bed. 'He'll be asleep in a few minutes, I don't suppose it would be considered improper for you to stay, not in the circumstances.'

Improper, did folks have nothing more to worry about than the proprieties? Llinos drew a chair to the bedside and took Philip's hand and smoothed it gently. 'There, go to sleep, rest now.'

'You are so kind, such a comfort to me, Llinos. I don't know how I would survive the night on my own.'

'I will stay with you, I promise,' Llinos said gently. She saw Philip's eyes close, his breathing became soft and even. In sleep he appeared younger, more vulnerable. There was the look of Eynon about him. Impulsively, Llinos bent and kissed his cheek.

'Sorry, miss.' The young maid was standing in the doorway looking at her curiously. 'Brought a blanket to put round you, if you need it, that is.'

Llinos shook her head. 'I will be all right, thank you. Just close the door to keep out the draught, will you?'

'Close the door, miss?'

'Yes, close the door.' Llinos wondered at the girl's stupidity, 'There's a draught from the land-ing, can't you feel it?'

'Yes, miss, of course, miss.' The girl left the room and closed the door and Llinos leaned back against the plush cushions of the chair. She kicked off her shoes, she was so tired, she must sleep.

She woke with the sunrise and sat up rubbing

her neck. Philip was still asleep, he lay on his back, his arm stretched out across the bed as though reaching for her.

Llinos poured water from the pitcher and splashed her face and hands. She was aching, she had not been able to rest properly in the upright chair. But at least she had kept her promise and remained with Philip through the night.

The maid entered the room just as Llinos was slipping her feet into her slippers. She bobbed a curtsy and put a tray of hot cordial down on the table beside the bed. She looked at Llinos with open curiosity and bobbed a curtsy once more before leaving the room.

The gossip spread through the Tawe Pottery and beyond the walls to the Savage Pottery next door and thence to the town. It was said that on the night of his wife's death, Philip Morton-Edwards had spent the night alone with Llinos Savage.

CHAPTER SIXTEEN

Llinos was standing next to Mr Wright watching the glaze running silkily from the plate he was holding when she heard the rattle of wheels against the stone floor. She looked up and was startled to see her father coming towards her. He trundled his chair awkwardly over the uneven floor, his face dark with anger. Walking behind him were two of his men. He made an impatient gesture towards Llinos. 'Bring her,' he said harshly.

The men caught her arms and, outraged, Llinos tried to pull away. 'How dare you lay hands on me!'

'Bring her, I said.' Lloyd Savage repeated the command and the men obeyed, drawing Llinos towards the door.

'What in the name of hell's teeth is going on here?' Mr Wright, his face red, took up a stand before Lloyd Savage's chair, staring down at him in outrage.

'I am Lloyd Savage and this young lady is my daughter. Out of my way before I take my stick to you, sir.'

'I am quite aware of who you are, sir, but you are acting with uncalled-for aggression towards your daughter. You should be ashamed of yourself.'

'Out of my way, fool!' Lloyd rammed his chair forward and Mr Wright moved smartly to one side.

'You just wait until Mr Morton-Edwards hears about this. He will not take kindly to your invasion of his property, sir, or your high-handed attitude to the young lady.'

Mr Wright was pushed roughly aside by one of the men.

'How dare you treat Mr Wright so roughly!' Llinos protested. No-one replied and she was marched unceremoniously over the short distance between the potteries. Once she was inside Pottery House she was taken upstairs and thrust into a bedroom. She heard the bolts shoot home and realized with a feeling of disbelief that she was a prisoner.

She hammered on the door, angry and bewildered. What did her father think he was doing? What had come over him?

'How dare you treat me this way, Father!' she called. 'Have I no rights at all?'

There was no reply, the house seemed silent, empty. She looked down at her hands. A spot of glaze dried against her palm, a good glaze, the best yet. And she was not there to see the china after the final firing. She felt like weeping tears of frustration.

She sank onto the bed and leaned back against the wall, tucking her legs under her skirts. She stared up at the soft sunshine slanting in between the curtains and thumped the pillows with her fists. 'How could you do this to me, Father!' she shouted, but no-one heard.

It was a long day. Llinos watched from the small window as the sun set over the river. She was hungry but she would not ask for food. In any case, she doubted anyone would hear her even if she called.

She was almost asleep when, at last, the door was opened. A manservant whom Llinos did not recognize stood on the threshold. 'Your father wishes to see you, Miss Savage.'

She was tempted to run past him, down the stairs and out into the street. She resisted the temptation, she would talk to her father, demand an explanation for his barbaric treatment. His first words startled her.

'Are you proud of yourself, madam?'

She saw the servant stand against the door as if to bar her exit.

'Proud of myself? I don't know what you are talking about! How dare you bring me here against my will, Father? Have I no right to my freedom, then?'

'You are the talk of the whole town! You, my daughter, sleeping with a man whose wife has just breathed her last. I can scarcely believe it of you.'

She sat down suddenly. 'You have been misinformed, Father.'

'You did not spend the night in the man's bedroom then, is that what you are saying?'

'No. I am saying I did not "sleep with him".

I slept in a chair at his side. He was distressed, he had just seen his wife die. Surely you can understand that?'

Lloyd Savage shook his head. 'So it is not true that a maid saw you kissing the man and then, come morning, saw you dressing?'

'Father, how could you believe this of me? I am your daughter, I am a respectable person, I do not deserve to be treated like a streetwalker.'

'Then why act like one?' He wheeled his chair to the window and looked out. 'I saw you once with Joe, in his arms, kissing him. You were behaving like a streetwalker then.'

Llinos looked at his back, straight and unyielding. 'Where is Joe?'

'He's left, gone to England. I expect he is as disillusioned with you as I am. I thought you were in love with the boy, what a fool I was! Joe did not own a pottery and he was a half-breed to boot.'

He turned to look at her, his face pale with anger. 'Oh, I see now that Joe was just a dalliance, your real aim was to win the favour of Philip Morton-Edwards.'

Despair washed over her. Joe was gone away, probably believing the worst of her; she would never see him again.

'I will never forgive you for this, Father,' she said. 'You have such little faith in me that you believe the gossip of servants. Now you even accuse me of wanting Philip's money. You must have a very low opinion of me.'

He just shook his head as though he was lost for words. She stared at him defiantly. 'All I did was comfort a bereaved man. I stayed with him all night, yes. I sat and watched at his side, that was all.'

Her father opened his mouth to speak but Llinos rushed on.

'And now you have ruined my life! You have taken me away from a position I enjoyed and, worse, you have sent away the only man I will ever love.'

Lloyd flinched as though she had struck him. For a moment, his gaze wavered. His shoulders slumped and his head rested on his chest. 'I can't believe a word you say, girl. I know I'm not an ideal father but you will obey me.'

'I might have to obey you, Father, but that won't make me love or respect you.'

'I can't help that. You are still a child in spite of your precocious ways. I know you would run away from school so I'm sending you to your aunt's house where you will have time to grow under the influence of a lady.'

'I will not go, Father,' Llinos said.

'You have no choice in the matter. Take her back to her room.'

The servant took her arms and propelled her up the stairs. He pushed her into the bedroom as though glad to be free of her and the bolts slid ominously into place. She peered through the window and saw Ben, his hair sparse and grey, and a lump rose to her throat as she remembered the happiness she had once enjoyed.

The days passed, the long tedious hours enlivened only once when she heard Philip Morton-Edwards' voice raised in anger outside the house. She could not see him but it warmed her that he had come to her defence. And then the silence had descended once more and she sank into a state of lethargic acceptance. Joe had gone, believing the worst of her; there was no purpose in life any more.

It was early morning, the dawn paling the blue of the night into daylight, when Llinos woke. She heard voices outside the house and rose quickly from the bed.

A carriage stood at the roadside, the horses patiently waiting, heads down, tasting the dried grass at the verge. The door was opened and the servant beckoned for her to come downstairs.

Her father was waiting for her. 'After breakfast, you are going to your aunt in Bristol.' He did not look at her. 'She has kindly sent her carriage to pick you up. I hope, in time, you will learn the manners of a young lady. At least under the care of Aunt Rebecca you will not be able to act like a serving wench. Mark my words, you will not find your aunt an easy companion.' He paused but Llinos was too dispirited to reply.

'Go and change into clothes appropriate for a young lady of your station in life. And, Llinos, don't try to cross me in this or it will be the worse for you.'

Later, in full view of the neighbours of Pottery

Row, Llinos climbed into the carriage and sat back in the seat along with two servants who were strangers to her.

Leaning forward to look through the window, Llinos saw the door close on her father's uncompromising face. She put her hand over her mouth forcing back the tears as the carriage jerked into movement and began the first stage of the journey from Swansea to Bristol.

'So, I hope you are happy.' Letitia stared at Joe, hostility in every line of her aged face. Beside her stood a box and a huddle of baggage. 'We shall be out of here this very day, have no fear.'

'There is no need to leave,' Joe said softly. 'I don't need the house or your possessions.'

'None of it is ours,' Letitia said. 'Father made sure of that. No, we will not stay and bear your charity, we have more pride than to live in the same house as Father's bastard half-breed son.'

'Your bitterness does you no good, sister.' Joe's mild tone belied the anger that burnt in his gut.

'I am not your sister. I never will be your sister. Your sisters are doubtless running wild in some outpost of the Americas, half clothed like the savages they are.'

'Savages sometimes come in the guise of a lady,' Joe said.

Letitia's gaze swerved away from his. 'Come, Charlotte, we will not stay under this roof a moment longer, we shall wait for our carriage outside.'

Charlotte paused for a moment, hesitating before putting a hand gently on Joe's sleeve. 'I'm sorry if Letitia's words hurt you, I'm sure your mother must have been very beautiful for Father to have fallen in love with her.'

The tightness of Joe's jaw softened. 'Your God go with you, Charlotte. Remember, if there is anything you need you must come to me.'

The house was silent. Joe wandered around the spacious rooms, dark with heavy panelling and rich carpets. Heavy drapes hung at the many windows. It was a magnificent house and it was his but it was not what he wanted.

Joe wanted the sun on his face, the wind through his hair. He wanted to hunt buffalo. Above all, he wanted Llinos.

He sat at his father's desk and opened the letter left there for him. Joe could imagine his father dictating the letter with difficulty before his illness had become acute. It outlined the modest provision he had made for his two daughters and Joe's eyes narrowed as he read the body of the letter.

To my son Joe I bequeath all my other worldly goods as specified in my will in the hope that he will return to the land of his birth and seek out his mother. If this is possible, I wish my son to offer his mother anything her heart desires. In conclusion, I would like to ask my son's pardon and beg that he might seek the pardon of the maiden I made my wife under the laws of the Mandan Indians.

A scrawled signature, barely decipherable, lay spiderlike across the paper. Joe folded it away and leaned back in his chair. The land of his birth, what would it be like now? He had left it as a child, left the lodges of his mother to learn to survive in the so-called civilized world. Could he return and belong once more to the tribe? He doubted it, too much time had elapsed, too many moons had passed.

And yet the same rivers would flow, the same buffalo would run, the same sun and sky and earth would greet him. He rose and walked outside. If he returned to the plains, he would be able to breathe in air that was free of scorn and prejudice, inhale the winds that did not carry the smell of death. He would sleep and make his decision in the morning.

He woke suddenly in the night. He had fallen asleep on the large sofa in the conservatory, admiring the stars in the softness of the night sky. He was alert, his eyes seeing not the darkness but the face of Llinos Savage. She was near him, he felt it, knew it. He rose and padded softly into the garden, pausing to think rationally about his feelings.

Before Joe had received a summons from his sisters, he had talked with Lloyd and he understood the captain's anger but he knew the gossips were wrong. Llinos would not do anything to shame herself or her father. Joe tried to say as much, but Lloyd was in no mood to listen. He had decided to send Llinos to her aunt in Bristol and nothing was going to change his mind.

Joe had the feeling that Lloyd would be happy to see the back of him. The captain had offered him a fine horse to take on his journey and Joe, wondering what could be wrong with Letitia and Charlotte, had accepted gratefully.

He had ridden almost non-stop to the border, reluctantly exchanging the rugged Welsh hills for the softer plains of the Marches. During the journey, he had thought deeply about Llinos.

He had seen in his mind's eye the way she was held captive in her own home. He had sensed her despair. And he knew that by now she would be on her way to Bristol, to be kept prisoner in the house of her aunt.

He thought of the lie of the land, of the route a carriage might take. To travel from Swansea to Bristol would mean at least one overnight stop. He closed his eyes, picturing the post houses along the roadways of Wales and through into Gloucester.

He returned to the house and made his way to his father's study. Joe lit a candle and carried it into the dusty room; there was a huge map on the wall and Joe needed to study it. His blood racing in anticipation, he looked at the skeletal lines of the map. He saw the hand-coloured hilly areas and traced the line of the rivers. He knew then where she would be resting.

He snuffed out the candle and closed the doors of his father's house behind him.

'Why did Maura leave me?' Binnie was sitting, head bowed, his thin features obscured by his work-roughened hands. Eynon shook his head impatiently.

'Look, Binnie, how do I know what was in Maura's thoughts? It seems to me that everything just became too much for her. She couldn't cope, not with the baby, the housework, nor with the way you left her day and night to her own devices.'

Binnie looked up sharply. 'You are blaming me?'

Eynon sighed. 'I'm not blaming anyone but facts need to be faced, Maura was not happy.'

'I wonder where she's gone.' Binnie rubbed at his stubbled chin. 'She might be gone to folks in Ireland, I suppose.'

'Or she might simply have returned to Greenhill whence she came,' Eynon said softly.

'You think so?' There was hope in Binnie's eyes. 'Perhaps I should go up there, have a look for her. What do you think?'

'I think you need to give her some time to herself.'

'Aye, perhaps you're right, but that bed is cold and empty without Maura in it.'

'Perhaps that was the trouble, bed was the

only place you had contact with each other. Maura talked to me more than she ever talked to you, Binnie, do you realize that?'

'I suppose I never thought about it.' Binnie rose and walked towards the window, staring out into the darkening day. Eynon watched him with a feeling of sadness. Life was hard for Binnie as well as for Maura. They had snatched at life without giving themselves the chance to grow up properly. But perhaps a failure in love was better than never having made the attempt at all.

And Binnie was not the only one who felt bereft; Eynon was missing Llinos badly even though she had been gone for less than a week. The way Lloyd had handled the situation was nothing short of barbaric but he was her father and he had his rights.

He rose abruptly. 'I'm going down the Castle Inn. Coming?' He opened the door and stared out at the sky streaked with scarlet as the sun finally set behind the hills.

Binnie rose from his chair and together they made their way down the slope towards town. There was a striking contrast between them of which neither was aware. Eynon was slim, with fine features and softly curling hair. Binnie was short and wiry with strong, irregular features. It was a strange, uncomfortable situation, Eynon Morton-Edwards in company with a lowly pot worker, but they were drawn together by a mutual feeling of loss.

The inn was filled with smoke. A fire blazed

in the huge open hearth and the corner seat was occupied by the two Anglican vicars.

Father Martin saw Binnie and nodded to him. Binnie returned the salute with little grace.

'Evening.' Eynon felt obliged to be polite, something that Binnie had no intention of doing.

'Fine red sky, augurs well for tomorrow.' He took some coins from his pocket and waved his hand to the landlord.

'Sit with us, gentlemen, our talk has become too insular, a little lightening will do us good.' The older man, Father Duncan, smiled and Eynon reluctantly took a seat opposite him.

Binnie stood awkwardly ill at ease for a moment and then sat down. 'Seen anything of Maura?' He spoke abruptly and Father Martin blinked behind his spectacles.

'Come now, Binnie,' the older vicar said amiably, 'we are not on duty here, we are having a quiet smoke and enjoying a short respite from the dragon of a housekeeper that Martin, in his rather dubious wisdom, saw fit to employ.'

'But . . .' Binnie stopped speaking as Eynon laid a restraining hand on his arm.

'Good crowd in here tonight,' Eynon said quickly, filling the awkward moment. 'I suppose as the night draws in, business will be even brisker. Better have our fill early, I think.'

Eynon felt and sounded inane but Father Martin smiled at him, looking rather like an overgrown baby. His face was round and pink and his mouth curved upwards in a smile.

'How are you managing up at the house without a woman's touch?' he said and amazement spread over his countenance as Father Duncan dug him sharply in the ribs.

'Llinos Savage found me some servants so I'm fine.' Eynon felt sorry for Martin; he seemed something of a misfit. In which case, they should get on very well, two misfits together.

'Ah, Llinos Savage, spirited girl, so spirited that her father has sent her packing.'

Eynon leaned forward. 'Aye, it seems she was taken from the Tawe Pottery quite roughly.'

Martin rubbed his chin. 'Well, that's understandable in the circumstances. I expect her father thought it best to put her in the care of a woman relative.'

'I don't suppose Llinos thought it was best,' Eynon said. 'She's independent, used to having her own way.'

'Well, not this time. You heard the gossip about her, of course.' Martin looked around quickly. 'It seems she spent the night alone with Mr Philip Morton-Edwards after his wife died.'

'Well done, Martin.' Father Duncan shook his head. 'I suppose it has escaped your notice that you are talking to Mr Morton-Edwards' son, has it?'

Martin clapped his hand over his mouth, his cheeks became pinker and his sparse eyebrows nearly disappeared into his hairline. 'Sorry, old chap, seems I'm forever putting my foot in it,' he said in confusion.

'Think nothing of it,' Eynon said. 'I've heard the story a dozen times and every version was different. I don't believe a word of it personally.' He was seething, he would have to speak to his father, tell him to his face how he despised him, tell him the scorn he felt for a man who would involve an innocent young girl in a scandal.

The silence seemed to stretch to eternity and Martin made an attempt to appear unflustered. 'The funeral is all arranged; I'm to conduct the service. I hope to see you there.' He stopped speaking as Eynon rose abruptly.

'I expect you will.' Eynon turned and without another word left the inn, leaving the open-mouthed vicar behind him. His father had not thought to inform him of the funeral arrangements but then Eynon was a fool to expect such consideration.

Eynon strode along the road towards the Tawe Pottery, his hands clenched against his sides. He pushed the door open and strode into the house and one of the maids rushed forward to take his hat.

'Where is my father?' Eynon said abruptly and the maid bobbed a curtsy pointing towards the dining-room.

Eynon pushed open the double doors and saw that his father was entertaining guests. 'I wish to speak to you, Father. Now.'

'So, you've honoured me with a visit,' Philip said coldly. 'Have you forgotten that tomorrow is Estelle's funeral?'

'I have just been informed of it by one of the vicars,' he said. Philip did not speak, he merely raised his eyebrows as though regarding a too-playful pup.

'Very well, Father, if you will not do me the courtesy of coming outside, I shall be obliged to speak to you here.'

One of the ladies took up her fan and waved it fiercely. With a sigh, Philip rose.

'Do excuse my son, he is not usually this eager to speak to me.' Philip led the way from the dining-room and closed the door. He turned to look at Eynon.

'What do you mean by barging in like this? Have you no tact, no sense of timing?'

'After what has happened to Llinos you talk of tact?' Eynon faced his father squarely; they were, he realized, of a height so that they looked each other in the eye.

'Her father has sent her away, I am saddened by it but I am not her keeper, Eynon, surely you understand that much?'

'And yet your selfish conduct is the cause of the gossip about the two of you,' Eynon said.

'Nothing untoward happened,' Philip said carefully, 'and if it had, it would be no-one's business but mine.'

'So why did you compromise her, Father? What were you thinking of?'

'Estelle had just . . . just passed away,' Philip said. 'I felt very low, naturally. Llinos was sympathetic, she . . .'

'So you were foolish enough to allow her to stay the night in your room? Didn't you stop to think of her reputation?'

'I was distraught . . .' Philip said.

Eynon held up his hand. 'No, you were selfish, as usual. So Llinos's father came and took her away and who could blame him?'

Philip shrugged. 'He came when I was out, took the girl back home by force, according to Wright.' He shrugged. 'What was I supposed to do?'

'You are a spiteful, vindictive man and I am ashamed that you are my father.' Eynon shook his head. 'You have no conscience, none at all. You might have ruined a young girl's life but what do you care?' He waved his hand towards the dining-room. 'Your wife dead only days and here you are entertaining, I just do not understand you.'

Philip turned on his heel. 'Nor I you. Now if you have finished your little tantrum, I will rejoin my guests.'

Eynon caught his father's shoulder. 'Father, as a matter of curiosity, why do you hate me?'

Philip turned and his gaze was full of scorn. 'Need you ask?' His voice was low, his mouth twisted into a sneer. 'You are only half a man, you have no strength. I will never get an heir from you so I shall have to get myself a son, a proper son.'

'You forget, Father, I am your heir whatever you think of me. I am your first-born, nothing you can do will ever change that.'

'Oh, don't you be too sure.' Philip walked into the dining-room and closed the door.

Eynon left the house and went out into the cool of the night air. His father was an evil man and a fool, nothing he could do would change Eynon's position in the scheme of things. One day, Eynon would inherit the house, the pottery and all the money that had belonged to the family of Eynon's mother.

He stood looking up at the Tawe Pottery for a long moment and then he moved into the row. His knock on the door of Pottery House brought an elderly manservant to enquire what he wanted.

He was invited into the hallway and stood there waiting for Lloyd Savage to put in an appearance. Eynon's welcome at the Savage household was much warmer than he might have expected.

'Eynon. Come inside, have you eaten?'

Lloyd was adept now at manoeuvring his specially adapted chair. Eynon nodded. 'I have, thank you.'

'Then we shall have a drink of porter and talk together, after all, you still have an interest in the pottery, don't you?'

Eynon seated himself in the comfortable leather chair and took the glass Lloyd handed him.

'My interest in the pottery is nominal, I can see that you have everything under control without any help from me. I came to enquire about Llinos,' he said and Lloyd nodded.

'I guessed as much. Your father was a fool, compromising the child's reputation the way he did. Well, Llinos is out of harm's way now, silly, headstrong girl.'

'And Joe?'

'Joe has gone. He had business of his own to attend to.' Lloyd tipped the glass to his mouth, savouring the liquid, rolling it round his tongue. 'It eases the night horrors, you know what I mean?'

Eynon nodded, he knew only too well, except that his own horrors were very much different to those of the man before him.

'So Llinos is all right?' Eynon sat back in his chair feeling suddenly deflated. He had expected another battle and Lloyd's geniality unnerved him. He was experiencing a crushing sense of disappointment. Even if he learned of Llinos's whereabouts, it was doubtful he would be able to see her.

'May I have her address? I would very much like to write to her.'

'I see no harm in that.' Lloyd wheeled himself to the desk and took out a sheet of paper. He scribbled an address and handed it to Eynon.

'If you do visit her, tell her I'm sorry I needed to use such tactics with her.' He shook his head. 'I had to take her from your father's pottery by force, it was not very pleasant. I don't suppose she will ever forgive me.'

313

'And I will never forgive my father for putting her in such a position.' Eynon accepted Lloyd's unspoken invitation, holding out his glass towards the bottle for Lloyd to refill it.

'Why do we need to battle with those we love?' Lloyd said. 'I only wanted what was best for Llinos, but of course she couldn't see that.' He looked at Eynon. 'She's grieving for Joe. Not even you could call Joe an ideal life partner for a girl as well-bred as my daughter, could you?'

Eynon paused for a moment to ponder what Lloyd meant by the 'even you'. 'I think it is the right of everyone, man or woman, to choose for themselves over something so important,' he said.

'Well, that's it, isn't it? Llinos is still a child, she is not a woman, not by a long chalk. She proved that by staying in your father's room all night alone.'

'Even so, she knows her own mind. I sometimes wish she didn't.'

'Poor Eynon, I know you are in love with her, I can see it in your face. Why don't you go after her, talk her into marriage with you. That's what you want, isn't it?' He gazed into his glass. 'I would never have thought I would accept the son of my bitterest rival as a suitor for my daughter but anything would be better than her marrying a half-breed.'

Eynon rose, forcing himself to be calm. 'I'm sorry I intruded on your privacy.' He swallowed the lump in his throat that might have been anger and then again might well have been tears. 'Thank you for the address.'

Outside in the coolness of the night air, Eynon felt the touch of rain on his face. It seemed that Lloyd felt as much scorn for him as his own father did.

He clenched the paper in his hand as though it was a talisman. He felt warm, suddenly here was a doorway to winning Llinos, he was sure of it. She would surely prefer marriage to him to being held prisoner for years to come. He glanced back once at the lights shining from the windows of the houses behind him. And then he walked away from the light into the darkness of the night.

CHAPTER SEVENTEEN

The rosy glow of dawn was bringing the trees into sharp focus. Dew gently dusted the grass beneath Joe's feet as he walked towards the house in the hollow of the valley. He had arrived too late at the coaching inn. Llinos and her party had already left. Fortunately, one of the grooms had overheard the servants talking and knew which direction the coach was taking.

Now Joe stood outside Avonbridge Hall. It was a sprawling, elegant building with high windows and many chimneys. He held his breath and closed his eyes. He pictured Llinos, her dark hair fanned like a silk cloak on her pillow, her beautiful eyes closed.

He would wake her with his mind, touch her with his longing and she would come to him. He looked up at the morning skies, he felt the earth beneath his feet, breathed in the scents and sounds of nature awakening around him and he knew it was good to be alive.

She came to him as he had known she would. She stood in her flimsy nightgown, her hair flowing around her shoulders, just as he had imagined her.

'Joe!' She stood looking at him for a long moment and then she walked slowly into his arms. He held her, kissing the glossy waves of silkiness as her hair cascaded across his face.

'I knew you were near, I knew you would come. I dreamed about you last night.' Her voice was husky with sleep.

He kissed her eyes, her hair and then he kissed her mouth. It was as though the rivers of his past, the rivers of pain, rejection, and loneliness had turned into sparkling, cascading fountains. He was this moment, he was the past, the future, he was eternity.

'I love you, Llinos, my little Firebird.' He felt her body strain against his and he wanted her, he would always want her. He had known her from time immemorial. She was his homeland; the grass on the plains. She ran free with the buffalo herds, she touched continents with the power of the four winds.

'I love you too, Joe.' She pulled his head towards her and he felt her heart beat like a tiny bird against his own. Now, he had the right to claim her. He was no longer penniless. He was a man of property, a man with prospects. He could take care of Llinos in the way her father could respect.

'Llinos Savage, come along inside the house at once!' The voice was cracked with age, fierce with outrage. Joe relinquished the soft sweetness of Llinos's lips and looked up.

A woman, old, with the map of time written across her face, her limbs gnarled like the twisting branches of the trees, was staring at him,

317

her eyes alive, filled with anger.

'Aunt Rebecca, don't be angry.' Llinos clung to Joe. 'We are in love. Joe's come for me and I won't be parted from him any longer.'

'Shame on you, girl.' Rebecca Savage twitched her shawl around her shoulders, covering her thin bosom. 'Come indoors this instant.'

She hobbled painfully towards the open French windows, her hand, clawlike, gripping her stick for support. Joe looked down at Llinos.

'I'll come with you.' He would explain to the old lady that he was offering Llinos marriage. He had not asked for his father's estate, had not even considered it his by right but if it was the key to his happiness with the woman he loved then so be it.

'Joe.' Llinos held his hand in hers. 'Why now, what's changed your mind?'

'My father has left me his estates. I have worldly goods to offer you now.'

'That never mattered to me.'

'I know.' He touched her cheek. 'But it mattered to me. And, I suspect, to your father. He will still see me as I am, a half-breed,' Joe said. 'But perhaps he will accept me now I have means.' He walked with her towards the house and he was conscious of her softness pressing against his side.

'Don't worry, Llinos, I think you will find that money and property can wipe out the most in-built prejudice.'

Inside, the house was bustling with life, maids

scurried from kitchen to bedrooms, carrying jugs of steaming water. How the rich lived in comfort by exploiting the poor never failed to amaze Joe. In his homeland every person, every tree, every twig was given honour.

Rebecca Savage sat in a chair, her shawl drawn tightly around her shoulders. Her eyes were sharp as they rested on Joe.

It was Llinos who broke the silence. 'Joe is the man I love, Auntie. I am going to marry him whatever anyone says.' Llinos touched her aunt's shoulder and Rebecca shrugged her hand away.

'It's all right, Joe's intentions are honourable. He owns lands, houses, he is very rich. Oh, come on, Auntie, don't frown like that.'

'Your father does not approve of him, child.'

'I will marry Joe whether Father approves or not.'

'Then you must return home to your father. I will have your bags repacked.' She shook her head. 'I did not expect your lover to turn up on my doorstep.'

She straightened her shoulders. 'You are an unruly and wilful girl and I will not have you under my roof another night.'

Her eyes flashed across the room at Joe. 'She will travel back to Swansea with you. One of my maids will accompany you. I didn't wish to be involved in the first place, now I can wash my hands of the whole sorry episode.' She rose with difficulty, refusing Llinos's help, and hobbled from the room.

Llinos looked up at Joe. He sensed the words trembling on her lips. 'You *do* want to marry me, don't you, Joe?'

It was what he wanted more than anything else in the world. She was part of him. She lived inside his head, his heart, his blood.

'Yes, I want to marry you,' he said. 'Now, go and get dressed. We shall leave for home before noon.'

Eynon felt out of place in his father's house, it was as though the very fabric of Ty Mawr were rejecting him. But one of the older servants had sent for him; Philip was sick and with Mrs Morton-Edwards newly laid to rest Eynon was needed to take charge.

He looked down at his father lying stricken in his bed; he seemed diminished by his illness. His skin was flushed an unhealthy red and his eyes were sunken, the flesh around them swollen.

His father, even in the throes of some fever, seemed to reject him. Whenever Eynon sat near, or smoothed away the tangled hair from his father's brow, Philip would move restlessly, as though trying to draw away from him.

Of course his father had never loved him, had found him weak, unlovable, but that did not alter the fact that they were tied by the bonds of blood. Eynon had a duty to discharge and he would do it to the best of his ability.

There was a light tapping on the bedroom door and the doctor entered, his face flushed from his ride. 'Morning, Eynon, how is our patient today?'

Eynon watched as the doctor examined his father, hoping there would be some change for the better. His hopes were dashed when the doctor turned to him, grave-faced.

'I'm sorry, Eynon, we can do nothing but wait it out. The fever should break soon and that will be the turning point. Would you like to call a second opinion, perhaps?'

'Thank you, Dr Rogers.' Eynon looked with affection at the old doctor who had cared for the family for as long as he could remember. 'I have every confidence in you, there's no need to call in any other doctor.'

Dr Rogers inclined his head. 'Thank you, Eynon.' He moved towards the door. 'Your father's heartbeat is rapid, it's an unpredictable organ at best. It can do all sorts of things for which we are not prepared.'

Eynon wondered if the doctor was speaking philosophically or medically.

'Your father is a strong man, I expect he will live to make old bones but you can never be sure. In the meantime, I know you are more than capable of looking after your father's affairs.'

Eynon nodded but he was trembling inside. The doctor's words reminded him that he would be responsible for the running of the pottery, the managing of the accounts. It was too sudden, he had no experience in that quarter, all he had known was painting and not even that since he had moved to his own home.

If Llinos was here, she would have known exactly what to do. He loved Llinos, he trusted her. He wished she was with him now. He would have travelled to Bristol to see her by now if his father had not been taken sick.

He sat alone in the darkness of the drawing-room and wondered what he should do. Binnie was used to the ways of the pottery, he could take charge for the time being. He might be a lowly potter, but Binnie Dundee was equipped with a keen mind and a wish to better himself.

Eynon would scarcely need to bother with the day-to-day running of the pottery. The key workers were in place; fine painters did the decorating, far better artists than he was. And under the care of Mr Wright, the experiments with the porcelain bodies were continuing in a most satisfactory way. No, all Eynon needed to do was keep an eye on things until his father was well again. Surely he could do that much, couldn't he? Why did he have to doubt himself always? He should be filled with confidence, ready and willing to step into his father's shoes. His father was right, he was a weakling, a moral coward, no wonder no-one looked up to him.

It had grown dark and restlessly Eynon rose and walked out into the garden. The moonlight silvered the trees and the small lake in the lower garden. Ty Mawr was a beautiful house with well-kept grounds and yet Eynon had never felt he belonged there. He glanced back at the house, at the glow from the window of his father's room, and he shivered. His father was normally so full of life and now he was lying on his sickbed with no-one to love him or care for him except the son he despised. It was strange how the world sometimes turned full circle. He breathed in deeply, suddenly lonely.

Through the dimness of the moonlight, Eynon caught sight of the flapping black robes of one of the vicars. As the man drew nearer, Eynon was relieved to see that it was Father Martin.

'I haven't yet thanked you for conducting the burial service, Father Martin,' Eynon said. 'You spoke so well, anyone would believe my father's wife was the best-loved lady in Swansea.'

Martin smiled his baby smile, his blue eyes crinkled with laughter. 'Well, so she was, of course. All my flock are well-loved, didn't you know that, sir?'

Eynon found himself smiling; he liked Martin, he was human, he made mistakes and he did not mind admitting it.

'Will you come inside and have a drink with me, I feel in need of company?'

'Most certainly I will, sir. Lead the way, I always knew I could smell fine brandy from a mile off!'

'Good. Please, Father, do me a favour, drop the formality and just call me Eynon?'

'I will if you will drop the formality and just call me Martin.'

The candles flickered in the draught from the door as Eynon led the way inside. He pushed open the doors of the sitting-room and gestured for Martin to enter. More candles flickered in the silver candelabra, washing the room with soft light.

'Please, Father . . . Martin, make yourself comfortable.' Eynon poured a good measure of brandy for each of them. 'This will warm the cockles of your heart.'

They drank in silence for a time, a comfortable silence, and Eynon began to feel his tension ease a little.

Father Martin leaned forward a little. 'You seem very much alone, Eynon. Perhaps you should find yourself a pretty wife who will fill your home with children.'

'The girl I want loves someone else.'

'Is she going to marry him?'

Eynon shook his head. 'I doubt it, I don't think her father would give his consent.'

'There's hope for you, then, Eynon.' Martin rolled the brandy around his teeth, savouring it. 'Remember, there are as many kinds of love as there are of flowers in the field. When I was younger, I was stubborn, I would not settle for second best and so I ended up alone.'

'Are you telling me to look around for "second best" if I don't get the girl I love?'

Martin smiled. 'Put it this way, I was in love once but I was disappointed. Instead of trying again, I turned my face away from all thoughts of love and became a vicar.'

'I don't fancy the Church as an occupation.' Eynon smiled. 'I think I would bore any congregation to tears.'

'Then you must channel your desires in some other direction.' Martin smiled. 'Or fall in love with someone else. Everyone is deserving of a little love and you seem to me to be a man of many qualities of which kindness and honesty are not the least.'

Eynon felt the fear that had held him ever since his father fell sick melt a little. 'I'm glad you came up here this evening,' he said. 'I don't feel so alone now.'

'You are never alone, my son. Your heavenly Father is always with you.'

Eynon smiled. 'You have become a cleric again.'

'I never stop being a cleric, it is my one joy and comfort to know that my heavenly Father loves me even if no-one else does.' He beamed his beatific smile and Eynon smiled too.

'Have another drink, Martin,' he said.

'Aye,' Martin said, 'let us fill our glasses, we might as well make a night of it.'

'That's fine by me.' Eynon rose to open a fresh decanter of brandy and for a moment stared into the depths of the amber liquid. Martin was right, it was time he began to make a new life for himself, find a new purpose.

'I heard a little bit of gossip today,' Martin said. 'Llinos Savage returned home last night escorted by the Indian fellow.'

Silently, Eynon digested the news: so Llinos was home and it had been Joe who had gone to fetch her. That was strange to say the least. Had Lloyd relented, had he welcomed Joe as a prospective son-in-law? Eynon doubted it.

'There is talk that Llinos has found a suitable husband, a local man of standing and property.' Martin smiled sheepishly. 'One of the maids up at the pottery overheard some talk, it seems, and gossiped about it to all who would listen.'

'I see.' Eynon refilled the glasses and lifted his high. He was suddenly filled with hope. 'Here's to the future, Martin,' he said softly.

It was a bright morning, Llinos had slept well. Now she faced her father, standing beside Joe, listening to him ask for her hand in marriage. She was so happy, so in love. She stood meekly to one side, allowing the menfolk to have their say. Her father listened in silence and when he did speak, his words were like a knife cutting into her.

'You are still a half-breed, Joe, nothing is ever going to change that.'

Llinos hugged Joe's arm to her side as though she could protect him from her father's cruelty.

'Father! How could you speak like that?'

Lloyd looked at her sharply. 'Face facts, girl, however much money he has, Joe is never going to be one of us. If you married him your children would be half-breeds, too. No, I won't have it,

I won't give my permission, it is as simple as that.'

'Then I shall go and live with Joe without your permission.'

'I see, as wilful as ever, Llinos. And you, Joe, will you take her against my wishes?' Lloyd stared up into the face of the man who had been his constant companion, the man who had saved his life, but he did not waver. The future of his only daughter was in the balance and he would not have her throw away her chance of happiness because of some girlish infatuation.

'Joe, don't listen to him!' Llinos said. 'We love each other, nothing can change that.'

'Stop it, girl.' Lloyd spoke harshly. 'You speak like the child you are. Show some restraint, some dignity. I'm sure Joe has the good sense to see that you are too young for marriage.'

Joe seemed suddenly remote. 'Your father is right, you are still very young.' He shook his head as she made to speak.

'You are mine and I am yours, never forget it.' He smiled. 'I shall wait patiently for you until the time is right for us.'

Llinos was afraid and angry. 'I don't know why my life should be ruled by men. Have I no say in any of it?' She turned to her father.

'You seem able to send Joe away but you will not have your way with me. I shall go back to Philip Morton-Edwards, I shall live in his house.'

'Be quiet, child,' Lloyd said sharply. 'Mr

Morton-Edwards is sick, he may be dying for all we know.'

Llinos felt a chill begin to grow inside her.

Lloyd nodded to her. 'You may think the world stands still because you are not part of it, Llinos, but you are wrong,' he said. 'Your views are insignificant, don't you understand that?'

'Father, do you realize how bitter you sound? Do you really hate the world and everyone in it so much?'

'Keep a civil tongue in your head, miss.' Lloyd's face flushed and he looked away from her. 'What have I to be happy about? I am half a man, I cannot love a woman, I can never walk in the fresh air and feel the sand of Swansea Bay beneath my feet. Why shouldn't I be bitter?'

'You are alive, Captain.' Joe spoke sternly. 'Have you forgotten so soon how many of our comrades were left at Mont-St-Jean?'

Lloyd looked down at his hands. 'No, I have not forgotten.' He spoke in a low voice. 'But you are right, Joe, of course you are. I am ungrateful sometimes, bitter often, but isn't it natural for a man to want to be whole?'

'It is also natural for a man to sit beneath the sun, to feel the rain on his face, to breathe in the sweet air and to be thankful.'

'You and your philosophies, Joe. You see how different you are from a white man? In spite of your father's efforts, you are a native to the bone.'

'Then perhaps I have the best of both worlds,

Captain.' Joe took Llinos's hand and kissed her fingers. 'I will go to settle my father's affairs — I have bills to pay, promises to fulfil. But I'll be back for you, my love, don't doubt it.'

She clung to him, her head buried against his shoulder. 'I don't want you to go.'

Joe held her away from him. 'It won't be for long. While I'm away, think hard about your life, be a fulfilled woman by the time I come for you and I will be happy.'

Llinos watched from the window as Joe walked away from Pottery Row and as he disappeared around the corner of the road, she felt as though he was taking part of her with him.

As Joe left the house, he was fighting the anger and disappointment of finding Lloyd still set against him. He strode along Pottery Row and took the path down towards the river. He would need to buy a horse and tack as well as provisions for the journey. It would be better to find lodging for a night or two and once he was ready, he would begin the journey back to his home on the Marches.

'Joe! I heard you were home.' Eynon was just dismounting from his horse at the gates of Ty Mawr. 'I've been for a gallop along the beach, it's good to feel the sea breeze in your face when you want to blow away the cobwebs.'

He gestured towards the house. 'I'm staying here for the time being, my father is not well.'

'I'm sorry to hear it, anything I can do?'

'I don't know. I'm hoping the fever will break soon,' Eynon said.

'I've got just the thing for fevers.' Joe dipped into his baggage. 'All you do is to distil . . .'

'Hey, hold on! I'm no good at that stuff. Why don't you come up to the house and mix the potion for me?'

'All right. In return perhaps you can direct me to a good lodging house.'

'You are looking for lodgings?' Eynon asked. 'So you are not staying at the Savage Pottery, then?'

'No, I'm not.'

'Well, look, you can stay here with me, there are plenty of rooms, goodness knows. Anyway, I'm in need of company.'

'How could I refuse such an offer?' Joe swung his bag from his shoulder and rested it on the ground. Beneath his feet, shards of pottery crunched against the drive, glinting like diamonds in the sunlight.

'Are you hungry, would you like a bite of something? I think the servants should have breakfast cooking by now.'

Joe followed Eynon along the drive and into the hallway of the big house. 'I'll need to go into the kitchen,' he said. 'I'll have to infuse some herbs in boiled water.'

'Go ahead. Don't mind the servants. Come and join me in the dining-room as soon as you are ready.'

Joe made the potion silently, aware of the cook

watching him with curious eyes. While the liquid cooled, he joined Eynon in the dining-room, realizing that he was hungry.

Eynon put down his gleaming cutlery, ignoring the fine dish of kidneys and the fresh crusty bread.

'I'm in love with Llinos and I want to marry her,' he said. Joe looked at him for a long moment and decided that honesty was the only answer.

'I know.'

'Good. You are going away, Joe? Does that mean you will not be courting Llinos yourself?'

Joe looked at him long and hard. 'Lloyd has rejected me as a son-in-law,' he said. 'But Llinos and I are meant to be together, it will happen.'

'Well, we'll see,' Eynon said. 'I'm hoping she will grow tired of waiting and will accept me.'

'I can't stop you doing what you think best, Eynon.' Joe smiled. 'Our fates are drawn for us, do you believe that, Eynon?'

'I don't know,' Eynon said. Joe saw him look around at the high ceiling and opulent hangings. 'Is this my fate then?'

Joe was silent and after a moment Eynon spoke again. 'I have always hated him, you know, my father.' He swallowed the contents of his cup. 'It's mutual. He doesn't want me near him, not even now when he's sick. I wish he could have loved me.'

Joe rose from the table. 'I think the potion will be ready now. Shall I ask one of the maids to take it to your father?'

'No.' Eynon pushed away his plate. 'I'll do it.' He left the room and Joe was alone with his thoughts.

Later, when Joe was preparing to walk into town, Eynon protested that he must not bother to buy a horse, he could take one from the Tawe stables.

'Good heavens, Joe, there are enough animals here to serve a regiment. Choose which one you like and you'll find anything else you need in the tack room in the yard.'

'That's very generous of you, Eynon, but won't your father protest?'

'My father is in no position to protest. By the way, the medicine you concocted has brought about an improvement already. Should I give my father more of it?'

'You can do, perhaps just before nightfall would be the best time. By morning we'll know if it has worked or not.'

In the evening, the two men sat together and talked. Eynon was drinking a great deal of brandy and his normally pale face became quite flushed.

'She can't marry you, Joe,' he said suddenly. 'It wouldn't do, you see. You are a fine chap, a handsome chap, but she deserves the best. I mean, what can you offer her?'

Joe smiled. 'I don't know, Eynon. Love, perhaps?'

'Ah, well, love is all fine and good but what

about material things, you might not think they count, Llinos might not believe they do either, not now but she will, later she will.'

'Eynon, I'm not going to argue with you,' Joe said. 'If you will excuse me I'm going to turn in, I'm tired.'

'All right, old boy. Sorry to be so hard on you but it won't do, you see. Llinos must marry one of her own sort.' As Joe left the room, he heard the clink of glass and knew that Eynon was pouring himself yet another brandy.

Later, Joe lay in the elegant guest room, facing the fire, seeing the glow of the flames around the logs. He marvelled at the colours which sprang from the wood, he saw pictures in the flames, pictures of a girl with long black hair and eyes that melted the heart of him. Llinos.

When he was with her he longed to undress her, to lie with her in the soft grasses of his homeland, to make her his own. And yet now, as he considered Eynon's reproachful words and thought of Lloyd's objections, he wondered if he was taking the wrong path. Joe sighed and shifted and turned his eyes away from the flames and when he slept, he dreamed of Llinos, dreamed he was touching, caressing her, dreamed they were one flesh. When he woke, the fire had died. Light was barely creeping into the bedroom.

He splashed his face with water and ran his fingers through his hair. Then he picked up his bag and let himself out of the house. He looked back once at Pottery Row, at the house behind the wall, and sent Llinos his message of love.

He moved out into the yard, heard the soft breathing of the horses in the stables and knew it was time to be on his way. The sun speared through the clouds and the breeze of morning touched his face and it was as though Llinos had answered him with a kiss.

CHAPTER EIGHTEEN

The pottery shed was filled with sunlight into which motes of dust fell like snow. Llinos watched as Mr Wright took one of the newly baked plates to the window and held it up to the light.

'What do you think, Llinos?'

She took the plate from him and examined it carefully, turning it around and then holding it at a level with her eye.

'No misshaping in the heat, that's one good thing. Some pitting on the glaze but not too much. I think we can call this one a success.'

'Thank heavens you came back to us when you did.' Mr Wright rubbed his hands against his apron. 'I've missed your common sense and your good ideas.'

'Thank you, Mr Wright.' Llinos felt extraordinarily pleased at the compliment. 'Mr Morton-Edwards is recovering slowly but he will need to take care of himself.'

Mr Wright turned his eyes up to heaven. 'Eynon does his best but he's no substitute for his father.' He smiled at Llinos. 'I thank the good Lord for sending us a lady who is prepared to make decisions!'

Llinos knew the old man was right, Eynon

was not interested in experimenting with china. He was not interested in the business at all. He seemed to have withdrawn into a shell since his father's illness. All Eynon seemed to want was to keep the pottery ticking over while he sat in the big house and brooded. It was not as if he could communicate with his father, the two were at loggerheads.

She thought of her own father, how she had hated him for his attitude to Joe. It was because of her father that she and Joe were still apart. She had stayed in her father's house, lived beneath his roof, but only on condition that she go back to work in the Tawe Potteries.

Llinos wiped her hands on the cloth tucked in her belt. 'I'd better be going,' she said. 'I've made Eynon promise to come with Binnie and me to Greenhill to see Maura. It's time Binnie made up his mind to marry the girl and stopped acting like a child.'

It did not escape her notice that Mr Wright was concealing a smile. To him she was just a young girl and a spinster to boot and yet Llinos knew she was much older than her years.

Binnie now was different, he had remained a child for far too long. It was only lately that Binnie Dundee had begun to grow into a man. When Binnie had seen Maura return to claim her child and take her daughter to the home which she had provided for her, only then had he been forced to face the fact that as a father he was abdicating his responsibilities.

Llinos left the sheds and brushed at her hair, feeling the grit from the china against her fingers. The soft breezes and the sunshine-dappled river made her think again of Joe; in truth, he was never far from her thoughts. She missed him, she dreamed about him, she ached to be with him. She took out his letter and read it again, even though the brief message was etched on her mind.

'My dear Llinos, I am going to America. This is something I must do but I will come back to you, I promise.'

It was signed in flowing script. Wah-he-joe-tass-e-neen.

Llinos returned the letter to her pocket, it was all she had of him now. Joe had forsaken her. He had left the shores of Britain and gone to America to find his roots. In all probability, he would also find a wife from his own people and never return to Britain. Joe was lost to her.

Would her father ever be sorry for his interference in her affairs? She doubted it. They scarcely spoke to each other these days.

Eynon was sitting in the garden. He looked up at her and his expression lightened. 'Llinos, come to spend some time with me?'

'I've come to tell you to get ready for our little jaunt to Greenhill,' she said. 'I've seen Binnie and persuaded him to try to talk to Maura.'

'I had forgotten.' Eynon caught her hand. 'And there I was thinking you wanted to be with me. You are a difficult woman at times!'

337

'Eynon, my love, I wish I could help you to find what you really want in this life but I can't, you know that.'

He patted the seat and she sat beside him and he rested his head against hers. 'Give it time, Llinos,' Eynon said. He smiled. 'I think your father would be pleased if you chose me, don't you think so?'

Llinos considered the matter. 'I think my father would agree to me marrying anyone so long as it wasn't Joe.' She caught the look of hurt pride that crossed Eynon's face. 'But he would be over the moon if it was you, of course,' she added hastily.

'Well then, think about it. You have lost Joe, he's gone away perhaps for ever, so why don't you marry me and then one day everything I have will be yours, including the new porcelain recipes?'

'It's impossible,' Llinos said, not even attempting to conceal her smile. 'The only man I'll marry is Joe.'

He caught her hand and kissed her fingers. 'Of course you'll always love him but he's not here and I am. Just don't say anything now, promise you will think about it.'

She chuckled. 'I'll think about it all right, think how mad you are, my dear, dear Eynon.'

'Oh, shut up. Come on, we'd better be starting out for Greenhill, it looks like rain and I don't want to be caught in a shower,' Eynon said easily.

The streets of Greenhill were awash with rain and mud. From the window of the carriage, Llinos watched as a child crouched against a bank and let forth a stream of urine that soon mingled with the rain and was gone.

As he stepped down from the carriage, Eynon exclaimed in disgust, 'Good lord, do these houses have no sanitation at all?' He stepped gingerly over a mound of human excrement.

'The people who live here are paid the lowest wages in the whole of the country,' Binnie said, his voice gruff. 'They are honest and hard-working, mostly Irish immigrants. They do the jobs that other people don't want.'

'Sorry.' Eynon made a face at Llinos and she smiled. 'I won't say another word,' Eynon added drily.

The house where Maura was living was at the end of a long court and from the outside, at least, it appeared clean and respectable, the windows gleaming from much polishing. Maura opened the door herself. She looked tired and she was dressed in clothes that were worn and patched.

'What are you doing here?' Her voice was sullen. Binnie moved towards her. 'Maura, I'm sorry . . .'

'Go away, I'm working.'

Llinos took charge. She moved past Maura into the house and the smell of stale cabbage made her wrinkle her nose in distaste.

She found herself in the strangest room she

had ever seen. Red silk, faded but still gaudy, hung against the walls. Plump cushions, decorated with brightly coloured heart designs, covered the floor.

'Hell, what is this?' Binnie spoke through gritted teeth. 'Have you sunk to being a whore, then, Maura?'

She lifted her head. 'I have not. I am a good churchgoing girl. The only time I played the whore was with you. That once was enough.'

'What then?' He caught her arm. 'What is all this . . . this rubbish!'

'Mind your own business! And what right have you to bring Llinos and Mr Morton-Edwards here, are you too much of a coward to come alone?'

'It was my idea,' Llinos said quietly. 'I thought we might be able to persuade you to come to work with us. Binnie has a position at the Tawe Pottery now, his wages are very generous.'

'I get my own wages here,' Maura said sullenly.

There was the sound of a door opening at the back of the house and Maura looked around anxiously. 'You'll have to go.' She made a gesture with her hands but no-one moved. The door opened and a tall, austere-looking woman swept into the room. She stopped abruptly.

'More visitors, what is it that ails you? Whatever it is, I have the remedy, be sure of that. I am better than any doctor, I can cure anything from gout to fevers of the brain.'

'No.' Llinos spoke. 'We are not sick, we've come to see Maura.'

'God, I need a drink.' The woman dropped her haughty manner and poured herself a liberal measure of gin, tossing it to the back of her throat in one gulp.

'I have a strange feeling about you.' She looked at Eynon. 'Mr Morton-Edwards, isn't it? Your father came to me for weed killer. Was it some more you're after? If so, the price has gone up, my stocks are running low.' She smiled briefly at Llinos. 'Plenty of unwanted weeds, or wives, about, or so it would seem.'

It was a strange thing to say but Llinos smiled politely as though she was paying a visit to the most respectable of ladies.

'I'm afraid we don't want to buy anything. We are just friends of Maura's on a visit. I do apologize for intruding.'

'Quite. Well, as you can see, Maura is busy. She has her work to do. I've agreed to let her bring the baby here but I can't keep her and the child out of charity, you understand?'

There was a gentle knocking on the door and Maura hesitated a moment before leaving the room.

'I'm Mrs Lane,' the woman said. 'If you ever need medicine, just come to me. Now, I have another patient to see to, I think you must excuse me.' She tugged at her plain linen skirt and the enveloping apron and then adjusted the lace cap on her head before following

Maura from the room.

Llinos looked first at Eynon and then at Binnie and a smile tugged the corners of her mouth.

'You two look as if you've been run over by a coach and pair! Perhaps you need some of Mrs Lane's remedies after all.'

Eynon took a deep breath. 'Well! I wouldn't like to get on the wrong side of her, that's for sure. What on earth did my father want to buy weed killer for? And why come to Mrs Lane?'

'Well, I don't want Maura working here for that woman!' Binnie broke in aggressively. Llinos held up her hand warningly.

'If you take that tack, you'll only make things worse. Leave the talking to me.'

When Maura returned to the room she looked flushed and embarrassed. 'You'd better go.' She looked down at her shoes, shifting uneasily from one foot to the other.

'Please, Maura, won't you reconsider? We need you to keep Eynon's house in order. He's been staying with his father, you see, and up at his own house the servants are doing just as they like.'

Maura looked at Binnie, her chin raised. 'And you, what do you say? Am I to live in sin with you in exchange for a decent job and food in my belly?'

Binnie took her hand and she snatched it away. 'I know it's a bit late in the day but, Maura, I want you to know I've been a blind fool. Please,

342

marry me, I love you. Look, I'll go on my knees to you.'

'Oh really, and how long will that last?'

'I mean it, Maura, we'll arrange the wedding right away.'

A glow began in Maura's eyes and her pale face became rosy. 'Do you mean it, Binnie? Do you really mean it?'

'On my life, I mean it.'

She smiled. 'Wait just a minute, I'll fetch the baby from her bed and shove my things in a bag and then I'll be with you.' She turned to smile impishly over her shoulder.

'We'll make our escape while Mrs Lane is busy.' Her smile widened. 'Otherwise she might just give us something nasty to swallow.'

Within ten minutes, they had left the house behind. Maura walked ahead with Binnie carrying the baby and Llinos slipped her hand through the crook of Eynon's arm. He looked down at her.

'I wish . . .' He stopped speaking as she held up her hand.

'No good wishing for the impossible. I've realized that very few of us get what we really want in this life.'

'Good heavens, Llinos, aren't you a bit young for such cynicism.'

'I'm not a cynic, just a realist. Come on, let's get out of this mud.' She looked up at the sky. 'I think it's going to rain again and if it does we'll really be in the mire.'

He tweaked her nose. 'You funny, sweet, dear little thing. I love you.'

'I know.'

It was her father who brought Llinos the news. He had wheeled himself to the entrance of the Tawe Pottery and sent one of the bin boys to fetch her. She was busy and resented the interruption and had been in two minds about refusing to see him, but at last she flung off her apron and walked towards the gates, a feeling of depression hanging over her like a cloud.

'Another letter came for you, Llinos. I've thrown it in the fire but I thought I should come and tell you what it said.'

'You've burnt it!'

'I felt I should.'

'How dare you, Father!'

'It's for your own good, Llinos. Joe's betrothed to some girl out in America. I was sorry after and tried to salvage some of it, see there's just the top of the first page, read it.'

She did. Carefully. 'I expect you're happy now,' Llinos said bitterly. She did not wait for him to reply, but turned and ran along the river bank away from the pottery. She headed for the curving bay, knowing that with the sea lapping the shore she might be able to think clearly. The beach was deserted, the only sound was of the seagulls screeching mournfully overhead.

The river was full flowing, the waters bright

in the sunlight. Joe sat with his people and realized that he no longer was one of them. He did not belong in England and it seemed he did not belong among the hills of Dakota either.

'We have not seen hide nor hair of you since you were a child,' Red Eagle said. His face was lined, his mouth pursed around the pipe was toothless. But his eyes were alert, intelligent, the eyes of a man who saw into the distance. 'But when you were born, you were betrothed to Sho Ka. Have you come to claim her?'

'No, I have not.' Joe's tone was firm. 'I have a woman of my own at home.'

'We hoped you would return to claim your bride when your mother called to you across the oceans.'

His mother was standing behind him. He turned and she looked down at him and smiled. She was still beautiful, her hair long and threaded with white. Her skin was smooth, her body strong and lithe.

'You are nearing your twenty-first year, my son.' Red Eagle spoke again. 'You are a man and should be planting the seeds of a new generation of Mandans. We need you here, Wah-he-joe-tass-e-neen. We need fresh blood to strengthen the tribe and to bring fire into the bellies of the braves once more.'

'I honour your laws, Chief Red Eagle,' Joe said. 'And I am conscious of the great gift you are offering me but . . .'

Red Eagle raised his hand. 'Say nothing more.

Sho Ka will be brought to your lodge when the moon falls below the river. You can look at her and see if you like her. If not, you are free to go.' He rose and walked sedately away, his head-dress of feathers swaying majestically in the breeze.

The men who had formed a circle around Joe melted away into the shadows and he rose to his feet and stared around him at the walls of the stockade. It was a well-thought-out construction with adequate space between the dome-shaped lodges. Around the perimeter was a stout fence guarded at all times by four tribesmen.

'Come, my son, we will talk.' Joe's mother came silently at his side. 'We have much to say to each other.'

Joe followed her across the sun-baked earth and ducked to enter the lodge. It was spacious, with skins covering the floor and walls. The earth roof was supported by four stout posts and cross-beams.

A brazier glowed with life and light casting shadows over the face of his mother and in spite of the love he felt for her, Joe wondered why he had come here to this foreign place.

'You should lie with Sho Ka, give her a child,' she said, and when he shook his head she put her hand on his arm.

'My son, it is ordained by a greater power than your own.'

'I am going to marry a girl from back home,' he said. 'I love Llinos, Mother.' He smiled. 'She is my Firebird, my joy, my destiny. Don't you understand how I feel? You loved my father once.'

She waved her hand impatiently. 'You have been a soldier?'

'Yes.'

'You were a saint then or did you enjoy women followers?'

He smiled. 'I was no saint.'

'Well then.'

'But I did not marry any of the camp followers, Mother.'

'Your marriage to the girl would only be sacred in the eyes of the tribe. As was mine to your father. But I see you are as stubborn as he was. Set in your own desires. You want this Llinos more than you want to fulfil your destiny here.' She paused.

'You have chosen, my son, I can see that your way is not with the Mandan tribe, at least not at this time. So,' she continued, 'I will arrange everything. Sho Ka will be happy and you can go home to make love to your Llinos.'

'Mother!'

She smiled at him, her dark eyes full of laughter. 'You'll see, it will all turn out well. Sleep now.'

He rolled himself in his blanket and settled on the floor. From a little way off he could hear the restless pawing of the horses. Some earth creature screeched in the night and then Joe fell asleep.

He was awakened by a warm body next to his. He opened his eyes slowly and looked into the face of a beautiful young girl. He sat up quickly.

Her hair was loose, it covered her eyes. Her skin was golden from the sun and she smelled sweet and clean. She put her finger to her lips, warning him to be quiet. 'I come to thank you,' she whispered. 'You have made me happy.'

He sat up and rubbed his hands through his long, loose hair and was relieved to see his mother entering the lodge.

'I told you everything would be fine, didn't I, son?' His mother sank onto the bank. 'Sho Ka is a sweet girl and she is in love with another brave.' She waved her hands and spoke in a strange tongue and Sho Ka crept silently from the lodge.

'They are very happy. Now you have rejected Sho Ka she can marry her brave. Tell me, son, have you lain with your Llinos yet?'

He shook his head.

'And why not? Because her custom demands that you walk in a church with her. What foolishness, the sky and the river and the hills and the earth are the place where the Great Spirit dwells, not some building created by man.'

'As you say, Mother, but it is our custom.'

'Ah, custom. Well Red Eagle knew you would not stay with us for ever and once you have gone, everyone will forget. Except me.'

Joe touched her cheek. 'I'm happy I came to

find you, Mother. My father always loved you, it was his dying wish that I told you how he felt. Well, I have done my duty and I've learned that my mother is a beautiful, clever woman. But I must go home soon, my life is not here on the plains, you understand?'

She touched his hand. 'I understand a great many things my son.' Her eyes shone. 'I understand that your father and I made us a fine boy child who has grown into a man, a man I can be proud of. When you go home to your Llinos, you go with my blessing and my great love.

'But you will be back, son. One day, your blood will mingle with my people and children will be born. It is your destiny. Now, let's go and bathe in the river before the rest of the tribe wakes and the sound of their voices fills the air. Let's have some quiet time together as mother and son should.' She touched his bare shoulder. 'I will not have you for long, I know that, but what time you've given me I'll hold very precious.'

As his mother led him outside into the bright morning sunshine, Joe looked at her and understood why his father had never forgotten her. Mint, his mother, was an extraordinary woman. She caught his eye and smiled and it was as if she knew exactly what he was thinking.

CHAPTER NINETEEN

'Come on, Llinos, give up your dreams of Joe, his letter confirms that Joe is never coming back.'

Llinos was walking beside Eynon across the vast sands of Three Cliffs Bay. The tide was on the ebb and huge rivulets of water created a silver pattern between the rocks.

'I just don't believe it.' Llinos bit her lip. 'I don't believe he's going to marry some Indian girl.'

'But your father showed you the letter, didn't he?'

'My father showed me a portion of a charred letter. I could barely distinguish the address and only fragments of the rest. In any case, even if Joe is married to someone else, what makes you think I'd want to marry you?'

She heard Eynon's sharp, in-drawn breath and regretted the harshness of her words. 'I'm sorry.' Llinos hugged his arm. 'I'm sorry for being such a horror. Since you returned home I've missed you dreadfully.'

Eynon was so kind, he wanted to give her his fortune, to take care of her; he was so generous and she was an unfeeling monster.

But then, were his motives so selfless? He could not conceal his joy that Joe was, apparently, promised to someone else. He, like her father, was prejudiced against Joe for all sorts of reasons.

'Do you think your father would lie to you, then?' he said.

'Eynon! Please! Allow me to make up my own mind about Joe.' There was a note of impatience in her voice. 'You are looking at this from your own point of view.'

'How can I help it? I want a wife and I want you, Llinos. Why should I defend Joe? He is a foreigner, his ways are different to ours, he even looks different. Just think about marriage to me, would it be so bad?'

She shook her head. It would never work. Already, she knew that she was born to passion. Her feelings when Joe had taken her in his arms had shown her that much and she felt no passion for Eynon, only friendship.

'I'm sorry, Eynon, I want more, much more than you could ever give me. I will only marry one man and that's Joe.'

'You might well end up an old maid, then.' Eynon spoke softly, not intending to give offence, but his words hurt nonetheless.

'I know.'

Eynon took her hand. 'You are probably right.'

'What about?'

'Everything. That Joe will come back to you and that marriage to me would be an unmitigated disaster.'

'Oh, Eynon, I didn't say that.'

He kissed the top of her head. 'I know. You and I are both fools, you know that? We are longing for that which we can never have. I am a weakling and I know you need a lusty man to share your bed.'

'Eynon!'

'Well, be realistic, Llinos. You are a hot-blooded girl. The only things I can offer are wealth and position and I realize that both those mean very little to you.'

His words were reflecting her own thoughts and she was uncomfortable that he knew her so well. 'Oh, to hell with everything!' She broke away from him and on an impulse kicked off her shoes. Lifting her skirts, she ran into the deepest part of the rivulet following its course towards the sea. She splashed the water in glittering droplets towards Eynon.

'You'll catch your death, you silly goose,' he called, standing tentatively on the edge of the stream. 'Come out of there!'

Llinos lifted her skirts higher and danced wildly through the shallow water. Her hair came loose and cascaded across her face. She felt the chill bite of the wind against her wet feet and danced faster.

At last she fell into a heap against the sand. She began to laugh and then, suddenly, she was weeping.

Summer moved into a heatwave, grass dried in the barren outcrops of rocks on the hills above the river. Mr Morton-Edwards sat most days in the garden wrapped in a cloak, his health still far from good. And Llinos Savage had taken charge of the Tawe Pottery with a vengeance.

Production of the blue-white porcelain dinner and tea services had increased. The rate of failures in the kiln, though still high, was not enough to prevent production.

The more elegantly decorated china was being shipped to London, the highly coloured flower and bird designs meeting with favour among the rich clientele of the town establishments.

Llinos, with Mr Wright, continued to experiment with the composition of the porcelain. She was determined to retain the almost translucent quality of the china while making a harder paste that would not shatter in the heat of the ovens. It was proving no easy task.

Eynon continued to try to persuade her to marry him and in the meantime had signed over to her some of his shares in the Tawe Pottery. Llinos had quarrelled with him over it but he was adamant, the gift was given, he told her and she would be churlish to throw it back in his face.

Gradually, as Philip Morton-Edwards began to recover from his illness, he began to take more interest in the running of the pottery. He expected Llinos to spend time with him, talking over matters of production. And though Llinos had worried that he would think her a scheming hussy, on the contrary, he had accepted that she now held shares in the pottery with a great deal of enthusiasm.

'My dear girl!' He was pale and thinner than before, but the sparkle of enthusiasm was back in his eyes. 'My first wife gave Eynon those shares as well as leaving him an enormous fortune; he can do what he likes with them. As for me, I am only too happy to have you on board. Left to Eynon, the pottery would have faltered and died.'

He touched her hand. 'I am very grateful to you for all you have done, but to lighten the load I have sent for my cousin Catherine to come and visit. I hope you don't mind, my dear?'

Strangely enough, Llinos did mind, she had become accustomed to being in charge. It was a position that suited her and she did not relish it being taken away. Still, it was doubtful that the cousin would wish to interfere in the affairs of the pottery.

Llinos realized that her life had fallen into a pattern: she had become busy and fulfilled, except that when she went to bed at home in Pottery House she was alone with her thoughts, and they were inevitably thoughts of Joe.

He was so far away from her, across vast oceans, living on another continent. It was in the dark hours that despair and anger against her father found release in dreams.

The Savage Pottery was also doing well, although the profits were and always would be far short of the fortunes made by the Tawe Pottery.

Lloyd Savage had kept his feet on the ground, ensuring that his workers produced solid, everyday products which would always be needed in kitchens of homes across the town of Swansea and the valleys beyond.

The terracotta jugs and bowls, glazed with yellow oxide, continued to sell well as did the transfer-glazed, blue and white tableware made of good strong earthenware.

Llinos made a point of keeping out of her father's way. When they were together, she scarcely spoke. She knew her attitude hurt him but Lloyd had a stiff-necked pride that would not allow him to admit he could be wrong, and she could be just as stubborn as he was.

It was after a particularly vivid dream about Joe that Llinos woke to the early morning with tears on her cheeks. She rose quickly and splashed cold water over her face and body and dressed in her sturdiest highwaisted dress. Her anger and pain were so intense that she needed to be outdoors, to breathe in the morning air.

The sun was already warm as Llinos made her way from along the row towards the Tawe Pottery. She heard her name being called and turned to see Eynon, his coattails flapping as he rode swiftly towards her.

'Llinos, I'm glad I've caught you.'

She held the reins of his animal as Eynon slid from the saddle. She watched Eynon delve through his pockets and for a moment her heart leapt, thinking he had heard from Joe. His first words dashed her hope.

'A letter from my Aunt Catherine,' he said breathlessly. 'Father has invited her to stay but she feels he is still too poorly to take on a couple of visitors and she wishes me to offer accommodation to both her and her god-daughter, Georgina Fairwater.' He made a face. 'I met her when she was a child, and a precocious little thing she was!'

He looked over the edge of the paper, his eyebrows raised. 'I'll read it to you. It begins . . . "My dear Eynon".' He made another face. ' "Dear Eynon" indeed, I haven't seen her in years. Anyway, I shall go on.

' "My Dear Eynon, My wish is to visit you at your establishment in Swansea. I shall be bringing Georgina with me and I believe that the two of you will get on very well together." You can see what she's after, can't you?'

'Lodgings for herself and this girl?'

'No, no, Llinos, you are missing the point. Aunt Catherine is hoping to make a match of it, me and Georgina, she thinks I'll fall in love and marry her goddaughter.'

Llinos nodded. 'You could be right. In any case, you can hardly refuse to let them come to Swansea, can you?'

'No. That's why I'm here. I want you to come and stay. You know the house, you know the servants. You'd be a sort of hostess to the ladies. I shall be going away for a while,' he smiled, 'making my escape, some would call it, and if

356

you were to take up a tenancy, all done legally, you'd be in charge.' He paused. 'Come on, you don't really want to go on living with your father, do you?'

'I suppose not,' Llinos said. 'But where are you going?'

'I don't know, anywhere out of Georgina's way! I won't leave at once, of course, I'll see the ladies settled in and all that. What do you say, Llinos? Please agree, you'd be helping me out.'

'I wouldn't mind renting your house but for heaven's sake, Eynon, I don't need to sign a legal document. No-one is going to attempt to push me out of there, are they?'

'You never know. I would like you to be legally entitled to stay for as long as you like. At least let me do this much for you as a friend, I know you're unhappy the way things are.'

'I don't know,' Llinos said again. 'Can't you let me think about this for a while, you have rather sprung it on me. In any case, how could I pay the rent? Be realistic, Eynon.'

'I am. You have wages for managing the pottery, don't you? And I will pay you as a sort of companion-cum-hostess. You see what I need, a buffer between me and dear Georgina while I'm home and a hostess when I'm not. Please, please, say yes. You would be doing me a favour.'

'I'll think about it. Now, while you are here, come and see the work of the new young artist

I've taken on, he's so talented you won't believe it. It's all right, your father hasn't been into the pottery for days, you won't have to meet him.'

'You and your china!' Eynon tethered his horse to the fence post and followed her along the lane to the pottery.

'Look, Llinos, the roses are out, perhaps Joe will come home soon.'

Her heart thumped rapidly for a moment. 'What makes you say that? Perhaps he has decided that his home is on the plains of America where he was born.'

'Perhaps.' Eynon fell silent and Llinos welcomed the silence; she could not bear to even talk about Joe. She missed him badly still. The months had not faded his memory from her mind or her heart. Without him, she was incomplete.

As she reached the entrance to the Tawe Pottery, she smelled the clay, the flux and the pungent odour of the glazes and squared her shoulders. She must put her longing for Joe out of her head, she had work to do.

'Why, Llinos, how nice of you to come and see me. I've missed your company very much.' Philip was looking a little better, Llinos thought.

'I'm disappointed that my cousin's god-daughter will be staying with Eynon. I had thought that Georgina would come over here to stay.'

'Well, Eynon's going away soon and I said I'd stay at his house, at least for the time being. It's not a permanent arrangement but I feel I owe it to him to be a sort of hostess to Miss Fairwater.' She frowned. 'In any case, it's difficult at home, my father and I are not getting along too well.'

Philip touched her hand. 'I wish you were my daughter. You are a fine woman, Llinos. We have become good friends, haven't we? I don't know what I'd have done without you. You have looked after my pottery with the nerve and skill of a woman twice your age.'

'I love the work,' Llinos said, 'and I'm pleased that you have faith in me.' How could people be so wrong about Philip? He was old and frail and needed looking after. Well, she was doing her best for him, she could do no more.

Two days after Llinos moved in to Eynon's house Georgina Fairwater arrived from England. She was accompanied by her elderly, fractious godmother and a mountain of bags and boxes. It occurred to Llinos that the tall, disdainful young woman, staring at her as though she was a butterfly on a pin, intended to take up permanent residence in Swansea.

'Where is Mr Eynon Morton-Edwards? Why is he not here to greet us?'

She flicked her gloves across the pale palms of her dainty hands, hands that had never touched clay or paint or glaze or indulged in any kind of work whatsoever by the look of them.

'I'm sorry, I don't know where Eynon is. I'm not his keeper.' Llinos's tone was sharper than

359

she intended and Georgina frowned down at her.

'What's your name, my dear?' Aunt Catherine asked.

'I'm Llinos Savage. I live here.'

'Do you indeed?' Georgina said. 'That's something we shall have to reconsider.'

'The fact that I live here is nothing to do with you.' Llinos was beginning to think she should have signed Eynon's piece of paper. 'This is Eynon's house, he alone decides who his guests are.'

Georgina's large blue eyes swept over her. 'Really? Get someone to take our things to our rooms, would you?'

'Sorry, I have work to do. I'm afraid you'll have to speak to the servants yourself.' Llinos left the house, slamming the door in a futile gesture of anger that nevertheless made her feel better.

As she flounced off down the drive, she was aware that she was being childish but somehow, she knew, with a deep certainty, that the peace she had hoped to enjoy in Eynon's home had vanished like the mist before the sun.

CHAPTER TWENTY

It was high summer when Binnie and Maura were married in the church that crested the borders of Greenhill. Maura looked beautiful in a cream velvet gown and cloak, her red hair upswept into a cascade of curls. Binnie was self-conscious in his new cut-away coat and fine polished boots, his hair parted and slicked down with water.

Llinos sat beside Eynon and watched as Father Martin conducted the service, his gentle voice rising and falling as he intoned the words.

'I never thought I'd see Binnie become a married man,' Llinos whispered.

'It was that or lose Maura altogether.' Eynon squeezed her hand. 'Aren't you tempted by all this to find yourself a wealthy husband?' He smiled down at her and Llinos shook her head at him.

'No, I am not!'

The wedding reception was held at Eynon's house. The place gleamed with cleanliness; in the kitchen cooks hovered over pans of steaming water and the mouthwatering aroma of roasting pork filled the house. Llinos, satisfied that everything was in hand, returned to the drawing-room.

Binnie crossed the room towards her. He had grown tall. His dark hair was groomed, his moustache neatly trimmed. He was still a young man but he had worked hard all his life and there were lines on his face that should have graced someone much older.

'I wish you every happiness, Binnie, you know that.' Llinos hugged him. 'You have a good job at the pottery and a fine house to live in, a healthy child and a very beautiful wife. You are to be congratulated.'

Maura did look beautiful. Her skin and hair glowed in the sunlight. Her eyes were warm as they looked across the room at her husband. He met her eyes and her smile was full of love.

'I should have done it long ago — I suppose.' Binnie's voice was heavy.

'You had to wait until you were sure,' Llinos said. 'You are sure — aren't you?'

He made a face at her. 'I don't know, Llinos. I know what I don't want and that is to feel trapped before I'm twenty years of age.'

'You feel — trapped?'

'If I'm honest — yes.'

'Wedding nerves. You'll see, everything will be just wonderful.'

'I wish I had half your optimism.'

Maura's happy laugh rose above the hum of conversation as a maid handed her the baby. Maura hugged her daughter close, her features softened with love.

'I suppose I should be grateful for everything.'

Binnie sounded doubtful. 'After all, as a boy coming from the workhouse, I've been more fortunate than most.'

'You can still have dreams, Binnie,' Llinos said. 'Being married isn't the same as being dead, mind.'

'How would you know?'

'Binnie! Come and see the baby. She's got another tooth!' Maura was alight with happiness.

'Go on.' Llinos gave Binnie a gentle push and watched him thread his way through the room crowded with Maura's relations. It seemed that Maura was forgiven now that she had become a respectable married woman.

Llinos let herself out through the French doors. It was chilly outside, the sun had vanished and grey clouds filled the sky.

'Things will work out for them, don't worry, Llinos.' Eynon was beside her. He put his arm around her shoulders. 'They'll have a comfortable enough life together, you'll see.'

Llinos shook her head. 'I'm not sure, Eynon, Binnie doesn't look at all happy.'

On an impulse, she put her arms around Eynon's waist and hugged him. He was thin beneath his clothes, his body slender with little strength.

'Thank you for being a friend, only you understand how I'm missing Joe. I want him so much, Eynon.'

'But will you ever get him, that's the question?

Try to steel yourself to the fact that Joe might never come home.'

Llinos closed her eyes, resentment at Eynon's words warring with her affection for him. She resisted the urge to give way to tears, knowing Eynon was right. Joe might be gone for ever.

Sometimes Eynon made her think a little too clearly but he was stability in her world, the world that had changed so much in the last few months. Soon even he would be gone from her life, at least for a while.

Eynon sensed her thoughts. 'You'll survive, people fall in and out of love all the time. And remember, I am always here for you, always. Anyway,' he said briskly, 'whenever you've had enough of the festivities, go upstairs out of it.' He smiled.

'You realize Aunt Catherine is sure we have a "love nest" here and as for Georgina, well, she is jealous of you already. If they spot us like this, arm in arm, their worst fears will be realized.'

Llinos did not reply, she was in no mood for banter. She stared across the grounds to where the trees stood tall in the sunlight.

'You mustn't think about me, Eynon. Live your life the way you want to, then at least one of us will be happy.'

A burst of laughter echoed from the warm cheeriness of the house and Llinos felt vulnerable and alone.

'Damn Joe! I sometimes wish I'd never met him.'

'I know exactly how you feel.' The irony in his voice was not lost on Llinos.

She looked up at him. His mouth was drawn down into a grimace. 'For heaven's sake,' she said, 'stop looking so sad. Let's go in and join the others before we start weeping on each other's shoulders.'

Llinos stayed at the celebration for as long as was polite but it was a relief to leave the noise of the crowd behind and relax in the privacy of her bedroom. She sank into a chair, thinking of Joe, trying to draw him to her with her thoughts, when a knock sounded on the door.

'Excuse me.' One of the maids stood hesitantly on the threshold. 'Miss Fairwater has been asking for you, Miss Llinos.'

'Oh? What does she want, Gladys?'

'Don't know, miss, bit put out she was, with all the noise and such from downstairs, says it's disturbing her godmother. She's asking can you go and see her.'

'I can't do anything about the noise,' Llinos said impatiently. 'And I haven't time to run at Miss Fairwater's beck and call. Will you bring me some nice hot tea, Gladys, please?'

When Gladys had gone, Llinos stretched her feet towards the fire. It was good to be alone, good to sift through the images of Joe she had stored in her mind. If she closed her eyes she could see him, feel him, taste the scent of him.

She tried to imagine him with a wife and a family around him but the image blurred and became misty and when she opened her eyes, they were filled with tears. He would come back to her, she knew he would, she prayed he would.

The door opened and Llinos, expecting Gladys with the tea, did not look round.

'I am so sorry to interrupt your solitude.' Georgina's voice was edged with sarcasm. 'I just wondered how you could be so rude as to leave me to languish alone in my room.'

Llinos sat up straighter. Beneath Georgina's hostile tone, she sensed a real feeling of loneliness.

'I'm sorry, perhaps I should have insisted you join me, but I didn't think you would be interested in the marriage of an orphan from the workhouse and an Irish girl from Greenhill.'

Georgina sank down in a chair. 'Everyone seems to be avoiding me, even dear Eynon. What have I done wrong?'

The maid came into the room with a tray and set it on one of the small tables. Llinos noticed that there were two cups and grimaced inwardly.

'I see you are going to join me for tea.' She heard the cold tone in her voice and swallowed hard. It was ungracious of her, she should at least make an effort to be civil to Georgina.

'Am I not welcome, then?'

'Please, you are most welcome. This is Eynon's house and if Eynon wishes you to stay then stay you must.'

Georgina sat near Llinos. 'Now we can have a cosy chat.'

Llinos tried to hide her impatience. 'Have some tea while it's hot.' She sat back in her chair, realizing quite suddenly that she was tired. It had been a long day.

'My godmother wishes me to marry Eynon,' Georgina said, putting down her cup with a dainty droop of her wrist. 'But he takes no interest in me. Is he in love with you?'

Llinos shook her head. 'Eynon and I are great friends.' She looked levelly at Georgina. 'I have no romantic interest in Eynon at all.'

'That's all right then. You and I have no need to be at loggerheads. I just thought that you and Eynon were lovers. It's a bit strange, you living here with him, I mean.'

'Why? We have ample servants to chaperone us, not to mention Binnie and Maura, who are our friends.'

'But Eynon takes care of you, doesn't he? I mean you can stay in his house whenever you like. Does he do all this out of friendship? Or does he offer you charity because he's sorry for you?'

'Don't be absurd, I don't need charity,' Llinos said sharply and then regretted her tone, knowing she had allowed Georgina to breach her defences.

Georgina was persistent. 'Perhaps you have grown accustomed to taking advantage of dear Eynon's good nature.'

Llinos flinched. Georgina had exposed a raw spot. She had worked hard to tell herself that she was doing Eynon a favour but did she really earn all that Eynon was giving her? She was living in comfort at his expense and giving him nothing in return. She saw the situation clearly in that moment and it was not a good feeling.

'Finish your tea.' She spoke more abruptly than she intended. 'I need to bathe and then I shall go to bed. I'm sorry if I seem inhospitable but I'm tired.'

Georgina rose to her feet, her face set. 'Now you are cross with me. I can't make you out, Llinos. You don't want Eynon, or so you say. You tell me you are not lovers and yet you enjoy all this.' Her hand encompassed the room. She moved towards the door.

'I'm sorry to be blunt, but I think you are a liar.' Her expression was hostile. 'Why would any man be so generous unless he was being paid in some way or another?' She smiled triumphantly. 'The whole town is talking about you, you do realize that, don't you?'

'Oh, and what are they saying?'

'They are saying that you are a kept woman and they are right, are they not?'

'I work for a living!' Llinos said. 'Oh, go away, you wouldn't understand!' She opened the door. 'Just leave me alone, Georgina. If you have any other questions, I suggest you address them to Eynon.'

The door slammed shut and Llinos closed her eyes in frustration. Damn Georgina! She had stirred up a cloud of questions in Llinos's mind.

Questions that must be faced and answered. Was she allowing herself to be a 'kept woman'? Could she blame the townspeople for talking about her that way?

She drank her tea and moved to the window, her face resting against the cold pane. She stared into the garden, at the shifting shadows thrown by the clouds racing across the moon. She saw the flash of silver in the fountain as the water cascaded into the ornate bowl below.

She was not being fair to Eynon and she was not happy at home. Surely she could find the courage from somewhere to change what she did not like about her life?

She did not sleep very well that night. She sat hunched against the pillows in the high, narrow bed and tried to sort out her mixed thoughts.

By the time the morning light was slanting through the tall windows, one thing was clear, she could not live on Eynon's charity for a moment longer.

Binnie sat up in bed and stared at the pink of the morning sky. Beside him, Maura lay, her hair spread around her face, her golden lashes touching her cheeks. She seemed like a beautiful stranger to him.

He might as well face it, he did not love her, he had never loved her. She had been his first taste of life, his first experience of love. But it had not been love at all, he recognized that now. What he felt for Maura had been nothing but the natural lust of a young man. He rose quickly and went into the small dressing-room. The water in the bowl was icy but he felt better when he'd splashed his face and hands with it. He looked into the mirror and saw a man old before his time. A married man.

Binnie stood for a moment, staring around him. He felt strangely removed from the everyday world. Panic engulfed him. He couldn't be tied down, not yet. Maura was a wonderful girl but she cared nothing for ambition. She had no urge to explore new worlds. Maura was content to live and work and bear children and live a humdrum life in which there was no excitement. Could he settle to that for the rest of his life? He could not.

Hurriedly, he packed a change of clothes and took some money from the drawer in the bedroom cabinet. He tip-toed across the bedroom, trying to sort out his muddled thoughts.

He descended the small stairs at the back of the house, hearing familiar sounds from the kitchen. The maids were at work, the fires would be lit and a good hot breakfast would be waiting for him. He was a very lucky man — so everyone told him.

Silently, he entered the gracious hall and put his bag on the floor.

'Morning, Binnie, how's the happily married man?' Eynon came into the hallway and stopped short.

'I'm all right.' Binnie had grown to like and

respect Eynon. The man was not strong, he lived an indolent life, but he did not set himself above others.

Eynon even ate in the kitchen sitting at the same table as the cook and the maid. This was an unheard-of practice among the higher orders, but then Eynon was not like the other rich businessmen of the neighbourhood.

'Where's Llinos? I want to talk to her,' Binnie said awkwardly, aware that his bag was standing near the door.

'She's left for the pottery already, she's nothing if not keen to earn her own living. What's wrong, Binnie? You look down in the mouth. Married bliss not all you hoped for?' Eynon said.

'It just don't feel right somehow, being married, I mean.'

'Doesn't,' Eynon corrected. 'It doesn't feel right.' He smiled. 'Marriage is a big step and, after all, you haven't given yourself time to get used to it, have you?'

Binnie squared his shoulders, knowing he would have to break the news to Eynon that he was leaving. He thrust his hands into his pockets and stared down at the toe cap of his boot. 'I've got to tell you something.'

Eynon sighed. 'I think I know what you are going to say, I can see you've packed your bag. You're leaving us. Don't you think you are being a little impulsive. What about Maura and the baby? Shouldn't you be thinking of them?'

'They'll be all right by here with you, won't

they? You won't throw them out into the street or anything?'

'No, of course not! But I can't be here all the time, you know, and Maura needs a husband and the child needs a father, don't you think?'

'I can't do it. She got a ring on her finger, the respectability she wanted,' Binnie said. 'Now I have to get away.'

'All right, if you are determined to go I can't stop you. Hold on here, would you?' Eynon disappeared into his study and returned after a moment with a purse of money.

'Call this your severance pay.' He smiled but it did not reach his eyes. 'It's more than you'd ever get out of my father.'

As Binnie hurried from the house and began the long walk into town, his spirits rose. He was relieved to be away from Eynon's house, more than relieved to be away from Maura. He felt suffocated by her love. He had made a mistake. He should not have married her. Well, it was behind him now.

Ahead of him, he caught sight of a familiar figure. He quickened his steps.

'Llinos!' he called. She hesitated for a moment and then stopped to wait for him. In her hand was a bag similar to his own.

'Binnie, trust you to catch me out when I'm running away.'

'So am I,' Binnie said, not taking her seriously. 'Running away, I mean. Where are *you* going?'

'I'm going to America to find Joe, to find out

if he loves me or not.' She looked at him, her head on one side.

'Llinos, you're mad! No woman travels alone and especially not to America.'

'Well, there has to be a first time for everything and I'm going. But you, Binnie, what do you think you are doing?'

'I can't stay, Llinos. Marriage is not right for me. I'm too young to settle down.'

'You don't mean it? Why, you've only just got married.'

He smiled. 'I do mean it. As you say, there's a first time for everything.' He measured his steps to hers as Llinos began to walk down the hill. She glanced at him, her eyes shadowed.

'I don't know what to say, Binnie. I can't agree that you are doing right to leave Maura. Why don't you give yourself a chance to think about it?'

'How long have you thought about going to America?'

'Well, I realize I can't keep living on Eynon's charity.'

'And when did that wonderful revelation come to you?' Binnie persisted.

'I scarcely slept all night. Georgina made me see sense. Oh, she was being spiteful but she was right, nonetheless.'

'So you decided this morning to leave? So did I. I can't live a lie for the rest of my life. In time I would come to hate Maura and all she stands for and she would hate me.'

The leafy lanes gave way to the roads at the edge of the town, where the shops and alley-ways sprawled in a confusion of cobbled streets and narrow courts.

Binnie kept step with her. 'Can I come with you, to America, I mean? I don't have a great deal of money. I could work my passage, though. I could help you to find Joe. Do you know where to start looking?'

Llinos nodded. 'I know where he is. He wrote to me, this is all I have left of the letter; my father tried to burn it.'

Binnie took the paper and looked at the date. 'It's been a long time getting here. Joe could be on his way home by now.'

Llinos shook her head. 'No. I don't think so.' She did not add that she would feel his presence, she would know without doubt if he was coming home.

Binnie looked at her in admiration. 'Well, Llinos, I take my hat off to you, there's not many women with a sense of adventure strong enough to carry them across oceans.'

'Don't praise me too soon, there's a passage to be booked, a captain to persuade.' She smiled. 'Though I must admit it will be that much easier if we appear to be a couple. I understand captains are not keen on lone, unattached females being on board ship.'

Binnie stared ahead of him as they neared the entrance to the docks. The water was filled with ships, some with sails unfurled waiting for the outgoing tide. Others were laid at anchor. Men called to each other as they loaded cargo into the holds. It was a strange place full of unfamiliar smells and the coarse language of the sailors.

'We should go to the shipping master's hut,' Llinos said. 'Make enquiries about sailings to America.'

Binnie was grateful for Llinos's clear-headed thinking. He followed her, taking her arm when she picked her way over boxes of fish and the upturned lobster pots that littered the dockside.

Llinos, with unerring instinct, found the building where the sailors and shipping line owners were filling in logs and booking out cargo. She took charge and Binnie watched her arrange matters with a briskness that would have done credit to a woman twice her age. Or any man for that matter.

Within the hour, Binnie found himself accompanying Llinos on board a four-masted barque heading out of Swansea harbour towards the Bristol Channel and the deep seas beyond. His new life was beginning and he embraced it with all the enthusiasm of a man freed from prison.

CHAPTER TWENTY-ONE

The river Missouri flowed sweetly, sunwarmed and golden. But summer was waning; it was time to go home. Joe walked the short distance to the stockade and stood at the door of the lodge where he had lived these past weeks with his mother.

In the clearing, the women were grouped around the fires baking clay pots beneath a covering of bark and branches and dung from the fields. It was all so different from the refinements of the Savage Pottery in Swansea and yet the end result was virtually the same. Jugs, basins, cooking vessels took shape, hardened by fire.

'You are thinking of leaving, son?' Mint appeared silently beside him, her buckskin boots making no sound on the soft ground. She smiled and her dark eyes glinted with merriment. 'There is no need to leave, Wah-he-joe-tass-e-neen — your bride, your Firebird is coming to you.'

Joe looked at his mother, his eyes narrowing. It was true he had felt that Llinos was near. Was she here, on the plains of America or was it a wish-thought, a dream?

Mint took his arm and guided him to the top of a small hill. 'Out there, see the cloud of dust? It is your little white squaw come to claim you.'

He did not ask Mint how she knew these things. The senses of his people were honed to a point of sharpness that was beyond him. The instincts of the Mandan Indians were unspoilt by the march of progress. Their minds were not blunted by the rigours of education as Joe's were.

'You will marry here, after all, my son.' Mint smiled as she caressed his cheek. 'Your seed will return one day and live among my people. It is the wish of the spirits.'

Joe was suddenly afire. 'I must go to meet her. Will you lend me a horse, Mint?'

'Take the black stallion but don't ride him too hard, he's getting to be an old man. While I wait I'll prepare a welcome. Sho Ka is bringing freshly baked bread and I'll cook some buffalo meat. Don't worry, we will make your white squaw welcome in our lodge.'

Joe looked down at his clothes, Indian clothes made of skins, decorated with beads, and wondered what Llinos would make of them.

'She will be here within the hour. Make haste, son.' Mint moved past him into the lodge, making a sweeping gesture with her hands. 'Don't stand there dreaming, go.'

Joe nodded his thanks to Black Crow as the brave swung wide the gate of the stockade. He had become friends with Sho Ka's mate, the two men of similar ages but from different worlds. A bond had been forged between them that would never be broken.

As Joe rode the stallion across the plains he

felt the softness of the breeze lifting his hair. He breathed in the scents of the plain, the sound of the buffalo, the calling of birds overhead. It was an open world, a world of big skies and great expanses of virgin land. But what would Llinos think of it?

He thought of her face, of her hair, her hands. His loins were on fire, he wanted Llinos, wanted to own her, to look into her soul. Now she had come to him nothing would keep them apart.

Llinos felt the thump of the horses' hooves as though it was inside her head. The wagon jerked from side to side with bone-shaking abruptness. It was growing hot and the dust rose in choking clouds. It was a frightening land, a land where great creatures roamed, staring with malevolent eyes at the procession of horse and wagon.

The sea journey had taken longer than Llinos had anticipated but she had taken to sailing as if born to it. Binnie on the other hand spent the entire journey in his cabin sick to his stomach at every lurch of the ship.

When night folded around the vast seas, Llinos had questioned her wisdom in undertaking a journey into the unknown. What would she do when she landed on the American continent? She had only the address on Joe's letter to guide her. Would she ever find the Mandan stockade?

In the sea port town of Troy, Llinos and Binnie had lodged for four days in a clean clapboard house near the docks. The plump landlady took her for Binnie's sister and Llinos saw no need to go into complicated explanations.

In the evenings, at supper served around the homely table, Llinos and Binnie had discussed their journey with the other lodgers. When they left, it was with repeated directions, instructions and good wishes to speed them on their way.

The wagon jerked over a rock and Llinos blinked, adjusting her vision to scan the unending land. She flicked the reins, encouraging her horse to walk on. Up ahead, Binnie rode uncomfortably on the small piebald; they would need two animals, they had been told, in case one of them went lame.

She had been glad she had saved the wages she had earned at the Tawe Pottery, for once embarked on her journey she found she needed every penny she had.

As she travelled along the strange alien land, she felt a twinge of guilt that she had left Swansea without a word to her father. She had left Eynon a brief note but she knew they would both be bitterly hurt by her disappearance. But she would write, soon, and tell them she was well and happy.

Binnie shifted his position on the horse and Llinos smiled, he was not used to riding without the comfort of a saddle. But saddles cost money, money Llinos could not afford.

Binnie reined in his horse. 'Perhaps I should give the poor creature a rest and ride in the wagon for a while,' he said. Llinos nodded. 'I can see that some poor creature needs a rest and it's not necessarily the horse!'

Like a sudden mist that rises from a river, Llinos felt a strange sensation that Joe was near. She stood up in the wagon and stared ahead of her.

'Wait, Binnie! There's someone coming towards us,' she said. 'It's a single rider.'

'I see him, it looks like a native.' His voice held a note of uncertainty and Llinos saw him finger the knife at his belt.

She felt her heart beat faster. Her hands gripped the side of the wagon.

'Lord in heaven!' Binnie exclaimed. 'He's riding like the wind. I hope the man means us no harm.' He straightened and stared ahead of him, his eyes fixed on the swiftly moving horseman.

Llinos held her breath, she saw him clearly now, the dark hair flying, the strong lithe body at one with the big black horse he was riding.

'Joe!' Llinos shouted his name and the breeze took the words and cast them around the heavens and, as if in response, the rider raised his hand in greeting.

He was close enough to be seen clearly now. His skin gleamed, more bronze than Llinos had remembered. His clothes were edged with strips of leather and his neck and hair were decked with feathers. But as he drew his quivering horse to a standstill Llinos saw that Joe's eyes were as clear blue as she had always remembered them.

She held out her arms and he took her, lifting

her easily onto his horse. She clung to him, tears running down her cheeks and into her mouth.

'Welcome to America.' His cultured voice was as much of a shock as it had been the first time Llinos had heard it. She clung to his waist, her face buried against his broad back. She knew the scent of him so well, she felt his muscles move beneath his coat and she was filled with happiness. He was hers, Joe had not forgotten her.

'Bring the wagon, Binnie,' Joe said. He turned the horse and rode the animal more sedately now. Llinos clung to Joe, wanting nothing more from life than she had in her arms at this moment. She was with the man she loved, the sun was shining above her, the breeze smelled sweet and even the strange-looking buffalo seemed to watch the progress of the small band with a more benign stare.

'My mother knew you were here,' Joe said. 'She is wise and beautiful, Llinos, nearly as beautiful as you.'

She snuggled closer to his body, her senses alive. Her eyes felt filled with stars, the sun pouring down was a benediction. Had anyone the right to be as happy as she was now? She did not need to ask how his mother had known she was coming. It was a case of like mother like son.

The journey seemed to pass in the blink of an eyelid. Soon, they were approaching the stockade. It was stoutly constructed and the wide gate was opening as the small party drew closer.

Inside the log fence was a neatly built village; it comprised seventy or more lodges. Women with long flowing hair decorated with beads were working in the open air and Llinos felt a jolt of homesickness as she breathed in the scent of baking clay.

'You see,' Joe said softly, 'the Mandans are potters, just like you.'

A woman came out to greet them. She stood looking up for a long moment, her dark eyes searching Llinos's face. At last she spoke in fluent English.

'Welcome to my lodge, my daughter.'

'This is my mother, her name is Mint. Mother, this is Llinos, my little Firebird.'

As Llinos slipped from the saddle, Mint took her in an embrace. The woman smelled of fresh grasses and herbs and her hair, streaked with white, hung in a glossy plait below her waist.

'Firebird is a good Mandan name. Welcome, come inside and rest.' The lodge was large and airy and Llinos blinked at the sudden dimness after the brightness of the sun outside. A brazier burned at the centre of the floor and two further braziers hung from beams. Richly coloured skins covered the walls and the floor had been covered with fresh straw.

Food was brought. Meat still sizzling from the fire, bread warm and crusty and small cakes of meal and barley were served to her.

'Where's Binnie?' she asked, her eyes drinking

Joe in. She was afraid to turn away from him in case he vanished.

'He will lodge with my friend Black Crow and his squaw Sho Ka.' Joe smiled at her. 'Don't worry, Llinos, he will be made to feel most welcome.'

He touched her shoulder. 'This is where I was born, Llinos. You can see how humble it is. You have met my mother, who is a true blood Indian woman. Do you still want to be my wife?'

She sighed heavily. 'How can you ask, can't you see it in my eyes that I want you more than I ever wanted anything in this world?'

He took her hand. 'Very well. Tonight you will sleep alone and tomorrow you can decide if you want to go ahead with the marriage ceremony.'

Llinos felt the colour flood into her face. She fanned her cheeks with her hand.

'Marriage ceremony?' Her voice was faint. 'Do you mean here?'

'Llinos, I know we might never have your father's blessing but will my mother's do?'

He put a finger over her lips. 'Think about it tonight and if, in the morning, you wish to make your vows, I will arrange it.'

'What sort of ceremony would it be?' Llinos could scarcely believe she was asking the question, everything seemed unreal, part of the dream she had dreamed so many times.

'An American Indian one, of course.' Joe smiled. 'But we can always have another ceremony performed by a minister of the church, if that's what you want.'

She knew what she wanted, it was to be in Joe's arms, to taste his mouth, to lie with him, to love him for ever. Mint reappeared at the door of the lodge.

'Will you come with me and the maidens to bathe in the river?' she asked in her soft voice.

Llinos looked down at her grubby skirts, felt the dust that matted her hair. She nodded. 'That sounds just wonderful.'

Some of the younger women were waiting in a group. One of them touched the long skirt of Llinos's dress and smiled, speaking in words that Llinos heard with a shock of recognition.

'Na pert.' It was the Welsh word for 'pretty'. Llinos looked at Mint.

'Some of us speak Welsh. It is told in our folk stories that your prince Madoc brought the language to us many years ago. Whatever the truth of it, the words are beautiful.'

The doors of the stockade were open and the girls surged forward, heading in small, chattering groups towards the banks of the river.

It was alarming at first to see the young Indian girls abandon their clothes and slip into the clear water. Mint nodded to Llinos.

'If you are too modest, keep on your shift, no-one will mind.'

One of the girls giggled as Llinos put a toe into the water. She tugged at the shift, her golden body gleaming with droplets and after a moment

384

Llinos shrugged off the last of her clothes and slid, naked, into the coolness of the river.

As the water closed over her shoulders, she looked up at the sky and turned to float on her back, her hair dragged by the flow away from her face.

The coldness was exhilarating; the strangeness of the open air, the scent of the long grasses on the bank and the huge sky above her, gave her a sense of unreality. And she felt a great sense of peace. She was here in a strange country, with strange people, and she was happy.

Later, curled in the softness of a bed of animal furs, Llinos slept and dreamed of Joe. She saw them in the pale English sunshine, inside the coolness of a church, and Joe was slipping a gold ring onto her finger. In the morning, when she awoke, he was beside her.

'The sun is rising. Come on, wake up. Llinos Savage' — he knelt beside her — 'will you marry me?'

She pressed her face against his shoulder and closed her eyes. 'Yes, Joe, with all my heart, yes.'

'I can't believe that my daughter would rush off across continents to be with a half-breed.' Lloyd Savage pushed his chair across the room and stared out of the window. 'What does it mean?'

'It means she must love Joe very much,' Eynon said gently. Lloyd turned to look at him.

'Couldn't you have stopped her?'

'Even if I'd known she was going, it wouldn't be my place to tell Llinos what to do. Anyway, I admire her courage.' Eynon had read the note Llinos left with sadness and anger. He had been forced to abandon his plans to go away and resigned himself to playing host to Aunt Catherine and the vacuous Georgina.

Still, he was not going to be browbeaten by Lloyd Savage. True, he felt sorry for the man and when Lloyd had begged him to tell him where Llinos was, he had brought him the brief note Llinos had left. He said nothing of his own pain at losing her. He had almost managed to convince himself that Llinos would marry him, given time, but now that hope was dashed for ever.

'What about money?' Lloyd demanded. 'You can't go halfway round the world without some resources at your disposal, can you?'

'I made enquiries at the docks, it seems she and Binnie boarded ship together. Try not to worry, Llinos had saved all her wages and Binnie had some money I gave him. Not much, I'll admit, but they'll get by, I'm sure.'

Lloyd shook his head. 'Why did my daughter never talk to me?'

'Perhaps you were too hard on her. She grew up quickly when her mother died. She ran the pottery and actually made a go of it even if it was in a very small way.'

'Aye, she had your help, though, didn't she?'

Eynon sighed. 'It seems you are determined not to give Llinos credit for anything. Do you blame her for her mother's death, perhaps?'

Lloyd slowly turned his chair. He looked at Eynon for a long moment. 'I think that is a foolish question. If I blame anyone, it's myself.'

'Then why are you so hard on her?'

'I wanted Llinos to have a decent education and I *didn't* want her marrying a half-breed. If that's being hard then I'm sorry but there it is. However fine a man Joe is, he's half American Indian, there's no denying that.'

'And he was a good friend to you.' Eynon was uncomfortable pursuing the matter but he felt he had no choice. He felt he must defend both Llinos and Joe.

'Yes, he was a good friend. He saved my life at the risk of his own. No man could ask for more than that.'

'Can't you see what you have done? You have forced the two people who love you most to go out of your life.'

Lloyd was silent for so long that Eynon wondered if he had heard. Lloyd looked up at him at last.

'You have a strange, unconventional way of looking at things, Eynon, but you are right, damn it! I was a fool and by my foolishness I have lost them both.'

He stared out of the window and Eynon watched him, aware that the captain was now white-haired and that the lines were drawn deeply into his face. Lloyd was growing old and he should have his family around him.

'Will she come back, do you think?' Lloyd asked.

'I don't think she will be able to keep away. The pottery is her love, her life. Well, it was until . . .' His voice trailed into silence.

'Until she fell in love with Wah-he-joe-tass-e-neen.'

'Or was it until you forced her out, sir?'

'Oh, to hell!' Lloyd said. 'Let's go down to the tavern in Wind Street and get some porter. I know you are missing the pair of them as much as I am.'

'Good idea.' He watched as Lloyd wheeled his chair towards the door.

'Hand me my coat, Eynon. Enough of sitting in here brooding. Let's drown our sorrows at least for tonight.'

It was crowded in the small tavern, smoke hung in a haze above the roughly hewn tables and the clatter of tankards on wood accompanied the sound of men's voices.

Looking around him, Eynon wondered if he had been wise to visit such a low establishment. The hubbub of voices was suddenly subdued as he wheeled Lloyd into position near the door. He took a deep breath and seated himself on a bench, holding up his hand for the attention of the landlord.

The man came forward quickly enough and addressed Lloyd Savage with a genial smile.

'Nice draught of ale, is it, sir, and perhaps some victuals to go with it?'

'Aye,' Lloyd nodded, 'I am hungry, come to think of it. Had no supper, had nothing all day, come to that.'

'Well, a respected businessman like yourself and a war hero into the bargain deserves better than that. How would you like one of the girls to cook you up a dish of ham along with a couple of chicken legs?'

Lloyd did not seem aware that the landlord was ignoring Eynon, not even giving him so much as a glance.

'Sounds good enough to eat!' Lloyd laughed at his own joke. 'And you, Eynon, what will you have?'

'Just a tankard of ale, thank you, Lloyd.'

The landlord lumbered across the room and within minutes a serving girl brought two drinks and placed them on the table. She looked at Eynon curiously, her dark eyes measuring him.

'You'll know me next time.' Eynon meant it to be a joke but the words almost stuck in his throat.

'Oh, we all know you, Mr Morton-Edwards.' A big man lumbered towards him and with a sinking of his heart Eynon recognized the man who had accosted him before when he'd been drinking with Joe.

'Not got your foreign friend with you this time, though, have you, laddie? Well, insults are never forgotten, not by me or my friends.'

'Hey, no need for that tone,' Lloyd said indignantly. 'Eynon Morton-Edwards is with me and that should be enough for any of you men, right?'

He glanced around him challengingly and, as abruptly as it had ceased, the flow of talk began again. The man faded into the crowd and yet Eynon could feel eyes upon him and he knew he was a marked man.

'What is it with men who can't hold their ale, all think they're heroes but where were they when Bonaparte was threatening us, hey?'

Lloyd took a long drink from the tankard. It was clear he needed no answer. When his food arrived, Lloyd ate hungrily, apparently unaware of the tension in the room.

Eynon drank sparingly. He had the feeling he would need all his wits about him when he left the tavern. He wished he had declined Lloyd's invitation. Lloyd, even crippled as he was, was twice the man Eynon would ever be and everyone in the room knew it.

The evening dragged endlessly. Lloyd gave up all attempts to talk to Eynon and fell into conversation with an old soldier who had fought in the early wars with France. He became animated, drinking heartily from the tankard the landlord kept replenished.

'We'd better be making for home,' Eynon said at last and Lloyd looked up at him through bleary eyes.

'You are right, yes, time to get to bed before

I fall asleep on my nose.' Lloyd chuckled. 'Come on then, give us a push back up the hill. I know I can rely on you, good chap, to see me safely home.'

Eynon took the full weight of the chair, the wheels catching in the pitted road. Lloyd fell into a doze, his head sunk onto his chest, and he began to snore. The night air was sharp with a wind blowing across the flatlands of sand stretching five miles around the bay to Mumbles Head. The tide was so far out that it was a blackness against the horizon.

Eynon felt the darkness wrap itself around him and he was afraid. He reached the Savage Pottery without incident and, breathing a sigh of relief, he took Lloyd inside.

The few servants Lloyd employed were no-where to be seen; they had no doubt retired for the night. Eynon lifted Lloyd from his chair with difficulty and almost fell with him onto the bed in the back room.

Beyond the windows, the ovens sent up a shimmering heat, the fires charged to bake the freshly made pots. Eynon pulled a blanket over Lloyd's sleeping form and hesitated for a moment. Perhaps he should stay for the night, curl up on the sofa in the parlour? He lifted his head and listened to the silence of the night. Was he a man or a mouse that he was afraid to go to his own home and his own bed?

He closed the door of the pottery house behind him and set out towards the west of the town.

The stars were bright, the moon hanging low over the sea. It was a beautiful night but Eynon was filled with apprehension.

He held his head high, staring straight ahead, waiting for something to happen. And yet when it did, he was unprepared. He turned a corner and was confronted by a silent ring of men.

'What do you want?' he demanded. 'If it's money, you are going to be disappointed — I have very little of it.'

The fist that connected with his jaw sent him sprawling. His head cracked against the cobbled roadway and the stars spun in the heavens.

Rough hands delved into his pockets. Eynon tried to rise but a booted foot caught him full in the mouth. He felt his lip split. A tooth became dislodged and he spat it out, gasping for breath.

'You can't hide behind your friends now, can you? Not such a big man when you're alone, eh?'

He recognized the voice with a shiver of apprehension. He lifted his head just as the boot caught him again in the ribs. He groaned and turned onto his stomach, trying to crawl away. The back of his collar was caught and he was hauled to his feet.

'Let's strip him, boys!' A thick voice, heavy with drink, seemed to ring in Eynon's head. 'Let's see if he's built like a man.'

To his horror, Eynon felt his clothes being ripped away, his shirt was torn from his thin chest and then he felt the blade of a knife against his belly as his trousers were cut from him.

'Look at the sniffling pup then, will you, got a bit of rope between his legs that's no good to anyone. Shall we cut it off?'

Eynon whimpered as the cold of the knife touched his groin. He was going to be killed, done to death in some dirty back street.

'No! We don't want the scandal of a dead man on our hands.' A voice, more commanding than the others, more cultured, rose above the noise. 'Give him a good hiding and have done with it.'

Fists began to pound him. Eynon fell to the ground, drawing his knees up to his stomach. One kick caught him in the kidneys and he moaned with pain. He did not know how long the beating went on but at last it stopped. He heard footsteps moving away as he drifted into unconsciousness.

He became aware of the coldness around him. He tried to open his eyes but they seemed stuck together. He struggled to his knees, fighting the waves of pain and nausea that threatened to overwhelm him.

'God help me,' he mumbled between swollen lips. He felt hands around his waist, a woman's hands. A shawl was thrown around his shoulders and a voice spoke close to his ear.

'Don't be afeared, it's me, Celia-end-house. Going home from a friend's sickbed, I was, when I heard the noise, like animals baying, it put the fear of God into me, I can tell you.'

She led him, half-conscious, unable to see, along the roadway. He stumbled several times and her arms held him upright.

'We won't be able to get far, Mr Eynon, but your father's house is only a few steps away.'

He no longer cared where he was. He did not even care if he lived or died. The humiliation he had suffered had been worse than the beating.

He was aware that he was indoors because he felt the warmth fold around him. He heard voices as if from far off and he was taken upstairs. He felt the coolness of sheets around him and then the heavier weight of blankets. He began to shiver and he heard Celia ask for hot water to be brought to him.

He felt the pain and the darkness and the futility of his life fall over him like a shroud and then a drink was being forced between his cut and swollen lips. It tasted bitter but it soothed him almost at once.

He heard his father's voice, harsh, without pity. 'The boy had it coming, I don't suppose he even fought back. He's a coward and he's no son of mine.'

Eynon began to drift, but this time the pain was receding. He was on a cloud being taken up to heaven where there was no longer any feeling.

'Sweet God in heaven, what have they done to the boy?' Lloyd had waited until he had seen Philip Morton-Edwards leave the house, he would ask no favours of his rival. Then several of the pottery workers had carried his chair upstairs so that he could see Eynon.

'He's still not regained consciousness.' Celia-end-house had taken charge of the sickroom, hampered by the bossy Miss Fairweather, who insisted on attending Eynon. The girl had no more sense than she was born with, she fluttered around the room, her fan waving furiously before her patrician face.

'Is he going to recover, do you think, Mr Savage?'

'Don't ask him, girl,' Celia said impatiently. 'Mr Savage don't know any more about the sick than you do. I don't know why you don't go back to Mr Eynon's house, I'm sure the old lady needs you there. In any case, you can't do no good here.'

Georgina sniffed but did not reply.

'He looks terrible!' Lloyd said. Eynon's face was unrecognizable. His eyes were closed, his mouth swollen so much that his lips had turned over on themselves, revealing a gap where his tooth had been.

'I've put witch-hazel on his body, poor boy. Skinny, he is, like a youngling. Needs caring for, he does, bless him.'

'I would have cared for him, if you would have allowed me to,' the pale Miss Fairweather said, pouting her full lips.

Lloyd shook his head. 'The boy's taken the beating of a lifetime. Saw men in better condition than this when they'd been hit by cannon fire. Looks like the lad might die.'

'No. I won't let him die,' Celia said doggedly. 'I will do my best for him, you can be sure.'

Lloyd leaned over the bed and tried to see in Eynon's battered face the boy who had laughed with him in the tavern a week ago. He felt anger surge through him.

'I'll get the bastards if it's the last thing I ever do,' he said. 'Call the servants to take me back downstairs. I'll get home to my own house, I can't do anything here. But I'll find whoever has done this and I'll kill him with my own hands.'

'Better still if you used that musket you keeps locked up there,' Celia said evenly. 'And I can tell you exactly who the bastards are, if you'll pardon my language.'

Lloyd looked at her for a long moment and then, slowly, he nodded. 'You are a sensible woman, Celia. It's about time I cleaned up that old gun of mine.'

He took one last look at the figure in the bed and doubted that Eynon would live long enough to know that he had been avenged. He sighed heavily. If only he had his legs, how he would enjoy hounding the men who had attacked Eynon. Well, if he could not go to them, he would just have to find a way to make them come to him.

CHAPTER TWENTY-TWO

It was her wedding day. Llinos woke to the sound of the birds and knew it was still early morning. Over the other side of the lodge Mint slept, one arm thrown across her face, her long hair spreading over her face. She was still a beautiful woman with a look of Joe about her and Llinos felt a constriction in her throat. Mint had been so kind, she had welcomed Llinos as her daughter with all the dignity and warmth of her nation.

As though aware of being observed, Mint opened her eyes and immediately she was wide awake. She rose and stoked the brazier with fresh logs, sending sparks flying across the lodge in all directions.

'The fire burns brightly, it's a good sign.' She looked at Llinos. 'We'll wash in the river before anyone else is awake.'

She smiled like a mischievous child and Llinos felt herself responding. Mint was a wonderful person, she combined the spontaneity of a child with the wisdom of the ages.

'Mint, am I doing the right thing?' she asked and her voice sounded small.

Mint squatted on the floor before her, pulling a covering over her shoulders. 'Let's think about it. You love Joe?'

Llinos nodded. 'Yes.'

'There is no doubt?'

'No doubt at all.'

'Then why are you worried?'

'My father would not consent under any circumstances to this marriage.' Llinos looked down at her hands; they were trembling. 'I am still a child in his eyes.'

'But you are a woman enough to want Joe's love — in all ways?'

Llinos met Mint's eyes. 'Yes.'

'Come to the river, talk to the Great Spirit as you wash away your old life. Then you must decide.'

Llinos followed Mint to the edge of the water and as she slipped into the coolness she felt the sun on her face and the softness of the breeze and knew that, beautiful as it was, the country of Joe's birth was foreign to her.

She floated on her back in the diamond glow of the water and her thoughts rippled like the river through her mind. She would like to marry Joe here in his native land if only to please his mother but before the marriage was consummated, the ceremony must be repeated in a church back home. Only then would she feel she and Joe truly belonged to each other.

Llinos washed the dust from her hair and, with a sense of freedom, dived beneath the crystal water. Her decision had been made. When she emerged from the river, she was refreshed, her mind clear.

'I must talk to Joe,' she said as Mint walked up the bank towards her, hair streaming with water, diamonds of moisture on her golden skin.

'You will be my son's wife today before his people but it will be a marriage of spirit only.' It was not a question. Llinos put her arms around Mint. She was taller than Mint by several inches.

'I will ask Joe to marry me in church. I want him to come home with me. Do you mind very much that I'll be taking him away from all this?' She looked up at the mountains, at the sparkling river and breathed the fragrant air that was so different from the stink and smoke of Swansea.

Swansea had its ugly face and yet there was an ache inside her for all she knew, all she had left behind. However dark and dirty her town, it was her home and she must return to it.

'My son is a man. He straddles two worlds, the world of the Indian and the world of the white man. Speak your thoughts to him and he will go with you, back to the cold and the rain and the confines of a land that is small beyond my imagining.'

'I'm sorry if I am a disappointment to you, Mint.' Llinos shivered a little. Her skin had dried in the breeze and quickly she began to dress.

'I knew you would want to go home but I will see you married in the custom of my people first, that will be joy enough for now.'

Llinos smiled. 'I pray that Joe will be willing

to wait until after the church service before we . . .'

'I understand. You will not feel properly married without the gold ring and the bells and the man of God saying words to you, it is only natural.'

Mint slipped her arm into the crook of Llinos's elbow. 'I will ask the spirits to speak to your father. Perhaps, after all, he will favour your union with Joe.'

Llinos doubted it. 'Perhaps.'

The village was awake, fires were lit within the stockade and the aroma of roasting meat permeated the air. Mint moved away. 'I've things to do, much to arrange.'

As Llinos walked towards the lodge she saw that Binnie was sitting on a log, watching the women kneeling before the fires baking the pots. He glanced up and rose to his feet, waving his hand to Llinos.

'Your hair is wet,' he said, smiling, and Llinos shook her head sending a spray of water over him.

'So it is. You are observant this morning.'

'And you are in a good mood. Llinos.' He was suddenly serious. 'This marriage, you know it will not be legally binding, not back home. Do you think you are doing the right thing?'

'Don't worry, Binnie. I mean to have a proper ceremony in a church later on.'

'So you will go through with the marriage, here, will you?'

'I see no harm in it.'

'I hope you are being fair to Joe.'

'Oh, Binnie, don't be such a misery! You know Joe as well as I do, I wouldn't do anything to hurt him. Where is he?'

Binnie shrugged. 'I haven't seen him this morning. Perhaps there are rituals, you know, paint, all that sort of stuff.' Binnie's voice betrayed his scorn for all things foreign. Llinos smiled.

'Aye, I expect we'll have a witch doctor make a human sacrifice or at least kill a pig or something before we tie the knot.'

'Don't make fun,' Binnie said. 'You don't know what heathen ways these people may have.'

'Well, I can't stop here talking to you all day, Binnie Dundee. It's my wedding day.'

In the warmth of the lodge, Llinos rubbed the river water from her hair. The drying curls felt soft and were scented with the perfume of the grasses from the river bank. Joe's country was beautiful but it was not home and never would be.

The day passed slowly. Of Joe there was no sign but great preparations were taking place outside in the village clearing. Skins had been spread on the ground and wide, glossy leaves held the feast of fish and meat.

Baskets of bread and fruit were set out along with jugs of amber liquid. Drums were beating softly, insistently, and Llinos began to feel apprehensive. Binnie was right, the ways of the

Indian people were foreign to her. What was she doing here taking part in some heathen ceremony?

Mint slipped silently into the lodge. 'I have come to help you dress for your wedding, daughter.' She had plaited her long hair and was wearing a band of bright beads of turquoise and black around her forehead.

'Mint, I'm afraid. I haven't seen Joe, where is he, why doesn't he come and talk to me?'

'It is not the custom, Firebird. You too have the custom where the man does not see the maid before the ceremony, is that not the way of it?'

'Yes, but I need to talk to Joe, to explain that we must wait until . . .' Her voice trailed away as Mint put a cool finger over her lips.

'You talk to Joe later, when you are alone in the lodge. Then you will be tied together for ever and no-one will set you apart.'

Llinos allowed Mint to dress her in the garments of an Indian maiden. Her hair was plaited and coloured feathers woven into it. A belt of polished stones was hung at her waist and ornaments around her neck.

The sound of drums echoed through the lodge and voices rose and fell with an easy, soothing rhythm. As Llinos was led into the clearing, she felt as though she had walked into a dream world.

Joe stood before her, magnificent in a feathered headdress. He was bare to the waist and his firm, golden body had been painted with strange symbols. He seemed remote, a stranger.

He smiled and he was her Joe again. She stood next to him. Tall as she'd become, she still reached only to just below his shoulder.

He took her hand. The ceremony had begun, now there was no turning back.

Maura placed the bowl on the table before drawing back the heavy curtains. She heard a groan from the bed and turned in concern to see Eynon trying to sit up.

'No, don't, you have some broken bones and the doctor said you must keep still. It was bad enough you insisted on coming home so don't go being difficult on me now, will you?'

He sank back onto the stained pillows and Maura saw that his nose had been bleeding again. Whoever had given him a beating had been ruthlessly thorough.

She began to bathe his face with warm water and he squinted up at her through his swollen eyes. 'Am I ever going to feel better, Maura? It's been almost a month since . . . since the accident.'

And a lifetime since Binnie had walked out on her. Maura bit her lip. He had left her flat as if the wedding had never taken place, how he must hate her. It had been something of a blessing when she had taken over from Celia-end-house; caring for Mr Eynon had taken her mind off her own problems.

'You're getting better every day. Sure, you're

young and strong, you'll mend well enough.' In spite of her cheerful words, she had reservations about his progress.

Eynon was weak. He still bore the bruises on his face and his broken nose had set crookedly. His ribs were slow to heal but it was the breaking of the big bone in his thigh that was causing the most trouble. Eynon had not been able to walk since the night of the beating. He was in constant pain, though he bore it gallantly.

Maura, who had harboured a sneaking impatience with Eynon's foppishness, now found herself with a new respect for him. He never complained and she rarely saw him low in spirits. She half smiled, they were two outcasts together, he despised as weak by the men of the town and she a scorned woman.

'I think I'll try to come downstairs for a while today.' Eynon's voice startled her. 'It's a little cold but the sun is shining and it's about time I faced the world again. You know, the only people I've seen these past weeks are Father Martin and you.' He caught her hand.

'I don't say much but I do appreciate all you've done for me. You've stayed with me in spite of everything.'

'Sure it works both ways, Mr Eynon. You've been good to me and the baby. I don't know what I would have done without you since Binnie walked out on me.'

'He's a foolish man but he will come to his senses one day, you'll see.'

'Maybe so, maybe not. And if he does, shall I want him?' She moved briskly round the room. 'Now, let's see if we can get help to bring you downstairs, shall we?'

Later, as Maura put her daughter down for her afternoon nap, she paused to peer into the garden. Eynon was stretched on a chair with a footstool to support his legs. He was covered in several shawls against the chill. He looked over his book and caught her eye and smiled.

The creak of wheels on the lane attracted her attention and she moved nearer to the window. Down below, she could see Captain Savage with one of his men who was pushing the chair towards the gate.

She admired the captain. He had got his own back on the men responsible for the beating by luring them into the market place with false promises of work. And then, in front of everyone in the place, he had scared the life out of them by firing shot at their feet. How folks had laughed when the captain had made the men dance. One of the men had cried for mercy, blaming Philip Morton-Edwards for the attack on Eynon. But no-one gave credence to the words of such a scoundrel. No-one except Maura.

'Come in, Lloyd, any news of Llinos?' Eynon's voice rose clearly to where Maura was standing.

Llinos. The very name brought the bright colour to Maura's cheeks. It was all Llinos's fault that Binnie had deserted his wife and child. She opened the window wider, aware that she was eavesdropping, but she could not help herself.

'Not a word from her, can you believe it?' Lloyd Savage spoke harshly. 'Well, I've washed my hands of her, Llinos is no longer my daughter.'

'You don't mean it, Lloyd,' Eynon said, but the captain was in no mood to listen.

'She's made her bed and she can lie on it. The gossips are saying she's run off with Binnie Dundee.'

'She hasn't run off with Binnie,' Eynon said, 'she's gone to find Joe.'

'You know that and I know that but to the townsfolk it looks like a wonderful scandal. In any case, if she comes home with the half-breed her name will be dragged further into the mud.'

'Don't be so hard on her, Lloyd.' Eynon spoke gently. 'She is young and impulsive. She's in love but she won't do anything improper, I understand Llinos well enough to know that much.'

'Aye, perhaps you're right but it doesn't help matters, does it? She could be murdered out there in that foreign country for all we know.'

'The Americans are very much like us,' Eynon said placatingly. 'Many of them are descended from English stock.'

'Aye but then there's the native American Indians. When I was in the war I heard tales about them that would make your blood run cold.'

There was silence for a moment and then

Eynon spoke. 'How's the sale of earthenware these days?'

'Very good,' Lloyd replied. 'I'm selling my products on a regular basis while your father's men waste their time trying to make porcelain that won't shatter in the ovens.'

'Ah, but the porcelain that survives the firing brings in a great deal of money, at least that's what my dear father claims.'

'I'd prefer a steady profit and a regular market,' Lloyd said. 'What about you, what are your plans for the future? Have you got any?'

'I'm going to recover my strength before I do anything,' Eynon said. 'I think Georgina has marriage in mind' — Maura heard Eynon chuckle — 'and that's where it will stay, in her mind!'

'Well, I don't know why you don't give it some serious thought, you can't spend the rest of your life pining for my daughter.'

'I know. But I love her, Lloyd, and while she's free there's hope.' Quietly, Maura closed the window and stood for a moment looking down at her sleeping daughter.

'Your father may have been led astray by Llinos Savage, my lovely.' She spoke bitterly. 'She is the devil in disguise, trapping all the men who come her way but your mammy will get her own back, one day, you'll see.'

It was quiet in the lodge. Llinos had been undressed, and flowers strewn over the bed she would share with Joe. She sat upright, staring into the brazier, trying to draw comfort from the brightness of the flames.

The plains had never seemed more alien to her than they did now. The strange sounds of creatures in the foliage and the low thud of the drums emphasized the fact that she was far from home.

Joe was enjoying a pipe with the men. Soon he would come into the lodge and he would expect her to be ready for him. There had been no opportunity to talk to him alone. From the time the strangely dressed Indian chief had conducted the ceremony, bride and groom had been surrounded by people.

She heard a rustle in the grass and Joe entered the lodge. He stood looking down at her for a long moment and then he fell onto his knees beside her.

'Llinos, my love.' He bent and kissed her mouth and she leaned against him, weak with love and desire. His mouth seemed to possess her, to draw her into a world where there was no logic, just emotion and sensation.

He touched her breast lightly and she drew away in panic.

'Hush, it's all right, I won't hurt you, my little Firebird.'

'Joe, we must talk.' She spoke desperately. He sat back on his heels.

'Have you some terrible confession to make?' He was teasing her and she shook her head.

'You know I haven't, Joe, but . . .'

He pressed her back against the softness of the shawls and skins that made up their bed. 'I love you, Llinos, I want you so much it hurts.'

'Please, Joe, listen to me.' She pressed her hands to his cheeks. 'I want to wait, Joe, until we get home. I want to be married properly before we . . . I want a church blessing and I want my father to be there. Oh, Joe, I'm sorry!' She felt tears burn her eyes, she was failing Joe, disappointing him. He rose and moved away from her and stood for a long moment, staring out through the entrance to the lodge into the night.

'Joe, please don't be angry with me.'

He came to her and took her in his arms as though she was a child and cradled her gently.

'I've waited this long for you, I can wait a little longer.' He touched his finger to the tip of her nose. 'But only a little longer, mind. Do you know what you are asking of me?'

She closed her eyes in gratitude. 'I am asking it of myself, too. I love you, Joe.'

'I know.'

She spent her wedding night wrapped in her husband's arms and when she woke in the morning he was there, smiling down at her.

'You snore.' He pulled at her hair and she swung away from him.

'I do not!'

'Yes, you do. I lay awake all night listening to you. Like a buffalo in pain, you were.'

She scrambled to her knees and aimed a playful blow at him. He caught her wrist and drew her close.

'You look so beautiful, my Firebird, with your eyes flashing and your hair tumbled. How can I resist you?'

Mint came into the lodge, carrying a large bowl of beans and a freshly baked loaf.

'I see you are behaving like a couple of children, not like the old married couple you are.' She sounded severe but her dark eyes were bright with laughter.

'Eat, you need to keep up your strength.' She looked up at him as Joe stood beside her, towering over her. He put his hands on her shoulders and looked into her face.

'I know, son, you will be leaving soon.'

'Will you come with us?'

Mint shook her head. 'I want to live out my old age here and have my bones buried under the mountains.'

'That day is a long time off, Mother.' Joe kissed her cheek. 'You run about the place like a young squaw.'

'I could not live in the coldness of your country, Joe. But you will make a name for yourself, you and Firebird. And your name will echo back to your people in America. So when you leave, son, it will be with my blessing.'

The days passed in a haze of happiness. Llinos knew that Joe's patience would not last for ever. He was a young, strong man and he needed a good wife. What made it worse was that she wanted Joe as much as he wanted her. A week after the wedding, she asked Joe if they could go home.

They were sitting at the perimeter of the clearing, away from the firelight. Binnie was spread out on the floor beside them, hands under his head as he looked up at the stars.

'You go home if you like,' he said. 'I'm staying here, in America.'

'Binnie, you can't mean it.' Llinos leaned over him and prodded his thin chest 'You wouldn't know how to make a living out here.'

'I don't mean here,' Binnie said. 'I'll come with you and Joe to the coast and I'll find work in Troy.'

'Joe, tell him, he must come with us.' Joe shook his head and remained silent.

'Binnie, I couldn't bear to think of you out here on your own.' Llinos spoke heatedly.

'Perhaps I'm meant to be alone,' Binnie said mildly. 'I didn't make much of a success at being a husband and father, did I? Anyway, America is full of opportunity for a young man and I am still young, Llinos.'

'I know you are. Oh, Binnie, think about it again when we get to the port. I'll bet you won't be able to watch Joe and me sailing for home without you.'

'We'll see.'

The wagon in which Llinos had ridden over the long tracts of virgin American soil had lain idle for months. One of the wheels needed attention and part of the boarding at the side had come loose.

Joe looked at it for a long time and then set to work. Llinos stood watching him until Mint took her arm and led her away.

'Your man will not disappear if you take your eyes off him for a minute, child! Come and see what your friend Binnie has done for us. Everyone is in the clearing behind the lodge, there is so much excitement, I think it calls for another celebration.'

Towards the edge of the stockade, a crowd of braves and squaws were standing in a circle, even one of the old chiefs had been tempted from his pipe and his lodge.

Binnie had been at work for several days, and now the results of his labour were evident in the strong lines of the stone kiln.

'Binnie! You clever old thing, you. That's the finest oven I've ever seen.'

'Aye, not bad, is it? I've had to chip the rocks into some sort of shape and I've bound them together with clay from the river. See how neatly my fires fit in around the edge.'

'Have you tried it yet?' Llinos peered eagerly into the dimness inside the kiln. Pots were stacked on shelves and already the warmth from the fires was changing the colour of the clay.

'I'll close up the door and by morning we'll know if it's worked or not.'

Binnie brushed the clay from his hands, leaving dry finger marks across his coat and trews. 'I can't see why it shouldn't work, mind. It's built on exactly the same principle as the kilns at home, except that it's much smaller, of course.'

Llinos hugged his arm. 'You are so good, Binnie, you'll make life so much easier for the Indians if your oven works.'

'Well, I've done my best, it won't be for want of trying.'

'I'm going to tell Joe,' Llinos said and behind her she heard Mint laugh.

'Can't keep away from him, can you, Firebird? Go on with you, then, but you'll be wasting your time. Joe knows all about it.'

'So I'm the last to know, am I?' Llinos shook Binnie's arm and he turned to look at her, a smile on his thin face.

'You wouldn't have listened. You've lived in the clouds since you married Joe.'

'I suppose you're right,' Llinos said. 'Well done, Binnie, I'm proud of you.'

It was a fine, bright day when Llinos helped Joe pack their few belongings onto the wagon. As a farewell present, the chief presented Joe with two fine horses, the most valuable gift he could give. Mint gave them shawls and skins and beads and held back her tears as she kissed them goodbye.

Binnie, too, received gifts in honour of his kiln, which had worked splendidly and was the pride of the village. He was given a horse and a small chest containing a ceremonial pipe.

The back of the wagon was filled with provisions and a half dozen skins of water. As the gates were opened, Llinos felt a constriction in her throat. She swallowed hard and made an effort to smile. Joe put his hand over hers.

'Don't grieve, we'll be back one day,' he said. 'But now, Llinos, my little bride, I am taking you home.'

CHAPTER TWENTY-THREE

Eynon sat outside in the garden. The house had begun to feel claustrophobic. He looked at the sheet of paper in his hand and he read the neat script again and smiled. Llinos was back on British shores.

He leaned back in the solid wooden seat and stared up at the trees. The branches stood naked against the sky but soon they would come into leaf and spring would warm the land. But even now the sun was shining, true, it was a pale winter sun, but Eynon breathed in the freshness, enjoying the moment.

Things were looking up. Georgina and Aunt Catherine had left to stay with his father; Eynon's home was his own again. And soon, now, he would be seeing Llinos.

Maura came out of the kitchen door, a tray on her arm. She looked thin and drawn. Her red hair was dull and lifeless. She was missing her husband, though she would deny it with her last breath.

'I've brought you some hot tea,' she said. 'Watch you don't get a cold now, you've not got your strength back yet.'

'Don't fuss, I'm well enough.' He tapped the letter. 'This is from Llinos, she's resting at Bristol after the long sea voyage from America. She's coming home, Joe too. The whole party will be back in Swansea in a few days.' He paused, realizing that Maura's colour had drained.

'Don't worry, I'm sure Binnie will want to sort everything out.'

She put the cup on the wrought iron table at the side of him. 'I don't know if I want Binnie back.' She met his eyes. 'I'm not sure if I love him or hate him right at this moment.'

If only he could say how much he wanted to see Llinos again, to say openly how much he loved her. He sighed, he had no choice but to believe she was lost to him for ever.

'Your father's coming up the path.' Maura spoke warningly.

Eynon felt his shoulders grow tense. 'Look out, here comes trouble,' he said softly.

'I see you have managed to crawl out of your bed, then, Eynon.' Philip sat on the carved wooden seat on the other side of the paved terrace, as far away from Eynon as possible. 'It's taken long enough. You don't seem to heal very well, do you?'

Eynon was used to criticism from his father and this time the implication was especially clear. Philip was saying that his son did not do anything very well.

'Perhaps you should go to Mrs Lane again, ask her for some of that weed killer. I believe you've used it once before, Father?'

'Mrs Lane? What do you mean? If it's an

accusation you are making you'd better be very careful.'

'I am not accusing you of anything, Father. Perhaps you have a guilty conscience. By the way, I didn't take any of that foul medicine you brought me.'

'Foolish boy! I don't understand you, are you insinuating that I'm trying to poison you?'

'I think we'd better change the subject,' Eynon said coldly.

'I think you are right. Now, I've been to see Duncan.' Philip took out his pipe and pressed down the tobacco with thick fingers.

'Father Duncan? So?' Eynon felt that something bad was about to happen.

'I've told him and that fop Martin to keep away from here. They are a bad influence on you.'

Eynon felt a cold anger inside him but he did his best to control it. 'You don't want me to have any friends, then, Father? Since those drunken thugs took it into their heads to give me a hiding, the only people I've seen are the servants and the two vicars, do you realize that?'

'And do you realize that I donate a great deal of money to our church. I think Father Duncan will have the good sense to listen to what I have to say.'

Eynon knew his father was right. However much sympathy the two clerics had for him they would need to do what was best for the church.

'I have enjoyed my discussions with Martin, Father. Do you want me to be totally alone?'

'There's no point continuing this discussion. I won't have you hiding behind the Church. Get on out there in the real world and be a man.'

Eynon was silent and Philip looked at him thoughtfully. 'Just think about it. You can cower here in your house for the rest of your life or you can face up to facts. No good ever came of being afraid to do what you want. Even if it means another beating, another six beatings, you must face the town, show you are not going to be intimidated. Of course, the next hiding you get might just finish you.'

Eynon shook his head speechlessly. Did his father hate him so much that he wanted him dead?

Maura came into the garden with a tray of tea. Philip smiled at her politely. 'I'm not staying, but thank you for the thought. How's the little one?' Philip was unfailingly polite to the Irish girl. It was his policy, always, to be seen as a benefactor; an upholder of the rights of the lower orders.

'Very well, sir, thank you, sir.' Maura was perhaps the one person who was not taken in by Philip's outward show of geniality. She bobbed several times, paying lip-service to Philip, but she did not raise her eyes.

'Very good.' Philip reached into his pocket and took out some coins. 'There, put these in the child's money box.'

Maura bobbed again. 'Thank you most kindly, sir.'

Philip stood before Eynon and quite deliberately picked up the letter from the table.

'Father, that's private, it's mine.'

Philip read the contents and flicked the paper into Eynon's lap. 'So the little Savage girl is coming back to Swansea, is she? Well, I for one will be pleased to see her, I might have a little surprise for her. I'll be off now. Good day to you, Eynon.'

Eynon watched as his father strode to the gate, unhitched his horse and swung himself into the saddle. 'What on earth is he up to now, Maura?'

Philip rode away without a backward glance and Maura looked into her hand and spat on the coins. 'Don't know, but it can't be anything good, can it?'

Eynon almost smiled at her small act of rebellion but then his father's words swept back into his mind. Perhaps it would be just as well to get right away from Swansea. He had given up the idea of ever persuading Llinos to be his wife. At least he could look for some solitude in his life, some peace.

He sighed and rose to his feet with difficulty. His body still ached, the bruises had faded but he was in constant pain. He pushed himself upright. If he wasn't very careful, he would begin to feel sorry for himself. He took one last look around the garden, at the fading sun and the winter earth and went into the house.

'I'm sorry, Martin, but the Bishop wants you to be transferred to Bangor in North Wales. It's a fine place, so I'm told, and they are in need of a good man.'

'This is part of a vendetta and you know it as well as I do.'

'Maybe, maybe not. In any case, ours is not to question why. When the Bishop gives an order we obey.'

'Morton-Edwards warned me to keep away from his son; I knew then I was asking for trouble, I could see it in his face.'

'Well, you did rather give the impression that you thought he was behind Eynon's . . . mishap. It's not up to us to point a finger.'

'I think Eynon is a good man, Father, and very much misjudged.' Martin spoke heatedly. 'He is not a coward even though he is a peace-loving man. In any event, he does not deserve that father of his.'

'Well,' Father Duncan said, 'that's as may be. Anyway perhaps you are being a mite over-sensitive, Martin. Philip surely has his son's best interests at heart. And he does give generously to the church.'

'But are you convinced by his show of goodness, because I am not.'

'Not altogether.' The older man stroked his chin. 'Still, none of us is without sin so I hesitate to cast stones.' He smiled. 'Or to make sudden judgements based on little more than a feeling

in my bones that the man is a scheming repro-
bate.' He puffed on his pipe. 'I'll be sorry to
lose you, you know that, don't you, Martin?
Now, let's not talk about the matter any more.'

It was evening when Martin made his way
across the valley to Eynon's house. He had been
a constant visitor since the attack on his friend
and quite obviously this had not gone unnoticed.

Philip Morton-Edwards was a wicked man. A
lion pretending to be a lamb. But it did not
wash, not with Martin. He had seen the scorn
in Philip's eyes when he talked about Eynon.
No, not scorn, it was stronger than that, it was
hatred. The man was a monster, he wanted to
control and manipulate everything and everyone.

'Martin, I'm glad to see you.' He was welcomed warmly into Eynon's cosy sitting-room.
A bright fire burned in the grate and the heavy
curtains were drawn against the chill of the night.

'There's been some dirty work afoot, Eynon.'
Martin slumped into a chair. 'I'm to leave Swansea. At the end of the week,' he said, stretching
his feet towards the fire.

'My father's doing, no doubt.'

'I suppose so. The order comes directly from
the Bishop. If your father has interfered, then
he has friends in high places.'

'I know that to my cost,' Eynon said ruefully.
'Where are they sending you?'

'North Wales, Bangor. I suppose I'll fit in
there, given time, but it's going to be so different

to Swansea.' He looked across the room. 'I'll be sorry to leave you at the mercy of your father but there's nothing I can do.'

'Don't worry, I'm going to sell up and leave Swansea, my friend. It's the only way out.'

'Won't your father object to that, too?' Martin frowned. 'It seems to me he won't rest until you are six feet under the earth. It's a strange world, all right. I will never work out the machinations of the minds of men, not if I live to be a hundred.'

'Have a glass of porter, it will do us both good.' Eynon rang the bell and the maid came at once, bobbing her head, her eyes curious as they rested on the two men.

'Bring me some porter, Jessie,' Eynon said briskly. 'And mind your manners, it's rude to stare.'

'Sorry, Mr Eynon. Didn't mean it, sir, jest never saw a proper vicar close-to before, me being a chapel girl.'

'All right, go on, fetch the porter and be quick about it.'

'Where's Maura, then?' Martin rubbed at his legs. He had developed bone ache of late; doubtless the sea air had something to do with the onset of the pain in his joints.

'She is with the baby, I expect. I try not to have her work in the evenings.'

'What will the girl do when you leave here?'

'I think that is her husband's problem.' Eynon smiled. 'I've had a letter from Llinos — she is back in England. She will travel up from Bristol in a few days' time.'

'And Binnie Dundee with her?'

'I presume so. Why, have you heard any different?' Eynon asked.

Martin shook his head. 'No, but never take anything for granted, my friend, it just does not pay.'

'Job's comforter!' Eynon looked up as the door opened. 'Good girl, Jessie, put the tray down, I'll see to it.'

He poured the reddish wine into the glasses and handed one to Martin. 'Here's to us both in our new lives.'

Martin took a sip of the drink, the taste was a mingling of spice and fruit. 'Mmm! Lovely.' He smiled. 'I was wondering, there may be a few properties for sale near where I'll be working in North Wales. Want me to look into it?' It would be good to have a friend nearby and Martin had become fond of Eynon.

'That's an idea worth exploring,' Eynon said. 'Yes, it might just be the solution.'

The door closed quietly behind Jessie but neither man noticed.

Llinos looked round the small room and felt a pang at the thought of leaving the comfort and security of the lodging house. Here, in this room, she and Joe had shared their thoughts and their dreams. Llinos had teased him and herself with the delights that would be theirs once they were truly married.

It had been a testing time for both of them. Joe had shown great restraint, it had been Llinos who was tempted to shrug off her hidebound ideas about a church wedding and make passionate love to Joe. But soon, she told herself, she would be his wife in the eyes of God and the Church, then everything would be wonderful. There came the sound of a light tapping on the door.

'Llinos, the coach is here.' Even his voice had the power to thrill her.

She picked up her bag and paused for a moment, taking a deep breath as though she was stepping out into a new world.

He smiled down at her, his hair tied back, his skin fresh. His eyes were so blue it was as though the sun was shining in them.

'I'm ready, Joe.' Outside, the sunshine was dappling the roadway between the trees. The ostler took the bags from Joe and flung them onto the roof. Llinos looked behind her at the low doorway and the mullioned windows of the old inn. It had been a wonderful few days. Days when she and Joe had talked together, made plans and grown closer than ever before.

Inside the coach it was dim and the cold upholstery creaked as Llinos took her seat. Joe settled beside her and, opposite, the plump woman with her two young sons moved her feet a fraction to accommodate Joe's long legs.

'Nice day for it.' She spoke in a pleasant West-

Country accent. 'The journey, I mean. Going to visit your folks, are you?'

Llinos wished she and Joe could be alone. She longed to kiss his mouth, to feel the heat of his passion for her.

'Returning home,' she said.

'Oh, been away have you, dear?'

Llinos took a deep breath. 'Yes, we've been visiting Joe's folks in America.'

'Fancy that, American are you, sir? I thought you looked sort of foreign, in a handsome way, mind. Good journey, was it?'

'Wonderful,' Llinos said.

'I expect your dear husband was made much of on board ship, such good looks. Are your folks rich, sir, like all those Americans?'

Joe's eyes sparkled. Llinos knew that look, it meant that Joe was going to exercise his wry sense of humour.

'It all depends on what you mean by rich. My mother owns the land, the buffalo herds, the sky, sun and moon. She's an American Indian. She wears animal skins, oh, and feathers in her hair, of course.'

'Oh dear. But your father . . . is he . . . ?' The woman's words trailed away and she coloured in confusion. Joe took pity on her.

'My father was an Englishman and so here I am, half Indian, half white.'

The lady sank back into her seat, clearly sorry she had begun the conversation. One of her sons stared across at Joe, leaning forward to get a better look. He finally slid from the seat and stood close to Joe, examining him from head to foot.

'You got no feathers in your hair, you can't be an Indian.' His tone was accusing.

'Billy, be quiet, don't be rude. Come and sit back down here at once.'

'I wear feathers when I'm home,' Joe said reasonably.

'Where do you live, then, if you're an Indian?'

'In America I live in a lodge, a sort of tent. Here, I live in a house.'

The young boy digested this in silence and his mother tugged at his sleeves, pulling them down over bony wrists.

'They grow so fast, these boys.' She was trying to appear unflustered. 'Got any youngsters your-selves?'

'Not yet,' Llinos said. She caught Joe's eye and smiled.

The coach jerked over the bumpy roadway obviously having a soporific effect on the lady opposite because, shortly, she began to snore gently.

Llinos put her head against Joe's arm and closed her eyes, wondering what sort of reception she would have when she arrived at her father's house. Would he welcome her or would he turn her away? There was no way of knowing how he would react. But surely by now he would have come to his senses? He must accept that she loved Joe and meant to be with him, otherwise her father would lose her altogether.

Joe kissed her hair. 'Try to sleep a little,' he said. 'It's going to be a long journey.'

Philip had been angry when Jessie came to him and told him what she'd overheard. She was paid handsomely for her trouble and as she bobbed a curtsy and made for the door she was smiling.

Philip thought the matter out. He did not want Eynon to go away, he wanted him here in Swansea where he could keep an eye on him.

He sat now in the vicarage and smiled sadly at Father Duncan. 'So you see, it would not be suitable for Father Martin to have any further communication with my son. It's unhealthy.'

'I'm not sure what you mean, why is it unhealthy?'

'My son is a weakling; he will grow to depend too much on the man. I want him to stand on his own two feet, to grow up and take responsibility for his own life. Until then I must keep an eye on him.'

'Well, sir, what do you suggest I do? If your son wishes to move away, I'm not clear what you expect me to do about it.'

Philip looked at the old priest; he had the feeling that the man saw right through him.

'Just make sure that Father Martin is sent far away, perhaps to England or Scotland, I don't know.'

'I have no power to do that, Mr Morton-

Edwards, it is a decision the Bishop must make.'

'Very well then, I shall speak with the Bishop myself,' Philip said affably. 'I mean to make an extra donation to the church fund this year in any case.'

'Right.' The vicar rose to his feet. 'God go with you, my son.'

Philip left the house feeling he had been subtly, but surely, dismissed. Well the old fart would soon learn it did not do to cross Philip Morton-Edwards. A word in the right ear, a hefty donation and everything would be arranged. Father Martin would be sent out of the country and Duncan would find himself pensioned off.

Later at Ty Mawr Philip sat at the dining table with Georgina and her godmother. As he had predicted, the girl had soon found Eynon was a dull companion.

Georgina's family was extremely rich, and Philip had begun to toy with the thought of proposing to the girl himself. She had good child-bearing hips and was not too intelligent. And she would certainly bring him a rich dowry both of money and lands.

He had harboured hopes of taking Llinos Savage as his next bride — until he had read her letter. He had been somewhat taken aback by her abrupt departure from Swansea but had been prepared to overlook what appeared to him a sign of her spirited nature.

However, it seemed she had taken part in some sort of marriage ceremony with the Indian. By now she was no longer a virgin and he, Philip Morton-Edwards, was too good to take any man's leavings, let alone those of some half-breed.

Still, life had its compensations. Rising, he took a small key from his breast pocket and unlocked the hidden drawer underneath the lid of the cabinet.

The bills of sale were growing satisfyingly large in number. Piece by piece, Philip was buying up all the land surrounding the Savage Pottery. Once the deal for the last piece of ground was settled, Savage would have to beg for a right of way into his own property.

Philip smiled to himself. Savage would be obliged to sell up and get out, there would be nothing else for him to do. He could hardly trade if there was no access to and from the gates of the pottery.

He sank back in his chair. Matters were working out very nicely in his favour. Soon, Eynon would be out of the way for good, Philip would see to it. Then he would inherit all the money that his first wife's family had left Eynon. Philip would be free to breed a fine family. All that remained was to choose the lady who was to become his wife. His options were not many, perhaps the answer was here at his own fireside.

In the dining-room, Georgina was staring moodily at her godmother. 'He's old, far too old for me.'

'Nonsense, child! In any case, from what I've heard you would find more life in the father than in the son. Eynon Morton-Edwards is something of a foppish young man, not very interested in ladies by the look of it and certainly not able to offer anyone protection. He can't even look after himself.'

'Well, I'm sure I could change him, make a man of him.'

'I doubt it, my dear. Some men are not cut out for marriage, you know. Some are too selfish by far to expend any energy on a woman.'

'I'm not sure that Eynon is like that.'

'Well, just take it from me, Georgina, Eynon will do you no good between the sheets.'

'God-Mamma!'

'I'm only speaking the truth, the boy is a weakling, you can see he has no stamina to speak of.'

'Well I don't want his father, that's for sure.'

'I wouldn't be so hasty, if I were you. You haven't exactly been the centre of attention at home, have you? Not since you were foolish enough to be caught in a most compromising situation with that young man, Frederick Haines. Well, he quickly left the scene, didn't he?'

'Oh, God-Mamma, people will forget all that in time.'

'No, they won't, that's why we came away. What you must remember is that Philip might be rather old for you, but he is a very rich and powerful man. As his wife, you would be given calling cards to all the best houses.'

Georgina looked thoughtful. 'I shall see Eynon tomorrow,' she said. 'I shall ask him if he intends to marry and if the answer is no, I shall think about what you say.'

'Very wise, dear, very wise.' Aunt Catherine rose unsteadily to her feet. 'I'm going to retire, I would advise you to do the same. I think Philip is probably consoling himself with the brandy bottle and men can be notoriously unsettled by drinking brandy.'

'I don't understand.'

'You don't understand much at all, do you, girl? Well put it like this, you won't get a wedding veil by giving a man what he wants before the ceremony.'

Georgina shrugged but she followed her god-mother up the wide curving staircase without demur.

'Good night.' She let herself into her room and closed the door, grateful to be away from the old lady's nagging. She sat before the mirror and stared at her face critically.

She wasn't bad-looking, she decided. She had very fair skin and rather sandy hair but her eyes were nice; hazel with flecks of green. Why had she been unable to get herself a husband? Well, if the worse came to the worse, perhaps she should think about accepting Philip Morton-Edwards. At least then she would not be left sitting on the dusty shelf while other girls her age were sprouting babies left, right and centre.

She heard Philip go to his room and tried to imagine him in his drawers. The thought made her giggle. Would he have a paunch like her grandfather? Would his chest be covered in greying hair?

Oh, lord, how awful! Could she really contemplate marriage to an old man? She thumped at her pillow, wishing it was Eynon's face. Why could he not have been a red-blooded man, willing, even eager to marry her? Fate could be so unkind.

Her last thought as she fell asleep was of Philip. He wasn't so bad, really, was he?

CHAPTER TWENTY-FOUR

Llinos felt her heartbeats quicken as the carriage entered Pottery Row. Everything seemed different, diminished, the houses crouched together in a huddle. Even the bottle kilns seemed smaller than she had remembered them. She knew why, of course. In contrast to the vast open plains of America, anything would appear small.

'Llinos! Welcome home, love.' Celia-end-house stood on the doorstep, waving her stick in welcome. She looked older, more frail than Llinos remembered.

'Nothing stays the same,' Joe whispered, and she smiled at him, knowing he had picked up on her thoughts.

Llinos alighted from the carriage and hugged Celia, feeling the thinness of the old lady beneath her layers of dark clothing.

'Your father will be glad to see you,' Celia said. 'He's been right miserable lately with a face like a bulldog on him.'

Llinos smiled wryly. 'Then I'll probably make him feel ten times worse!'

'Go on with you.' Celia looked shyly at Joe. He was an enigma to her, she was never quite sure how to talk to him. Llinos came to her rescue.

'I've been staying with Joe's folks in America.'

Celia's eyes opened wide. '*Duw!* America, is it?' She looked round. 'Where's our Binnie, then? Gone home to his wife, is he?'

Llinos was saved from replying by the sound of her father's wheelchair rumbling over the rough ground. She turned, her heart in her throat, not knowing what sort of reception she was going to get.

'Llinos, my little girl, you've come home then.' Her father's voice was mild. He held out his arms and hope filled her heart. It seemed he had forgiven her.

'Father! I'm so glad to see you.' She hugged him, breathing in the familiar smells of clay and oxide mingled with the tobacco from the pipe in his pocket.

'Come on in, girl, let's talk in private.' He did not look at Joe, not once, and Llinos bit her lip.

'I'll talk to him on my own, shall I?' she whispered to Joe. 'I'll try not to upset him.'

'No,' Joe said, 'we are together now, one.' He followed Llinos into the house.

'Have you come to your senses, Llinos?' Lloyd Savage was looking up at her, his eyes almost begging her to understand his rejection of Joe. He did not look away from her face but focused all his attention on his daughter. A bitter sense of disappointment filled her.

'You didn't expect me to be with Joe these past weeks and to change my mind about him, did you?'

'But I thought he was going to marry some Indian woman in America.'

'No, Father, and please don't talk about him as if he weren't here.'

'All right, then, tell me the worst, what have you done?'

'There is no worst, Father.' She knelt down beside his chair and took his hand. 'Please try to understand, I love him.'

Lloyd shook his head. 'You haven't done anything foolish, have you, Llinos?' He smoothed her hair. 'Speak to me, Llinos, tell me the truth.'

'Joe and I are married according to the customs of the Mandan tribe.'

She saw her father's face crease in anger and she spoke more forcefully. 'Before you begin to chastise me for being a loose woman again, let me tell you that we have not lived as man and wife. We decided to wait until we have a proper church wedding.'

'Thank God.' He kissed her hand. 'Let's get you settled in, then.' He rang the bell and almost immediately a young girl Llinos had never seen before bobbed her way into the room.

'Wenna, make up two guests rooms, would you?'

Llinos put her arm through Joe's. 'I'm sorry, my love,' she said softly. He looked down at her and after a moment untangled her arm from his.

'Lloyd, you can't pretend I don't exist,' he said. 'Llinos loves me and I love her. We intend to be together whatever you say.'

435

Lloyd shook his head and waved his arms as though fending off a troublesome fly.

'Please Father —,' Llinos began but Lloyd interrupted her.

'Hush, Llinos, I have to tell you right away that the pottery is in trouble, bad trouble.'

She sighed softly. 'What sort of trouble, Father?'

'The land surrounding ours has been bought up, lock, stock and barrel.'

Llinos frowned. She did not understand, it was land that was not fit for anything but supporting manufactories.

'What does it mean, Father?'

'It means I can't trade, there is no access, the pottery is ruined.'

'You mean someone has bought Pottery Row? But that's impossible.'

'Apparently not,' Lloyd said sombrely. 'Of course, it's Philip Morton-Edwards who is behind this. He's always wanted me out of the way and he'll stop at nothing to ruin me.'

Llinos could not believe Philip would be so devious. He had been unfailingly kind to her. He had trusted her with his recipes for the porcelain bodies. Why was everyone so ready to condemn him?

'But, Father, he's so rich, why would he want you ruined? What threat is the Savage Pottery to him?'

'He is an evil man, Llinos, and you are too young and trusting by far.' He glanced briefly at Joe. 'You can't see bad in anything or anyone.'

Llinos rubbed her hands along her skirt to smooth out the creases. 'Oh, I've seen evil all right, Father. You forget I lived with Mr Cimla. I saw him beat Binnie to within an inch of his life and in the end it was Mr Cimla who caused my mother's death.'

Lloyd was silent for a long time. He looked up to her then, his eyes filled with tears. 'I'm sorry. I'm being selfish, of course, you must live your own life. I'm not denying that but you must think about your future very carefully, my dear.'

He looked up at her, his face twisted with pain. 'All I ask is that you don't turn your back on me, not now, Llinos, I'm so worried, so alone.'

'Of course I won't turn my back on you, Father. Joe and I'll stay and help you sort out your problems, won't we, Joe?'

Lloyd turned his face away from her. 'You can't expect me to welcome as your husband the man who was only my batman.' He spoke in a low voice. 'He served me, waited on me, polished my boots, cooked my meals. Apart from being a foreigner, Joe is a menial.'

'Father!' she said, aghast. 'How can you talk like that about the man who saved your life?' Both men remained silent and looking into Joe's eyes Llinos knew he was not going to speak up in his own defence.

'I need Joe,' she said softly. 'I love him, Father.

We will be married as soon as possible, take it or leave it.'

Lloyd sighed heavily. 'He can stay here with us, of course. I realize that you think you love him and want to marry him.' He reached out and she went to him.

'Just promise me this, that you'll wait a little while, that you'll help me to get my life back into some sort of order.'

'I don't know if I can promise you that, Father.' Llinos tried to smother her anger. Her father did not know what he was asking. Her whole being ached to belong to Joe, to lie with him, to be his wife.

She looked at her father. He had grown old, old and frightened. 'I just don't know. I feel torn, do you understand that? Torn between the two men I love.' She moved towards the door.

'I'm going to my room. I think I can find it without help from anyone, thank you,' she added, as her father lifted his hand to the bell. She hurried through the hall and up the familiar stairs. The woodwork was polished, the carpet was freshly brushed. But Llinos could see nothing for the tears that blinded her.

Joe stared out of the window at the throbbing heat of the kilns and tried to be calm. He had been installed in a large, cold back bedroom. It was comfortable enough but it marked his place in the scheme of things as Lloyd saw them. He was a foreigner, a half-breed and second best was good enough for him.

Joe moved to the narrow bed and flung himself down, his arms beneath his head. The door opened and Llinos entered the room, frowning as she looked around her.

'Joe, I'm sorry about . . . well, about everything.'

He did not speak. He was tempted to just get to his feet and walk out of her life for ever, he seemed to bring her nothing but tears and unhappiness.

He lay back, his eyes closed as if to shut her out, and he felt the depression in the bumpy mattress as she sank down beside him.

'Joe, look at me. In the morning, I shall find out exactly what has been going on.' She spoke briskly now and he knew she was hurt by his lack of response. He could read her thoughts. Joe, patient, wise Joe, would wait for ever. Well, would he?

'My father is an old man, you can see he's in pain and his very livelihood is threatened. I can't just think of myself now, can I?'

He remained silent, this was something she must work out for herself if she was to grow. After a moment, she rose and left the room, closing the door with a thud behind her. Joe stared up at the light glancing across the ceiling and thought with longing about clear rivers and rich grasslands and the wide open spaces of America.

'So Binnie didn't come home after all.' Maura's voice was low, tear-filled. Eynon tried to think of something comforting to say but failed.

Eynon was sitting with Llinos in the small drawing-room and in that instant he was angry with her. Maura stood before him, her shoulders slumped, and as he looked into her eyes he saw the tears welling over. He coughed to hide his embarrassment.

Damn Llinos! Her impetuous behaviour had acted as a spur to Binnie to leave his wife, sometimes Llinos could be so irresponsible. Now it was left to Eynon to explain matters to Maura.

'Binnie has remained behind in America, he intends to find work there. I expect he'll send for you when he's set up.'

Maura looked at him and he could see she did not believe a word he said. 'I'll get you some tea, sir. Shall I bring it into the drawing-room?'

'Yes, please, Maura.'

Llinos was playing with a necklace that hung against her pale skin. She looked very beautiful, flushed from her walk across the valley. Eynon ached with despair, how could he love her so much knowing she felt nothing for him?

'Eynon, I'm sorry, it wasn't pleasant for you breaking the news to Maura.' She held out her hand and he took it. Her fingers were slender and delicate and yet she could wedge and mould clay with the strongest of workers. She was a remarkable woman but she needed to grow up, face facts. If she married Joe she would never be accepted in polite society.

'Will you go back to America?' he asked, looking out through the window, trying not to see how lovely she was.

'One day, perhaps. Eynon, look at me.' Her voice trembled and suddenly, she appeared vulnerable.

'Eynon, I seem to be hurting everyone but I love Joe and I will be with him, whatever happens.'

Eynon shrugged without speaking. Llinos changed the subject abruptly and the moment of intimacy vanished.

'My father is in trouble, someone is buying up the land around the Savage Pottery. Any idea who it could be?'

'My father, who else?'

'Eynon! Why should it be your father?'

'It has his stamp, he can't bear to see anyone content and happy. He's had Father Martin sent away just because we were friends. Oh, yes, he's the one out to ruin the Savage Pottery, no doubt about it.'

'I'm sure that's not true,' Llinos said. 'Your father has riches enough and he has the wonderful recipes for porcelain. I'm sure he's far too busy to concern himself with the land around our pottery.'

She was so sweet, so trusting, and in some ways so immature. Had she learned nothing from her years of hardship? How could he warn her about his father when she did not want to listen?

'I'll be moving near to Martin's parish soon,' he said, 'that will annoy my father, show him he does not always get his own way.'

'Oh, Eynon, I'll be so sorry to see you leave Swansea.' Her beautiful eyes, dark and mysterious, stared into his. Something had changed between them, he was on edge with her. The old ease of their friendship had gone.

'I doubt that, you managed quite well without me while you were in America.'

'That was different,' she said. 'It was only a temporary arrangement.' She leaned forward, the beads swinging against the sweetness of her breasts.

'What's happened to you? The gentle, kind Eynon I knew is gone. You've become cynical.'

'I haven't changed my feelings for you, Llinos,' he said softly.

She rose and hugged him, her cheek against his and he felt his gut turn to water. Soon, she would marry Joe. He should be happy for her but all he felt was pain.

'This is a pretty scene, I feel quite envious of you, Eynon.' His father's voice was like a deluge of cold water. Eynon tensed but he made an effort to act normally as he drew away from Llinos.

'You don't believe in being announced, do you, Father?' He felt the words choke in his throat as Llinos greeted Philip warmly, taking his hands in hers.

'It's good to be back among my friends,' she said. 'How are you, Philip?'

'Very well, my dear.' He held her away from him. 'And you are more beautiful than ever. Send for some more tea, Eynon. I would like to join you, that's if I'm not intruding.'

'Of course you are not intruding,' Llinos said cheerily and moved to accommodate him on the sofa beside her.

'I have news for you, son.' Philip rested his arm along the back of the sofa. 'I've managed to get your friend Martin the most wonderful advantage.'

'Really, Father? What could that be?' Eynon felt cold, his father was ruthless. He manipulated everyone and somehow got away with it. It was amazing that Llinos could not see through him.

'He's to go to work in London, in one of the big churches there. It's one of the greatest honours any young man could hope for.'

'I see.' Eynon was aware of Llinos looking at him sympathetically. She leaned past Philip and rested her hand on Eynon's arm.

'Oh, Eynon, I know it's disappointing for you but I'm sure you're happy for Martin.'

'Yes, very happy.' Eynon spoke listlessly. His father had dangled a juicy carrot before Martin's eyes and he had taken it.

'I'll just ask Maura to make fresh tea.' Llinos

left the room and Philip sat back, his lean face full of amusement.

'Let that be a lesson to you, boy. Everyone has a price.'

'So you keep telling me.' Eynon was suddenly tired. His father could control any situation and turn it to his own advantage. Eynon was beginning to think that the only escape from his father was the grave.

'Don't look so down-hearted, son.' Philip rested his hand on Eynon's shoulder. 'I shall always take care of you, you know that.'

Eynon looked at his father in surprise before he realized that Llinos was in the doorway, Maura following her carrying a tray. His father was clever, Eynon gave him that.

He sat up straighter, fighting a battle against a rush of anger and losing. 'Right,' he said in a hard voice, 'let's all have a cup of tea and a jolly chat, shall we? Tell us, Father, who have you got it in for this week? Whose reputation are you going to ruin just to amuse yourself?'

He was aware of Llinos, her eyes wide with reproach, but he no longer cared. 'Damn you, Father!' He stood up and stared at his father for a long moment before leaving the room.

He hated his father, hated his own flesh and blood, surely that was wrong? Well, the hate was there and would not go away. It was about time he found some courage and stopped trying to run away from his father, about time he stood up to him instead.

Suddenly, he felt released, free of the tyranny his father had imposed on him all these years. His father had interfered once too often and Eynon was tired of it. Now it was time to plan his revenge.

'I must apologize for my son's behaviour, Llinos. Perhaps you will allow me to take you home in my carriage.'

'That's very kind but I think I would enjoy the walk, Philip.'

'Llinos, you have not allowed my son to influence you against me, surely?'

'No, of course not.' Llinos spoke the truth, she had seen the caring way Philip had rested his hand on his son's shoulder. Seen the pain in his eyes when he broke the news about Father Martin. He had expected praise from his son and instead he had received a rebuke.

'I don't know what's wrong with Eynon lately,' Philip said thoughtfully. 'I try to make him happy but he is a strange boy. I suppose it's all my fault.'

Llinos shook her head. 'No, it isn't.' How could it be Philip's fault? He had given his son every advantage. He was allowing him to live his own life where some fathers, her own included, wanted to dictate to their children.

'Did I do wrong getting Father Martin the post in the city?' Philip sounded wistful. 'I thought I was giving the young man a helping hand. I just don't understand, all I want is for Eynon to be proud of me, to be happy.'

Llinos took his hand. 'Don't be troubled, Philip, I'm sure everything will sort itself out.'

'You're right, of course you are. Now, tell me about your adventure. I understand from Eynon that you actually got married in America.'

Llinos smiled. 'Well, I did get married according to the laws of the Mandan Indians. However, Joe and I are going to have a proper church wedding when the time is right.'

'And Joe, is he not jealous of your friendship with Eynon?'

'No, he's not, Joe feels only liking and respect for Eynon.'

'Well, that's very tolerant of him.' Philip leaned towards her. 'Llinos, are you really going to marry this man, this Indian fellow? It's not too late to change your mind. I'm sure you could make a highly successful marriage if you wished, one that would be accepted in polite society.'

'I don't give a fig for "polite society", I only want to be happy.'

Philip looked at her thoughtfully. 'Your father, what does he say about it all?'

She shrugged. 'Well, he's not pleased. So I have made up my mind to spend a little time with him before I marry Joe. I'll try to persuade Father that what I'm doing is right.'

'Very noble, my dear.'

Llinos touched his arm. 'Could you tell me something, Philip?'

'I will if I can, my dear.'

'Do you know who is buying up the land

surrounding the pottery?'

Philip's eyebrows rose. 'Buying up the land, whatever for? Nothing will grow on it for years, it's worse than useless. A man would have to be a fool to throw away good money like that.'

Llinos congratulated herself that she had been right. Whoever was hedging her father in, trying to ruin his business, it was not Philip Morton-Edwards.

'Still, that's what's happening. Could you try to find out about it for me, please?'

'I'll do my best but these lawyer chaps are sticklers for keeping their noses clean. Confidentiality and all that.'

Llinos sighed. 'I'd better get back, my father is a lonely man these days. He depends on me more and more.'

Philip nodded. 'I know and you are a very dutiful daughter. Take care of yourself, Llinos. You have shadows under your eyes that tell me you are not altogether happy.'

At the gates to Eynon's house, Llinos turned and waved to Philip. There was no sign of Eynon. She sighed and began to walk towards home.

Maura folded the bedsheets with angry stabs of her fingers. The linen smelled fresh and clean but she did not notice. She was angry, very angry. If Llinos Savage had not interfered in her life Binnie would be home where he belonged, supporting his wife and child.

She put the sheets away in the drawer of the huge chest on the landing and then returned to the kitchen.

The cook looked over her shoulder. 'Better keep an eye on the babe, she looks flushed to me.'

Maura had left her daughter on a thick blanket on the floor. The little girl had been sleepy all morning but Maura had thought nothing of it.

'Oh, Cookie, look, Bridget's got spots all over her.'

The cook bent over the child and frowned. 'Looks like the measles,' she said.

All at once, the sounds of the pots boiling on the stove, the clatter of cutlery as Jessie the kitchen maid cut up the vegetables for dinner, faded into the background.

Maura felt a cold fear grip her. Measles was bad, she had seen the epidemics of it when she lived at Greenhill. Most children died of the sickness.

But her baby had not been anywhere near Greenhill. Bridget lived in clean surroundings, ate good food. How could she have caught the disease? Cookie must be wrong, she had to be wrong.

'Go see Mr Eynon,' Cook said. 'Ask him if we can have the doctor. I'll get the baby up to bed.'

Eynon was slow in responding to her knock and Maura waited outside his door in a fever of impatience. As soon as she saw him the words poured from her lips.

'Mr Eynon, the baby's right poorly, Cook thinks Bridget's got the measles, she says we should have a doctor.'

'I'll get one of the boys to ride into town to fetch Dr Rogers or if he's out one of the other doctors will come, don't worry. And, Maura, remember, little children are up and down, one minute they're sick, the next they are fine again.'

It seemed an eternity before the doctor arrived. He looked into Bridget's mouth and touched her brow and examined the spots on her plump belly without a word. Maura waited anxiously for him to say something.

'Yes, it's measles, I'm afraid. The child must be kept in complete isolation. Build up the fire, cover her up with blankets, sweat the fever out of her.'

A cold chill gripped Maura. She wanted Binnie desperately, wanted the only other human being on earth who had any part in bringing the baby into the world. But her husband was on the other side of the ocean.

It was the early hours of the morning when Maura woke from a restless sleep. The room was silent, the candle had flickered and died. Maura lit it with shaking fingers. The baby was quiet, the hoarse breathing had ceased. Maura screamed and ran in a frenzy down the stairs, hammering on Eynon's door.

He came at once. 'What's happened?'

'Eynon, the baby isn't breathing, I'm so frightened.'

Maura followed Eynon across the landing and up the small stairs to the servants' rooms. Cook was already there, a bonnet tied askew on her grey hair. As she stood aside for Eynon to go into the bedroom she was shaking her head.

'Bridget!' Maura fell on her knees beside the bed. 'My little girl, look at mama, come on, now, open your eyes.'

Maura began to cry. 'Why isn't Binnie here?' She looked up at Eynon. 'He's always run away from his responsibilities. It's all the fault of that Llinos Savage, her and her big ideas! I hate her. Oh, sweet Jesus, spare my baby!'

It was Eynon who drew her away and tried to calm her. Maura wanted to say some prayers but they had become a jumble in her mind. She looked towards the bed, at Bridget's face. It was pale, serene and beautiful.

'My baby,' she mumbled, her tongue suddenly cleaving to the roof of her mouth. 'My baby.'

'There, there,' Cook said gently, 'the little one's gone to a better place.'

Maura heard the sound of screaming, it rang inside her head, deafening her. And then, all was darkness and peace.

The funeral of Bridget Dundee took place several days later. Eynon Morton-Edwards had paid for the very best in funeral accoutrements. The coffin was polished oak, the handles solid brass.

The hearse was drawn by two splendid greys. But there was no-one to witness the pomp and grandeur, it seemed the entire township had taken fright and those who were not sick were remaining indoors, hiding away.

Maura stood with Eynon and listened to the prayers of Father Duncan. He had retired from his post but he was the only one who would conduct the service. It began to rain but Maura did not feel it. Her baby was dead and it felt like her own life was ended.

When Eynon led her back to the carriage, she followed him obediently. At the gate of the cemetery, she saw Llinos Savage carrying a beautiful bouquet of roses.

'I'm so sorry,' she began.

'Go away. Just go away, leave me alone,' Maura said. 'All this is your fault and I hope you suffer the flames of eternal damnation.'

Eynon half lifted her into the carriage and, sunk in misery, she closed her eyes. The world had turned dark and grey. She was alone in her grief and it was all because of one woman, Llinos Savage.

'This is no-one's fault, you know that really, don't you?' Eynon was speaking to her but she could not hear him. She saw his mouth open and close but she was deaf to his words, locked into her own world of misery.

As soon as they reached the big house, Maura climbed wearily up the stairs and fell on the bed. She was tired, so tired. She felt like death. But she would not die, she needed to live. To pay back those who had done her wrong, Binnie, her husband who had walked out on her, and Llinos Savage, who had taken him away from his wife and child.

At last she slept but her dreams were tortured. She saw her baby, pale and limp like a rag doll, floating in a stream of cold water. She woke suddenly and she was shivering, her throat hurt and she knew she had caught the dreaded sickness.

The night turned to day and back to night again; people came and went. Water was forced between her lips. Fever raged through her body. But her will was strong. By the tenth day after the burial of her child, Maura Dundee's fever broke.

CHAPTER TWENTY-FIVE

Binnie was beginning to adjust to life in the village of West Troy even though, at first, it had all seemed foreign to him. The scenery, even the weather, was so different from that at home. But Binnie had been quick to spot the unmistakable signs of the pottery business in the tall kilns that hummed with heat and life on the edge of the village. That fact alone was enough to convince him that he had done the right thing in deciding to settle in Troy Village.

He had found lodgings in a rambling clapboard house near the docks with an elderly couple and their three daughters. Mrs McCabe had looked him over long and hard before renting him a room and it amused Binnie to realize that the woman saw him as a potential husband for one of her girls.

Still, he congratulated himself on finding himself a comfortable niche. His room was kept spotlessly clean, his food, if strange to his taste, was plentiful and well cooked. And the company was most welcome.

Binnie had only lodged with the McCabes for a few days before he learned that Dan McCabe was himself the owner of a pottery, a large flourishing concern a mile or two from the house.

Binnie told himself that lady luck was with him for once.

This feeling was reinforced when Binnie discovered that Mr McCabe was looking for an experienced foreman. A foreman who might one day become a son-in-law.

It worked to Binnie's benefit that there seemed to be a dearth of single men in Troy. He realized at once that the shortage of husband material accounted for the welcome he had received into the McCabe household.

And once Dan became aware of how knowledgeable Binnie was concerning the process of creating good earthenware, Binnie's position in the household was secured.

After only a month Binnie was made foreman at the McCabe Pottery and was in charge of production from the wedging of the clay to the temperature of the kilns. He had fallen on his feet, at last.

In his spare time, he explored the countryside on horseback, familiarizing himself with the surroundings of his new home. The village of West Troy was located in Albany County, on the west bank of the Hudson River opposite the City of Troy. A distance easily covered on the back of a fine horse, should Binnie be tempted to discover the pleasures of the city. So far he had resisted the bustle of the city streets for the quietness of the village and the sweet company of the McCabe girls.

If Binnie missed anything of his old life, he

thought, staring at his reflection in the mirror in his neat bedroom, it was the green of the grass and the softness of the countryside that spread beyond the boundaries of Swansea.

He did not miss Maura or his child at all and though it plagued his conscience sometimes that he had deserted them, he usually managed to put it out of his mind.

Some nights when he lay in bed, dreaming of the warmth of a woman beside him, he remembered his wife as she had been when he first met her. Maura with her bright hair and ivory skin had been so beautiful, so passionate, so willing. But she had turned into a drudge, her mind filled with the baby and the cleaning. He was too young to settle for such a mundane life.

He finished his toilet and drew on a clean shirt. That was another bonus; for a nominal sum, his laundry was washed and pressed. He looked at himself again in the speckled mirror and was pleased with the image that he saw there. He had filled out, his shoulders were broader, his frame strong and his muscles well defined. He had become a man.

The sound of cheery American voices greeted him as he descended the stairs. The big kitchen was usually the centre of activity. Here the family ate and played, here the fire burned brightly at all times.

As Binnie entered the room, the youngest of the McCabe daughters smiled up at him. Josephine was fair and pale, her complexion unaffected by the sun. Josephine took great care to keep her face shaded when outdoors by wearing a big bonnet covered with its scattering of cotton rosebuds.

'Evenin', Mr Dundee.' Josephine smiled up at him and moved her skirts shyly to one side so that he could take the seat next to her. 'How you been doin' at work today?'

'Fine.' He sat down. 'I've checked out so many pots and jugs that I think I'll see them in my sleep.'

'Have some pie, Binnie.' Mrs McCabe handed him a plate and the rich aroma of meat rose appetizingly and he realized how hungry he was.

'Have some sweet corn and potatoes, Mr Dundee.' Hortense was the oldest of the girls. Her dark hair was tied back in a severe knot. She was by no means a beautiful girl but there was something about her eyes and about the seductive swell of her breasts beneath her bodice that made Binnie feel glad he was a man.

Melia, not to be outdone, handed him a jug of lemon juice, her blue eyes smiling into his. He sat back in his chair, it was good to be waited on. He was a welcome guest, much admired, and it was a wonderful feeling.

After supper, Dan McCabe took his fiddle out onto the porch and began to play a haunting tune. The women busied themselves clearing up the dishes and Binnie, knowing he would never be allowed to lift a finger to help, joined Dan under the starlit sky.

'Here.' Dan handed him a jug. 'Take out the cork and get a sniff of that.'

Binnie did as he was told and the strong smell of liquor rose to greet him. 'Good stuff?'

'The best. Get some down your throat and pass the jug to me and whatever you do, don't let on to the womenfolk that I got this here liquor in the house.'

Binnie knew that he had reached a new stage in his relationship with the McCabe family; he was being accepted by the man of the house and his position as a friend established.

'Beautiful!' he said appreciatively. Binnie took another drink and passed the jug to Dan. 'Where do you get it?'

'Make it myself.' Dan's uneven teeth showed beneath his straggling moustache. 'Got a still out back. The women think it's for making potions and such. They only drink it when there's a chill on them.'

'You've got a good life here, Dan, what with your pottery, your comfortable house, a fine hard-working wife and three pretty daughters.'

'Aye, well I got it all with these.' Dan held out his big hands, the fingers broad and callused. He was a man who had worked hard for what he possessed.

He looked around him. 'Built this house myself. Such carrying of timber, such sawing and such cussing you never did see. But I got it done. Out here, a man's got to be a man, especially when there's womenfolk to pay mind to.'

457

He looked at Binnie thoughtfully. 'My only regret is that I never got me a boy of my own, a son to foller in my footsteps.'

'You have three lovely girls, I expect they'll give you plenty of grandsons.' As soon as Binnie spoke, he realized that Dan was making plans for one of those girls, plans that involved Binnie Dundee.

He toyed with the idea of telling Dan the truth, that he was a married man with a child, but the words stuck in his throat. He would be a fool to ruin the good thing he had going here.

'You'll be looking for a wife right soon, I 'spects. You seem like a fine red-blooded fella to me, the kind that needs a good woman around.'

'You're not wrong.' Binnie spoke ruefully. 'It's a very long time since I've had the pleasure of bedding a woman. Oh, excuse me, Dan, I hope I haven't offended you or anything.'

Dan laughed out loud. 'Lord, you won't offend me, boy. I've had more women than slices of Mrs McCabe's pie. Still, you are a young sprat and the blood is wild. My advice to you is to keep away from the whore-house. One of them gels gets their claws into you and before you know it you are facing the preacher man, taking on other men's leavin's.'

'I'm sure you're right, Dan. In any case, I'm not that desperate. I can wait until the right girl comes into my life.' Binnie had hoped his words would discourage Dan from thinking of him as a prospective son-in-law but they had the opposite effect.

'Good for you, boy. You got your chance to meet fine respectable gels right here under your nose. An' if you marries into the McCabe family, you gets all the help you could want regarding the building of a property and all. You think about it, son. Here, have another swig of this.'

Later, the women joined the men on the porch and Dan began to play some melodies on the battered fiddle. The girls' voices were sweet and harmonious and, relaxed by the home-made liquor, Binnie began to feel that marriage to one of them would not be such a bad idea. So he was already married to a woman back home but how could anyone find out about it?

As he listened to the music, Binnie warmed to the idea of marrying into the McCabe family. He would get himself a good home, a pretty, amenable wife and an easy living, what more could any man want? He pushed the thought of Maura to the back of his mind, that was his old life. Here, in America, he was beginning afresh.

'So, Lloyd.' Eynon was sitting opposite Lloyd Savage in the sitting-room of Pottery House. 'What I would like is to take a more active part in the running of the pottery.' He could see that Lloyd had become older, he looked careworn, tired.

'You know the problems we are having with someone buying up the surrounding land?' Lloyd said. 'We might not have a pottery to run in a few weeks' time.'

'I have ideas about that,' Eynon said. 'But leave that with me, Lloyd, I think I will be able to sort it all out for you.'

'In that case, you are welcome in the camp.' Lloyd smiled. 'Most welcome. I think it's about time I gave up, handed over the reins, I'm getting too old for all this aggravation.'

Eynon rose and picked up his hat and stick. 'How is Llinos?'

'All right,' Lloyd said. 'She's been looking after me, I've told her to go back to work if she wants to but she won't have it. I expect she's in her room. Do you want to see her?'

'No, don't disturb her, this was not a social call, not really. All right, Lloyd, with your permission, I'll get working on the problems right away.'

'That's good to hear,' Lloyd said. 'I wish you luck in whatever it is you are planning, Eynon.'

Outside in the row Eynon handed a coin to the boy who had been looking after his horse.

'Thank you, Watt, it is Watt, isn't it? You've grown so much I hardly recognize you.'

'Yes, sir, Mr Morton-Edwards, thank you, sir.' Watt pocketed the coin quickly and handed over the reins with reluctance; it had been pleasurable to stand caressing the neck of the big creature instead of carrying loads of waste clay to the bins.

Eynon was about to ride away when Joe came

silently out of the gates of the pottery and stood still, like a shadow beside the high wall.

Eynon's first instinct was to act as though he had not seen Joe, but such behaviour was unbecoming to his new-found determination to face life head on.

'Joe, good day to you.' Curse Joe! He was a handsome devil with his black hair and high cheek-bones and fine strong frame. And yet Eynon could not dislike him even though Joe was, perhaps, the one impediment between him and Llinos.

'You are looking well, Eynon,' Joe said, smiling. 'You seem different, stronger. I never did give you those lessons in defence I promised, did I?'

'No, you did not. How about making up for it now?' Eynon said. 'That's if you are not too busy.'

'I'm not busy at all.' Did Joe sound a little disgruntled with his lot?

'Well, what if you come up to my place, say three times a week, early in the morning would be fine.'

'What if I come up there every day? That way you will learn the art of defending yourself much more quickly.'

'Right, Joe, it's a deal. I'll see you tomorrow at sunrise.'

As Eynon rode away, he felt happier than he had done in a long time. He was becoming stronger and soon he would be strong enough to fight any battle that came his way.

It was a week later when Philip Morton-Edwards arrived at Eynon's house, his face reddened by the wind, his eyes gleaming with anger.

'What do you think you are up to, Eynon?' Philip stared at his son as though he had grown horns. Eynon would have smiled if the situation had not been so serious. 'I understand you have bought the waste land to the rear of the potteries and intend to build a roadway there. Is that correct?'

'Yes, that's correct. You see, I've changed my mind, Father, I'm fed up with being your whipping boy.'

'What are you babbling on about now? I just fail to understand you, boy. Changed your mind about what?'

'You are not usually so slow, Father, I'm not going to run away any more, not from you or from life. I'm taking you on, I'm going to beat you at your own game. Now do you understand?'

'You are a fool! If you challenge me, you will lose, Eynon. Believe me, if it comes to a fight I will not give any quarter just because you are my son.'

'Oh, I know that. Indeed, you will be twice as determined to beat me, twice as vindictive. Well, I'll not tell you what I'm up to, you'll just have to wait and see. One thing I will tell you, you are going to learn that you can't always have what you want. You finally pushed me too far and now I want to get even with you for all the insults, all the cruelties you have ever inflicted on me.'

Philip slapped his boot with his riding crop. 'Well, my boy, there's many ways to catch a fox but you won't be sharp enough to catch this one.' He strode towards the door and paused. 'I know that half-breed is working with you, I've had reports of him coming up here every day. What for? Neither of you is up to any good. Well, he'll be my first target, just to show you I mean business. Good day to you, son, and good luck!'

Eynon watched his father whip his horse and the animal plunged forward, heels flying. Eynon took up his coat and hat, noticing that Jessie had not come running the way she did when his father called. On reflection, Jessie saw and heard too much: perhaps Philip paid her to keep her eyes open, it would explain a great deal.

He left the house, deciding to walk into town. It was a fine day and a walk would strengthen his legs. He had made good progress in the last few days, finding he was quick to learn Joe's lessons in defence. Strength, as Joe kept insisting, began in the mind.

Eynon made his way downhill into the valley and out onto the busy streets that led to the Savage Pottery. He needed to see Lloyd and while he was at the pottery he would have a word with Joe, he would warn him about Philip's threats. Not that Joe would be worried by them, he was well able to take care of himself.

Eynon stepped out more briskly, taking great gulps of fresh air, it was a fine day with the sun shining and it was good to be alive.

Llinos had woken to the early-morning light and as she stared around the bedroom, aware of the sun slanting in through the bright curtains and the smell of beeswax polish rising from furniture, she had the feeling that something was wrong.

Her father was already in the garden, tying up a trailing rose-bush. He looked better, Llinos thought, more rested, and she wondered what was responsible for the improvement. Hopefully, it was her return home.

'Morning, Father.' She kissed the top of his head. 'What a heavenly scent of roses, aren't they lovely?'

He grunted some response and Llinos patted his shoulder. 'Had breakfast yet?'

He shook his head.

'I'm sure the cook is seeing to it,' she said, 'I'll go and find out.' She stared around her, wondering why her feelings of pessimism were persisting. Perhaps after a cup of warm milk and some food she would feel better.

There were only two places laid in the dining-room. Llinos lifted her head, suddenly aware that the house felt empty in spite of the clatter of dishes from the kitchen and the sound of the groom outside tacking up one of the horses.

She felt her heart freeze. She stood quite still

for a moment and then, galvanized by fear, she ran upstairs to the back bedroom. It was empty.

She opened cupboards and drawers with frantic haste. All were bare. She sank onto the neatly made bed, her head in her hands and the tears forced hot trails between her fingers.

'Joe!' She spoke his name but she knew there would be no reply. Joe had gone away. He had simply packed his few belongings and left and she had the feeling that he might never return.

'Llinos! Come down here, have a look at this.' Her father was calling from the bottom of the stairs. He sounded anxious and she wiped her eyes, not wanting him to see her tears.

She descended the stairs two at a time. 'Father, what is it, have you seen Joe?'

He was standing in the hall, holding out a letter and she took it with trembling fingers. The words did not make sense, the letter was not from Joe but from a solicitor. Llinos swallowed hard and tried to concentrate.

'They can't do this to us, Father,' she said at last.

'They've already done it.'

Llinos stared at the official-looking document, trying to think clearly. 'So we may not even have access to the end of the road without the permission of this . . . this Mrs Sanders. Who is she, anyway?'

'That's easy enough to work out.' Lloyd sounded bitter. 'Morton-Edwards has got a dupe to front the scheme for him so that no speck of dirt can fall on his precious name.'

'That's not true, Father. I spoke to Philip about it and he was as concerned as we are.'

'Can't you see further than your nose, girl?' Lloyd sounded weary. 'The man is a Janus, he has two faces.'

'No, Father, you're wrong, I know you are.'

'I'm not wrong.'

Llinos took the letter and went slowly into the drawing-room, trying to sort out her bewildered thoughts. She sank down into a chair and read the letter again, staring at the fine sloping handwriting. The tone was official, warning the proprietors of the Savage Pottery not to trade across the land to the fore and the side of the buildings. Furthermore, an injunction had been taken out to prevent any building work being carried out on the land to the rear of the property.

'So what are we supposed to do, fly up into the air with our pottery?' Llinos said angrily.

'I can't fight any more,' Lloyd said. 'That man has beaten me. I had looked to Eynon to get us out of this, but so far there has been no word from him.'

'Father, I know you are worried sick about this, but I have to ask, have you seen Joe?' Llinos knelt beside him and hugged him, feeling the bristles on his chin rough against her cheek.

He seemed not to have heard her. 'I'm old and sick and in pain. I'd be better off dead.'

'You mustn't say that. What would I do without you?' Llinos was close to tears again.

'You would marry Joe. From what you've told me he's a wealthy man now, a man of property. I should not have stood in your way in the first place.'

Llinos bit her lip. Why did her father have to say all this now when it was too late?

Lloyd rubbed his face and frowned. 'Where is Joe?'

'I don't know, Father, but he'll be back soon, I'm sure.'

'Yes, of course he will.' Lloyd sounded unsure, his memory was bad now and sometimes he grew confused.

'Excuse me, miss.' Wenna looked into the room. 'Mr Morton-Edwards the younger is at the door. Shall I show him in?'

'Yes, of course,' Llinos said heavily. 'He's used to us, he's more of a friend than a visitor.'

Eynon came in through the door, bringing a breath of fresh sunny air with him. 'Eynon, thank God you've come,' Llinos said.

'Why? What's wrong?' he asked.

'Look, read this letter.'

'It's my father, of course,' Eynon said. 'He's reacting to my plan to make a new road for us from the pottery into town. He's madder than ever.'

'Oh, Eynon! Why do you blame Philip for everything bad that happens?'

Eynon sank down onto the lumpy horsehair sofa. 'Mrs Sanders is my Aunt Catherine, Llinos. Now do you understand?'

'She won't listen to anyone.' Lloyd waved his hand dismissively. 'I'm past talking to her, she's headstrong and stubborn, she will go her own way whatever I say.'

'Where's Joe gone?' Eynon asked. 'My father intends to punish him, he thinks Joe is involved in my plan to build the road.'

Lloyd looked at him vaguely. 'He's gone away for some reason or other. I can't remember why.' Lloyd sighed. 'Everyone I care about seems to be deserting me.'

'That's not true, Father, I haven't deserted you. Joe hasn't either, I'm sure.' Llinos was not sure at all, not sure of anything any more.

Some time later, Llinos stood at the window of her bedroom staring out into the garden. Behind the house, the pottery was still in full production. The crocks were piling up, stocked in the sheds. The goods must be sold soon or the pottery would begin to lose money.

She would see Philip, beg him to talk to Mrs Sanders who now owned the roadway and the surrounding land. Perhaps she could offer Mrs Sanders a cut of the profits. It was not fair but at least that way they would survive.

She sank down on the bed and put her hands over her eyes. 'Joe.' She whispered his name softly and at once he seemed to be there, in the room with her. She breathed in his scent, felt his presence so strongly that she opened her eyes. The room was empty, all she could see was the fluttering of the curtains against the open window.

Joe stood in the large drawing-room of the house that had been his father's and searched the faces of his sisters. Neither of them would meet his eye.

'Well, Letitia, Charlotte, I came as soon as I got your letter. What can I do for you?'

'You did say we could come here whenever we liked, didn't you, Joe?'

It was Charlotte who spoke, her small voice trembling. Letitia was stiff-necked with pride as always and looked at him disdainfully.

'Of course I did and I meant it. This is your home, too.'

'We've lost all our money.' Charlotte blurted the words. 'The money you so generously gave us, Joe, we lost it all.'

She began to cry and Joe crouched before her, touching her hands lightly. 'It's all right, Charlotte, this is your home, remember?'

He looked at Letitia; she was watching him and her eyes narrowed. Joe straightened.

'I mean it, Letitia. There are no strings, no catches, I promise.'

Letitia heaved a great sigh. 'I will never agree that it was proper for Father to leave you everything, not when we had looked after him all his life. But I will admit I might be wrong about you, you are not a fortune-hunter.'

'Just as we were wrong about Mr Abbot,'

Charlotte said, dabbing at her eyes with a small square of lace.

'We were gullible fools, I can do nothing else but admit it,' Letitia said.

'Tell me exactly what happened, Letitia. Who is this Mr Abbot?'

'He was selling us a property.' Letitia spoke tersely. 'We saw the house and liked it. The solicitor Mr Abbot recommended took the money and gave us the key, only, when we went to take up residence in the house, someone was already living there. We were fools, fools!'

For a moment her iron reserve deserted her. She sniffed and coughed and after a moment sank into a chair. 'We have never needed to handle business on our own before, what are we going to do?'

Joe felt anger burn in his gut. What sort of man defrauded two defenceless women? 'Tell me all you know about this Mr Abbot. I'll find him and get your money back.'

'You watch him, Joe, he's a slippery customer,' Charlotte said breathlessly. 'I didn't like him from the start, his eyes were too close together.'

'Tell me, Letitia.' Joe's voice was deceptively calm.

'I'll tell you where his office is but you must promise not to try to see the man tonight. Another day will make no difference, I doubt he'll bother to run away, he holds us in such scorn.'

Joe nodded. 'Very well, we shall leave it for

470

tonight and in the morning I'll find this Mr Abbot.'

In his room, Joe sank onto the bed and closed his eyes. Cocooned in the silent darkness he was free to think about Llinos. She was in his pulse, in his heart and soul. He loved her as he could love no other woman. In the eyes of his native kinsmen, Llinos was his wife. She should not have chosen her father above her husband whatever the reason.

He turned on his side. All the same, Lloyd Savage was a beaten old man. He needed his daughter now if he had never needed her before. And Joe had felt obliged to come to the aid of his sisters. The future of all of them was in the hands of fate and the gods.

He woke early, it was still dark and his first thought was of Llinos. He longed to touch her hair, to feel her skin cool against his. Their lives were inextricably joined, they belonged together. When he had dealt with Mr Abbot, he would return to Swansea.

Downstairs, the house had an air of chill about it. Joe realized that the fires had not been lit for days. He smiled, he could not see Charlotte being any good at menial tasks. Letitia on the other hand was the sort of woman who could do anything she turned her mind to. All the same, he would suggest that Letitia employ help in the house.

He bathed in the coldness of the river at the end of the garden and emerged tall and magnificent into the early-morning sunlight.

The breeze was sharp against his skin, the water ran from his hair and into his eyes and so he did not see his attackers creep up on him. He heard them nevertheless. He heard the soft whinnying of a horse and the cracking of twigs that betrayed a heavy man to his left. The soft whisper of leaves indicated another man to his right.

He ran the short distance down the bank and dived cleanly into the water. He surfaced to the sounds of cursing and when he shook the water from his eyes, he saw two men brandishing heavy clubs.

'The bastard foreigner, he's got away from us!' One of the men began to run along the bank and Joe submerged himself beneath the water. He swam downstream and emerged on the banks where the river curved away from the house. Stealthily, he made his way round to the spot where the men had paused to argue, voices loud against the silence of the morning.

'He's drowned I tell you, the river's done the work for us.'

'We don' know that, Gifford. I says we wait a while and then look for him at nightfall. If we let him go Mr Morton-Edwards will not pay us, you know that.'

Joe moved swiftly. He caught the bigger of the two men at the side of the neck and the man fell to the ground without making a sound.

Joe heard the whoosh of the club as Gifford

aimed a blow at his head. He ducked, turned and hit the man on the point of his jaw. It should have felled him but Gifford shook his head and came forward again, the club swinging in a protective arc around his body.

Joe dodged sideways, his wet feet slipping on the grass. As Gifford advanced on him Joe saw the cruel spikes jutting from the end of the club.

'I'll get you, you bastard!' Gifford growled the words low in his throat like an animal. 'I'll beat your head in before I'm finished.' He looked at his fallen companion, who was shaking his head as though to clear it.

'Get up, Soames, for Gawd's sake!'

Joe backed against a tree and braced himself to lash out with his feet. Gifford came closer and raised the club above his head, intending to smash it against Joe's skull.

A loud blast of shot rang out and a cold voice carried clearly across the garden.

'Put down that weapon, I am an excellent shot.' Letitia stood firm, a pistol held firmly in her hand.

Gifford dropped the club. 'Come on, Soames, let's get the 'ell out of here. I didn't reckon on getting shot or nothin'.'

The men disappeared into the trees and Joe looked after them thoughtfully.

'Please, Joe, put on some clothes, you look like a heathen.' Joe turned and saw Letitia's shoulders shake and he knew she was laughing.

'You know something, Letitia, you are not half

the dragon you make yourself out to be.'

Later, when he entered the drawing-room, he found Charlotte sitting near the fire, luxuriating in the warmth. 'I've made some tea for us,' she said. 'Letitia is cleaning Papa's gun.'

'It's all done and the pistol is locked away.' Letitia came into the room. 'Who were those men, Joe? Did Mr Abbot send them, perhaps?'

Joe looked at her and shook his head. 'I don't think so.'

Charlotte handed round the tea. 'Let's forget all the nasty people, shall we? Perhaps they were just itinerants looking for someone to rob.'

She smiled and drew a shawl closer around her thin shoulders. 'Isn't this cosy? You know, Joe, I think we are all going to get on very well, after all.'

Joe smiled. 'I hope so.'

He drank the weak, tepid tea, his thoughts racing. He wondered why Morton-Edwards had sent men after him. Why on earth should Eynon's father want him out of the way?

'Will you go looking for Mr Abbot today?' Charlotte asked and Joe forced his thoughts back to the problem in hand.

'Yes, I've enough information to find this man, always supposing he hasn't gone into hiding.'

But then, why should he? As Letitia had pointed out, Abbot did not expect any retaliation from two old ladies.

Joe rose to his feet. 'I'll be on my way.' He smiled at Letitia. 'But I don't expect to be long.

When I return, Charlotte, perhaps you will make me more of your wonderful tea.'

He left the house and stood for a moment, staring up at the cloud-filled sky. At such times, he longed for the open plains of America and the sunlight and the rivers and in the winter the white of the snow, pure and virgin. There a man was free from intrigue and no-one harmed a neighbour unless it was in self-defence.

Joe set out for the small town which was set in the curve of the river only half a mile from the house. He felt he would have little trouble finding Mr Abbot and his crooked accomplice, who was probably no more a solicitor than Joe was. And when he did catch up with them, they would both pay dearly for their sins.

CHAPTER TWENTY-SIX

Pottery Row was alive with voices, angry voices. The bailiffs stood stolidly waiting as furniture was carried from the houses into the street.

Celia-end-house caught Llinos's arm as she came out of the gate.

'We're all being evicted! Oh, my lord, Llinos, can't you do anything to stop it?'

Llinos watched in bewilderment as a table and a group of chairs were dumped into the roadway. 'I don't know what to do, Celia, I only wish I did.'

The rattle of pots and pans made a cacophony of sound in the air of early evening. A kettle fell and bounced along the cobbles, the noise a knell of doom in Llinos's ears.

'Fifty years I've lived here,' Celia wailed. 'Born here, I was, and I thought I would die here.' She leaned heavily on her wooden stick, watching as her precious box of herbs was dumped on top of a pile of chairs.

One of the bailiffs caught Celia's arm. 'Come along, missis, you got to get your stuff out of here.'

Llinos looked at him, her eyes steely. 'Take this lady's belongings to the Savage Pottery. At least that's still ours.'

The man recognized quality when he saw it and touched his hat. 'I'll get that done, right away, miss.'

Celia hung on to Llinos's arm. 'There's good of you, love, I thought it was the workhouse for me.'

Llinos led Celia into the grounds of the pottery. The old woman was trembling, her face parchment white.

'I'll have to do something,' Llinos said more to herself than to Celia. 'I can't let this go on. Celia, go inside, tell my father you're to stay with us. I won't be long.'

The evening sun was slanting through the trees, dappling the countryside with patches of light and shadow. Llinos lifted her skirts and stepped across the pool of water left by an early-morning shower. She crossed the yard and climbed over the boundary between the two potteries; she must see Philip, he was the only one she could turn to.

Georgina Fairwater was in the garden of the Ty Mawr, her large bonnet shading her eyes, but as she watched Llinos draw nearer, her shoulders were tense.

'Miss Savage, how kind of you to come over, but as you see, I'm cutting flowers for the table. We shall be eating supper within the hour.'

Llinos read her well. 'I don't intend to stay long, don't worry.'

'Oh, I'm not worried. Indeed, I'm glad you've called, you can congratulate me.' She held out her left hand. A clear blue sapphire gleamed against her skin. 'Philip has proposed, I'm going to be his wife.'

'Congratulations,' Llinos said drily. 'He's quite a catch.'

'I thought you might think so.' Georgina sounded smug. 'Well, you'd better come inside.'

Llinos bit back the retort that she had every intention of doing so and followed Georgina into the house. The scent of beeswax hung in the air rich and pleasant, the sun shone through the huge window above the staircase sending spears of light onto the polished wood of the curved banister. It was all peace and quiet, a far cry from the chaos of Pottery Row.

'Philip, darling, we have a visitor.' Georgina's voice trilled girl-like across the expanse of hall-way and after a moment Philip appeared in the door of his study.

'Llinos! My dear, how good to see you. Please, come into the drawing-room, have a glass of cordial with us.'

'Philip, darling, supper is almost ready.'

'I wanted to see Llinos, anyway, Georgina; you know that, darling.'

'Oh, yes, of course, you intend to give her notice, don't you?'

Llinos glanced at Philip, expecting him to deny he would do any such thing. He remained silent.

'Might I speak to you alone?' Llinos said as Georgina hurried past her into the drawing-room.

'Will you excuse us, my dear?' Philip said. 'We shan't be long.' He closed the door on Georgina's retreating figure and gestured for Llinos to take a seat.

'What's wrong, Llinos, why have you come?'

'What's wrong? Don't you know? I'm surprised you haven't heard the noise from here,' Llinos said. 'People are being evicted from their homes, furniture thrown into the street.' She sank into a chair and twisted her hands together in her lap.

'My father's going out of his mind with worry. What is happening to us, Philip, why are you doing this?'

Philip sat opposite her. 'It's my cousin Catherine,' he said, 'she's old, confused. I'll try to speak to her again, get her to see sense.'

Llinos looked at him, wondering whether to believe him or not. 'It's urgent, Philip, our stocks of clay and coal are almost gone, we've laid off most of the workers. We are going under. At this rate we'll soon be bankrupt.'

'Surely not. Your young man, I understand he is a man of some means, can't he help you?'

'He's not returned from England. In any case, if he gave us money for supplies, we couldn't bring them in.'

Philip rubbed at his chin. He was silent for a long time and then he looked at Llinos. 'I can't offer much hope for the tenants of the houses in the row but there is a solution to your problem.'

'What solution?' Llinos said suspiciously. She leaned forward. 'Tell me.'

'I could buy the Savage Pottery. It's adjacent to my own pottery. With a little readjustment I could combine the two premises and any goods and stock would enter and exit through my property.'

He paused, frowning thoughtfully. 'You would have to vacate the house, of course.'

Llinos swallowed hard. 'It's a way out, I can see that, but it's rather harsh, isn't it, Philip?'

Philip smiled. 'Look, my dear, it was just an idea. Perhaps I don't really want any more land; I have enough as it is.'

Llinos swallowed hard. 'I'll put it to my father, see what he thinks.' She sighed. 'I'd better be going.'

The door was pushed open and Llinos had the distinct impression that Georgina had been listening outside.

'Oh, Philip, my darling, you really must not be so charming to the ladies,' she gushed. 'You don't realize how handsome and captivating you can be.' She slid her hand into his arm and looked at Llinos. 'Does he?'

'Thank you for your time,' Llinos said, ignoring her. 'I do hope I haven't delayed you too long from your supper, Philip.'

As she walked back across Philip's land, her head was spinning. It could work. If Philip bought the Savage Pottery, she and her father would at least survive. She could rent a small house in town on the proceeds of the sale.

Her father was sitting slumped in his chair. He looked up at her, his eyes dull. 'We're finished,' he said. 'It's over, the Savage Pottery is no more.'

Suddenly she felt weary. 'Father,' she said softly, 'there is a way, we don't have to lose everything.'

'What way?'

'We could sell the pottery.'

'Oh, yes, and who would buy a pottery with no access to it by road? Don't be foolish, girl.'

'Listen, Father.' She spoke more firmly now. 'I've talked to Philip, he would buy the . . .'

'Ha!' Lloyd Savage glared at her. 'I might have known! This is exactly what he wants, to do me out of my home and my livelihood. And you, girl, are stupid enough to be taken in by him.'

Llinos swallowed her anger. 'Perhaps it *is* all Philip's fault. Perhaps he's planned this down to every last detail but what choice do we have? We must sell.'

He rubbed his eyes wearily. 'I know you are right but I would burn the place to the ground rather than let that swine have it.'

'Oh, Father!' Llinos said impatiently. 'It's a solution, just think about it for a moment.'

'You are so gullible girl,' Lloyd said. 'Oh, go away, leave me, I can't think straight.'

Llinos sighed, shaking her head and after a moment left him alone. It was dark in the hallway, the sun had finally set. She made her way slowly upstairs. In her bedroom, she stood in the window, staring out, trying to make sense of her muddled thoughts.

Her father and Philip Morton-Edwards had always been rivals. Maybe her father and Eynon were right and she had been wrong about Philip all along?

If only Joe was here. He was wise, he would hold her in his arms, kiss her, make her feel free and light, make her feel like a woman.

She stretched out on top of the quilt, not even bothering to take off her shoes. Her mind ran round in circles as she tried to think of a way to save the pottery. But in the end, there was only the glaringly obvious solution, that they sell out to Philip Morton-Edwards.

'You are a clever darling, aren't you?' Georgina sat beside Philip and leaned against his shoulder, staring up at him admiringly. Men, especially old men like Philip, were so susceptible to flattery.

'Well, it was a master stroke, although I say it myself. I have got what I want at last, the land adjoining my pottery. Now the pottery will be the biggest one for miles around. Bigger even than some of the Staffordshire potteries. Yes, I am clever, aren't I?'

Georgina nuzzled her cheek against his. 'And I am lucky, having such a wonderful man as you. I think I've been in love with you from the moment I saw you, Philip, darling.' It was a blatant lie but Philip did not see through it. He took her hand and kissed it; he was like a grateful puppy but then she was bringing him a great deal of money. He would have not only a share of her fortune but the use of her lithe young body. For those privileges, he would pay dearly.

Georgina knew she gave the impression that she was light-hearted without a brain in her head, but she had listened well to her father. Before he had died, he had taught her a great deal about people. He was a wise man, a man who had been a doctor and a philosopher. He showed her how she could hide some of her fortune in an account in Switzerland, the country of his birth.

'Remember, when you marry, your fortune becomes the property of your husband,' he had told her gravely. 'But a husband cannot control what he does not know about.'

Dear Papa, he had been the one man she could respect. Perhaps the only man she would ever love unconditionally. He would have congratulated her on her stroke of genius in persuading Philip to put the land around the Savage Pottery in her godmother's name. The townspeople might know very well that Georgina Fairwater had come to stay in Swansea but no-one would pause to think that her godmother, Aunt Catherine, went by the name of Sanders. Thank heaven the old woman had taken to her bed early and had not been present when Llinos Savage arrived. Catherine was getting old and sometimes she let things slip that were best kept secret.

'You are very quiet, my dear.' Philip's voice roused her from her reverie.

'I was thinking how wonderful it will be when we are married,' she lied. 'How I long to be Mrs Morton-Edwards.'

'And you will be, my dear, very soon.'

'How soon, my darling?'

Philip laughed and took her in his arms. 'You are an eager young thing, aren't you? But then, your blood is hot. I shall match your passion, my dear, I think you will find I'm as good a lover as any young buck.'

She lowered her eyes. 'You forget, Philip, I'm an innocent. I know nothing of men or of their passions.'

She could have laughed out loud at her own audacity. She had taken a stable boy as her amusement when she was but fourteen years old.

'I will teach you about love and I shall be a good teacher. You will bear me sons, strong healthy sons.'

'But what about Eynon?' Her eyes were round. 'Much of his fortune is from his mother's family, he will inherit everything, won't he?'

'Not if I can get around it. And I will, I swear I will. I will have him declared insane if I have to.'

She was exultant, convinced now that she had been wise to follow her godmother's advice. She would have Philip's fortune to add to her own — eventually.

'Shall we set a date for our wedding, darling?' she asked, rubbing her fingertips over the back of his hand. He took her in his arms and kissed her lingeringly. She was surprised at his ardour. Well, it was something she would encourage. If he over-exerted himself so much the better. His early demise would be very gratifying. As for Eynon, the weak-kneed fop, let him rot in Bedlam for all she cared. Though, come to think of it, there might just be a better way of getting rid of him, she must ponder on it.

As Philip's hand strayed to her breast, she pushed him gently.

'No, my darling, we mustn't get carried away. We must be properly married before . . .' She tried to force some colour into her cheeks . . . 'you know.'

'My dear little Georgina, you *are* an innocent. Very well, I will make the arrangements for our marriage to take place as soon as possible.'

She buried her face against his shoulder. 'I'm so happy, my darling.' She smiled to herself. She had Philip just where she wanted him. Her little tricks had trapped him. He had seen past her rather ordinary face and glimpsed the magnificent figure beneath her clothes. And that was all she had allowed him, a glimpse. If he wanted to taste her fruits, he would have to put a ring on her finger first.

485

'I'm sure there has been some mistake.' Abbot sat behind his desk fiddling nervously with a sheaf of papers.

'I hope so.' Joe spoke affably. 'Mistakes can be rectified.' He sat back in his chair and waited. He could see the sweat break out on the other man's brow. The silence lengthened, still Joe waited. He had learned as a child that the best way to stalk a prey was in silence.

'I will investigate the matter as soon as possible,' Abbot said at last. Joe sat immovable. Abbot coughed.

'If you will leave the matter with me, I'll look into it,' he said.

Joe rose slowly and stood staring down at the man. His shirt was frayed and spotted with the remains of his breakfast. His hair was in need of attention. He was as shabby as his surroundings.

'Just bring me the money my sisters gave you.' Joe leaned against the door. He had no intention of leaving.

'But I'll have to speak to the bank — there are formalities in a case like this.'

'I'll wait here.'

Abbot looked around him, it was clear he was worried about leaving Joe alone in the office. He rose to his feet, he was still uncertain.

'If you could come back in, say . . . an hour, perhaps?'

'No.' Joe folded his arms across his chest. He

could have smiled at the dismay on Abbot's face.

'Oh, very well.' Abbot moved from behind his desk, keeping a safe distance from Joe. 'I'll be back.'

'Come alone. If you have anyone with you, that crooked solicitor, for instance, I'll hit you first and then ask questions.'

Abbot darted out and Joe watched him as he scurried along the street. He had no illusions about the man. He probably had no intention of returning, at least not until Joe had given up waiting and left.

Joe began to make a systematic search of the office. Quickly and efficiently he opened drawers and cupboards finding only layer upon layer of dusty papers.

He paused and looked around him. Abbot must hide his money somewhere, he was not the sort of man to use the services of a bank.

High on the wall was a long clock. It was covered in dust and clearly had not worked in years. Joe took a chair and stood on it and lifted the clock from its robust hangings. The back was screwed into place and was obviously an addition to the original casing.

Joe drew a knife from his belt and set to work on the screws. They were not tightly threaded and it was an easy job to remove the back from the clock.

He lifted out of the false back of the clock four leather pouches and put them on the desk. He had found Abbot's hoard of money.

Joe took only the amount that Abbot had tricked out of the two sisters. He had no doubt that the rest of the money represented ill-gotten gains and, on an impulse, he took the pouches into the street and began to scatter the gold coins into the roadway.

It took no time at all for folk to gather round, picking up the coins and hiding them away in pockets and gloves and bags. As the last pouch was emptied, Joe saw Abbot appear at the edge of the crowd, his dark brows raised in curiosity. When he saw what Joe was doing, he howled like a wounded animal and tried to dash into the centre of the crowd.

He was pushed back and Joe walked to where Abbot stood, tears dripping down his red face.

'Have any luck in the bank?' he said, and Abbot lunged towards him, his hands raised like claws. Joe easily side-stepped him and Abbot fell into the dust bawling like a baby.

Joe, with one last look at the pathetic Abbot, mounted his horse and made for home. When he handed the money to Letitia she looked up at him questioningly.

'Keep it, put it aside in case you might need it. It took a bit of persuading for Abbot to part with it, but I convinced him in the end.'

'Well done.' Letitia was a woman of few words but those words made Joe smile.

Later, they sat down to a hot supper. Letitia looked across the table at Joe and took a deep breath.

'You will be leaving for home soon?' She regarded him steadily. 'I will be sorry to see you go.'

'You have read my mind. It's about time I left.'

'Marry the girl,' Letitia said bluntly. 'If you know she's the one for you then nothing else matters.'

Joe smiled. 'Will you come to the wedding?'

It was Charlotte who answered. 'Oh, Joe, a wedding, try keeping us away!'

It was early the next morning when Joe set out for Swansea. The mists were rising from the river, spiralling upwards to a leaden sky. But he felt light-hearted, he was going home. To Llinos.

'Father's gone to a meeting, I can't help thinking there will be trouble,' said Llinos.

She was sitting with Eynon in the parlour of Pottery House. A cheerful fire crackled in the grate and outside, the wind lifted the branches of the old oak trees. Sitting in the corner, silently sewing, sat Celia, her thin figure hunched into a shawl.

He took Llinos's hand. 'Listen to me, you don't realize what a dangerous man my father is.'

'Surely not dangerous, Eynon. I'm willing to concede that he might be devious, crooked even but not dangerous.' She paused. 'I'm surprised I haven't heard from him in the last few days.'

'He's gone to London with Georgina. They

are to be married there with a great deal of pomp and ceremony, I understand.'

'How does that affect you, Eynon?'

'It means I will have two enemies wanting to be rid of me instead of one.'

'But what good would it do anyone to "get rid of you" as you call it?'

'Silly, innocent Llinos. I'm worth quite a bit of money. My father and his sweet little bride want their hands on it. What's more, with me out of the way, Georgina's sons would inherit Father's estate.'

Llinos rubbed her eyes. 'I can't believe that anyone could be so wicked, Eynon.'

Eynon shook his head. 'Believe it! My father sent two men to England after Joe.'

'Joe?' Her throat was suddenly dry. 'But why?'

'He believes Joe is with me in the deal to buy the land behind the pottery.'

'Did they hurt him? Is Joe all right?'

Eynon smiled. 'I'm sure he is. In any event the men came running back to Swansea with their tails between their legs. Oh, don't worry, Joe can look after himself.'

Llinos heard the crunch of wheels on the ground outside and inwardly braced herself.

'Father's back from the meeting at the inn.' She moved to the door. 'If the people of the row find out that your family is behind the evictions, they'll be out for blood.'

'I know,' Eynon said. 'But Aunt Catherine is just a cover, a name to hide behind. I doubt she

490

realizes half of what's going on under her nose.'

The door opened and Lloyd was wheeled into the room by one of the men from the row.

'Lovely fire you got there, Miss Savage.' Jim Cooper pushed the chair near the blaze. The smell of ale was heavy in the small room.

'We've come to an agreement,' Lloyd said, holding his hands out to the blaze. 'We are not going to take this lying down.'

'What can we do, Father?' Llinos asked. It was Jim who replied.

'We are going to man the roadway, day and night,' he said. 'We'll make sure that the pots gets out and the supplies get in. We are not going to be done out of our homes and our jobs by some scum with more money than sense.'

'Here! Here!' Celia said loudly. 'The women-folk will be right with you, don't you worry.'

'Won't you be breaking the law?' Llinos asked worriedly.

'We have to do something, Llinos. We can't just sit on our backsides and make no protest while our living is destroyed.'

'I'll be behind you all the way, Lloyd.' Eynon was leaning forward eagerly. 'My father has blocked the building on the land behind the pottery for the time being, but I have money enough to pay lawyers and I will. It's about time justice was done.'

'Good lad.' Lloyd held out his hand and Eynon shook it. 'Tomorrow,' Lloyd continued, 'the men are returning to work. Anyone who uses violence will be met by violence.'

'Father, are you sure that's wise?' Llinos pulled her chair close to his.

'It's a question of survival, Llinos,' Lloyd said. 'We have our pride and we intend to fight. If we fail at least we can say we tried.' He touched her hair. His voice softened. 'Anything is better than sitting around doing nothing.'

'I know we have to do something, Father,' Llinos said, 'but are you sure this is the right way to tackle the problem?'

'What other way is there?'

Llinos knew by the set of her father's face that he would not be shifted from his purpose. Her heart sank, why were men so intractable?

Eynon rose. 'It's time I was getting back home.' Jim Cooper took his cue from Eynon.

'Aye, me too, I'll see you in the morning, Captain Savage, bright and early.'

Eynon waited for Jim to leave and then he came back to the fireside. 'My father has been very cunning, Lloyd, but perhaps we can outwit him, play him at his own game.'

'How, just tell me that, Eynon?' Lloyd looked up eagerly at the younger man.

'I'll talk to my aunt, ask her to allow the people of the row to return to their houses. I will also ask her to sign a document allowing you free access.'

'Why should she do that?'

'My father is away, so is Georgina — I will

never have a better time to approach the old lady.'

'All right, go ahead. I'll keep the men quiet in the morning. We'll wait for you to come to us.'

Eynon smiled at Llinos. 'Don't look so worried, this will all work out, you'll see.'

Llinos was worried. From the little she had heard of Mrs Sanders, the lady was not one to give in so easily.

Later, as she lay in the darkness, Llinos put all thoughts of the pottery out of her mind. She concentrated on Joe. She saw in the darkness the outline of his strong face, saw the hair sweep his shoulders, felt his arms, strong around her. She wanted Joe so badly it hurt.

She knew he felt she had let him down. They had been married by the laws of the American Indians and should have been married in church as soon as they returned to Swansea. If she had done as Joe wished, she would be lying with him now instead of alone with only her imaginings for company.

She sat up abruptly, the bedclothes slipping away from her. Joe was here! She knew it, felt it. She pulled on a robe and padded to the window. A slant of moonlight fell across the yard and after a moment she saw him, a shadow among the shadows. Was he really there or was her imagination playing tricks on her?

She hurried downstairs and opened the back door to the yard. Then she was in his arms. She breathed in Joe's scent, touched his skin, his hair. Neither of them spoke. He held her close, his lips against her hair. Slowly, he tipped her face up to his and his mouth was hot against hers.

Llinos felt a surge of an emotion that was more than happiness, more than desire. 'Joe.' Her voice was hoarse. 'I love you so much!'

He cupped her face in his hands and kissed her again. She wanted more of him. She wanted to possess him. To be one with him.

He kissed her throat, the rise of her breasts between the edges of her robe. Passion flared through her. She responded to him, pressing herself against the hardness of his body.

When he moved from her she felt cold. 'Joe . . .' Her voice trailed away. How could she ask him to come to her bed? She could not be so immodest. And yet everything in her yearned to have him hold her in his arms again.

'Go to bed now.' He spoke softly. 'I shall sleep in the kitchen, near the fire.' She felt rather than saw him smile.

'I shall keep the flame alight, don't you worry, my Firebird.'

She did not want to leave him but if she stayed with him any longer, she would forget modesty, forget pride. She would beg him to make love to her. She turned and ran upstairs. If she gave in to her feelings now, she would make a mockery of all the protestations she had made about waiting for a proper church wedding.

She sank onto her bed and clenched her hands together. 'Damn and blast my stupid scruples.' Her whisper hung for a moment on the air and then there was only the silence of the night.

CHAPTER TWENTY-SEVEN

Philip Morton-Edwards was a happy man. He had found in his new wife the perfect woman. After the first few nights of their marriage when she was understandably modest, she had responded to his demands with an eagerness that pleased and excited him.

Admittedly, she was plain of face but her body was young and strong; her breast full and ripe, her hips curved pleasingly. Best of all, she enjoyed experimenting as much as he did. With her he did not need to resort to threats or coercion as he'd done with Estelle. Even better, Georgina was not very bright, he could influence her in any way he chose.

He was sitting at his desk in the den, staring out of the window at the garden beyond. He could see his land spread out before him and he felt a glow of satisfaction. Soon, he would own the Savage Pottery and there was nothing Lloyd Savage could do to prevent it.

One little task remained unattended to, that was the matter of Eynon. The boy had shown more grit than Philip had expected. Perhaps it would have been advisable to allow the boy to trek off to North Wales and live near the vapid cleric.

Martin would never have inspired Eynon to show such courage and strength. No, the fault for that lay with the foreigner Lloyd Savage had brought home with him.

Philip had been angry and disappointed when the men he had sent to England had failed to get rid of the Indian, but perhaps it was just as well. It was just possible that this half-breed Indian could yet prove useful. It was something he would ponder over.

He turned the pages of the order book he'd brought in from the manufactory. Business was booming, the porcelain wares, though still throwing up a great deal of waste, paid well. The plain pottery side of the business had begun to flourish simply because Lloyd Savage had been prevented from trading.

'Philip, darling, could I interrupt just for a moment?' Georgina was standing in the doorway. Her bodice was low-cut, the waist high, all of which served to emphasise the lovely swell of her breasts. Philip was immediately roused. He was proud of his reaction, not bad for a man in his middle years.

'You can interrupt me any time you wish, my dear. Come in.' He held out his arms and his new wife came into them with an eagerness that was gratifying. Her breasts brushed against his face and he buried his head against her softness.

'Darling, the door is open, the maids might see us.'

Philip pushed her bodice aside with his chin

and his mouth fastened onto a pink nipple. He cared not a fig for the servants. If they saw anything then the fault was theirs, they should not be snooping.

The thought of being observed stimulated him. He pushed up the thin material of Georgina's dress and pressed against her. She began to respond in a most gratifying way. Her head was flung back, soft moans escaped from her rosy lips. He laughed, she was as roused as he by the thought that someone might see them. Yes, this marriage was working out in a most satisfactory way.

Though Philip did not know it, Georgina was of a like mind. 'It's working rather well, isn't it, God-Mamma?' Georgina was seated in the window staring out at the early-evening sky. The old lady was positioned next to the ornate lamp, stitching at a sampler.

'It seems that way,' she said. 'He thinks you stupid, me too. So did his son, coming cap in hand expecting me to give him all he asked for. Well, I showed him the rough side of my tongue.'

She smiled enigmatically. 'Did I hear sounds of passion earlier this morning?'

'You did, and afterwards my dear husband was so exhausted he needed to lie down in his bedroom.'

'Well, keep up the good work, dear, but don't kill him off too quickly. Allow the man time to settle with that son of his.'

She smiled. 'Play your cards right, my dear, everything will be yours. That is, everything except for the Savage Pottery.'

Georgina arched her eyebrows. Her godmother tapped her hand with her fan.

'Just a little payment for my support, wouldn't you say?'

The ringing of the doorbell echoed through the house and Georgina heard the patter of the maid's footsteps across the hall. She frowned as she heard a male voice raised in anger.

'It's Eynon,' she said. 'I hope Philip has revived enough to tackle his son.'

Eynon came into the drawing-room and looked around him. 'Where's Father?'

'Sit down, Eynon, please.' She spoke sweetly. 'Your father will be down in a moment. He has been resting. He's not as young as he used to be and the exertions of coping with a new wife have tired him.'

Eynon sank into a chair and Georgina studied him dispassionately. He was a good-looking man. Thin, perhaps, but his legs beneath his breeches were satisfyingly muscled. His shirt was open at the neck and the pale column of his neck rose to a well-proportioned face and curling fair hair. She wondered what it would be like to lie with him.

'How's your friend, you know the one, the half-breed, Joe, I think they call him? Handsome devil, isn't he, at least Llinos Savage thinks so.'

Eynon looked at her coldly without replying.

499

Georgina continued speaking, unabashed by his displeasure. 'Such a strong face and those broad shoulders, I can see why she thinks so much of him.'

She leaned closer and whispered to him so that her godmother could not hear. 'I expect he's a wonderful lover, unlike you? Never had a woman, have you, Eynon, dear?'

Eynon looked at her with loathing. 'You are disgusting.' He turned his face away but she could see she had hurt him and she was not about to let him off the hook so easily.

'I wonder if he is actually in love with that Savage trollop.' She put her head on one side. 'What goes on between the three of you when you are alone? I would love to know.'

Philip entered the room, his robe carelessly thrown around his thickening body. Grey coarse hairs sprouted from his chest and he looked older than his years. Georgina congratulated herself; her eagerness between the sheets was taking its toll on him.

'Darling!' She rose and slipped her hand through his arm. 'Your son has come to see us, don't you think that's good of him?'

'What do you want, Eynon?'

'Look, Father, can't you stop all this? What's the gain in turning folks from their homes and preventing the Savage Pottery from working? Have you no honour?'

Philip disentangled himself from Georgina's hands. 'Why don't we go into my den and talk this over, man to man?'

'Oh, no, darling, I want to hear what you have to say, too.' Georgina pouted but Philip shook his head.

'We don't want to upset Catherine, do we?'

Georgina followed them and stood outside the half-open door listening unashamedly.

'You see, this is the way of it, Eynon. I want sons, good strong, honest-to-God sons. You, unfortunately, will never carry on the Morton-Edwards name, you must see that. You lost your chance when you let the Savage girl slip away from you.'

'So what do you suggest, Father, that I give in to you and relinquish my right to my inheritance and all will be well with the people of the row?'

'What if I say I will arrange for the people to rent their homes once more.' He paused. 'In addition, I will call my men off the Indian fellow.'

Georgina could hear Eynon's hissing breath. 'That won't work, Father. I will tell the whole town what you are up to. I'll even tell them how you murdered Estelle.'

Georgina took a step backwards. Murder? That was something she had not suspected. Still, it was all very interesting and it was good to be forewarned of just how far Philip could go.

'What are you talking about?'

'I'm talking about Mrs Lane, the herbalist woman in town. I'm talking about weed killer that you bought from her some time before Estelle died.'

'Who would believe you, Eynon, tell me that?' Philip laughed shortly.

'Estelle told Llinos of her suspicions, as well as me. You're on thin ice, Father.'

Philip shook his head. 'No-one is going to believe a word you say. I didn't murder Estelle, such a suggestion is absurd.'

'Just be careful, Father, one day you will go too far and then your entire house of cards will come crashing down on your head.'

'Go away, Eynon. Talking to you has the same effect on me as squashing a gnat. You are merely an irritation. Get out of my house and stay out.'

The door swung wide and Eynon brushed past Georgina as though he had not seen her. She waited for the slamming of the front door and then she went into the den. It was time to tell Philip what was on her mind.

'That boy is a changeling, I'm sure he's not your son,' she said. 'You are so masculine, my darling, so vigorous and he is a fop. Are you sure your wife did not trick you into marriage?'

She saw the light dawn in Philip's face and hid a smile. He would take the suggestion she had made so casually and mould it to make it work for him and never realize it was she who had planted the seed.

'You're right, he can't be any son of mine, I will repudiate him.' Philip thrust his hands into the pockets of his robe. He still needed some guidance from her and Georgina touched his arm lightly.

'Think back, darling, perhaps Eynon wasn't your wife's child either. Perhaps he's a substitute planted by your first wife to stop you getting all the money from her family.'

'That would be just the sort of thing she would do,' Philip said. 'Most of her relatives were dead and had already willed their estates to any son she might bear. My first wife had a great deal to gain by having a child.'

'Think back, darling, did you see a great deal of your wife through her pregnancy?'

Philip rubbed his chin. 'No, I did not. She went off to Gloucester for weeks on end. When she returned the boy was in her arms. I thought it strange she was not here for the birth.'

Of course, he had thought no such thing but it was politic to encourage him. 'There, you see? Give it some more thought, darling. Is there anyone of the family left to deny or confirm your story?'

Philip smiled. 'No, I don't think there is.'

Georgina could see that he was pleased with the story that was unfolding in his mind. She put her arms around him and kissed his cheek.

'You are so kind, my love, many a man would never have accepted the boy in the first place. You did not wish to doubt your wife and so you put your fears to the back of your mind. But now, the truth is staring you in the face. Eynon does not look like you, he does not behave like you. He cannot be your son.'

She smoothed back his grey hair. 'Perhaps you should go to Gloucester, see if you can bribe, er . . . coax someone into admitting the child was theirs and was given up to a rich lady in order to have a better life, you know, darling, that's the sort of story that always touches people's hearts.'

'I'll do that, my darling. I'll go first thing in the morning.'

'Oh, my love, I know you are right to go away when your whole future lies in the balance, but I'm going to miss you so much! Don't be away for long or I'll die of loneliness.' Georgina pressed her lips to his and he held her for a moment before gently easing her away.

She smiled. 'I can see you want to prepare for the journey. I'll make myself useful and tell the maid which clothes to pack for you.'

'The maids know what I'll need, darling.' He took her hands and kissed her fingertips.

'No, I shall see to it myself. I want to make sure you are well equipped to face the weather. I can't have you falling sick, can I?'

As she left the study and made her way upstairs, Georgina was exultant. If all went well, Eynon would be discredited, his riches forfeit. She smiled. Before very much longer, she would be a young, very rich widow.

The men had gathered in one of the sheds in the yard of the Savage Pottery. Their voices, loud and angry, carried to where Llinos was sitting at the kitchen table. Joe was with them and she knew he would keep tempers in check with his air of calm.

The cook was stirring a huge pot of *cawl*, the smell of the rich lamb soup permeating the room. Later, the men would all be served with a hot meal, possibly their first since they had been evicted from their homes.

Llinos made her way outside, pausing in the doorway to draw her cloak more firmly around her shoulders. Her father had told her to stay indoors but she must know what was going on.

Her father was speaking. 'You can count on me to give you all the support I can muster.'

'But will we get our homes back, Mr Savage?' Jim Cooper stepped forward. 'There are eighteen families been done out of house and home by this Sanders person.'

'Morton-Edwards,' Lloyd said, 'is the real culprit, he is determined to ruin me, to ruin all of us.'

'We can't fight 'im, Mr Savage, he's too rich, too powerful, we might as well give up the ghost here and now.'

Lloyd tried to interject, but the mumbling became louder until the men were arguing between themselves.

Llinos watched worriedly as Joe made his way to the front of the crowd.

'Quiet!' His voice carried clearly above the noise. 'Let us be calm about this.'

'What's it got to do with you, you're a bloody foreigner,' Jim Cooper said.

'Listen to him, Jim,' Lloyd interjected. 'Joe is a well-educated man. He has a good head on his shoulders. What's more, as an outsider, he can see the facts of the matter more clearly.'

'All right, listen.' Joe paused and looked round; he had the men's attention. 'Before you were evicted did any of you fail to pay your rent on time?'

There were murmurs of dissent from the crowd. Celia-end-house lifted her hand.

'I did. I owed the landlord one week's money but it wasn't my fault, he never called to collect it.'

'Are you aware that by law you should have a leasing agreement?'

'No, we wasn't.' One of the men pushed his way to the front of the crowd. 'But where's all this getting us? The new owner can't be responsible for what the old landlord did.'

'The law is complicated, I agree, but I believe that you, as tenants, have security of tenure for the term of your lease, whoever owns the land.'

'What does all that gobbledegook mean?' Celia asked. It was Lloyd who answered her.

'It means that the new landlord can't throw you out into the streets. You all have a perfect right to go back into your houses and live there in peace until the lease expires.'

'I did sign a lease.' Jim Cooper's voice rose with excitement. 'It was for nearly a hundred years.' He looked round him. 'Well, I'm not a hundred yet, not by a long chalk!'

'Right, men.' Lloyd lifted his hand to acknowledge Celia's presence. 'And ladies, how about moving back into your houses?'

The crowd surged out of the yard, the men calling loudly to each other. Lloyd looked up from his chair.

'Joe, you are a genius, do you know that?' He wheeled forward and held out his hand. 'I'm proud of you.'

Llinos felt her throat constrict with tears. She swallowed hard, the old friendship between the two men had been renewed.

'What about the roadway to the pottery? How do we stand with access, Joe?'

'I would imagine that the same terms apply. The people of the row need to have access and no-one can deny that the members of the Savage family are residents in the row.'

'I'm going inside to search for the bill of sale. I'll check the terms that applied when I bought the pottery land,' Lloyd said. 'I was a fool not to have looked into the legalities of the matter before this.' He began to wheel himself away and then paused.

'What are you two waiting for, haven't you got a wedding to arrange?'

Llinos looked into Joe's face. His eyes were startlingly blue. His hair hung darkly down his back, he was exotic and handsome and she loved him.

'I can't wait any longer, when can we get married?'

'As soon as we can arrange it.' Joe held out his hand. 'In the meantime, let's go inside and join your father, otherwise I might forget my manners and make love to you here in the pottery yard.'

'What do they think they are doing?' Georgina appealed to her godmother, her face flushed with anger. 'How dare those . . . those people move their rubbish back into the houses you own?'

'Someone has apprised them of their rights as tenants,' Mrs Sanders said crossly. 'I feared this would happen.' She took a handkerchief and dabbed at her forehead. 'One thing is certain, we'll have to let them be. We can't lower our dignity to go outside and quarrel with that rabble.'

Georgina drew a cloak over her shoulders. 'Well, I can! I'll go and speak to them, there's more than one way of coping with the situation and I do not intend to use aggression, so don't worry.'

'You can't go out there, you might not be aggressive but they might, the barbarians.'

'They won't harm me, don't be foolish. I'm Mrs Morton-Edwards.' She smiled. 'I might not be able to use force but I have other methods. You'll see.'

Georgina walked sedately up the slope towards Pottery Row, her maid tripping behind her.

When she reached the row, she stood and waited for the men to notice her. They had been busy returning furniture to the houses and now they were joined by their womenfolk.

'Look, it's 'er, the new Mrs Morton-Edwards. What does she want round here? Up to no good, I'll bet a farthing,' Celia said loudly.

Jim Cooper's wife tapped his shoulder and jerked her head in Georgina's direction. Jim walked towards her.

'Mrs Morton-Edwards, what can we do for you?'

She smiled warmly. 'I'm here looking for workers. My husband has expanded his potteries and he needs more skilled men and women. He is, of course, offering well above the average wage as well as other benefits.'

'You won't get us out of our houses again, not by threats or bribes, missis,' Celia said loudly. 'We got right on our side, we got leases, mind.'

Georgina held out her hands. 'Have I come equipped to evict you? I have no armed men with me. No, I come to offer a genuine opportunity to the people who live on my godmother's property.'

'Why were we evicted in the first place, then?' Jim asked, folding his big arms across his chest.

'That was a mistake. It was made in my husband's absence while he was away on business. Mrs Sanders becomes confused at times, she is old. But I'm here to apologize and to invite you to take up a new position with the best pottery in Swansea.'

'We got a good position now, missis,' Jim Cooper said loudly.

'But' — Georgina paused — 'I'm also offering you your homes rent-free for as long as you work for us.'

'*Duw!* We can't turn that offer down flat. We got to think about it, man.'

Jim turned and stared angrily at the speaker. 'Speak for yourself, Dennis Anderson. My answer is no.'

'Well my answer is yes.' Dennis Anderson was an older man, his hair greying. 'I can't afford to turn down the chance of more wages and a rent-free house, even if you can.'

'And what about when they sack you?' Jim challenged. 'How long would you keep your house then?'

'Why would they sack me? I'm a blutty good worker.' He turned to Georgina. 'I apologize for my language, Mrs Morton-Edwards, but I got carried away, like.'

'No-one is going to get sacked,' Georgina said loudly. 'So long as the work is done satisfactorily, you all have a secure position in my husband's pottery. How secure would your future be if you remained with the Savage Pottery? It's finished, don't any of you understand that?' Georgina smiled.

'I'll leave you to think it over. Those who wish to take me up on my offer can start work first thing in the morning. In the meantime, please feel free to return to your homes in peace.'

Her head was high as she walked away. She smiled, she'd had them in the palm of her hand. Appeal to the greed in man's nature and you could usually get what you wanted.

'Did those ruffians behave themselves?' The old lady was standing anxiously in the window of the sitting-room staring across the intervening land towards Pottery Row.

'Of course they did. Oh, some clever person had apprised them of their rights but I've handled it. I've offered them a job and their hovels back, rent-free.'

Mrs Sanders looked at her for a long moment and her face broke into a smile. 'You are a clever girl. This way, Lloyd Savage is still going to be beaten. Philip will be pleased.'

Georgina sank into a chair. 'I'll be pleased if he displays the same wit and finds some midwife to lie about his first wife and the particulars surrounding Eynon's birth.'

'He will. Philip is a resourceful man, be careful you don't underestimate him.'

'We'll see.' Georgina rested her head back against the plush upholstery of the chair. 'And when I've sucked him dry like an orange and when I'm done with him, I'll find myself a vigorous young man to share my bed.'

'You'll take a lover?' The old lady's voice rose a little. Georgina smiled at her.

'I'm certainly not going to take another husband. I have no intention of handing over all my worldly goods again, not to anyone.'

Mrs Sanders leaned over and patted her knee. 'You know something? I'm certainly glad that you and I are on the same side.'

Joe stood on the top of Kilvey Hill and stared out over the vast expanse of the sea. The scent of the soft breeze mingled with Llinos's sweet perfume as she came to stand beside him.

'I was so impressed with your cleverness,' she said, resting her head against his shoulder. 'How did you know all that about tenancy agreements and leases and such?'

'My father had me educated properly, remember?' Joe smiled down at her; she was slight, feminine with her dark hair blowing free of her bonnet. Her lips were rosy, her cheeks flushed. She was so beautiful. He found it difficult to keep his hands from tracing the line of her breasts and the slimness of her waist.

He thanked the Great Spirit that the last obstacle to his marriage to Llinos had been removed. Lloyd was a man of few words, he had never been effusive but now, in his own blunt way, he had given them his blessing.

'I'm surprised we've had no trouble from Philip Morton-Edwards,' he said, forcing his thoughts back to practical matters.

'I think he's still away.' Llinos nuzzled against his arm. She was tall for a girl but she only just came up to his shoulder. He felt a curl of her hair lifted by the breeze touching his face and he ached with love for her.

He moved away, unable to trust himself. 'I wonder why so many of the men stayed off work this week. I have the feeling that someone might have used coercion, threatened the men in some way.'

'I can't see that,' Llinos said. 'Who would do that? As I said, Philip is still away. In any case, Jim Cooper isn't the type to be intimidated, is he?'

'No, he's not. But Jim turned up for work as usual this morning. Something is wrong. I feel it.'

'Perhaps our neighbours are all drunk with some home-made brew, it's the weekend and a time for celebrating. They'll probably make a start back to work on Monday.'

'I don't think so.' Joe felt the itch at the back of his neck, heard the rushing of ancient rivers and he knew that danger was waiting for himself and, worse, for Llinos.

'Why don't you go to visit my sisters?' He saw her look of surprise and smiled. 'They should be invited to our wedding, don't you think?'

'Yes, I do think. Now that you've closed the breach between you, they would be most welcome.' She came near and pressed close to him and he looked into her dark eyes and felt he might never think clearly again. Llinos, his Firebird. She had become woven into the fabric of his being. They had not yet lain together but they were part of each other.

'But I am not going away and leaving you, not now.'

'Why not now?'

'Because you know something is going to happen. In that strange mysterious way you have of seeing the truth, you sense danger for us.'

He put his arms around her and she buried her head beneath his chin. 'You are too perceptive by far, Llinos Savage.'

'Look at the pot calling the kettle black!'

He felt her arms wind around him. His bones seemed to melt as her softness fitted against the contours of his own body. The breath swooped away from him as if the big eagle had come down from the skies and taken the air from him.

'My place is with you, Joe,' she said simply.

CHAPTER TWENTY-EIGHT

Binnie sat on the wooden porch of the McCabe house listening to the haunting sound of the fiddle. Beside him, like fallen flower petals, were the McCabe sisters, each of them vying for his attention.

It was a heady feeling to be wooed by three lovely girls. Dangerous too, he acknowledged. It sometimes troubled his conscience that he was a married man but then no-one in America knew that. In any case, why should he spoil his prospects at the McCabe pottery by admitting to a foolish mistake he had made when he was too young to know better?

'Would you like some blueberry wine, Binnie?' Josephine smiled at him, her large eyes staring into his.

'I'll fetch you a cup, Binnie.' Melia flounced through the doors into the kitchen, her curls bobbing on her shoulders. A little way off, in the shadows, Hortense remained silent, her hands resting in her lap. Binnie kept glancing at her, admiring the stillness of the girl, the dignity of her.

'You are very quiet tonight, Hortense.' Binnie moved over to sit beside her. The perfume drifted from her, he glimpsed the womanly swell of her breasts beneath the bodice of her gown and immediately he was roused. It was a long time since he had lain with a woman and a man had needs. Binnie moved, embarrassed by his obvious reaction to Hortense. She glanced at him, her eyes all-knowing, and smiled.

'You plannin' to stay in our country long, Binnie?' She spoke softly.

'For ever!' he said emphatically. 'When the sun shines here, it really shines. The air is fresh and clean and you can drink from the springs that cut like silver ribbons through the hills.'

'That's so poetic,' Hortense said. 'You'll be thinking of setting up a home of your own, then, I expect.' She glanced sideways at him. He was taken aback.

'I suppose so.'

'Daddy would help you build a fine house for yourself, Binnie, best timber an' all.'

Binnie swallowed hard, he had not thought of moving out of the McCabe household where he felt so comfortable. But it could be he was out-staying his welcome.

'You like me, don't you, Binnie?' Hortense spoke practically, with no hint of seductive-ness.

'Of course I like you. You are a very desirable woman.'

She met his eyes. 'And you are a well set-up young man. Well versed in the pottery business, too. You are a good strong practical man who could look after a wife and family. Am I right about that, Binnie?'

'Well, yes, I suppose so.'

'In that case, why don't we get wed?'

He looked at her sharply, there was no hint of a smile in her eyes. Hortense was deadly serious.

'What would your folks have to say about that?' The words seemed to stumble from his mouth. 'After all, you haven't known me very long, have you?'

'Long enough,' Hortense said. 'And in a country this size, a woman often don' know the man she's to marry hardly at all.' She regarded him steadily.

'Now, I have seen you bathe and I have seen you eat. Both you do with commendable good manners.' She studied him for a long moment. 'I know you would like to bed me, it's plain enough in your eyes for anyone to see.' She allowed herself a smile. 'Even Daddy has made remarks.'

Binnie felt the hot colour rise to his cheeks. He had not realized how transparent he was.

'There's a young man from over at Troy City wants to wed me. He's presentable enough but a bit slow.' Hortense tapped her head. 'I would prefer you for a husband, Binnie, but you will have to declare yourself soon or it will be too late.'

'Declare myself?'

'Ask my daddy if you can have me in marriage. If he say yes, then the preacher man will call and we will be man and wife before you can spit.'

Binnie felt a surge of excitement: married to Hortense, his future would be secure. Dan McCabe was rich by any standard, not only did he own the pottery but he also had a huge timber business. Apart from the material considerations, there was the need in him that was becoming urgent.

He leaned closer to Hortense. 'Would it be proper for me to ask him tonight when we have our last drink on the porch?'

'That would be an ideal opportunity, Binnie.' She rose from her chair and bending down to where he was sitting on the steps, she dropped a kiss on his forehead, affording him a fine look at her golden, sun-kissed breasts. 'I'm going to help Momma clear up after supper,' she said. 'And I'll drop a little hint about our forthcoming nuptials.'

She left him and before the other girls could settle round him Binnie pushed himself to his feet and strode away towards the creek that flanked the edge of the McCabe land.

He ran his hand around his collar, suddenly feeling the heat of the night. Was he mad? He was already married, how could he even contemplate taking another wife?

But what was the alternative? Sooner or later the McCabes would lose patience with him. Dan had made it clear enough that he was expected to take one of the daughters as his wife.

'To hell with it!' He spoke softly into the fragrant air. He was ready for a commitment now, not like the first time when Maura had forced him into a marriage he did not want.

Later, he sat on the porch with Dan and tried to swallow the hard lump of anxiety that had stuck in his throat. At last, Dan gave him an opening.

'You like my Hortense, then? Good choice, she's a bright girl, good at figuring and a head too smart for a girl. She's strong and will bear good young 'uns. Aye, if I was a man choosing a wife, Hortense would do for me.'

Binnie coughed. 'I wanted to talk about that, Dan.' The younger man rose to his feet. 'Dan, you know me for an honest man and a good worker.' He coughed again and Dan laughed.

'Don't put yourself through the tortures of hell, boy! Of course you can marry my girl.' He rose and clapped Binnie on the back.

'You treat her right an' don't raise a hand to her unless she backchats you and you'll do fine as a son-in-law.'

He moved to the door. 'Bring out the drinks, Momma, we got ourselves a fine son at last.'

Binnie and Hortense were married within the month. The occasion was celebrated hugely; most of the villagers had attended the ceremony, all of them dressed in their Sunday best. Binnie found the actual marriage ceremony short and to the point, conducted as it was by the local clergyman. It had been a relief when he had slipped the thin band on the finger of his new wife and stepped out of the heat of the small church into the fresh sunshine.

'Well, I'm Mrs Dundee now.' Hortense looked up at him with a smile. 'You will find me a good wife and a willing mate, Binnie. But I will not be put aside for any other woman, do you understand that?'

Binnie looked into her eyes. 'I have no intention of playing the fool, Hortense. I didn't do it before we were wed, so why should I do it after?'

'You are right on that point,' Hortense agreed. 'But in this country where there are many women without a man, these infidelities do occur. Look at my daddy, he's had a little woman from way back.'

'Has he?' Binnie was genuinely shocked and Hortense laughed.

'Yes, well, Momma has never liked the bedroom activities and so she don't mind. I would mind.'

Binnie drew her into his arms. 'Does that mean you like the bedroom activities then?'

'I don't know yet but I'm sure looking forward to finding out.'

Hortense smiled and drew away from him. 'But now, Mr Binnie Dundee, we got to be with our guests, it's only polite.'

It was midnight before Binnie could lead Hortense away from the festivities and carry her over the threshold of their new home.

Dan McCabe's men had worked like beavers to construct the neat, two-bedroomed house in readiness for the wedding day and now they all stood watching as Binnie carried his new bride inside and closed the door.

'Shall I light the lamps?' Binnie set Hortense down and she laughed low in the darkness.

'Not yet.' She drew him towards the bedroom and he could hear the sound of her slipping off her clothes. He slid under the blankets and felt her softness against him. She wound her arms around him and as he kissed her mouth for the first time, Binnie knew that he was in love. Hortense was his woman and he would treat her gently, he would be good and kind to her always, he would never want to leave her.

It was the early hours of the morning before Hortense rose from the bed and sighed softly into the darkness. She lit a lamp and stood it in the window and Binnie sat up sharply as a great roar went up from outside the house.

'That's the sign they were waiting for,' Hortense said. 'Now they know I'm truly your wife, the celebrations will be over, they'll all go home to bed.'

'Come back here, wife,' Binnie said. 'Our celebrations are only just beginning.'

'We've been betrayed,' Lloyd said flatly and Llinos rested her hand on his arm as though she could protect him from his own pain. 'The bastards have left me, all of them except old Ben and Jim Cooper have gone to work for that twicer Philip Morton-Edwards.'

'Father, they were afraid, they almost lost their houses and their jobs. You can't really blame them.'

'I do blame them. Is there no such thing as loyalty any more?'

Llinos sighed. 'We must think of a way of getting our workers back, Father.'

'What can I offer them, Llinos? I have nothing more to give.'

'Don't say that.'

'It's true.' Lloyd rubbed his eyes. 'I might as well lie down and die right now. I'm finished. Philip Morton-Edwards has won the battle.'

Lloyd was white, his face thin and drawn. Suddenly, he looked old and ill. He wheeled his chair away from her and along the corridor to his room at the back of the house. He closed the door against her with a snap of finality and Llinos put her hand to her lips, fighting back the tears.

Outside, the air was soft and warm but Llinos felt cold. She wrapped her arms around her body and stared at the empty sheds, at the silent yard which, at this time of day, usually thronged with activity. At the kilns, cold now, unused, the fires no more than ashes.

She squared her shoulders. She would speak to Philip, talk to him reasonably. She couldn't believe he would have gone this far, not unless he allowed his wife to speak for him now.

As she drew her cloak around her shoulders, Joe came silently behind her and stood looking down at her. He shook his head.

'You can't reason with such people.' He spoke gently. 'They are bent on having their own way.'

'I don't think Philip is like that,' Llinos protested. 'I'm going to make one last attempt to talk to him, face to face.'

Joe said nothing and Llinos clasped her hands together.

'Do you think I'm wrong? I must at least try to sort this out amicably.'

He kissed the tip of her nose. 'Whatever you feel you must do, then do it.'

Llinos covered the short distance between the potteries with brisk steps, her mind in a whirl. Philip was a reasonable man, he would have to listen to her, wouldn't he?

It was Georgina who greeted Llinos. She was sitting in the drawing-room, her eyes alight with malice. She did not rise, neither did she offer Llinos a seat.

'I would like to see Philip . . . Mr Morton-Edwards. I have something I must discuss . . .' Llinos began but Georgina's tinkling laugh stopped her mid-sentence.

'You must appreciate that my husband is a busy man. From time to time he needs to go away on business. Anything you have to discuss you shall have to discuss with me.'

Llinos felt anger surge within her but she struggled to keep a rein on her temper.

'You have offered my father's workers more pay, is that why they came to you?'

'Of course it is. How naïve of you to even ask. In addition, they had their little hovels back rent-free so they came running. You did not expect loyalty from the lower orders, surely?'

'I did not expect double-dealing from a lady,' Llinos said tartly. Georgina's eyebrows rose.

'Oh, make no mistake, Miss Savage, I will look after my own interests, do not doubt it.'

'When will Philip be back?' Llinos asked desperately.

Georgina shook her head. 'If I knew, I would not tell you. In any case, it makes no difference. You and your tin-pot manufactory are finished. Do you understand me, finished?'

'Why are you so vindictive towards me and my father?' Llinos asked. 'What have we ever done to harm you?'

'Grow up, Miss Savage, business is business and if your little place falls by the wayside that is no concern of mine. My only purpose in employing these people is to guard my husband's interests.'

Llinos moved towards the door. 'I can see there's no point talking to you.'

Georgina rose to her feet in a sweeping movement and came towards Llinos.

'You are not much of a businesswoman, are you? And certainly not much of a lady to consort with a half-breed however handsome he might be.'

Llinos smiled suddenly. 'That half-breed, as you call him, is a man of substance. He has lands and a great deal of property in England. He is also very clever.' She paused and her smile widened. 'And, of course, unlike your husband, he is young.'

Georgina swirled away from her, the colour rising to her cheeks. 'Please leave my house.'

'Look.' Llinos made one last attempt to appeal to Georgina's better nature. 'I want the pottery to survive because of my father. It is his livelihood and he does not deserve to have it taken away from him. But then, I can't expect you to understand any of that, you have no finer feelings.'

She left the house and walked briskly towards Pottery Row; the sooner she was off Morton-Edwards' land the better. As she crossed the opening to the yard of Tawe Pottery, she caught sight of Jim Cooper. He lifted his hat to her and she stood waiting for him to come closer.

'Miss Savage, I've been trying to talk to the men, to get them back to work at the Savage Pottery. They are not all that happy at Tawe Pottery, some of them are grumbling already about Morton-Edwards not paying as well as expected.'

He fell into step beside her. Llinos smiled up at him. 'Well, I'm grateful to you for trying, Jim. Grateful for your loyalty and support, I know it's cost you dear.'

'Well if them buggers don't want to speak to

me, then that's their loss.' He sighed. 'It's my missis feels it most. Loves a gossip she does and only Celia-end-house will bother with her.'

'We'll work something out, Jim, I'm sure.'

When she returned home, Joe was waiting for her. He took her hand. 'Let's walk to the top of Poppets Hill.'

A pale sun was shining between the clouds. Llinos looked up at Joe. He was magnificent. His hair swung to his shoulders, his head raised as though to see into the distance. His high cheek-bones gleamed golden, splashed with light. Her heart moved with pride. Joe loved her. She was the richest woman in the world.

A carriage rattled past and Llinos was aware of faces. Georgina and her godmother were peering through the window at her. She smiled, no doubt they were discussing what a hussy she was, flouting convention by walking out alone with a man.

At the top of the hill, the roadway petered out and Llinos felt the softness of grass beneath her feet. Below her, spread out like a giant picture, lay the town. And beyond the huddle of buildings, the sea fanned out towards the horizon, blue beneath the unexpected sunlight.

'It's so beautiful.' Llinos spoke softly. 'The sun shining through the rain clouds, the sea sparkling as if hundreds of candles were alight beneath the water.' She looked up at Joe.

His eyes met hers. 'Nothing could be as beautiful as you, Llinos.'

'Let's sit here for a while,' Llinos said. 'Let's forget the potteries, forget everything. Let's just enjoy being together. We've had little enough time for that, goodness knows.'

They sat on a fallen log, Joe's arm warm around her. Llinos sighed and rested her head against his shoulder.

'This is the closest I'll ever get to a heaven on earth.' She closed her eyes. She would not think, would not worry, she would just enjoy the moment.

Lloyd turned his chair towards the window and looked outside at the bleak emptiness of the yard. He clenched his fist, the knuckles showing white. He had never felt so angry, so impotent. Philip Morton-Edwards had beaten him. The man had destroyed his trade, stolen his workers, ruined what was left of his life. He hated him with an intensity that brought sweat out in beads on his forehead.

He rubbed his face in frustration, sometimes he felt he would go mad. Here he was, half a man, he would never lie with a woman again, never know a woman's love. He was a useless object, his life was not worth living.

His thoughts were racing, he wanted to kill Philip Morton-Edwards, to see him suffer, to see him lose everything.

A knock on the door snapped him out of his crazy thoughts. He turned away from the window and propelled himself along the passage.

'Jim, what can I do for you?'

'I've thought of a way out of this mess.' Jim came into the room, a big man with huge arms and a chest like a barrel.

'I'm listening.'

'This morning, I took in some lodgers, five in all.' Jim smiled. 'Potters, they are, come down from up the North of England.' He paused. 'Seems there are too many potters up there and not enough jobs.'

'Well I don't know, Jim, we have stocks enough of pots, pots that no-one wants. Morton-Edwards has taken our markets from us.'

'I know, but these men, they've brought with them new methods, more up-to-date than our own. Now we have access along the row again why not make one last stab at it? The folks of Swansea will jump at the chance of good solid tableware, I'll bet on it.'

Lloyd felt his pulse run fast with hope. 'Will these men defect to that bastard Morton-Edwards, though?'

Jim shook his head. 'Not after what I've told them about the man. We have the beginnings of a good band of workers and in any case some of our old workers are ready to come back to us; Morton-Edwards is paying them less than you did.'

He looked at Lloyd, waiting for his reply. Lloyd smiled.

'It's certainly worth a try.' He glanced up at Jim. 'Well done, Jim! We'll beat the old sod yet.'

Jim's face was shining with satisfaction. 'I've passed the word on in town that we need more workers, it won't matter if they're unskilled, they'll be useful for the wedging and the fetching and carrying.'

'Sit down, Jim, have a glass of porter. I think we should talk about a rise, it's about time I appreciated you.'

Jim waited until Lloyd poured the drinks and then he leaned forward in his chair, his big arms resting on his knees.

'These Staffordshire potters, they've brought some of the patterns with them. One of them was designing up in England, worked at several manufactories, all over the place, real experienced he is. He says there's a good china paste that will not fracture in the oven and it's more delicate than the rough earthenware we're making now. Perhaps we should experiment with it.'

'Make better porcelain than Morton-Edwards, my Lord, that would be something!' Lloyd said. 'Beat the man at his own game. I wonder if we could pull it off?'

'We could if we could stop production at the Tawe Pottery for a week or so,' Jim said. 'We'd be in there, getting all the orders from the big houses. We could approach the inns in the area, the better ones are ripe for some new china.'

'Yes, that would work if only we could find a way . . .'

'What if I was to dam up the river?' Jim broke in excitedly. 'It's high tide soon and the rains are coming if I'm any judge. As the Tawe Pottery is on the lower slope of the hill, we could flood the place, easy enough. It would do no lasting harm but it would sure as hell delay things a bit.'

Lloyd nodded. 'Why not? Morton-Edwards has played enough dirty tricks on me to last a lifetime, it's about time I paid him back in the same coin.'

Jim smiled. 'I wouldn't like to see his stock of clay when the water got to it!'

'You're a good man, Jim. I won't forget you gave me your help when I most needed it.'

Jim drained his glass. 'No need for thanks, Captain, you and me go back a long way. I'll be off now and do a bit of reckoning on the tides.'

When he was alone, Lloyd returned to his spot before the window. The bottle kilns of both potteries were almost side by side but the Tawe Pottery, as Jim had pointed out, was on slightly lower land.

Lloyd looked up at the leaden skies; there was rain up there for sure. It could be the elements were on his side for once. He puffed on his pipe and sat back in his chair. Perhaps he was not so useless after all. He could still think, he had his brain, didn't he? He could still reckon up the accounts, order materials, make out bills of sale. Sometimes he forgot things, sure, but a good manager would cover for him.

The Savage Pottery would survive, china

would be produced once more, the ovens would be fired for baking, the yard would throng with workers. He raised his fist.

'You will not beat me after all, Morton-Edwards,' he said softly.

CHAPTER TWENTY-NINE

Georgina sat in the window staring out into the garden. She was well pleased with herself as she recalled her husband's triumphant return home.

She had greeted him in the hall with arms outstretched, clinging to him, very much aware that he looked every minute of his fifty-five years. She pressed her lips close to his, closing her eyes, trying to force some warmth into her embrace. After a moment, she had drawn away from him.

After his journey, he had rested himself in bed for a whole day and now she waited anxiously for him to speak. She caught his arm.

'Come, darling, tell me all that's happened.' Her tone was genuinely enthusiastic.

Philip led the way into the sitting-room and nodded abstractedly towards Mrs Sanders. 'Afternoon, Catherine, have you been looking after my affairs while I've been away?'

She nodded, ascertaining that he required no answer, and he sank down into a chair and rubbed his hand through his greying hair so that it stood on end. He looked like some absurd wild man and Georgina sat opposite him trying not to look too closely at the lines that seemed to have deepened in his face in his short absence from home.

The taunts Llinos Savage had flung at her seemed to be graphically illustrated in her husband's aged appearance. She thought of the half-breed Llinos had boasted about. He was tall, handsome and very rich. Indeed, her own lot was not, in comparison, such a wonderful one. Still, Philip could not last long. Soon, she would be free of him and free of his brat of a son, too.

'Did you achieve anything?' she urged, irritated by Philip's slowness to volunteer information.

'I did.' He had taken a folded paper from his pocket. 'This was signed and witnessed before a notary.' He smiled and something of the handsome man he must have once been flashed into his face. 'It testifies that my first wife deceived me, she was barren just like my second wife.' He sounded bitter. 'She took a child from the lower orders, from a family by the name of Cowper, and foisted him on me as my own.'

Philip spoke so convincingly that, for a moment, Georgina almost believed she was hearing the truth. But of course, it was all lies, a plot to throw Eynon out of the nest. Still, so long as Philip continued to be convincing, his story would be believed.

He held out the document and she took it with trembling fingers. It looked official enough, Philip must have offered the Cowpers a very large bribe indeed, enough to make their story believable in the eyes of the law.

'Excellent.' She handed it back to him, gleefully anticipating the moment when she would tell Eynon the news. She would not be able to restrain herself for very long.

She rode out that very evening, seated in the carriage with her godmother at her side.

'We'll show that brat of Philip's just where he stands, God-Mamma.' She spoke with satisfaction.

'What if it's true?' Catherine said so softly that, for a moment, Georgina wondered if she had heard correctly.

'What do you mean?'

'I mean it's very strange that you are Philip's third wife and still there is no other child but Eynon. Could Philip be the barren one, do you think?'

Georgina laughed out loud, clinging to the door handle as the carriage bumped over the stony ground.

'That's wonderful!' she said. 'Do you know, God-Mamma, I think you just could have hit the nail on the head.' She righted her bonnet.

'Well, if that is so, I shall make sure I get with child by some other man before much longer. And I think I will enjoy the experience, Philip is too old by far for me.'

It was at the door of his house that Georgina confronted Eynon. His servant had gone to announce her and instead of being invited in as she had expected, Eynon had come out to her, making it obvious she was not welcome. She

534

did not mince her words.

'You are a bastard.' She spoke loudly enough for the servants within the house to hear what she was saying.

'Philip has come home from England with proof that your mother was barren. You are a changeling, foisted on Philip. I always knew there was something strange about you.' She laughed. 'Now I understand what it is. You are from the lower orders, Eynon, what do you think of that?'

'I don't believe you.' Eynon had become very pale. He leaned against the porch of his house and stared down at her with eyes that were shadowed.

'Well, it's true. The proof is with your father's lawyer right now.'

'With Timothy Beresford?' He could hardly speak; she knew she had shocked him and she meant to thrust the barb deeper.

'I don't know how much your so-called mother's family left you, Eynon, but whatever it is you will have to forfeit it. Perhaps you should try to make a good marriage before it is too late, before the whole world knows about your origins.'

He stared at her with something almost like pity in his eyes. 'You must be a very unhappy woman, Georgina,' he said, and then he shut the door in her face.

She was returning home in her carriage when she heard the sound of hooves pounding against the dry earth. The rider thundered past, coattails flying, and she recognized the pale gold hair and the slim form of Philip's son. Eynon, it seemed, was riding hell for leather into town.

'Good lord, God-Mamma, where do you think he's going?'

'To see this lawyer chap, I imagine, to find out the truth of the matter,' Catherine said. 'I can't help feeling a little sorry for the boy.'

Georgina stiffened her shoulders. 'With luck, the fool will fall and break his neck, that would save everybody a great deal of trouble!' she said savagely.

'I think I shall return home to England at first light tomorrow,' Catherine said. 'I find all this intrigue very tiring.'

'Well, maybe it's a good idea,' Georgina said. 'I suppose it's all too much for you, at your age.'

She did not see the angry look her godmother flashed her way and if she had, she would not have been disturbed by it.

It was with a sense of relief that Georgina saw her godmother into the carriage that would take her home. Catherine could be a little tiresome and anyway, once out of the way, Catherine might forget that she had ever wanted any part in the potteries.

It was towards evening when Philip entered the room. He smelled of the china sheds and she wrinkled her nose at him.

'Darling, do you have to come in here straight from work?' She turned her face for his kiss, which landed on her cheek. 'You have underlings to see to things at the pottery, you should not bother yourself with it all.'

'For heaven's sake, stop talking to me as if I'm in my dotage, woman.'

'Sorry!' Georgina made a face behind Philip's back. He looked up at her sharply.

'I have done all you asked, now when are you going to do your part and provide me with an heir? Am I not vigorous enough for you?'

'Of course you are, darling, you are a wonderful lover, don't be so touchy.'

'Well, madam, answer me, are you with child yet?'

She knelt before him, her arm around his waist, her eyes downcast.

'I have not had my . . . how shall I put it? My monthly curse. It could well be that you have made me . . . well, you know.'

'Do you mean it?' Philip's mood changed. 'My dear girl.' He drew her onto his knee. 'You do look a little pale. I have been unnecessarily harsh with you.'

'Darling, you are tired and worried about work, that's what it is. I know you had to sack some of the men and now they are running back to the Savage Pottery. I'll never understand these people.' She understood right enough, Philip was overbearing, he had become hard, unreasonable and the men did not like it. And also, they did not like the cut in wages that he had imposed on them.

'Aye.' He shook his head and she could clearly see the bald patch that was growing larger every day. She closed her eyes and turned away.

'Those idle workers don't know a real boss when they see one. A touch of the birch they need to keep them at it,' he said.

She swallowed her anger but she could think of nothing reassuring to say. She changed the subject.

'I went to see Eynon yesterday.' She spoke softly, sensing that Philip needed to be humoured. 'I told him about the unfortunate circumstances of his birth.'

'You did what?' Philip rose to his feet, unbalancing her. She looked up at him, he was white with anger.

'Who do you think you are, woman? You have no right to run my life, I'm not a child. I should have been the one to talk to Eynon. You take too much on yourself.'

'But, Philip, I did very well while you were away, I made all the workers from the Savage Pottery come over to us.'

'And how long did that last?' Philip said sourly. He walked to the cabinet and took out the bottle of brandy. 'In any case, they were useless, bone idle. I want real men to work for me, not Lloyd Savage's leavings.'

'Oh, Philip!' Georgina was unable to hide her exasperation and Philip looked at her with narrowed eyes, his displeasure plain to see in the tight set of his mouth.

Georgina hastily recovered from her mistake. 'I wish you wouldn't upset yourself so over these people. They are not worth it. You are right, we can do without that sort.'

Inside, she was seething. Had Philip never heard of diplomacy? These men from Pottery Row could have proved valuable allies. Now Philip had alienated them, they would undoubtedly carry tales to Lloyd Savage. Philip was losing his grip. He was growing old and crotchety, quarrelling with his own shadow. The sooner he gave up and handed the reins to her, the better it would be for everyone.

She sank back in her chair. For now she must play the game of loving wife to this old, tired man standing before her. And it was not a role she relished.

'I'm sorry, Eynon, you have to accept this.' Timothy Beresford was seated behind his desk, his spectacles caught in a slant of sunlight giving him a blind look. He rested his fingers heavily on the document before him. 'It's the truth.'

'But knowing my father he has bribed these people, can't you make other enquiries, Timothy?'

'Eynon, I knew your mother well, we were very close friends, she told me everything. Do you understand me?'

'Are you saying she admitted the truth?'

Timothy Beresford sighed. 'Wild horses wouldn't have dragged this from me but now I have no other choice. You are the son of a serving woman by the name of Jane Cowper, father unknown. By the time your mother arranged all this, she had realized that she did not love your father, had never loved him.' He paused, considering his words.

'Indeed, she had found him to be greedy and cruel and she was determined he would not profit from the large fortune her family owned. So her will and those of her dead brothers are made in your favour. You will never want for anything.'

Eynon sat in silence, not hearing Timothy's words. It was all too difficult to comprehend. He had loved his mother more than any other living soul; had loved a stranger, a woman who wanted him only to spite her husband.

'Thank you for your honesty, Tim.' Eynon rose to his feet. 'Give me a few days to think all this out, will you?'

'Of course. I have not replied to Philip, not yet, I too have a great deal of thinking to do.' He paused. 'Eynon, may I just say one thing? Your mother loved you, loved you as much, no, more than if she had borne you herself.'

Eynon sighed. 'I am in no state to distinguish truth from lies. Thank you for talking to me.'

He left the building, not seeing the sun rising high in the sky or the long street that stretched towards the beach. He was picturing his parents, his true parents, and realizing how little they must have thought of him to give him away without a second thought.

'We'd better be getting back.' Joe drew Llinos to her feet and the breeze whipped her hair around her face. She looked fresh and beautiful, her eyes as dark as those of any Indian maid. He had the urge to lay her down in the sweet heather of the hillside and make love to her. 'Come on, let's go before I do something rash.' He was trying to make light of his feelings but he could see by the glow in Llinos's eyes that she was aroused as he was.

He drew her close and kissed her hair, her eyelids, her mouth. His lips moved to her neck and to the softness of her breasts. He felt fire spread through him, desire like molten gold ran through his veins.

'Llinos, my little Firebird, how can I resist you when you look at me like that?'

The pounding of horses' hooves at first seemed to be the drumming of blood in his head. Joe felt the prickling of the hair rising at the back of his neck. A sense of danger hung heavily in the air.

Then he saw him: Eynon, his hair flying, was riding his horse as though the demons of hell were after him. The animal was foaming at the mouth, eyes rolling. Eynon was heading the animal straight for the rocky headland that fell away into a wide gorge.

Joe measured the distance with his eyes, the

flying hooves were coming closer. He was all native now, his senses alive. As he sprung towards the crazed animal, he heard Llinos scream. He caught the reins and held on, dragged across the ground close to the pounding hooves, too close. The world dissolved around him and he was drawn through a tunnel of flashing lights that faded abruptly into complete darkness.

Llinos stood for a moment, paralysed with fear. She saw Joe being dragged along the ground, watched horrified as the animal lashed out, hooves flying. Joe rolled sideways and lay quite still.

The horse, crazed with fear, tried to turn away from the abyss, the creature reared, mane streaming, then fell heavily, slender legs beating the air. Slowly, the horse rolled over, crushing Eynon beneath its broad back.

Llinos started to run, she cried out and the wind took her words and tossed them over the mountainside. She could scarcely breathe as she fell onto her knees beside Joe.

'My love!' She drew his head to her breast and rocked him as though he were a baby. 'Joe, Joe!'

As if in answer to her voice, she felt him stir against her, a small trickle of blood was making a rivulet along his forehead.

Slowly, he opened his eyes and blinked as though to clear his head.

'I'm all right,' he said. 'Don't cry, Llinos.' He

sat up, rubbing his hand across his eyes. 'Go and see to Eynon.'

'Joe, I don't want to leave you.'

'I'm just dazed, I'll be all right in a minute.'

Reluctantly, Llinos left him and hurried to where Eynon was lying spread-eagled across the grass. His arms were flung outwards across the ground, his leg was trapped beneath the body of his horse.

Llinos bent over him, fighting a sense of un-reality. It was like living in a nightmare. 'Eynon!' There was a gash across his jaw and his eyes were beginning to swell. Llinos tried to pull him free of the animal and he groaned in pain.

'He's alive,' Llinos called over her shoulder. Joe was already on his feet. He limped across the intervening ground and knelt beside the fallen horse.

He took out his knife and began to dig the earth away from beneath Eynon's trapped leg. Feeling the movement, Eynon opened his eyes and groaned. He tried to get up but Joe put a restraining hand on his shoulder.

'My grey,' Eynon said. 'Is he . . . ?'

'He feels nothing. Lie still, I'll have you free before you know it.'

As Joe dug away the earth, Llinos held Eynon's hand, talking quietly, encouraging him to keep up his spirits.

The sun was dying in the sky by the time Joe was able to pull Eynon free of the dead horse. As he did so, Eynon cried out in agony. From the angle of his foot it was clear a bone was broken.

Joe worked rapidly. He found two stout branches and bound the injured leg with the reins he had taken from the dead horse.

'You stay here with him, Llinos.' Joe rested his hand on her shoulder. 'I'll go and fetch help.'

'Joe, are you sure you're all right?' She looked up at him anxiously and he smiled.

'I'm not ready to die, Llinos, not just now.'

She watched as he walked away, still limping, and then she sat on the ground, edging closer to Eynon. She lifted his head into her lap and caressed his cheek.

'Silly, Eynon, riding like a mad thing,' she said. 'You could have killed yourself!'

Eynon sighed heavily and after a moment looked up at her.

'I'm a bastard, Llinos, illegitimate.' The words fell into the silence and hung there for what seemed an eternity.

'Who told you that?' Llinos said at last. 'No, don't tell me, Georgina has been talking to you, hasn't she?'

He nodded.

'And you believed her, just like that? Didn't you think to find out the truth, Eynon?'

'I have. I spoke to Timothy Beresford, he confirmed it. My mother' — he laughed shortly — 'the woman I thought was my mother, took me from a poor family and brought me up as her own. She did it just to get back at my father.' He sighed.

'I believe her money is mine, she's willed it to me,' he said, 'but that's not important, it's just the thought that nobody cared enough to love me for myself. Not my real mother who gave me away nor my adopted mother.'

He glanced remorsefully at his horse. 'I should have been lying there dead.'

Llinos touched his cheek. 'I love you and I'm sure your mother must have loved you, too. Things are not always as simple as they seem. When you are poor, a great deal of what you do is forced on you.'

He sighed. 'Do you know, Georgina actually smiled as she smashed my life into pieces. How can people be so unkind, Llinos?'

'Greed, spite, fear. Any number of reasons.'

The darkness was creeping round them, spreading shadowy fingers over the uneven ground and turning the rocks below into a chasm of blackness. Llinos was relieved when at last she heard the sound of carriage wheels coming towards them.

Joe was riding a wagon across the uneven land and Ben and Jim Cooper were with him, both men holding lanterns.

As he drew in the reins, Joe smiled down at her and in the dim light she saw the heavy bruising on his temple and fear caught her by the throat. How easily she might have lost him. He turned to the men at his side.

'Help me to lift Mr Morton-Edwards into the wagon, carefully now, Jim, you don't know your own strength.'

Eynon bit his lip as he was lifted bodily and placed on a blanket, his broken leg stretched before him.

'Soon have you back in civilization, Eynon,' Joe said. He put his hand around Llinos's waist. 'Climb in.' She rested her head for a moment on his chest, feeling his heart beat rapidly beneath his shirt.

'Go on, get in. I'll see you later.'

'Later?' She looked up at him.

'I'll stay behind, deal with the horse.'

Llinos sat beside Eynon and he caught her hand, grimacing in pain. 'I think the fall has jarred the big bone in my leg, the one I broke before,' he said through clenched teeth.

'It won't be long now, we'll have you down at the doctor's house in no time.'

She stared over the edge of the wagon. Joe was beside her. looking into her face, his hair flying loose in the breeze. They touched hands briefly and then the cart jolted into movement. When Llinos looked back, Joe was a distant figure on the horizon.

When at last Llinos was able to take Eynon home, Maura was standing in the doorway, the candles behind her filling the hall with light.

'Old Ben rode over to tell me what happened.' She ignored Llinos and spoke directly to Eynon.

'I've got a bed set up in the side room. It will be light in there and you can look out onto the garden. If it's fine, I can open the French doors for you to get a breath of fresh air.'

Eynon forced a smile. 'Thank you, Maura, I appreciate your kindness.'

'Go away with you! I'm doing what I'm paid for and nothing more.'

'If that's a reminder that you haven't been paid for weeks, point taken.'

'Looks like the doctor took good care of you,' Maura said drily. 'If you can smile and joke you must be feeling better.'

Maura's back was turned deliberately, shutting Llinos out. Maura had always been impertinent and yet now there was something sad and lost about her. She turned to Llinos abruptly as if sensing her thoughts.

'You'll be getting married soon, I hear.' Maura looked at her with hooded eyes. 'The half-breed, is it?'

'Do you have to be so unpleasant? Can't you just wish me luck, Maura?'

'Aye, maybe so but then I don't hold with marriage. Married one day and deserted the next, fine judge I am of men.'

Llinos turned away. 'If you don't mind, Eynon, I'd better get back home,' she said. 'I'll come and see you tomorrow.'

He held up his hand. 'Llinos, thank you and, Joe, tell him . . .' His words trailed away and Llinos smiled.

'I know. Now, don't worry, everything is going to be all right.'

She stepped out briskly along the roadway, glad of the breeze against her hot cheeks. She was exhausted, the accident had upset her more than she was willing to admit.

Llinos reached the banks of the river Tawe and paused for breath. The walk was much longer than she had anticipated. She sat down on a fallen log and looked at the swiftly flowing river, the water was rising, it must be high tide. Llinos closed her eyes, feeling the calming effect of the rushing water drain away her tension.

'Llinos, what are you doing here?' Philip was beside her suddenly, his face shadowed in the moonlight.

Startled, she looked up at him. 'I'm fine, thank you. I've walked a long way and I'm tired, that's all.'

He sat beside her, his booted feet jutting out before him. He looked older than she remembered, his hair was thinning and the lines had deepened around his mouth.

'Philip, there's been an accident.'

'What sort of accident?'

'Eynon had a fall from his horse. He's got a broken bone but the doctor says he will make a complete recovery.'

He frowned. 'When did this happen? Why am I always the last one to know what's going on?'

'Joe and I were on the spot,' Llinos said. 'Eynon is all right, there's nothing to worry about. He's very upset, of course. Philip, did your wife have to be so cruel breaking the news about his birth the way she did?'

'If the truth hurts, so be it,' Philip said harshly.

She looked at him closely. 'Georgina was wrong about one thing, Eynon is not penniless.' She smiled. 'His mother made a will, it's all legal, the lawyer told him so.'

'Well, I shall see about that! In any event, Eynon is not my son, and I'm glad, do you hear me, glad! Now I know why I have never cared for him.'

'You never cared for him because you are a cruel, sadistic man and greedy to boot,' Llinos said angrily.

Philip seemed to slump sideways and suddenly he was leaning heavily against her. She touched his shoulder.

'Philip, are you all right?'

'No, I don't think I am. Will you walk to the house with me, I feel quite ill.'

Llinos hesitated but she had no choice but to comply. Already tired, she found progress over the uneven ground was intolerably slow, and Philip was breathing heavily. He must be very sick indeed to ask her for help. The sooner she got him home the better.

It was a relief when the grounds of the Tawe Pottery came into sight. Llinos guided Philip towards the door and, as it swung open, the maid looked at them with raised eyebrows.

'Call your mistress,' Llinos said. Philip grasped

her arm and drew her into the sitting-room. Georgina rose to her feet, staring in open-mouthed surprise at them.

'Philip is not feeling well,' Llinos said abruptly. She helped him to a chair and he held on to both her hands. To her surprise, his grip tightened, became stronger and when she struggled to pull away, he held her fast.

'She is a meddlesome nuisance.' He glanced at his wife. 'But she has reminded me of some very interesting information.'

'What information is that, darling?' Georgina stared at Llinos as though she was little more than a creature to be trampled underfoot.

'There is a will made by my conniving first wife. Her brothers were involved in all this and Timothy Beresford, too, for if I'm any judge he always did have a soft spot for my wife.'

'Let me go!' Llinos said, trying to free herself, but Philip's grip became cruel, his nails biting into the flesh of her wrists.

'I'm afraid you are not going anywhere,' he said reasonably, though his eyes seemed to burn like coals in his head. 'At least not until we've dealt with these wills, if they exist at all.'

'What's to stop me talking to people when you do release me?' Llinos said hotly.

'Once I've attended to the matter, you can do your worst, my dear. No wills, no proof. I'm sure you understand.'

He looked up at his wife. 'I'll take her down to the disused shed and lock her in there. She can scream her head off and no-one will hear.'

Llinos saw Philip lift his hand. Saw it clench into a fist. And then the world exploded into a myriad of colours that slowly faded away into blackness.

'Good work, men,' Jim said. 'That's the explosives in place.' He was waist deep in river water. 'It's high tide tonight,' he said. 'With luck it will flood all the buildings of the Tawe Pottery. We'll show Philip Morton-Edwards that we can play dirty tricks just as well as he can.'

He looked across the narrowest part of the river. The bank rose to a height of about ten feet. The blast, he judged, would cut a swathe in the earth and allow the water to gush into the pottery. The water would eventually find its own level but it would flood landwards just long enough to cause trouble for that bastard Morton-Edwards.

The best part of it was that no-one would be harmed. The houses were too high to be flooded. After an hour or two the tide would be on the ebb and the river would return to normal.

'What about the Savage Pottery?' Old Ben looked doubtfully along the line of the water.

'That will be all right. It's further along the bank and quite a bit higher. Only Morton-Edwards will be affected, don't you worry.'

Ben sighed. 'I wish I was as sure about that as you, Jim. Looks right dangerous to me.'

'I know this river like the back of my hand,'

Jim said. 'I've fished it since I was a little lad. Everything will go to plan, you'll see.'

'It's going to rain,' Ben said.

'That's what I'm hoping for. Stop worrying.'

'Might flood the whole damn place,' Ben mumbled, but Jim ignored him and waded onto the bank, pulling off his breeches.

'Watt, get me that clean pair of trews, there's a good lad. And for Gawd's sake let's get off to the Angel for a drink, the cold's getting into my bones.'

Jim followed the trail of men walking along the bank of the Tawe towards the road. He paused and glanced back at the river. Already the water was building up. It should do the trick very nicely.

It took the crowd of men little over half an hour to walk to the Angel and as the last man stepped inside, the first drops of rain began to fall.

CHAPTER THIRTY

Joe looked up at the sky. It was beginning to rain; he had been sitting at the grave of the dead horse and making prayers to the spirits for far too long. Clouds were racing across the sky, the moon trembling between the clouds.

He rose to his feet, and began to run. The wind threw the rain into his face like the darts of an enemy. And yet he smiled as he imagined Llinos indoors, sitting near a blazing fire, her small feet tucked up beneath her.

His breath caught in his throat, soon, very soon, he would have the right to take her in his arms, opening the floodgates on the passion that had burned so long for release.

The rain was coming down harder now, cold needles against his skin. Ahead of him was the friendliness of candlelight behind windows. And yet there was an air of foreboding in the rushing clouds that now extinguished the moon.

When he arrived at Pottery House there was no sign of Llinos, neither was Lloyd at home. The fires burned brightly in the empty rooms. The candles flickered, sending shadows leaping along the walls. The servants were in the kitchen, huddled round the huge open grate, the logs spitting and hissing as rain touched their heat with icy fingers.

'Where's Mr Savage, Sally?' Joe asked the young maid who was kneeling before the fire, fresh logs in her hands. The girl looked at him and frowned.

'I don't rightly know, sir, I think he's gone down the Angel with the men from the pottery. I know old Ben was going and Jim Cooper. Talking about work, I reckon.'

She knelt placing the logs strategically on the fire. 'Miss Savage has not been back since before teatime, leastways I 'aven't seen her.'

She was probably still up at Eynon's house, nursing the injured boy. Joe felt a twinge of unease but he brushed it aside.

'Shall I fetch you a bite of supper, sir?' The scuttle hung from Sally's smudged hands, there was the shadow of dust across her face. Joe shook his head.

'No, thank you. What you can do is bring water upstairs for me to bathe.' He would wash away the earth of the horse's burial mound and then he would go to Eynon's house.

Upstairs, he glanced through the windows. There was something in the air tonight, something he could not understand, and he did not like it. The sooner he fetched Llinos home, the better.

'Will it work, Jim?' Lloyd sat back in his chair, aware of the cruel ache in his legs. His wound was plaguing him again, so badly that he needed an extra toddy of rum to dull the pain.

'Sure it'll work. I know the moods of the Tawe so well, sir. When I sets off the explosives, the bank will cave in and the water will run towards the Tawe Pottery sure enough.'

'I hope you are right. Ben, what do you think?'

Ben rubbed at the whiteness of his whiskers. 'I don't know, Captain Savage.'

'Doubtful, are you?'

'The banks will go, all right, and the water will run. But the river has her moods and she might run too far and flood the lot of us.'

'Naw, nothing will go wrong, I guarantee it,' Jim said. He lifted his arm. 'Landlord, bring more rum, the nights are getting colder or I'm growing old.'

Lloyd allowed the landlord to refill his own mug. The rum shimmered enticingly, promising him sleep and release. He looked at Jim, he was a good man, he had always shown a great deal of common sense. Jim knew what he was talking about and yet a strange sense of uneasiness persisted and Lloyd wheeled his chair a little nearer to Ben's.

'I hope this is going to work.'

'Aye, I suppose it will be all right. What else can we do, we can't let the man get away with his wickedness, can we?' Ben puffed on his pipe. 'Trying to put decent people out of house and home and then bribing them to work for him. It's not right.'

'Well, those who went to work for him have found him out,' Lloyd said. 'I think they have all realized that Morton-Edwards is a ruthless man, he'll stop at nothing to ruin me, but I'll beat him yet.'

Ben smiled. 'He'll have a rude awakening when the water ruins all his stock, turns his pots back into clay. Won't do the porcelain much good either, the lot will be smashed, if we're lucky.'

The door swung open, letting in a rush of cold air. Lloyd looked up to see Joe framed in the doorway, his shoulders large beneath the cloth of his coat, his hair tied back so that it hung darkly down his back. He was a handsome man, his noble face gleaming red gold in the candle-light. It was no wonder Llinos had lost her head over him.

Well, he would not make a bad husband. Joe had money now, a large house of his own. In any case, Llinos loved the man, perhaps in the end that was what was important.

'Joe, come and join us, have a mug of rum to warm you up.' He shifted to allow Joe to sit close. 'Where have you been, sweet-talking my daughter, is it?'

'There was an accident,' Joe said quietly. 'Eynon came off his horse, broke his leg. Llinos came back to town with him in the wagon. I stayed behind to give the animal a decent burial.'

Joe was a strange man, talking about a horse as though it had a mind and a soul. He was filled with strange beliefs in spite of his excellent English education but then, he was still an Indian half-breed, when all was said and done.

Joe's eyes met his, it was as if the man knew exactly what he was thinking. It was Lloyd who looked away. Joe rose to his feet.

'I'm going over to Eynon's house now to fetch Llinos home. I've taken the horse and trap, I hope that's all right.'

'Of course it's all right.' Lloyd could feel the rum warming his blood, bringing the heat to his cheeks, loosening his tongue. 'You'll do me as a son-in-law in spite of everything.'

Joe remained silent, his eyes were unreadable. Lloyd moved restlessly. 'Well, get on with it then, fetch my girl home. I want her safe to-night.'

Joe's farewell nod included the rest of the men and Lloyd saw that all of them, with the exception of Ben, were still wary of him. To them Joe was an outsider and not even a proper Englishman.

He watched as Joe walked to the door, light on his feet as though he wore no shoes. He recalled a moment during the war when Joe had been scouting. He had walked in that same sure-footed manner as he had stalked the enemy. In that moment, Lloyd wanted to call Joe back, to ask him if planning to flood the Tawe Pottery was the right thing to do. But it was too late, Joe had swung through the door and into the darkness.

'Come on, Jim, let's have another drink, it's my turn to call.' Lloyd spoke with a cheerfulness that was forced. But Jim did not notice.

'Last one,' he said, 'then I'm off to do the necessary.' He was drinking heavily. Perhaps Lloyd should caution him to take it steady. But no, Jim was a grown man and Lloyd was not his keeper. In any case, the pain was creeping back. Lloyd needed more rum, not more worry. To hell with it, he intended to forget everything and drink himself into a stupor.

It was cold outside the light and warmth of the Angel Inn, and Jim Cooper turned up his collar as he made his way along the low road beside the river. The lamp swung crazily in his hands, almost dousing the candle inside. He had drunk a little more rum than was good for him but he was still up to the job in hand.

He stumbled and dropped the bag containing the black powder. Cursing, he fumbled for it, and, picking it up, he staggered along the road, unaware of the trail he was leaving in his wake.

He reached the spot on the bank where he wanted to set his charge and sank down on his knees in the mud.

His fingers were slow, clumsy. He felt sick, the rum seemed to rise to his head, drumming in his ears. He shook his head to clear it but the action only made it worse.

'Jim!' The voice reached out to him in the

darkness. Fuddled, Jim looked up towards the road.

'Captain Savage, is that you?'

'Yes, Jim, it's me.' His voice was faint and Jim realized dimly that the wheelchair would be dangerously close to the bank.

'I've changed my mind. Come back out of it, you're in no fit state to handle that stuff.'

'Go away.' Jim waved his hand in the air. 'Get back, it's not safe for you to be down by here, man.'

He swayed a little, that would have to do. The charge was set in a good place, just near enough to make trouble but not to do any real harm.

He staggered as he tried to rise. The lamp tilted and fell onto the ground, igniting the trail of powder. Jim knew he should run. His feet seemed to sink into the mud, he could not move, it was a nightmare. And then the world exploded into a glowing ball that engulfed him.

Llinos slowly became aware of the cold and the darkness that seemed to be pressing in on her. She struggled to sit up and realized that her wrists were bound in front of her with a tough rope that bit into the flesh. When she tried to move, she realized her ankles, too, were bound.

She struggled to push herself into a sitting position and leaned back against rough boards. As her eyes became accustomed to the gloom she realized she was in a small shed and from the sound of rushing water nearby, she knew she must be somewhere on the banks of the river.

Her jaw ached and she remembered in a flash of fear mingled with anger the way Philip had punched her. She could not believe that she had been fooled by him for so long. They had all warned her, Joe, her father and Eynon but, headstrong to the last, she would not listen to sense.

From outside, she heard the sound of the wind moaning in the trees and rain drumming against the roof of the shed. A storm was building up and Llinos shivered. What if the river rose? It was high tide tonight and if the rain continued to fall, the river could overflow the banks. How close to the water was she?

But she was being foolish, Philip might be greedy, unfeeling even, but even he would not leave her there to drown. All he wanted was time to destroy the wills that were made in Eynon's favour. Then he would let her go. Wouldn't he?

She began to work at the ropes on her wrists. She pulled against the knots with her teeth but they were securely tied. She managed to turn over onto her knees and she gasped trying to ignore the pain of the ropes biting into her flesh. She paused for breath and then made an effort to push herself to her feet.

If she could reach the small window, perhaps she could attract attention and get help. But the window was too high for her to see anything. She rested her head against the wooden planks and tried to think calmly.

She needed something to stand on. She peered

around in the gloom and saw a box lying near the door. She edged her way across the floor towards the box. With her feet, she shuffled the box awkwardly towards the window.

The rain was beating down more fiercely now, she could feel the dampness as water trickled in through holes in the shed roof. She took a deep breath and attempted to climb onto the box. She did not make it. She fell heavily to the floor and lay there breathless, trying to clear her head.

She moved her feet and felt that the ropes around her ankles were looser. She leaned over almost double and pulled at the knot. She could hardly move her hands, they were so tightly tied, but her heart leapt with hope as she felt the rope at her feet break. With one more tug, the rope fell from her ankles.

She peered through the dimness of the shed and found a piece of broken bottle. She rubbed the rope at her wrists against the sharp edge of the glass. Once she caught the skin of her inner arm and felt the warmth of blood oozing from the wound. She seemed to be getting nowhere and all the time the sound of rushing water was coming closer. It seemed that an eternity passed before the ropes fell from her chafed wrists, but at last she was free.

To her dismay, she found that the door was securely locked. Frantically, she pushed her weight against it but it did not budge. She stood on the box and looked outside. She could see nothing but sweeping rain and darkness. No-one would be fool enough to be out on a night like this, it was hopeless.

Llinos closed her eyes and thought of Joe, willing him to find her. She concentrated hard, trying to send him her thoughts and for a moment, she was with him on the sweeping plains, touching his golden skin, feeling his hair brush her hands.

The noise of an explosion crashed through the night. It was like the booming of a cannon, the very earth seemed to tremble. The shed vibrated and pieces of timber tumbled down onto her head. She might have screamed, but if she had no-one would have heard her. The rushing, swirling flood of water was like a monster coming to devour her.

'What in the name of all that's holy was that!' Philip looked down from the carriage and pair towards the river. He had taken the low road to town, intending to visit the chambers of Timothy Beresford at once. Georgina grumbled about the rain but was determined to keep watch while he found a way into the building and destroyed any paperwork that might be there.

'It sounds like an explosion of some sort.' White-faced, Georgina leaned closer to him. 'My God, Philip, the water's rising up the sides of the carriage, turn back, for heaven's sake!'

'Not on your life, rain and flood water will not stop me now!' Philip flicked the reins angrily, lashing out with the whip, and one of the animals reared in fright.

'Do something, Philip, don't be a fool!'

'I'm going on,' he said. 'I'll beat that no-good weakling who claims to be my son, you see if I don't.'

'Philip, the water's getting higher, we'll be drowned! For heaven's sake see sense.' She clutched at his arm and tried to pull the reins away from him. He slapped her hard and she fell back in her seat, numbed with shock.

He tried to urge the animals into a gallop but they were wild-eyed, trembling as the water surged with the sound of thunder behind them. Philip whipped the animals mercilessly, anger raging through him. He would deal with Eynon and then he would deal with the Savage family. His enemies would learn that it did not do to cross Philip Morton-Edwards.

A flash of fire seemed to run along the bank through the mud. There was a series of small explosions and suddenly the terrified horses broke free of the shafts.

The carriage lurched sickeningly to one side. Georgina screamed. The carriage overturned and slid with almost indecent haste towards the swollen river. The last thing Philip heard was his wife's terrified voice as the cold waters of the Tawe closed over his head.

Llinos gasped as the water overwhelmed her but she had the sense to catch a thick spar of wood and cling to it. The shed had disintegrated and the water dragged at her, threatening to swamp her, but she held on to the spar, shaking water out of her eyes and mouth.

The river seemed to rise in tumult around her, huge, dark waves engulfed her time and time again until she felt her strength drain away.

And then, abruptly, the water receded, sucked back from the shore as though by a giant hand. Llinos tried to see through the darkness, there was a gaping hole in the bank to her left and as she watched, the river flowed through it towards the land where the potteries stood.

She could hear cries coming from Pottery Row. She saw the flicker of storm lanterns as if they were small pinpricks in the darkness.

Llinos was lifted on a wave and dashed back into the trough again, the coldness of the water stealing her breath. And then, slowly, the waters became calmer. Llinos took a deep ragged breath and began to swim towards the bank, still clinging to the spar.

Her arms were stiff, her wrists sore from the bite of the rope. She was half drowned but she was alive.

She felt something drag at her legs and screamed as a body appeared beside her on the surface of the water. It was Jim Cooper. She tried to catch hold of him but the suck of the river took him away from her.

Llinos pushed her way towards the bank. She was in danger of being carried downstream, she was growing weaker. She was going to die, she would never be Joe's wife, never walk with him on the golden plains of America.

Hands were around her then, holding her. As the water cascaded over her head, she knew that Joe was there with her. She was being drawn towards the shore and a great hope filled her.

Gasping, she hauled herself upwards, sliding in the mud, her hands grasping at grass and roots in an effort to draw herself away from the rushing water. Joe was kneeling beside her, holding her. 'Oh, Joe!' She touched his face wonderingly, he was here, he had brought her out of the river.

The next few seconds seemed to flash by as she heard a voice calling to her from the blackness.

'Llinos!' The cry resounded in her ears: it was her father. She stared into the dark of the river just as the moon emerged from behind a cloud. Lit from above as if with a lantern, she could clearly see her father, floundering in the water.

He was clinging on to what was left of his wheelchair, she could see one of the wheels spin away into the depths. Her straining eyes caught sight of the thin figure of Watt thrashing about in the water. The boy was holding her father's head, trying desperately to keep the helpless man afloat.

She watched Joe dive cleanly into the river and her heart knocked against her ribs so hard she felt she would die. She looked frantically around her for someone to help but no-one seemed to know what was happening. She saw figures rushing from buildings. Women were screaming, running with children in their arms. There was no hope of anyone hearing her voice even if she called.

She turned back to the river and sucked in her breath as she saw Joe swimming towards the bank, pulling Lloyd behind him. Watt was doing his best to help, his head just visible above the water.

Llinos held her breath, willing Joe to safety. The river was calmer now, falling back along the banks. The water eddied away from her, swirling, carrying debris like a weapon.

As Joe drew nearer, Llinos leaned over and caught her father's jacket. He fell against the muddy bank, breathing harshly. Watt slumped beside him, his wet hair plastered to his face. His teeth were chattering and he was shivering as though he had the ague.

Joe was still in the water. Llinos caught his hands, trying to pull him ashore, but a sudden wave swept up the bank and she was engulfed. The river pounded against her, she could not see. She could not breathe. She was dragged like a doll into the fury of the swirling river.

She was losing consciousness. She felt Joe's arms around her, holding her. Her hands fluttered and came to rest on his bare shoulders. She and Joe were encapsulated in a shimmering light, they were being lifted upwards out of the darkness.

As the water parted over her head, she dragged in a great gulping breath. She did not know if she was alive or dead but she knew that wherever she was, Joe was there too.

It was as if a great eagle had swooped down from the darkness of the sky and plucked her from the river. She was flying through the heavens, light as the feathers of a dove.

She felt a warm breath on her face. 'Welcome back to life, my little Firebird.' Joe was lifting her easily in his arms. She saw over his shoulder the gleam of the morning sun, the rays spreading through the clouds like fingers of hope. This was the beginning of a new day.

The people of the row would begin again, homes would be salvaged, pottery would be made once more in the kilns of Swansea. Life would go on.

Llinos clung to Joe, her wet hair against his, their breaths mingling. She buried her face in the warmth of his neck and as he carried her away from the morning-kissed river, she knew that this was the beginning of a new life. A life she would spend with the man who was more dear to her than life itself. The man she would follow to the ends of time.

We hope you have enjoyed this Large Print book. Other G.K. Hall & Co. or Chivers Press Large Print books are available at your library or directly from the publishers.

For more information about current and upcoming titles, please call or write, without obligation, to:

G.K. Hall & Co.
P.O. Box 159
Thorndike, Maine 04986 USA
Tel. (800) 257-5157

OR

Chivers Press Limited
Windsor Bridge Road
Bath BA2 3AX
England
Tel. (0225) 335336

All our Large Print titles are designed for easy reading, and all our books are made to last.